Ready-to-Run
Visual Basic® Algorithms

Second Edition

Ready-to-Run
Visual Basic® Algorithms

Second Edition

ROD STEPHENS

WILEY COMPUTER PUBLISHING

John Wiley & Sons, Inc.
New York • Chichester • Weinheim • Brisbane • Singapore • Toronto

Publisher: Robert Ipsen
Editor: Carol A. Long
Assistant Editor: Kathryn A. Malm
Managing Editor: Marnie Wielage
Electronic Products, Associate Editor: Mike Sosa
Text Design & Composition: Benchmark Productions, Inc.

Library of Congress Cataloging-in-Publication Data:
Stephens, Rod, 1961–
    Ready-to-run visual basic algorithms / Rod Stephens. –– 2nd. ed.
      p. cm.
    Includes index.
    ISBN 0-471-24268-3 (paper : alk. paper)
    1. BASIC (Computer program language).   2. Microsoft Visual BASIC.
  I. Title.
  QA76.73.B3S8338   1998
  005.26'8--DC21   97-53196
                                      CIP

Printed in the United States of America
10 9 8 7 6 5 4 3 2 1

CONTENTS

INTRODUCTION

Programming for Windows has always been a daunting task. The Windows Application Programming Interface (API) provides a powerful but dangerous set of tools for building Windows applications. In a way, the API is like a bulldozer: If you use it properly you can build amazing things, but without the proper skills and care you will probably wreak havoc and destruction.

Visual Basic has changed all that. Using a point-and-click interface, Visual Basic allows you to build complete applications quickly and easily. Using Visual Basic you can write and test sophisticated applications without ever using the API directly. By freeing you from API worries, Visual Basic lets you concentrate on the details of your application.

Even though Visual Basic makes building a program's user interface much easier, you must write the rest of the application yourself. You must write the code that takes input from the interface, processes it, and presents the results. That is where algorithms come in.

Algorithms are formal instructions for performing complicated tasks on a computer. A searching algorithm, for example, might explain how to locate a particular customer record in a database of 10 million records. The quality of the algorithms you use can make the difference between locating needed data in seconds, hours, or not at all.

This book describes algorithms in Visual Basic. It contains many powerful algorithms, completely implemented in Visual Basic. It analyzes techniques for managing data structures such as lists, stacks, queues, and trees. It also describes algorithms to perform common programming tasks like sorting, searching, and hashing.

To use these algorithms successfully, you must do more than copy the code into your program and press F5. You must understand how different algorithms behave under different circumstances. You must also determine which circumstances apply in your situation. Finally, you must use that information to select the algorithm that best fits your needs.

This book describes algorithms in plain English. It explains their typical and worst-case behaviors so you will know what to expect when you use them in your programs. This approach will help you recognize worst-case behavior when it occurs so you can rewrite or replace the algorithm. Even the best algorithm will not help you if you use it under the wrong circumstances.

Each algorithm is also implemented in ready-to-run Visual Basic source code that you can easily plug into your programs. The code is provided on the accompanying CD-ROM, along with example applications. These examples show how a program can use the algorithms, and they demonstrate important characteristics of the algorithms themselves.

What This Package Includes

This book and CD-ROM package will provide you with the following:

A solid introduction to algorithms. After reading the book and running the example programs, you will be able to use sophisticated algorithms in your Visual Basic projects. You will be able to critically evaluate new algorithms written by you or others.

A large collection of source code that you can add to your programs. Using the code on the CD-ROM, you can quickly add powerful algorithms to your applications.

Complete, ready-to-run example programs that allow you to test the algorithms. You can use these programs to gain a deeper understanding of how the algorithms work. You can modify the programs to learn more about the algorithms, or you can use them as a basis for building your own applications.

Intended Audience

This book covers advanced Visual Basic programming topics. It does not teach Visual Basic itself. If you have a good understanding of the fundamentals of Visual Basic, you will be able to concentrate on the algorithms rather than becoming bogged down in the details of the language.

This book teaches important programming concepts that you can generalize to solve new problems. The algorithms use powerful programming techniques such as recursion, binary subdivision, dynamic memory allocation, and network data structures that you can apply to your unique problems.

Even if you have not yet mastered Visual Basic, you will be able to run the example programs and compare the performance of different algorithms. Most importantly, you will be able to select the correct algorithms for your needs and add them to your Visual Basic projects.

Visual Basic Version Compatibility

The best algorithms depend on fundamental programming concepts, not the idiosyncrasies of a particular version of a programming language. The first edition of this book was written using Visual Basic 3. After several years, the original algorithms still work in Visual Basic versions 4 and 5.

Some of the concepts introduced in Visual Basic 4 make understanding, implementing, and debugging certain algorithms easier. Object references, classes, and collections allow simpler implementations of these algorithms. Classes can wrap the functionality of some algorithms into neat packages that are easy to add to a program. While these concepts are not absolutely necessary for implementing these algorithms, they provide too great an advantage to ignore.

For these reasons, the algorithms in this book have been written for use with Visual Basic 4 and 5. They are stored on the CD-ROM in Visual Basic 4 format. If you load them into Visual Basic 5, the development environment will tell you that it will save files in Visual Basic 5 format, but you will not need to make any changes. All of the algorithms have been tested using Visual Basic 4 and Visual Basic 5.

The CD-ROM also includes Visual Basic 3 source code from the first edition. These programs show how you can implement algorithms without the latest object-oriented features. Collections and objects make programming easier, but they make some of the newer programs slower than the older versions.

If you ignore classes, objects, and collections, however, you miss out on some truly powerful features. These additions allow you to reach new levels of program modularity, reusability, and design. You should strongly consider using these features, at least in your initial designs. Later, if you discover performance problems, you can modify your programs to use the faster, more primitive techniques.

Programming languages often grow, but they rarely shrink. A remarkable example is the goto statement in the C language. This statement is awkward, dangerous, and almost never used by the vast majority of C programmers, but it has remained in the language since the 1970s. In fact, it was incorporated into C++ and more recently Java, even though the creation of a new language provided an ideal excuse to drop it.

Similarly, future versions of Visual Basic will continue to add new features to the language, but they are unlikely to remove the building blocks needed to implement the algorithms described in this book. Whatever they add, Visual Basic 6, 7, and 8 will surely provide classes, arrays, and user-defined data types. Most, if not all, of the algorithms explained in this book should run unchanged for many years to come.

Chapter Overviews

Chapter 1, "Fundamental Concepts," covers those concepts you should understand before you begin to analyze complex algorithms. It explains the techniques you need to theoretically analyze the complexity of algorithms. Some algorithms that perform well in theory may not do as well in practice, however, so this chapter also deals with practical programming considerations like paging and the use of collections versus arrays.

Chapter 2, "Lists," shows how to build several kinds of lists using arrays, objects, and pointer faking. These data structures are useful in many programs, and they are used throughout the rest of the book. Chapter 2 also tells how to generalize linked list techniques to build other, more complicated data structures such as trees and networks.

Chapter 3, "Stacks and Queues," describes two special kinds of lists: stacks and queues. These data structures are used in many algorithms including several described in later chapters. Chapter 3 ends by presenting a simulation that compares the performance of two kinds of queues that might be used at an airline check-in counter.

Chapter 4, "Arrays," explains several special kinds of arrays. Irregular, triangular, and sparse arrays allow you to use convenient array representations while reducing memory usage.

Chapter 5, "Recursion," discusses a powerful tool, recursion. Recursion can also be confusing and dangerous. Chapter 5 explains when recursion is appropriate and shows how you can remove recursion when necessary.

Chapter 6, "Trees," uses many of the techniques presented earlier, such as recursion and linked lists, to examine the more complicated topic of trees. This chapter covers different tree representations like the *fat node* and *forward star* representations. It describes several important tree algorithms such as tree traversal.

Chapter 7, "Balanced Trees," examines a more advanced topic. Balanced trees have certain properties that keep them evenly balanced and efficient. Balanced tree algorithms are surprisingly simple to describe but quite difficult to implement. This chapter uses one of the most powerful of these structures, a *B+tree*, to build a sophisticated database.

Chapter 8, "Decision Trees," discusses problems that can be described as searching for a solution within a decision tree. For even small problems, these trees can become enormous, so searching them as efficiently as possible is essential. This chapter compares several different techniques that make searching for solutions manageable.

Chapter 9, "Sorting," deals with what is probably the most heavily studied topic in algorithms. Sorting algorithms are interesting for several reasons. First, sorting is a common task in programming. Second, different sorting algorithms have their own strengths and weaknesses, so no single algorithm works best in all situations. Finally, sorting algorithms demonstrate a wide variety of important algorithmic techniques such as recursion, heaps, and the use of random numbers to minimize worst-case behavior.

Chapter 10, "Searching," examines a topic closely related to sorting. Once a list has been sorted, a program may need to locate items within the list. This chapter compares several methods for locating items in sorted lists as efficiently as possible.

Chapter 11, "Hashing," discusses a technique for storing and locating items even more quickly than is possible using trees or sorting and searching. The chapter covers several hashing techniques, including chaining, buckets, and several kinds of open addressing.

Chapter 12, "Network Algorithms," describes another category of algorithms. Some of these algorithms, like shortest-path calculations, apply directly to physical networks. The algorithms can also be used indirectly to solve other problems that may initially seem unrelated to networks. For example, shortest path algorithms can divide a network into districts or identify critical tasks in a project schedule.

Chapter 13, "Object-Oriented Techniques," explains techniques made possible by the classes introduced in Visual Basic 4. These techniques use an object-oriented approach to implement behaviors that are unnatural for "traditional" algorithms.

Appendix A, "Using the CD-ROM," describes the contents of the CD-ROM. It explains how you can load the example programs, and it tells how you can get help if you have trouble with the CD-ROM.

Appendix B, "List of Example Programs," summarizes the example programs provided on the CD-ROM. You can look through this list to see which programs demonstrate particular algorithmic techniques.

What's on the CD-ROM

The CD-ROM contains the Visual Basic 4.0 source code for the algorithms and example programs described in this book. The code is saved in Visual Basic 4.0 format so that it can be used by the largest number of readers possible. You can load these files into Visual Basic 4.0 or later. The algorithms have been tested using Visual Basic 4.0 and Visual Basic 5.0

The example programs described in each chapter are contained in separate subdirectories beneath the Src directory. For example, programs demonstrating algorithms described in Chapter 3 are stored in the Src\Ch3 directory. Appendix B lists the programs described in this book.

The CD-ROM also includes the source code for the programs in the book's first edition. Those programs are compatible with Visual Basic 3.0 so they are stored in Visual Basic 3.0 format. You can load these programs in Visual Basic 3.0 or in later versions of Visual Basic. The old versions are stored in subdirectories of the OldSrc directory. For example, the OldSrc\Ch3 directory contains programs that relate to Chapter 3 in this edition of the book.

The older programs demonstrate many of the same topics covered in this edition of the book, but they use Visual Basic 3.0 code. For example, they do not use collections or classes. This makes some of the algorithms a bit harder to understand, but many of them give better performance.

In particular, the newer versions of the tree and network algorithms use collections and classes extensively. Although this approach makes the programs easier to understand, it also makes them slower. The older programs use forward star tree network representations (see Chapter 6, "Trees," for more about forward star) to achieve better performance.

Hardware Requirements

To run and modify the example applications, you need a computer that is reasonably able to run Visual Basic. Almost any computer running any Windows operating system will do. You also need a compact disk drive to load the programs from the CD-ROM.

Algorithms run at different speeds on different computers with different configurations. A 200 megahertz Pentium Pro with 64Mb of memory will be faster than a 386-based computer with 4Mb of memory. You will quickly learn the limits of your hardware.

Changes in the Second Edition

As far as this book is concerned, the biggest recent change to Visual Basic is the introduction of classes. Classes allow you to think of certain problems in a new way. This approach makes understanding and implementing many algorithms more natural and therefore easier. The changes in this edition take advantage of classes. They fall into three categories.

Replacing pointer faking with classes. Even though all the algorithms written in the first edition still work, many that were implemented using pointer faking (described in Chapter 2, "Lists") are easier to understand using classes.

Encapsulation. Classes allow a program to wrap the features of an algorithm into a tight package that a program can use easily. For example, classes allow you to create several linked lists without writing redundant code to manage each list separately.

Object-oriented techniques. Classes also make understanding certain object-oriented algorithms much easier. Chapter 13, "Object-Oriented Techniques," describes techniques that would be difficult to implement without classes.

How to Use This Book

Chapter 1, "Fundamental Concepts," gives background material used later throughout the book so you should start there. You should read this material even if you do not need an in-depth understanding of the algorithms right away.

Chapter 2, "Lists," and Chapter 3, "Stacks and Queues," explain different kinds of lists used by programs later in the book, so you should read these chapters next.

Chapter 6, "Trees," discusses material that is used in Chapter 7, "Balanced Trees," in Chapter 8, "Decision Trees," and in Chapter 12, "Network Algorithms." You should read Chapter 6 before you tackle these later chapters. You can read the remaining chapters in any order.

Table I.1 shows three possible plans of study that you can use, depending on how broad you want your introduction to algorithms to be. The first plan covers basic techniques and data structures that you will find helpful in your programs. The second plan also describes fundamental algorithms, like sorting and searching algorithms, which you may need to build more advanced programs.

The final plan shows one order in which you could cover the whole book. While Chapter 7, "Balanced Trees," and Chapter 8, "Decision Trees," follow logically from Chapter 6, "Trees," they are more difficult than some of the later chapters so in this plan they are studied a little later. Chapter 7, "Balanced Trees," Chapter 12, "Network Algorithms," and Chapter 13, "Object-Oriented Techniques," are probably the most difficult chapters in the book, so they are left for last. Of course, you can also read the book in order from the front cover to the back cover if you like.

Why Visual Basic?

One of the most common complaints about Visual Basic is that it is slow. Delphi, Visual C++, and many other compiled languages are faster, more flexible, and more powerful than Visual Basic. With this in mind, it is natural to ask, "Why should I implement complex algorithms in Visual Basic? Wouldn't it be better to use Delphi or C++? Or at least to implement algorithms in those languages and make them available to Visual Basic programs through libraries?" Implementing algorithms in Visual Basic makes sense for several reasons.

First, building a complete application in Visual C++ is much more difficult and dangerous than building one in Visual Basic. If your program does not handle all of the Windows programming details correctly, your application, the development environment, and possibly all of Windows will crash.

Second, building a C++ library for use by Visual Basic involves many of the same dangers as writing a Windows application in C++. If your library and Visual Basic program do not cooperate in just the right way, you will again crash your program, probably the Visual Basic environment, and perhaps Windows as well.

Third, many algorithms are efficient enough to give good performance even in a slower language like Visual Basic. For example, the countingsort algorithm

Table I.1 Plans of Study

Coverage	Chapters												
Basic techniques	1	2	3	4									
Fundamental algorithms	1	2	3	4	5	6	9	10	13				
In-depth coverage	1	2	3	4	5	6	9	10	11	8	12	7	13

described in Chapter 9, "Sorting," can sort 1 million long integers in less than 2 seconds on a 133 megahertz Pentium. You might be able to make the algorithm run a little faster using a C++ library, but the Visual Basic version is fast enough for most applications. Visual Basic 5's compiled executables make the gap between the languages smaller than ever.

Finally, by implementing algorithms in *any* programming language, you learn more about algorithms in general. As you study the algorithms, you will learn techniques you can use in other parts of your programs. Once you have mastered an algorithm in Visual Basic, it will be much easier for you to reimplement it in Delphi or C++ if you find it absolutely necessary.

FUNDAMENTAL CONCEPTS

This chapter presents background material that you should understand before you begin the serious study of algorithms. The chapter begins by asking, "What are algorithms?" Before you get deeply into programming details, it is worth spending a few moments to step back and consider exactly what algorithms are.

The chapter then introduces *complexity theory,* the formal study of the complexity of algorithms. Using complexity theory, you can evaluate the theoretical performance of algorithms. This approach lets you compare different algorithms to each other and predict their performance under different circumstances. The chapter gives several examples that show how to apply complexity theory to small problems.

Some algorithms that perform well in theory may not do as well in practice, however, so the chapter ends with a discussion of several real-world programming considerations. Excessive paging or poor use of object references and collections can ruin the performance of an otherwise fine application.

Once you have mastered the concepts in this chapter, you will be able to apply them to the algorithms throughout the rest of the book. You will even be able to use them to analyze programs of your own so you can judge their performance and anticipate problems before they turn into disasters.

What Are Algorithms?

An algorithm is a set of directions for performing a particular task. When you give someone instructions to fix a lawn mower, drive a car, or bake a cake, you create an algorithm. Of course, these sorts of everyday algorithms are described in imprecise terms like these:

```
Make sure the car is in park.
Make sure the parking brake is set.
Turn the key.
Etc.
```

[1]

You assume that the person following the instructions can handle the millions of little details such as unlocking the door, opening the door, sitting down behind the wheel, fastening the seat belt, finding the parking brake, and so forth.

When you write an algorithm for a computer, you cannot assume that the computer will understand anything you do not tell it explicitly. The computer has a very limited vocabulary (a programming language), and all your instructions must be phrased using that vocabulary. To deal with this situation, you need to use a more formal style for writing computer algorithms.

It is an interesting exercise to try to write an algorithm for a common, everyday task in a formal style. The car driving algorithm, for example, might begin like this:

```
If the door is locked then:
    Insert the key in the lock
    Turn the key
    If the door is still locked then:
        Turn key the other way
Pull up on the door handle
Etc.
```

This piece of code only gets the door open; it does not even check that you are opening the right door. If the lock is sticky and hard to open, or if the car has an anti-theft system, the algorithm can become extremely complicated.

Algorithms have been formalized for thousands of years. Around 300 B.C. Euclid wrote algorithms for bisecting angles, testing whether triangles were equal, and performing other geometric tasks. He started with a small vocabulary of axioms such as "parallel lines never intersect," and from those he built algorithms for complicated tasks.

This sort of formalized algorithm is appropriate for mathematical purposes where it must be shown that something is true or that some task can be accomplished, but the speed of the algorithm is unimportant. For problems where someone must actually execute the instructions, like sorting a million customer records using a computer, efficiency becomes a critical part of the problem.

Analyzing Algorithms—How Fast Is Fast?

Complexity theory is the study of the complexity of algorithms. There are several ways in which you can measure the complexity of an algorithm. Programmers usually focus on an algorithm's speed, but other factors are also important. How much memory, disk space, or other resources an algorithm uses can also be an issue. A fast algorithm will not be of much use if it requires more memory than your computer has available.

Space versus Time

Many algorithms provide a trade-off between space and time. You can solve the problem quickly, using a lot of memory, or more slowly, using less memory.

One type of shortest-path algorithm provides a good example. Given a network, like the network of streets in a city, you can write an algorithm to compute the shortest distance between any two points in the network. Instead of calculating these distances whenever you need them, you could precompute the shortest distances between every point and every other point and store the results in a table. When you need to know the shortest distance between any two points, you look the value up in the table.

This example would allow you to look up distances almost instantly, but it would require a huge amount of memory. The street network for a large city like Boston or Denver might contain a few hundred thousand points. The table needed to store all of the shortest-distance information would have more than 10 billion entries. In this example, the space versus time trade-off is clear: By using an additional 10 gigabytes of memory you can make the program much faster.

This special relationship between time and space gives rise to the idea of *space-time complexity*. In this sort of analysis, an algorithm is evaluated in terms of both time and space, and the trade-offs between them are studied.

This book concentrates mostly on time complexity, but it points out any unusual space requirements. Some algorithms, like the mergesort algorithm discussed in Chapter 9, "Sorting," require extra scratch space. Other algorithms, like heapsort, also discussed in Chapter 9, require a fairly natural amount of space.

Big O Notation

When you compare different algorithms, it is important to understand how complexity relates to the size of the problem itself. One algorithm may need 1 second to sort a thousand numbers and 10 seconds to sort a million numbers. Another algorithm might need 2 seconds to sort a thousand numbers but only 5 seconds to sort a million. In that case, you cannot instantly declare one program better than the other. Which is better depends on the data you are sorting.

Although it is interesting to know the exact speeds of each algorithm, it is more important to understand the relative behaviors of the algorithms for problems of different sizes. In this example, the first algorithm sorts small lists faster, but the second algorithm sorts large lists faster.

You can relate an algorithm's speed and size using "Big O" notation. An algorithm has complexity $O(f(N))$, pronounced "order F of N," if the time required by the algorithm goes up at the same rate as the function $f(N)$ when the problem size N gets large. For example, consider the following code that sorts N positive numbers.

```
For I = 1 To N
    ' Find the largest item in the list.
    MaxValue = 0
    For J = 1 to N
        If Value(J) > MaxValue Then
            MaxValue = Value(J)
```

```
        MaxJ = J
    End If
Next J
' Print the largest item we just found.
Print Format$(MaxJ) & ":" & Str$(MaxValue)
' Zero the item so we do not pick it again.
Value(MaxJ) = 0
Next I
```

In this algorithm the variable I loops from 1 to N. Each time I changes, the variable J also loops from 1 to N. For each of the N times the outer loop is executed, the inner loop is executed N times. The total number of times the inner loop is executed equals N * N or N^2. This gives the algorithm complexity of $O(N^2)$ ("order N-squared").

When calculating Big O values, you should use only the fastest growing part of the run time equation. Suppose an algorithm has a run time given by $N^3 + N$. The Big O notation for that algorithm would be $O(N^3)$. Looking at only the fastest growing part of the function allows you to study the behavior of the algorithm as the problem size N gets large.

When N is large for a routine with run time $N^3 + N$, the N^3 term dominates and the entire function starts to look like N^3. When N = 100, the difference between $N^3 + N = 1,000,100$ and $N^3 = 1,000,000$ is only 100, a 0.01 percent difference. Notice that this is true only for large N. When N = 2, the difference between $N^3 + N = 10$ and $N^3 = 8$ is 2, a 20 percent difference.

You should also ignore constant multiples in Big O notation. An algorithm with run time $3 * N^2$ would be considered $O(N^2)$. This makes it easier to understand relative changes in the problem size. If you increase N by a factor of 2, the 2 is squared in the N^2 term, so the run time would increase by a factor of roughly 4.

Ignoring constant multiples also makes it easier to count the steps executed by the algorithm. In the previous sorting example, the inner loop is executed N^2 times, but how many steps should you count for each inner loop? You could count only the If statement because only it is executed every time through the loop. You could calculate the total number of times the statements within the If are executed and count those, too. Then there are the statements inside the outer loop but outside the inner loop, like the Print statement. Should those be counted, too?

Following these different counting methods you might decide the algorithm has N^2, $3 * N^2$, or $3 * N^2 + N$ complexity. With Big O notation these are all the same. They all reduce to $O(N^3)$, so it does not matter exactly which statements you count.

Looking for Complexity

The most complex parts of a program are usually in program loops and subroutine calls. In the previous sorting example, two loops executed all of the algorithm's statements.

When a subroutine calls another subroutine, you must think more carefully about how much work that other subroutine is doing. If it is performing a constant amount of work, like printing a number, then you do not need to worry too much about it for Big O purposes. On the other hand, if it is executing O(N) steps, then the function may be contributing significantly to the algorithm's complexity. If the subroutine call is executed within a loop, the effect may be even greater.

For example, suppose a program has a subroutine called Slow with $O(N^3)$ complexity and another subroutine Fast with $O(N^2)$ complexity. The complexity of the program as a whole depends on how the two subroutines are related.

If Fast calls Slow each time it runs through its loops, then the complexities of the subroutines combine. The combined complexity is the product of the two. In this case, the complexity is $O(N^2)$ times $O(N^3)$ or $O(N^3 * N^2) = O(N^5)$. The following code fragment shows this sort of behavior.

```
Sub Slow()
Dim I As Integer
Dim J As Integer
Dim K As Integer
    For I = 1 To N
        For J = 1 To N
            For K = 1 To N
                ' Do something here.
            Next K
        Next J
    Next I
End Sub

Sub Fast()
Dim I As Integer
Dim J As Integer
    For I = 1 To N
        For J = 1 To N
            Slow            ' Call subroutine Slow.
        Next J
    Next I
End Sub

Sub MainProgram()
    Fast
End Sub
```

On the other hand, if the main program calls the subroutines separately, their complexities add. In this case, the total complexity is $O(N^3) + O(N^2) = O(N^3)$ in Big O notation. The following code fragment has this complexity.

```
Sub Slow()
Dim I As Integer
Dim J As Integer
Dim K As Integer

    For I = 1 To N
        For J = 1 To N
            For K = 1 To N
                    ' Do something here.
            Next K
        Next J
    Next I
End Sub

Sub Fast()
Dim I As Integer
Dim J As Integer

    For I = 1 To N
        For J = 1 To N
                ' Do something here.
        Next J
    Next I
End Sub

Sub MainProgram()
    Slow
    Fast
End Sub
```

Complexity of Recursive Algorithms

Recursive routines are routines that call themselves. They introduce complexity in a subtle way. In many recursive algorithms it is the number of times recursion occurs that determines the complexity of the algorithm. While a recursive routine may seem simple, it can contribute greatly to the program's complexity if it calls itself many times.

The following code fragment shows a subroutine that contains only two statements. When called for input N, however, this subroutine executes N times. That makes the complexity of this piece of code O(N).

```
Sub CountDown(N As Integer)
    If N <= 0 Then Exit Sub
    CountDown N - 1
End Sub
```

Multiple Recursion

A recursive algorithm that calls itself more than once is *multiply recursive*. Multiply recursive routines can be harder to analyze than singly recursive algorithms, and they can contribute much more complexity.

The following subroutine is similar to the previous subroutine CountDown except it calls itself twice instead of once.

```
Sub DoubleCountDown(N As Integer)
    If N <= 0 Then Exit Sub
    DoubleCountDown N - 1
    DoubleCountDown N - 1
End Sub
```

Because the routine calls itself twice, you might expect that it would have twice the run time of subroutine CountDown. That would give this routine a run time of 2 * O(N) = O(N). Unfortunately, the truth is more complicated.

If you let $T(N)$ be the number of times the routine is executed with input N, it is easy to see that $T(0) = 1$. When the routine is called with input 0, it simply exits.

For larger values of N, the routine recursively calls itself twice with parameter = $N - 1$. The number of times the routine is executed is $1 + 2 * T(N - 1)$. Table 1.1 shows some of the values generated by the equations $T(0) = 1$ and $T(N) = 1 + 2 * T(N - 1)$. If you look closely at these values, you will see that $T(N) = 2^{(N + 1)} - 1$, giving the routine a run time of $O(2^N)$. Even though subroutines CountDown and DoubleCountDown look similar, DoubleCountDown requires many more steps to execute.

Indirect Recursion

A recursive routine can also call itself indirectly by calling a second routine that then calls the first. Indirect recursion can be even harder to analyze than multiple recursion. The Sierpinski curve algorithm discussed in Chapter 5, "Recursion," uses four subroutines that are both multiply and indirectly recursive. Each of these routines calls itself and the other three routines up to four times. It is a fair amount of work to show that this algorithm runs in time $O(4^N)$.

Space Complexity of Recursive Algorithms

Space complexity is particularly important for some recursive algorithms. It is very easy to write a recursive subroutine that allocates a little bit of memory

Table 1.1 Values of the Runtime Function for Subroutine DoubleCountDown

N	0	1	2	3	4	5	6	7	8	9	10
T(N)	1	3	7	15	31	63	127	255	511	1023	2047

each time it is called. That space can add up if the routine enters a long series of recursive calls. For this reason, you should perform at least a casual space complexity analysis of recursive routines to make sure they do not use huge amounts of memory.

The following subroutine allocates more memory each time it is called. After 100 or 200 recursive calls, the routine will use up all of the computer's memory and the program will stop with an "Out of memory" error.

```
Sub GobbleMemory(N As Integer)
Dim Array() As Integer

    ReDim Array (1 To 32000)
    GobbleMemory N + 1
End Sub
```

Even if a routine does not explicitly allocate memory, the system allocates memory from the *system stack* for bookkeeping purposes whenever the routine is called. When the routine returns, the memory is returned to the stack for later use.

If a subroutine enters a long series of recursive calls, it can exhaust the stack even though the computer still has memory available. If you execute the following subroutine, it will quickly exhaust the available stack space and halt your program with an "Out of stack space" error. You could then use the debugger to check the value of the Count variable to see how many times the subroutine called itself before the stack was exhausted.

```
Sub UseStack()
Static Count As Integer

    Count = Count + 1
    UseStack
End Sub
```

Variables that you declare locally within a subroutine may also be allocated from the stack. If you modify the previous UseStack subroutine so that it allocates three variant variables each time it is called, the program will run out of stack space sooner.

```
Sub UseStack ()
Static Count As Integer
Dim I As Variant
Dim J As Variant
Dim K As Variant

    Count = Count + 1
    UseStack
End Sub
```

Chapter 5, "Recursion," has much more to say about recursive algorithms.

Average Case and Worst Case

Big O notation is used as an upper bound on the complexity of algorithms. Just because a program has a certain Big O complexity does not mean the algorithm always takes that long. Given the right data, many algorithms take far less time than analysis indicates they might. For example, the following code shows a simple algorithm that locates an item within a list.

```
Function LocateItem(target As Integer) As Integer
    For I = 1 To N
        If Value(I) = target Then Exit For
    Next I
    LocateItem = I
End Sub
```

If the target item is at the end of the list, the algorithm will need to search all N items in the list before finding the item. That will take N steps, so this is an O(N) algorithm. This is the longest the algorithm could possibly take, so it is called the *worst case analysis* of the algorithm.

On the other hand, if the target number happens to be at the very beginning of the list, the algorithm will stop almost immediately. It will execute only a couple of steps before it finds the number and stops. This makes the algorithm's *best case* run time a constant or O(1). Generally a best case like this one is not very interesting because it will be unlikely to occur in real life. It is more interesting to look at the algorithm's *average* or *expected case* behavior.

If the numbers in the list are initially mixed randomly, the target item could appear anywhere in the list. It could be near the end of the list, and it could be near the beginning. On the average you would need to examine N / 2 of the items before finding the one you wanted. This makes the average case behavior of this algorithm O(N / 2), which is the same as O(N) in Big O notation.

For some algorithms, the worst case and expected case results are different. For example, the quicksort algorithm discussed in Chapter 9, "Sorting," has worst case behavior $O(N^2)$ but expected behavior $O(N * \log(N))$, which is much faster. Algorithms like quicksort go to great lengths to ensure that worst case behavior is as unlikely as possible.

Common Complexity Functions

Table 1.2 lists some of the functions that commonly occur in complexity calculations. The functions are listed in increasing order of growth, with the functions at the top of the list growing more slowly than the functions at the bottom. This means algorithms with run time complexities involving functions near the top of the list will be faster than those with run time complexities involving functions near the bottom.

Table 1.2 Common Complexity Functions

Function	Notes
f(N) = C	C is a constant
f(N) = log(log(N))	
f(N) = log(N)	
f(N) = N^C	C is a constant between 0 and 1
f(N) = N	
f(N) = N * log(N)	
f(N) = N^C	C is a constant greater than 1
f(N) = C^N	C is a constant greater than 1
f(N) = N!	i.e., 1 * 2 *...* N

It also means a complexity equation that contains more than one of these functions will reduce to the last one in the table when it comes to Big O notation. For example, $O(\log(N) + N^2)$ is the same as $O(N^2)$.

Whether an algorithm with a run time shown in Table 1.2 is fast enough depends on how you use it. If you run the algorithm once per year on a fairly small data set, $O(N^2)$ performance is probably acceptable. If you run the algorithm interactively on large data sets with a user watching, O(N) may not be fast enough.

Usually run times involving N * log(N) and smaller functions are very fast. Run times involving N^C for small C, like N^2, are acceptably fast if the amount of data is limited. Run times involving functions like C^N and N! are so slow that these algorithms are usable only for very small problem sizes.

An interesting way to think about the relative sizes of these functions is to consider the time it would take to solve problems of different sizes. Table 1.3 shows how long it would take a computer executing 1 million algorithm steps per second to execute some slow algorithms. The table shows that only very small problems can be solved when the complexity is $O(C^N)$ and only the tiniest problems can be solved when the complexity is O(N!). An O(N!) problem where N is only 24 would take more time to solve than the current age of the universe.

Logarithms

Before reading further, you should review a little bit about logarithms because they play an important role in many algorithms. The logarithm of a number N in a base B is the power P that satisfies the equation $B^P = N$. For example, when you see the equation $\log_2(8)$ you should think "2 to what power equals 8?" In this case $2^3 = 8$, so $\log_2(8) = 3$.

Table 1.3 Times to Execute Complex Algorithms

	N = 10	N = 20	N = 30	N = 40	N = 50
N^3	.001 sec	.008 sec	.027 sec	.064 sec	.125 sec
2^N	.001 sec	1.05 sec	17.9 min	1.27 days	35.7 years
3^N	.059 sec	58.1 min	6.53 years	$3.86 * 10^5$ years	$2.28 * 10^{10}$ years
$N!$	3.63 sec	$7.71 * 10^4$ years	$8.41 * 10^{18}$ years	$2.59 * 10^{34}$ years	$9.64 * 10^{50}$ years

You can convert between different log bases using the relationship $\log_B(N) = \log_C(N) / \log_C(B)$. If you wanted to convert $\log_2(N)$ into base 10, for example, you would have $\log_{10}(N) = \log_2(N) / \log_2(10)$. The value $\log_2(10)$ is a constant that is approximately 3.32. Because you ignore constant multipliers in Big O notation, you can ignore the $\log_2(10)$ term. In fact, for any base B, the value $\log_2(B)$ is a constant. That means for purposes of Big O notation, all log bases are the same. In other words, $O(\log_2(N))$ is the same as $O(\log_{10}(N))$ or $O(\log_B(N))$ for any B. Because all log bases are the same, the log base is usually omitted in Big O notation, so $O(\log_2(N))$ is written $O(\log(N))$.

Binary representations are natural in programming, so the logarithms used when analyzing run times are usually base 2. To make the notation easier, the chapters that follow assume that $\log(N)$ means $\log_2(N)$. When a different log base is needed, the base is written explicitly.

The Real World—Fast versus FAST

Even though it is useful to ignore small terms and constant multiples when studying complexity, it is often important to consider them when actually writing programs. These numbers become particularly important when the problem size is small and the constants are large.

For example, suppose you have two algorithms that can accomplish the same task. One runs in $O(N)$ time, and the other runs in $O(N^2)$ time. For large problems the first algorithm will probably be faster.

Looking closely at the run time functions, however, you may find that the first is $f(N) = 30 * N + 7000$ and the second is $f(N) = N^2$. In this case, the second algorithm will execute fewer steps for problems where N is under 100. If you know that your problem size will never exceed 100, you might be better off using the second approach.

On the other hand, not all algorithm steps are equally fast on a computer. If the first algorithm uses fast memory operations and the second uses slow disk accesses, the first algorithm might be faster in all cases.

A number of other factors further confuse the issue. The first algorithm might require a huge amount of memory that your computer may not have. The second algorithm may be much more complicated, so it might take you days longer to implement, and it might become a debugging nightmare in the future. Real-life issues like these can sometimes make complexity analysis seem almost pointless.

Complexity analysis is still useful for understanding the general nature of an algorithm. The analysis usually shows you where the bulk of the computation takes place. Knowing which parts of the algorithm determine the overall performance lets you decide where improvements will give you the greatest benefit.

Sometimes the best way to determine which algorithm is better is to test them. When you compare algorithms like this, it is very important that you use data that is as similar to the real data as possible. Many algorithms behave quite differently when they execute on different sets of data. If you test the algorithms on unrealistic data, you may be unpleasantly surprised when you run the program in the real world.

Paging

A particularly important real-world consideration is *paging*. The Windows operating system reserves a certain amount of disk space that it can use for *virtual memory*. When all of your real memory fills up, Windows writes the contents of some of that memory onto the disk. This process is called paging because Windows writes the memory in chunks called *pages*. Windows then uses the real memory that was copied to the disk for other things. When a program needs to access items written to disk, the system copies them back into real memory.

Because accessing a disk is much slower than accessing real memory, paging can slow the performance of an application tremendously. If a program jumps back and forth across huge amounts of memory, the system will page often. All that reading and writing to the disk will slow the application.

Example program Pager allows you to allocate bigger and bigger arrays until the system begins paging. Enter the amount of memory you want the program to allocate in megabytes, and click the Page button. If you enter a small value like 1 or 2, the program will be able to allocate the array in real memory so the program will run quickly.

If you enter a value close to the amount of physical memory on your computer, the program will start to page. You will probably hear your disk drive start working overtime when this happens. You will also notice that the program takes much longer to run. A 10 percent increase in array size may result in a 100 percent increase in run time.

Program Pager can access its memory in one of two ways. If you click the Page button, Pager examines its array from the beginning to the end. When the program visits part of the array, the system may have to page to load that part of the array into real memory. Once that page is in real memory, the program continues to visit that part of the array until it is finished with the entries on that page.

On the other hand, if you click the Thrash button, Pager accesses the memory randomly. By jumping randomly through the array, the program greatly increases the chances that the next item it needs has been paged to the disk. In that case, the system will need to page it back into real memory. This excessive paging is called *thrashing*.

Table 1.4 shows times required by program Pager to examine various amounts of memory on a 90 megahertz Pentium with 24Mb of real memory. Your run times will be different and will depend on the kind of computer you have, the amount of real memory you have, the speed of your disk drives, and the sizes of other programs running on your system.

Initially the time needed by the tests increases about as quickly as the memory allocated does. When paging begins, there is a sudden dramatic increase in run time. Notice that the paging and thrashing tests have very similar behavior until paging occurs. When all of the memory allocated fits in real memory, it takes the same amount of time to access items in an orderly or random fashion. Once paging begins, however, random access to the memory is much less efficient.

You can do a few things to help minimize the effects of paging. Most important, do not waste memory. If you can keep memory usage to a reasonable level, you will never have to worry about paging. Remember that other programs including Windows also use memory while your program is running, so you will not be able to use all the physical memory on your computer. The computer that generated the data in Table 1.4 paged heavily when the program allocated 20Mb of memory even though it had 24Mb physically available.

Sometimes you can write your program's code so it deals with memory in natural chunks before moving on to other parts of memory. The mergesort algorithm described in Chapter 9, "Sorting," manipulates data in large chunks. Each of these chunks is sorted, and then the chunks are merged together. The orderly way mergesort moves through memory minimizes paging.

Table 1.4 Run Times in Seconds for Program Pager

Memory (Mb)	Paging	Thrashing
2	3.79	3.73
4	7.58	7.47
6	11.37	11.20
8	15.49	14.94
10	18.90	18.62
12	22.85	22.36
14	26.47	26.15
16	30.26	29.88
18	34.51	37.46
20	132.37	12,155 (estimated)

The heapsort algorithm, also described in Chapter 9, "Sorting," jumps freely from one part of its list to another. For very large lists, this will cause thrashing. On the other hand, mergesort requires extra storage space while heapsort does not. If the list is large enough, the extra storage mergesort uses may force it to page.

Pointer Faking, Object References, and Collections

Some languages, like C, C++, and Delphi, allow you to declare variables that are *pointers* to memory locations. These locations can hold other pieces of data like strings, arrays of doubles, or user-defined data structures. A particularly useful way to use a pointer is to have it point to a data structure that contains another pointer. That pointer points to another data structure containing a pointer, and so forth. Using data structures that contain pointers, you can create all sorts of exotic lists, graphs, networks, and trees. Later chapters examine some of these complex structures.

Visual Basic 3 and earlier versions provided no way to create pointer variables directly. All a pointer needs to do, however, is point to another piece of data. If you create an array of data structures, you can use integers as pointers to the entries in the array. The data to which a pointer points is the array entry with the corresponding index. This technique is called *pointer faking*.

References

Visual Basic 4 introduced classes. A variable representing an instance of a class is a reference to an object. For example, in the following code, the variable obj is a reference to an object of class MyClass. Because this variable is not declared with the New keyword, it initially does not refer to any object. In the second line of code, the New statement makes obj point at a new object.

```
Dim obj As MyClass

    Set obj = New MyClass
```

References are Visual Basic's version of pointers.

Visual Basic objects use *reference counting* to make object management easier. Each object has a count that indicates the number of references the program has to it. When a new reference points to the object, the count is increased. When a reference no longer points to an object, the count is decreased. When the reference count reaches zero, Visual Basic knows the program can no longer access the object. At that point, Visual Basic destroys the object and reclaims the memory it occupied.

Later chapters have more to say about references and reference counting.

Collections

In addition to objects and references, Visual Basic 4 introduced collections. You can think of a collection as a fancy array. Collections provide certain useful features like the ability to grow and shrink over time and the ability to search for an object using a key.

Performance Issues

Pointer faking, references, and collections are mentioned here because they can have a big impact on performance. References and collections make certain operations easier, but they come with a large amount of overhead.

Example program Faker demonstrates some of the trade-offs between pointer faking, references, and collections. When you enter a number and click the Create List button, Faker builds lists of items in three different ways. First, it creates objects to represent the items and adds references to the objects to a collection. Next, it uses references within the objects themselves to create a linked list of objects. Finally, it builds a linked list using pointer faking. Do not worry about how linked lists work just yet. They are explained in detail in Chapter 2, "Lists."

If you click the Search List button, Faker searches the lists for every item present. If you click the Destroy List button, Faker destroys the lists and frees their memory.

Table 1.5 shows the times it took Faker to perform these tasks on a 90 megahertz Pentium. Creating and destroying collections took the longest by far. This extra time is the price you pay for the convenience of collections.

Collections provide indexes into the list. Part of the extra time to fill the collection is spent preparing the index. When the program destroys its collection, the references stored in the collection are freed. The system updates and checks the referenced objects' counts to see if they still have references. In this case they do not, so the objects themselves are also freed. All this work takes a lot of extra time.

Creating and destroying the list is so fast using pointer faking that the time is unnoticeable. Pointer faking builds lists using large arrays that are easy to allocate and erase. With pointer faking, the system does not need to deal with references, reference counts, and freeing objects.

On the other hand, searching a collection is faster than searching the reference linked list or a pointer faked linked list. This is because the collection uses a fast hashing scheme for its index while the other lists use a slow sequential search. Chapter 11, "Hashing," explains how you can add hashing to your program without using collections.

Table 1.5 Times in Seconds to Create / Search / Destroy Lists

List size	1000	2000	3000
Reference collection	0.77 / 0.33 / 0.60	1.53 / 0.60 / 2.25	2.42 / 1.05 / 5.93
Reference linked list	0.11 / 1.49 / 0.06	0.33 / 6.32 / 0.17	0.60 / 14.66 / 0.22
Pointer faking	0.00 / 1.48 / 0.00	0.00 / 5.77 / 0.00	0.00 / 13.07 / 0.00

Although pointer faking generally provides better performance, it is more confusing than using references. If a program needs only a small list, references and collections may be fast enough. If the lists are large, you may get better performance using pointer faking.

Summary

Analyzing the performance of algorithms lets you compare different algorithms. It allows you to predict how algorithms will behave under different circumstances. By pointing out the parts of an algorithm that contribute most to run time, analysis helps you define the places where extra work may give the largest improvements.

Programming is full of trade-offs that are critical in real-world applications. One algorithm may be faster than another, but only if it can use a huge amount of extra memory. Another algorithm using collections may be easy to implement and maintain, but it may be slower than a more complicated algorithm that uses pointer faking.

Once you have analyzed the available algorithms, understand how they behave under different circumstances, and know how they are influenced by real-world trade-offs, you can select the one most appropriate for your situation.

LISTS

There are four main ways to allocate memory in Visual Basic: by declaring variables of the standard data types (integer, double, etc.); by declaring variables that are of user-defined data types; by creating instances of a class using the New keyword; and by creating and redimensioning arrays. There are also a few more unusual ways, such as creating a new instance of a form or control, but these do not offer much help in creating complex data structures.

Using these methods you can easily build static data structures such as large arrays of a user-defined type. You can even modify an array slightly using the ReDim statement. Rearranging data, however, can be quite difficult. To move an item from one end of the array to the other, for example, you need to rearrange the entire array. You would shift every item in the array over one position to fill in the spot left by the item you moved. Then you would place the moved item in its new location.

Dynamic data structures allow you to make this sort of change quickly and easily. With only a few steps, you can move an item from any position in the data structure to any other.

This chapter describes methods for creating dynamic lists in Visual Basic. Different kinds of lists have different properties. Some are simple and provide only limited functionality. Others, such as circular lists, doubly linked lists, and threaded lists, are more complex and support advanced data management features.

Later chapters use the techniques described here to build stacks, queues, arrays, trees, hash tables, and networks. Be sure you understand this chapter before you read the later material.

List Basics

In its simplest form, a list is a group of objects. It holds the objects and allows your program to examine them. If that is all you need a list to do, you can use an array to store the list. You can use a variable NumInList to keep track of the number of items in the list. Whenever your program needs to examine the items, it can use NumInList to determine how many items are present. It can then visit the items using a For loop and perform whatever actions are necessary.

If you have a program that can use this simple strategy, use it. This method is effective and, due to its simplicity, is easy to debug and maintain. Most programs are not this straightforward, however, and require more complicated versions of even simple objects like lists. The sections that follow discuss some of the ways you can build more powerful lists.

The first section describes ways to make lists that can grow and shrink over time. In some programs you may not be able to determine beforehand how large a list might need to be. You can handle this situation with a list that can resize itself as needed.

The next section discusses *unordered lists* that allow you to remove items from any part of the list. Unordered lists give you more control over the list contents than simple lists do. They are also more dynamic because they allow you to change the contents of the list freely over time.

The following sections discuss *linked lists,* which use *pointers* to create an extremely flexible data structure. You can add or remove items from any part of a linked list with very little effort. These sections also describe some linked list variations such as circular, doubly linked, and threaded lists.

Simple Lists

If your program needs a list that never changes, you can build it easily using an array. It is then a simple matter to examine the items when necessary using a For loop.

Many programs use lists that grow and shrink over time. You could allocate an array big enough to handle the list at its largest, but that may not always work very well. You may not know ahead of time how large the list will become. There may also be a small chance that the list will become huge. In that case, allocating a gigantic array would be a waste of memory most of the time.

Collections

A program can use a Visual Basic collection to store a resizable list. The Add method adds an item to the collection. The Remove method removes an item. The following code fragment shows a program adding three items to a collection and then removing the second item.

```
Dim list As New Collection
Dim obj As MyClass
Dim i As Integer

    ' Create and add item 1.
    Set obj = New MyClass
    list.Add obj

    ' Add an integer.
```

```
i = 13
list.Add i

' Add a string.
list.Add "Fun with collections"

' Remove item 2 (the integer).
list.Remove 2
```

Collections try to provide support for all applications, and they do a remarkably good job. They are easy to use, they can retrieve items indexed by a key, and they give reasonable performance when they do not contain too many items.

Collections have some drawbacks, though. For large lists, collections can be slower than arrays. If your program does not need all the features provided by a collection, using a simple array may be faster.

The hashing scheme collections use to manage their keys also imposes a couple of restrictions. First, collections do not allow duplicate keys. Second, a collection cannot tell which key is associated with a given item. It can tell what item has a given key, but it cannot tell what key goes with a specific item. Finally, collections do not support multiple keys. For instance, you might like your program to be able to search a list of employee data using either employee name or Social Security number. A collection could not support both lookup methods because it can manage only one key.

The following sections describe methods you can use to build lists that do not have these restrictions.

A Resizable List

Visual Basic's ReDim statement allows you to resize an array. You can use this ability to build a simple resizable list. Start by declaring an undimensioned array to hold the list items. Also declare a variable NumInList to keep track of the number of items in the list. To add an item to the list, use the ReDim statement to make the list large enough to hold the new item. To remove an item, use ReDim to shrink the array and free the memory that you no longer need.

```
Dim List () As String          ' The list of items.
Dim NumInList As Integer       ' The number of items in the list.

Sub AddToList(value As String)
    ' Resize to make room for the new entry.
    NumInList = NumInList + 1
    ReDim Preserve List (1 To NumInList)

    ' Then add the new item to the end of the list.
    List (NumInList) = value
End Sub
```

```
Sub RemoveFromList ()
    ' Resize the array to free unused memory.
    NumInList = NumInList - 1
    ReDim Preserve List (1 To NumInList)
End Sub
```

This simple scheme works well for small lists, but it has a couple of drawbacks. First, the array must be resized frequently. To create a list of 1000 items, you would need to resize the array 1000 times. Even worse, as the list gets larger, resizing it may take longer because Visual Basic needs to copy the growing list into new memory.

To reduce the number of times the array must be resized, add extra entries to the array whenever you resize it. When you enlarge the array, add 10 entries instead of 1. When you add new items in the future, the array will contain unused entries where you can place the items without resizing. You need to resize the array only when it runs out of unused entries.

In a similar fashion, you can avoid resizing each time you remove an item from the list. You can wait until there are at least 20 unused items in the array before resizing. When you do resize the array, be sure to leave 10 empty entries so you can add more items without being forced to resize again.

Note that the maximum number of unused items (20) should be larger than the minimum number (10). This minimizes the number of times you need to resize the array when you add and remove items.

With this scheme, the list will usually hold a few unused items. The number of unused items is small, however, so not much memory is wasted. The unused items give you insurance against resizing the array when you later add and remove items from the list. In fact, if you repeatedly add and remove only one or two items from the list, you might never need to resize the array.

```
Dim List () As String        ' The list of items.
Dim ArraySize As Integer     ' The size of the array.
Dim NumInList As Integer     ' The number of items in use.


' If the array is full, resize to give it 10 unused entries.
' Then add the new item to the end of the list.
Sub AddToList(value As String)
    NumInList = NumInList + 1
    If NumInList > ArraySize Then
        ArraySize = ArraySize + 10
        ReDim Preserve List(1 To ArraySize)
    End If
    List (NumInList) = value
End Sub


' Remove the last item from the list. If there are more than
' 20 unused items in the list, resize the list to free unused memory.
```

```
Sub RemoveFromList()
    NumInList = NumInList - 1
    If ArraySize - NumInList > 20 Then
        ArraySize = ArraySize - 10
        ReDim Preserve List(1 To ArraySize)
    End If
End Sub
```

For very large arrays this may still not be a good solution. If you need a list
holding 1000 items and you typically add 100 items at a time, you will still spend
a large amount of time resizing the array. An obvious strategy for handling this
situation is to increase the extra resize amount from 10 items to 100 or some even
larger value. Then you could add 100 items at a time without frequent resizing.

A more flexible solution is to make the amount of extra space depend on
the current size of the list. When the list is small, the extra space added is
small. The array would be resized more often, but it does not take too long to
resize a small array. When the list is large, the amount of extra space added is
larger, so the array would be resized less often.

The following code tries to keep about 10 percent of the list array empty.
When the array fills completely, the program enlarges it by 10 percent. If the
amount of empty space in the array grows beyond about 20 percent of the array's
size, the code makes the array smaller.

Whenever the program resizes the array, it always adds at least 10 items, even
if 10 percent of the array size is smaller. This reduces the number of resizes necessary when the list is very small.

```
Const WANT_FREE_PERCENT = .1     ' Try for 10% free space.
Const MIN_FREE = 10              ' Min free space when resizing.
Global List () As String         ' The list array.
Global ArraySize As Integer      ' Size of the list array.
Global NumItems As Integer       ' The number of items in the list.
Global ShrinkWhen As Integer     ' Shrink if NumItems < ShrinkWhen.

' If the array is full, resize it.
' Then add a new item to the end of the list.
Sub Add(value As String)
    NumItems = NumItems + 1
    If NumItems > ArraySize Then ResizeList
    List(NumItems) = value
End Sub

' Remove the last item from the list.
' If the array contains too many unused entries, shrink it.
Sub RemoveLast()
```

```
    NumItems = NumItems - 1
    If NumItems < ShrinkWhen Then ResizeList
End Sub


' Resize the list to give it 10% empty entries.
Sub ResizeList()
Dim want_free As Integer
    want_free = WANT_FREE_PERCENT * NumItems
    If want_free < MIN_FREE Then want_free = MIN_FREE
    ArraySize = NumItems + want_free
    ReDim Preserve List(1 To ArraySize)

    ' We will shrink the array if NumItems < ShrinkWhen.
    ShrinkWhen = NumItems - want_free
End Sub
```

The SimpleList Class

To use this simple list strategy, a program would need to know all the details of the list. It would need to keep track of the size of the array, the number of entries currently in use, and so forth. If the program needed to create more than one list, it would need multiple copies of all these values and duplicated code to manage the different lists.

Visual Basic classes can greatly simplify this task. The SimpleList class encapsulates this list scheme to make list management easy. The class provides Add and Remove methods for the main program to use. It also provides NumItems and ArraySize property get procedures so the program can tell how many items are in the list and how much memory the list occupies.

The ResizeList subroutine is declared private within the SimpleList class. This hides the list resizing from the main program because only the class code ever needs to use this routine.

Using the SimpleList class, it is easy for an application to create more than one list. It simply uses the New statement to create one object for each list. The objects each have their own variables so they can each manage their separate lists.

```
Dim list1 As New SimpleList
Dim list2 As New SimpleList
```

Example program SimList demonstrates the SimpleList class. Enter a value in the text box and click the Add button. The program will add the item to its list. The SimpleList object will resize its array if necessary. Whenever the list is not empty, you can press the Remove button to remove the last item from the list.

When the SimpleList object resizes its array, it displays a message box telling you how large the array is, how many items in the array are unused, and the value ShrinkWhen. When the number of items in use in the array falls below the value ShrinkWhen, the program resizes the array to make it smaller. Notice that when the array is almost empty, ShrinkWhen sometimes becomes zero or negative. In that case, the array will not be resized, even if you remove all the items from the list.

Program SimList adds 50 percent of the current array size as empty entries when it must resize the array, and it always keeps a minimum of 1 empty entry when it resizes. These values were chosen so that you could easily make the program resize the array. In a real application, the percentage of free memory should be smaller and the minimum number of free entries should be larger. Values more like 10 percent of the current list size and a minimum of 10 unused entries would make more sense.

Unordered Lists

In some applications you may need to remove items from the middle of the list, though you can still add new items at the end. This will be the case when the order of the items is not particularly important, but you may need to remove specific items from the list. This kind of list is called an *unordered list*. It is also sometimes called a *bag* or *sack*.

An unordered list should support these operations:

- Add an item to the list

- Remove a specific item from the list

- Determine whether a specific item is in the list

- Perform some operation (print, display, etc.) on all of the items in the list

You can easily modify the simple scheme presented in the previous section to handle this kind of list. When you remove an item from the middle of the list, you shift the remaining items one position to fill in the hole left behind. Figure 2.1 shows this operation graphically. Here the second item is removed from the list and the third, fourth, and fifth items are shifted to the left to fill in the hole.

Removing an item from an array in this way can take quite a bit of time, particularly if the item removed is near the beginning of the array. To remove the first item in an array containing 1000 entries you would need to move 999 of the entries one position to the left. A simple *garbage collection* scheme will allow you to remove items much more quickly.

Instead of removing items from the list, mark them as not in use. If the items in the list are simple data types like integers, you might be able to use a specific

---

Figure 2.1 Removing an item from the middle of an array.

garbage value to mark items. For integers you might use the value –32,767. For a Variant you could use the value Null. You assign this value to any item that is not in use. The following code fragment shows how to remove an item from this kind of integer list.

```
Const GARBAGE_VALUE = -32767

' Mark the item as garbage.
Sub RemoveFromList(position As Long)
    List(position) = GARBAGE_VALUE
End Sub
```

If the items in the list are structures defined by a Type statement, you can add a new IsGarbage field to the structure. When you remove an item from the list, set the value of the item's IsGarbage field to True.

```
Type MyData
    Name As String         ' Data.
    IsGarbage As Integer   ' Is this entry garbage?
End Type

' Mark the item as garbage.
Sub RemoveFromList(position As Long)
    List(position).IsGarbage = True
End Sub
```

To keep things simple, the rest of this section assumes that the data items are variants and that you can mark them with the garbage value Null.

Once the list contains entries marked as garbage, you must modify other routines that use the list so they can skip the garbage values. For example, you might change a subroutine that prints the list like this:

```
' Print the items in the list.
Sub PrintItems()
Dim I As Long

    For I = 1 To ArraySize
        If Not IsNull(I) Then    ' If it's not garbage
            Print Str$(List(I))  ' print it.
        End If
    Next I
End Sub
```

After you use a garbage marking scheme for a while, the list may become full of garbage. Eventually subroutines like this one will spend more time skipping garbage entries than examining actual data.

To solve this problem, you can periodically run a *garbage collection routine.* This routine moves all of the nongarbage entries to the beginning of the array. You can then add the remaining entries to the unused items at the end of the array. When you need to add more items to the list, you can reuse these entries to avoid resizing.

Adding the reclaimed garbage entries to the other unused entries may make the total amount of unused space quite large. In that case you may want to resize the array to free some unused space.

```
Private Sub CollectGarbage()
Dim i As Long
Dim good As Long

    good = 1    ' The first good item goes here.
    For i = 1 To m_NumItems
        ' If it's not garbage, move it to its new location.
        If Not IsNull(m_List(i)) Then
            m_List(good) = m_List(i)
            good = good + 1
        End If
    Next i

    ' This is where the last good item is.
    m_NumItems = good - 1

    ' See if we should resize the list.
    If m_NumItems < m_ShrinkWhen Then ResizeList
End Sub
```

When you perform garbage collection, you move items near the end of the list toward the beginning to fill in the space occupied by garbage entries. That means the positions of the items in the list may change during garbage collection. That in turn means other parts of the program cannot rely on the items in the list staying in their original positions. If other parts of the program must access items by their positions in the list, you will need to modify the garbage collection routine so it can update those other parts of the program. Generally, this sort of thing can be confusing and can lead to big maintenance problems later.

There are several ways you can decide when to run the garbage collector. One way is to wait until the array reaches a certain large size. For example, when a list contains 30,000 entries, you could run the garbage collector.

This method has some drawbacks. First, it uses a lot of memory. If you add and remove items frequently, you will fill a lot of array entries with garbage. If you waste enough memory like this, the program might spend time paging when the list could fit completely in real memory if you rearranged it sooner.

Second, if the list starts to fill with garbage, routines that use it will become extremely inefficient. If an array of 30,000 items contains 25,000 pieces of garbage, a subroutine like PrintItems described earlier would be terribly slow.

Finally, garbage collection for a very large array can take quite a bit of time, particularly if scanning the array causes your program to page. This may cause your program to freeze for several seconds while it cleans house.

To help solve this problem, you can create a new variable GarbageCount to keep track of the number of garbage items in the list. When a substantial fraction of the list's memory contains garbage, you can start garbage collection.

```
Dim GarbageCount As Long          ' Number of garbage items.
Dim MaxGarbage As Long            ' This is set in ResizeList.


' Mark the item as garbage.
' If there is too much garbage, start garbage collection.
Public Sub Remove(position As Long)
    m_List(position) = Null
    m_GarbageCount = m_GarbageCount + 1

    ' If there's too much garbage, collect the garbage.
    If m_GarbageCount > m_MaxGarbage Then CollectGarbage
End Sub
```

Example program Garbage demonstrates these garbage collection techniques. It displays unused items in the list as "<unused>" and entries marked as garbage with "<garbage>." The GarbageList class the program uses is similar to the SimpleList class used by program SimList, except it performs garbage collection.

Enter a value and click the Add button to add an item to the list. To remove an item, click on the item and then click the Remove button. When the list contains too much garbage, the program performs garbage collection.

Whenever the GarbageList object resizes its list, it presents a message box that tells you the number of used and unused items in the list and the values MaxGarbage and ShrinkWhen. If you remove enough items so that more than MaxGarbage items in the list contain garbage, the program runs the garbage collector. Once the garbage collector is finished, the program shrinks the array if it contains fewer than ShrinkWhen used items.

Program Garbage adds 50 percent of the current list size as empty entries when it must resize the array, and it always keeps a minimum of 1 empty entry when it resizes. These values were chosen so you can easily make the program resize the list. In a real program the percentage of free memory should be smaller and the minimum number of free entries should be larger. Values more like 10 percent free and a minimum of 10 entries would make more sense.

Linked Lists

Linked lists provide an alternative list management strategy. A linked list stores items in data structures or objects called *cells*. Each cell includes a pointer to the next cell in the list. Because the only types of pointers Visual Basic provides are references to objects, a linked list in Visual Basic must use objects for its cells.

The cell class should define a NextCell variable that indicates the next cell in the list. It should also define variables to hold whatever data the program needs to manipulate. These variables could be declared public within the class, or the class could provide property procedures to get and set the variable values. For example, in a linked list of employee records, these fields might store employee name, Social Security number, job title, and so forth. The Declarations section for the EmpCell class might look like the following:

```
Public EmpName As String
Public SSN As String
Public JobTitle As String
Public NextCell As EmpCell
```

A program uses the New statement to create new cells. It assigns their variable values and uses their NextCell variables to connect them.

The program should keep a reference to the top of the list. So it can tell where the list ends, the program should set the NextCell value for last item to Nothing. For example, the following code fragment creates a list representing three employees.

```
Dim top_cell As EmpCell
Dim cell1 As EmpCell
Dim cell2 As EmpCell
Dim cell3 As EmpCell

    ' Build the cells.
    Set cell1 = New EmpCell
    cell1.EmpName = "Stephens"
    cell1.SSN = "123-45-6789"
    cell1.JobTitle = "Author"

    Set cell2 = New EmpCell
    cell2.EmpName = "Cats"
    cell2.SSN = "234-56-7890"
    cell2.JobTitle = "Lawyer"

    Set cell3 = New EmpCell
    cell3.EmpName = "Toole"
```

```
cell3.SSN = "345-67-8901"
cell3.JobTitle = "Manager"

' Connect the cells to make the linked list.
Set cell1.NextCell = cell2
Set cell2.NextCell = cell3
Set cell3.NextCell = Nothing

' Save a reference to the top of the list.
Set top_cell = cell1
```

Figure 2.2 shows a schematic representation of this linked list. Boxes represent cells, and arrows represent references to objects. The small box with an X in it represents the value Nothing that marks the end of the list. Keep in mind that top_cell, cell1, cell2, and cell3 are not actually objects—they are references that point to objects.

The following code uses the linked list built by the previous example to print out the names of the employees in the list. The variable ptr is used as a pointer to the items in the list. It starts at the top of the list. The code uses a Do loop to move ptr through the list until it reaches the end. During each loop, the routine prints the EmpName field for the cell pointed to by ptr. It then advances ptr to indicate the next cell in the list. Eventually ptr reaches the end of the list and is set to Nothing, and the Do loop stops.

```
Dim ptr As EmpCell

    Set ptr = top_cell    ' Start at the top of the list.
    Do While Not (ptr Is Nothing)
        ' Display this cell's EmpName field.
        Debug.Print ptr.EmpName
```

Figure 2.2 A linked list.

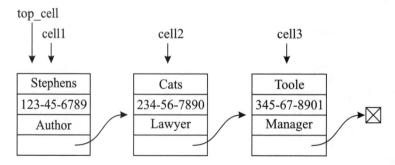

```
' Advance to the next cell in the list.
    Set ptr = ptr.NextCell
Loop
```

If you execute this code, you will see a result like this:

```
Stephens
Cats
Toole
```

Using a pointer to point to another object is called *indirection* because you use the pointer to manipulate data indirectly. Indirection can be very confusing. Even for a simple arrangement like a linked list, it is sometimes hard to remember which reference points to which object. In more complicated data structures such as trees and networks, a pointer may point to an object containing another pointer. With a couple of different pointers and several levels of indirection, you can easily become confused.

To make things a little easier, this book uses pictures like the one in Figure 2.2 to help you visualize the situation whenever possible. Many algorithms that use pointers are easy to describe using pictures like this one.

Adding Items to a Linked List

The simple linked list shown in Figure 2.2 has several important properties. First, it is very easy to add a new cell to the beginning of the list. Set the new cell's NextCell value so that it points to the current top of the list. Then set top_cell to point to the new cell. Figure 2.3 shows the picture corresponding to this operation. The Visual Basic code for this operation is quite simple.

```
Set new_cell.NextCell = top_cell
Set top_cell = new_cell
```

Compare this to the code that you would have needed to add a new item to the beginning of an array-based list. There you would need to move every entry in the array one space to make room for the new item. This O(N) operation could

Figure 2.3 Adding an item to the top of a linked list.

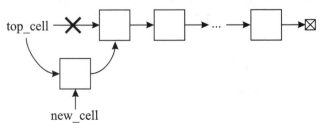

top_cell

new_cell

take a long time if the list is long. Using a linked list, you can insert a new item at the top of the list in just two steps.

It is also easy to insert a new item in the middle of a linked list. Suppose you want to insert a new item after the cell pointed to by variable after_me. Set the new cell's NextCell value to after_me.NextCell. Then set after_me.NextCell to point to the new cell. Figure 2.4 shows this operation graphically. Once again the Visual Basic code is straightforward.

```
Set new_cell.NextCell = after_me.NextCell
Set after_me.NextCell = new_cell
```

Removing Items from a Linked List

It is just as easy to remove an item from the top of a linked list as it is to add one. Simply set top_cell to point to the next cell in the list. Figure 2.5 shows the picture corresponding to this operation. The source code for this operation is even simpler than the code for inserting an item.

```
Set top_cell = top_cell.NextCell
```

When top_cell is moved to the second item in the list, the program may no longer have any variable referencing the former first object. In that case, that object's reference count will be reduced to zero and the system will destroy the object automatically.

Removing an item from the middle of the list is also easy. Suppose you want to remove the item after the cell after_me. Simply set that cell's NextCell value to point to the following cell. Figure 2.6 shows this operation graphically. The Visual Basic code is straightforward.

```
after_me.NextCell = after_me.NextCell.NextCell
```

Figure 2.4 Adding an item to the middle of a linked list.

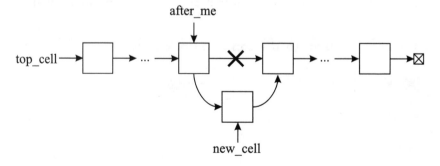

Figure 2.5 Removing the top cell from a linked list.

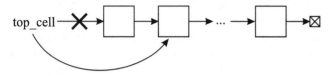

Again you should compare this code to the code needed to perform the same operation using an array-based list. You can quickly mark a removed item as garbage, but this leaves garbage entries in the list. Routines that manipulate the list must be complicated to take this into account. They may also be slowed by excessive garbage, and eventually you will need to run a garbage collector.

When you remove an item from a linked list, you create no gaps in the list. Routines that manipulate the list still start from the top and follow the list to its end, so you do not need to modify those routines.

Destroying a Linked List

To destroy a linked list, you might think you need to move through the list setting each call's NextCell value to Nothing. Actually the process is much simpler: You simply set top_cell to Nothing.

When the program sets top_cell to Nothing, the reference count of the first cell in the list is reduced to zero so Visual Basic destroys that cell.

As it destroys the first cell, the system notices that the cell contains a reference to another cell in its NextCell variable. Because it is destroying the first cell, it reduces the reference count of that other object. That makes the reference count for the second object in the list zero, so the system destroys it, too.

When the system destroys the second object, it reduces the reference count of the third, and so forth until every object in the list has been destroyed. As long as the program does not contain other references to the objects in the list, it can destroy the entire list with the single statement Set top_cell = Nothing.

Figure 2.6 Removing an item from the middle of a linked list.

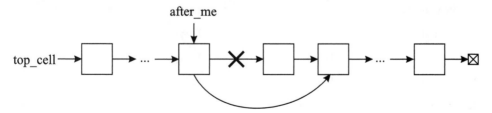

Sentinels

The routines for adding and removing items are different depending on whether you want to add or remove an item from the top or middle of the list. You can make both of these cases behave in the same way and eliminate some redundant code, if you introduce a special *sentinel* cell at the very top of the list. The sentinel cell should never be removed. It contains no meaningful data—it is used only to mark the top of the list.

Now instead of having to deal with the odd case of adding an entry at the very top of the list, you can add the new item after the sentinel. Similarly, you do not need to worry about the special case of removing the first item in the list—you simply remove the item after the sentinel.

Using a sentinel makes a small difference now. Sentinels play important roles in many more complex algorithms. They allow a program to treat special cases, like dealing with the top of a list, as if they were nothing special. You can write and debug less code, and the algorithms are more consistent and easier to understand.

Table 2.1 compares the difficulty of performing some common operations using array-based lists with garbage collection and linked lists.

Linked lists are usually better, but the array-based list is superior in one area: memory usage. Linked lists require you to add an extra NextCell field to every data item. Each of these object references takes an additional four bytes of memory. For very large arrays, this may take up a lot of space.

Example program LnkList1 demonstrates a simple linked list with a sentinel. Enter a value in the text box, and click on an item in the list or on the sentinel. Then click the Add After button, and the program will add the new item after the one you selected. To remove an item from the list, click on an item and click the Remove After button.

Encapsulating Linked Lists

Program LnkList1 manages its linked list explicitly. For example, the following code shows how the program removes an item from the list. When the subroutine

Table 2.1 Comparison of Array-Based Lists and Linked Lists

Operation	Array-Based List	Linked List
Add item at end	Easy	Easy
Add item at top	Hard	Easy
Add item in middle	Hard	Easy
Remove item from top	Easy	Easy
Remove item in middle	Easy	Easy
List nongarbage items	Medium	Easy

begins, the global variable SelectedIndex gives the position in the list of the item before the one that should be removed. The variable Sentinel contains a reference to the list's sentinel.

```
Private Sub CmdRemoveAfter_Click()
Dim ptr As ListCell
Dim position As Integer

    If SelectedIndex < 0 Then Exit Sub

    ' Find the item.
    Set ptr = Sentinel
    position = SelectedIndex
    Do While position > 0
        position = position - 1
        Set ptr = ptr.NextCell
    Loop

    ' Remove the next item.
    Set ptr.NextCell = ptr.NextCell.NextCell
    NumItems = NumItems - 1

    SelectItem SelectedIndex ' Reselect the item.
    DisplayList
    NewItem.SetFocus
End Sub
```

To make using linked lists easier, you can encapsulate the linked list functions in a class. Example program LnkList2 does just that. It is similar to the LnkList1 program except that it uses a LinkedList class to manage its list instead of performing the management tasks itself.

The LinkedList class manages all the internals of a linked list. It provides subroutines that add and remove items, return the value of an item given its index, return the number of items in the list, and clear the list. This class makes the linked list behave as much like a regular array as possible.

This makes the main program much simpler. For example, the following code shows how LnkList2 removes an item from its list. Only one line of this code is actually involved in removing the item. The other lines display the new list. Compare this code to the previous subroutine.

```
Private Sub CmdRemoveAfter_Click()
    LList.RemoveAfter SelectedIndex

    SelectItem SelectedIndex ' Reselect the item.
    DisplayList
    NewItem.SetFocus
```

```
        CmdClearList.Enabled = LList.NumItems > 0
End Sub
```

Accessing Cells

The LinkedList class used by program LnkList2 allows the main program to use the list much as it would use an array. For example, the Item subroutine shown in the following code returns the value of an item given its position.

```
Function Item(ByVal position As Long) As Variant
Dim ptr As ListCell

    If position < 1 Or position > m_NumItems Then
        ' Out of bounds. Return Null.
        Item = Null
        Exit Function
    End If

    ' Find the item.
    Set ptr = m_Sentinel
    Do While position > 0
        position = position - 1
        Set ptr = ptr.NextCell
    Loop

    Item = ptr.Value
End Function
```

This routine is fairly simple, but it does not take advantage of the list's linked structure. For example, suppose a program needs to examine each of the objects in the list in order. It could use the Item subroutine to access the items one at a time, as shown in the following code.

```
Dim i As Integer

    For i = 1 To LList.NumItems
        ' Do something with LList.Item(i).
            :
    Next i
```

Each time the Item subroutine executes, it loops through the list looking for the next item. To find item I in the list, it must skip over I − 1 items. To examine every item in an N item list, it will skip over $0 + 1 + 2 + 3 + \ldots + N - 1 = N * (N - 1) / 2$ items. When N is large, the program will waste a large amount of time skipping items.

The LinkedList class can make this operation faster using a different access scheme. It should use a private m_CurrentCell variable to keep track of its position in the list. It then provides a CurrentItem subroutine to return the value of the current item. MoveFirst, MoveNext, and EndOfList routines allow the main program to manage the list's current position.

For example, the following code shows the MoveNext subroutine.

```
Public Sub MoveNext()
    ' If there's no current cell, do nothing.
    If Not (m_CurrentCell Is Nothing) Then _
        Set m_CurrentCell = m_CurrentCell.NextCell
End Sub
```

Using these routines, the main program can visit every item in the list using the following code. This code is slightly more complicated than the previous version, but it is much more efficient. Instead of skipping $N * (N - 1) / 2$ items to visit every cell in an N item list, this code skips no items. When the list contains 1000 items, this saves almost half a million steps.

```
LList.MoveFirst

Do While Not LList.EndOfList
    ' Do something with LList.Item(i).
        :
    LList.MoveNext
Loop
```

Example program LnkList3 uses these new techniques to manage a linked list. The program is similar to program LnkList2 except that it accesses its list items more efficiently. For the small lists used by this program, the difference is not noticeable. For a program that accesses every element in a large list, this version of the LinkedList class is more efficient.

Linked List Variations

Linked lists play a part in many algorithms, and you will see them throughout the rest of this book. The following sections discuss a few specialized variations of linked lists.

Circular Linked Lists

Instead of setting the NextCell field of the last item in a list to Nothing, you could have it point back to the first item in the list. This makes a *circular list*, as shown in Figure 2.7.

Circular lists are useful when you need to loop through a set of data items indefinitely. At each step in the loop, the program simply moves a cell pointer to the next cell in the list. For example, suppose you had a circular list of items containing the names of the days of the week. Then a program could list the days of the month using the following code.

Figure 2.7 A circular linked list.

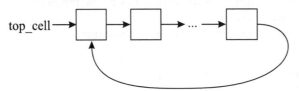

```
' Code to set up the list, etc. goes here.
    :
' Print a calendar for the month.
'
' first_day is the index of the day of the week structure for
' the first day of the month. For example, the month might
' start on a Monday.
'
' num_days is the number of days in the month.
Private Sub ListMonth(first_day As Integer, num_days As Integer)
Dim ptr As ListCell
Dim i As Integer

    Set ptr = top_cell
    For i = 1 to num_days
        Print Format$(i) & ": " & ptr.Value
        Set ptr = ptr.NextCell
    Next i
End Sub
```

Circular lists also allow you to reach the entire list starting from any position in the list. This gives the list an appealing symmetry. The program can treat all the items in the list in pretty much the same way.

```
Private Sub PrintList(start_cell As Integer)
Dim ptr As Integer

    Set ptr = start_cell
    Do
        Print ptr.Value
        Set ptr = ptr.NextCell
    Loop While Not (ptr Is start_cell)
End Sub
```

Circular Reference Problems

Destroying a circular linked list requires a little more attention than deleting a
normal link list does. If you simply set the top_cell variable to Nothing, your program will no longer be able to access the list. Because the last cell has a NextCell
value pointing to the first cell, however, the first cell's reference count is not zero,
so it will not be destroyed. Every item in the list is pointed to by some other item,
so none of them can be destroyed.

This is a *circular referencing* problem. Because the cells point to each other,
none can be destroyed. The program cannot access any of them, so the memory
they occupy is wasted until the program ends.

This is not the only way a program can run into circular reference problems.
Many networks contain circular references. Even a single cell with its NextCell
variable pointing to itself can cause this problem.

The solution is to break the circular chain of references. For example, your
program could use the following code to destroy a circular linked list.

```
Set top_cell.NextCell = Nothing
Set top_cell = Nothing
```

The first line breaks the circle of references. At that point no variable points to
the second cell in the list, so the system reduces its reference to zero and destroys
it. That reduces the reference count for the third item to zero, so it is also
destroyed. The process continues around the list until every item has been destroyed
except the first one. Setting top_cell to Nothing reduces its reference count to zero,
and the last cell is destroyed.

Doubly Linked Lists

You may have noticed during the discussion of linked lists that most operations
were defined in terms of doing something *after* a particular cell in the list. Given a
particular cell, it is easy to add a new cell after it, delete the cell after it, or list all
the cells that come after it. It is not as easy to delete the cell itself, to insert a new
cell before the cell, or to list the cells that come before it. With only a small
change, however, you can make these operations easy, too.

Add a new pointer field to each cell that points to the *previous* cell in the list.
Using the new fields you can create a *doubly linked list* that lets you move forward
and backward through the items. Now you can easily delete a cell, insert before a cell,
and list cells in either direction. Figure 2.8 shows a picture of a doubly linked list.

Figure 2.8 A doubly linked list.

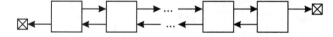

The DoubleListCell class used for this kind of list might use the following variable declarations.

```
Public Value As Variant
Public NextCell As DoubleListCell
Public PrevCell As DoubleListCell
```

It is often useful to keep pointers to both the top and bottom of a doubly linked list. Then you can easily add items at either end of the list. It is also sometimes useful to have sentinels at both the top and bottom of the list. Then as you manipulate the list, you need not care whether you are working on the top, middle, or bottom of the list.

Figure 2.9 shows a doubly linked list with sentinels. In this picture the sentinels' unused NextCell and PrevCell pointers are set to Nothing. Because the program recognizes the ends of the list by comparing cell pointers to the sentinels rather than by looking for the value Nothing, setting these values to Nothing is not absolutely necessary. It is still a good practice, however.

The code for inserting and removing items from a doubly linked list is similar to the code presented earlier for dealing with a singly linked list. The routines need to be changed only slightly to handle the PrevCell pointers.

You can now write new routines to add an item before or after a given item and to delete a particular item. For example, the following subroutines add and remove cells in a doubly linked list. Notice that these routines do not need to access either of the list's sentinels. All they need are pointers to the node to be added or removed and a node near the point of insertion.

```
Public Sub RemoveItem(ByVal target As DoubleListCell)
Dim after_target As DoubleListCell
Dim before_target As DoubleListCell

    Set after_target = target.NextCell
    Set before_target = target.PrevCell
    Set before_target.NextCell = after_target
    Set after_target.PrevCell = before_target
End Sub

Sub AddAfter(new_cell As DoubleListCell, after_me As DoubleListCell)
```

Figure 2.9 A doubly linked list with sentinels.

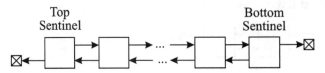

Top
Sentinel

Bottom
Sentinel

```
Dim before_me As DoubleListCell

    Set before_me = after_me.NextCell
    Set after_me.NextCell = new_cell
    Set new_cell.NextCell = before_me
    Set before_me.PrevCell = new_cell
    Set new_cell.PrevCell = after_me
End Sub

Sub AddBefore(new_cell As DoubleListCell, before_me As DoubleListCell)
Dim after_me As DoubleListCell

    Set after_me = before_me.PrevCell
    Set after_me.NextCell = new_cell
    Set new_cell.NextCell = before_me
    Set before_me.PrevCell = new_cell
    Set new_cell.PrevCell = after_me
End Sub
```

If you look again at Figure 2.9, you will see that every adjacent pair of cells forms a circular reference. That makes destroying a doubly linked list a little harder than destroying singly linked or circular lists. The following code shows one way to empty a doubly linked list. It begins by setting all of the cells' PrevCell pointers to Nothing to break the circular references. This essentially converts the list into a singly linked list. When the sentinels' links are set to Nothing, all the items are freed automatically, just as they are in a singly linked list.

```
Dim ptr As DoubleListCell

    ' Clear the PrevCell pointers to break circular references.
    Set ptr = TopSentinel.NextCell
    Do While Not (ptr Is BottomSentinel)
        Set ptr.PrevCell = Nothing
        Set ptr = ptr.NextCell
    Loop
    Set TopSentinel.NextCell = Nothing
    Set BottomSentinel.PrevCell = Nothing
```

If you build a class to encapsulate a doubly linked list, its Terminate event handler can destroy the list. When the main program sets its reference to the list object to Nothing, the list will automatically free its memory.

Example program DblLink manipulates a doubly linked list. It allows you to add items before or after a selected item, and it lets you delete a selected item.

Threads

In some applications it is useful to traverse a linked list using more than one possible ordering. In different parts of an application you might want to list employees ordered by their last names, salaries, Social Security numbers, or job classifications.

Normal linked lists allow you to examine the items in one order only. Using a PrevCell pointer, you can create a doubly linked list that allows you to move forward or backward through the list. You can extend this idea further by adding more pointers to the data structure to allow you to display the list in other orders.

The set of links that makes up one of these orderings is called a *thread*. Do not confuse this term with the multi-processing threads provided by Windows NT.

A list can contain any number of threads, though at some point the extra work of maintaining the threads is not worth the effort. A thread ordering employees by last name would make sense if your application uses that ordering frequently. A thread ordering employees by middle initial would probably not be useful because your program would probably never use it.

Some orderings do not make good threads. A thread ordering employees by gender, for example, would not be a good thread because the ordering is easy to obtain without it. To list the employees ordered by gender without the thread, you simply traverse the list along any other thread while printing out the names of the female employees. Then you traverse the list again printing out the names of the male employees. You would need only two passes through the list to produce this ordering.

Compare this to the case where you want to list employees ordered by their last names. If the list did not include a last name thread, you would have to search the list for the name that came first, then search for the name that came second, and so forth. This is an $O(N^2)$ process that is much less efficient than the $O(N)$ method for ordering employees by gender.

Generally, an ordering will make a good thread if you need to use it often and if it would be hard to build the same ordering whenever you need it. An ordering will make a bad thread if it is easy to re-create at any time.

Example program Threads demonstrates a simple threaded employee list. Fill in the last name, first name, Social Security number, job class, and gender fields for a new employee. Then click the Add button to add the new employee to the list.

The program contains threads that order the list by employee last name forward and backward, by Social Security number, and by job classification forward and backward. You can use the option buttons to select the thread by which the program displays the list. Figure 2.10 shows program Threads listing employees ordered by name.

The ThreadedCell class used by program Threads defines the following variables:

```
Public LastName As String
Public FirstName As String
Public SSN As String
Public Sex As String
Public JobClass As Integer
```

```
Public NextName As ThreadedCell        ' By name forward.
Public PrevName As ThreadedCell        ' By name backward.
Public NextSSN As ThreadedCell         ' By SSN forward.
Public NextJobClass As ThreadedCell    ' By job class forward.
Public PrevJobClass As ThreadedCell    ' By job class backward.
```

The ThreadedList class encapsulates the threaded list. When the program uses the AddItem method, the list updates all its threads. For each thread the program must insert the new item in its proper order. To insert a record with last name "Smith," for example, the program loops through the list using the NextName thread until it finds an item with a name that should come after "Smith." It then inserts the new entry in the NextName thread before that item.

Sentinels play an important role in finding where new entries belong in the threads. The ThreadedList Class_Initialize event handler creates top and bottom sentinels and initializes their pointers so they point to each other. It sets the data values for the top sentinel so they come before any valid real entries for all the threads.

For example, the LastName variable can contain string values. The empty string "" comes alphabetically before all valid string values, so the program sets the top sentinel's LastName value to the empty string.

Similarly Class_Initialize sets the data values for the bottom sentinel to be bigger than any valid values in all of the threads. Because "~" comes alphabetically after all other visible ASCII characters, the program sets the bottom sentinel's LastName value to "~."

By giving the sentinels the LastName values "" and "~," the program avoids the need to check for special cases where the new item should be inserted at the top or bottom of the list. All valid new values will fall between the sentinels'

Figure 2.10 Program Threads.

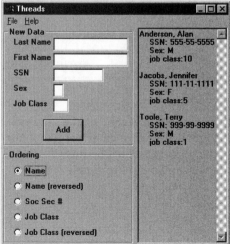

LastName values, so the program will always find the new item's correct position without worrying about searching past the bottom sentinel and falling off the list.

The following code shows how the ThreadedList class inserts a new item in the NextName and PrevName threads. Because these threads use the same key, the cells' names, the program can update them at the same time.

```
Dim ptr As ThreadedCell
Dim nxt As ThreadedCell
Dim new_cell As New ThreadedCell
Dim new_name As String
Dim next_name As String

    ' Save the new cell's values.
    With new_cell
        .LastName = LastName
        .FirstName = FirstName
        .SSN = SSN
        .Sex = Sex
        .JobClass = JobClass
    End With

    ' See where the new cell belongs in the NextName thread.
    new_name = LastName & ", " & FirstName
    Set ptr = m_TopSentinel
    Do
        Set nxt = ptr.NextName
        next_name = nxt.LastName & ", " & nxt.FirstName
        If next_name >= new_name Then Exit Do
        Set ptr = nxt
    Loop

    ' Insert the new cell in the NextName and PrevName threads.
    Set new_cell.NextName = nxt
    Set new_cell.PrevName = ptr
    Set ptr.NextName = new_cell
    Set nxt.PrevName = new_cell
```

For this to work, the program must ensure that the new cell's values always lie between the sentinel values. If a user somehow managed to enter "~~" as a last name, for example, the loop would run past the bottom sentinel because "~~" comes after "~." The program would then crash when it tried to access the value nxt.LastName when nxt was set to Nothing.

Other Linked Structures

Using pointers you can build many other useful kinds of linked structures such as trees, irregular arrays, sparse arrays, graphs, and networks. A cell can contain any number of pointers to other cells. For example, you could use a cell containing two pointers, one to a right child cell and one to a left child cell, to create a binary tree. A BinaryCell class might include the following declarations:

```
Public LeftChild As BinaryCell
Public RightChild As BinaryCell
```

Figure 2.11 shows a tree built from this kind of cell. Chapter 6, "Trees," has much more to say about trees.

A cell can even contain a collection or linked list of pointers to other cells. This allows a program to link a cell to any number of other objects. Figure 2.12 shows examples of other linked data structures. You will see structures like these later, particularly in Chapter 12, "Network Algorithms."

Pointer Faking

Visual Basic's references allow you to easily create linked structures like lists, trees, and networks, but references come with quite a bit of overhead. Data structures built using references are slowed by reference counting and other memory allocation issues.

An alternative strategy that often provides better performance is *pointer faking*. In pointer faking, a program allocates an array of data structures. Rather than using references to link the structures, the program uses indexes into the array. Visual Basic can locate an item in an array more quickly than it can resolve an object reference. That gives pointer faking better performance than corresponding object reference methods.

On the other hand, pointer faking is less intuitive than reference methods. This may make implementing and debugging complex algorithms like balanced tree and network algorithms more difficult.

Figure 2.11 A binary tree.

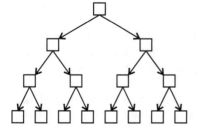

Figure 2.12 Linked structures.

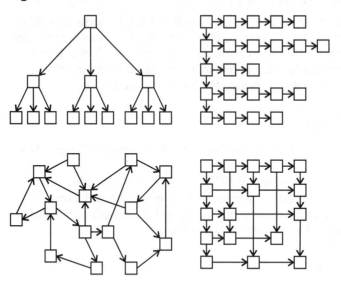

Example program FakeList manages a linked list using pointer faking. It allocates an array of simple data structures to hold the list's cells. The program is similar to program LnkList1 except that it uses pointer faking.

The following code shows how FakeList allocates its array of cell structures:

```
' The cell data structure.
Type FakeCell
    Value As String
    NextCell As Integer
End Type
```

```
' The array of linked list cells.
Global Cells(0 To 100) As FakeCell
```

```
' The list sentinel.
Global Sentinel As Integer
```

Because faked pointers are integers, not references, a program cannot use the value Nothing to indicate the end of the list. Program FakeList uses the constant value END_OF_LIST defined to be -32,767 to indicate a pointer that does not point to any cell.

To make finding unused cells easier, program FakeList keeps a separate garbage list containing the unused cells. The following code shows how the program initializes the empty linked list. It sets the sentinel's NextCell value to END_OF_LIST. It then places all the unused cells on the garbage list.

```
' Linked list of unused calls.
Global TopGarbage As Integer

Public Sub InitializeList()
Dim i As Integer

    Sentinel = 0
    Cells(Sentinel).NextCell = END_OF_LIST

    ' Put all the other cells on a garbage list.
    For i = 1 To UBound(Cells) - 1
        Cells(i).NextCell = i + 1
    Next i
    Cells(UBound(Cells)).NextCell = END_OF_LIST
    TopGarbage = 1
End Sub
```

To add a new item to the linked list, the program uses the first cell available in the garbage list. It initializes the cell's Value field and inserts the cell into the list. The following code shows how the program adds an item after the currently selected item.

```
Private Sub CmdAddAfter_Click()
Dim ptr As Integer
Dim position As Integer
Dim new_cell As Integer

    ' Find the insertion position.
    ptr = Sentinel
    position = SelectedIndex
    Do While position > 0
        position = position - 1
        ptr = Cells(ptr).NextCell
    Loop

    ' Get a new cell from the garbage list.
    new_cell = TopGarbage
    TopGarbage = Cells(TopGarbage).NextCell

    ' Insert the item.
    Cells(new_cell).Value = NewItem.Text
    Cells(new_cell).NextCell = Cells(ptr).NextCell
    Cells(ptr).NextCell = new_cell
    NumItems = NumItems + 1
```

```
    DisplayList
    SelectItem SelectedIndex + 1 ' Select the new item.
    NewItem.Text = ""
    NewItem.SetFocus
    CmdClearList.Enabled = True
End Sub
```

After removing a cell from the list, program FakeList places the removed cell on the garbage list so it will be easy to reuse later.

```
Private Sub CmdRemoveAfter_Click()
Dim ptr As Integer
Dim target As Integer
Dim position As Integer

    If SelectedIndex < 0 Then Exit Sub

    ' Find the item.
    ptr = Sentinel
    position = SelectedIndex
    Do While position > 0
        position = position - 1
        ptr = Cells(ptr).NextCell
    Loop

    ' Skip the next item.
    target = Cells(ptr).NextCell
    Cells(ptr).NextCell = Cells(target).NextCell
    NumItems = NumItems - 1

    ' Add the removed cell to the garbage list.
    Cells(target).NextCell = TopGarbage
    TopGarbage = target

    SelectItem SelectedIndex ' Reselect the item.
    DisplayList
    CmdClearList.Enabled = NumItems > 0
    NewItem.SetFocus
End Sub
```

Pointer faking usually provides better performance than object referencing techniques, but it is more complicated. For that reason, you initially may want to build your applications using object references. Then, if you find the program spends a large percentage of its time manipulating references, you can convert it to use pointer faking if necessary.

Summary

Using object references, you can build flexible data structures such as linked lists, circular linked lists, and doubly linked lists. These lists allow you to add and remove items quickly from any position.

By adding extra references to a cell class, you can extend doubly linked lists to create threaded lists. By extending these ideas further, you can create more exotic data structures, including sparse arrays, trees, hash tables, and networks. These are described in detail in the following chapters.

STACKS AND QUEUES

This chapter continues the discussion of lists started in Chapter 2, "Lists," by describing two special kinds of lists: stacks and queues. A stack is a list where items are added and removed from the same end of the list. A queue is a list where items are added to one end and removed from the other. Many algorithms, including several presented in later chapters, use stacks and queues.

Stacks

A *stack* is an ordered list where items are always added and removed from the same end of the list. You can think of a stack as a stack of objects on the floor. You can add items to the top and remove them from the top, but you cannot add or remove an item from the middle of the pile.

Because of their Last-In-First-Out behavior, stacks are sometimes called *LIFO lists* or *LIFOs*. For historical reasons, adding an item to a stack is called *pushing* the item onto the stack, and removing an item from a stack is called *popping* the item off the stack.

The first array-based implementation of a simple list described at the beginning of Chapter 2, "Lists," is a stack. You use a counter to keep track of where the top of the list is. You then use that counter to add and remove items from the top of the list. The only minor change made here is that Pop, the routine that removes an item from the stack, saves the item in a parameter. This makes it a little easier for other subroutines to retrieve an item and remove it from the stack in one step. Other than this change, the following code is similar to the list code presented in Chapter 2.

```
Dim Stack() As Variant
Dim StackSize As Variant

Sub Push(value As Variant)
    StackSize = StackSize + 1
    ReDim Preserve Stack(1 To StackSize)
    Stack(StackSize) = value
```

```
End Sub

Sub Pop(value As Variant)
    value = Stack(StackSize)
    StackSize = StackSize - 1
    ReDim Preserve Stack(1 To StackSize)
End Sub
```

All of the previous discussion about lists also applies to this sort of stack implementation. In particular, you can save time if you do not resize the array every time you push or pop an item. Example program SimList, described in Chapter 2, "Lists," demonstrates this sort of simple stack implementation.

Programs often use stacks to hold a sequence of items that the program will manipulate until the stack is empty. Operating on one item might cause others to be pushed onto the stack, but eventually they will all be removed. A simple example is an algorithm to reverse the order of the items in an array. Here each item is pushed onto the stack in order. Then each item is popped off the stack in reverse order and written back into the array.

```
Dim List() As Variant
Dim NumItems As Integer

' Initialize the array.
    :

' Push the items onto the stack.
For I = 1 To NumItems
    Push List(I)
Next I

' Pop the items from the stack back into the array.
For I = 1 To NumItems
    Pop List(I)
Next I
```

In this example, the stack may change length many times before it is eventually emptied. If you know ahead of time how big the array needs to be, you can avoid these resizings by making the stack big enough to hold all the items at the start. Instead of resizing the stack as it grows and shrinks, you can allocate it at the beginning and destroy it when you are finished.

The following code lets you preallocate a stack if you know how large it must be. The Pop routine does not resize the array. When the program finishes using the stack, it should use the EmptyStack routine to deallocate all of the stack's memory at once.

```
Const WANT_FREE_PERCENT = .1      ' Try for 10% free space.
Const MIN_FREE = 10               ' Min unused space when resizing.
Global Stack() As Integer         ' The stack array.
Global StackSize As Integer       ' Size of the stack array.
Global LastItem As Integer        ' Last index in use.

Sub PreallocateStack(entries As Integer)
    StackSize = entries
    ReDim Stack(1 To StackSize)
End Sub

Sub EmptyStack()
    StackSize = 0
    LastItem = 0
    Erase Stack        ' Free the array's memory.
End Sub

Sub Push(value As Integer)
    LastItem = LastItem + 1
    If LastItem > StackSize Then ResizeStack
    Stack(LastItem) = value
End Sub

Sub Pop(value As Integer)
    value = Stack(LastItem)
    LastItem = LastItem - 1
End Sub

Sub ResizeStack()
Dim want_free As Integer

    want_free = WANT_FREE_PERCENT * LastItem
    If want_free < MIN_FREE Then want_free = MIN_FREE
    StackSize = LastItem + want_free
    ReDim Preserve Stack(1 To StackSize)
End Sub
```

This sort of stack implementation is quite efficient in Visual Basic. The stack does not waste much memory, and it does not resize very often, particularly if you know how big it needs to be before starting.

Multiple Stacks

You can manage two stacks in the same array by placing one at the top of the array and the other at the bottom. Keep separate Top counters for the two stacks, and make the stacks grow toward each other, as shown in Figure 3.1. This method allows the two stacks to grow into the same memory until they bump into each other when the array is completely full.

Unfortunately, resizing these sorts of stacks is not easy. When you enlarge the array, you must shift all the items in the upper stack so that you can allocate new items in the middle. When you shrink the array, you must first shift the items in the upper stack before you redimension the array and reclaim the unused memory. It is also difficult to extend this method to handle more than two stacks.

Linked lists provide a more flexible method for building multiple stacks. To push an item onto a stack, you insert it at the top of its linked list. To pop an item off a stack, you remove the first item from the linked list. Because all items are added and removed from the top of the list, you do not need sentinels or doubly linked lists to implement this sort of stack.

The main drawback to linked list stacks is that they require extra memory for the cells' NextCell pointers. A single array-based stack containing N integers requires only 2 * N bytes of memory (2 bytes per integer). The same stack implemented as a linked list would require an additional 4 * N bytes of memory for the NextCell pointers, tripling the size needed to manage the stack.

Example program Stacks uses several stacks implemented as linked lists. Using the program you can push and pop items onto and off of each of the lists. Example program Stacks2 is similar except that it uses a LinkedListStack class to manage its stacks.

Queues

A *queue* is an ordered list where items are added at one end of the list and removed from the other. A group of people waiting in a store checkout line is a queue. New arrivals enter at the back of the line. When a customer reaches the front of the line, the cashier helps that customer. Due to their First-In-First-Out nature, queues are sometimes called *FIFO lists* or *FIFOs*.

You can implement queues in Visual Basic using techniques similar to the ones used to implement simple stacks. Allocate an array, and keep counters that indicate where the top and bottom of the queue are. QueueFront indicates the index of the item at the front of the queue. QueueBack indicates where the next

Figure 3.1 Two stacks in the same array.

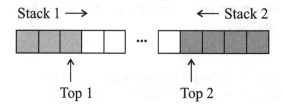

Stack 1 ⟶   ⟵ Stack 2

Top 1   Top 2

new item should be added to the queue. As items enter and leave the queue, you resize the queue array so that it grows at one end and shrinks at the other.

```
Global Queue() As String         ' The queue array.
Global QueueFront As Integer     ' The next item to be removed.
Global QueueBack As Integer      ' Where the next new item goes.

Sub EnterQueue(value As String)
    ReDim Preserve Queue(QueueFront To QueueBack)
    Queue(QueueBack) = value
    QueueBack = QueueBack + 1
End Sub

Sub LeaveQueue(value As String)
    value = Queue(QueueFront)
    QueueFront = QueueFront + 1
    ReDim Preserve Queue(QueueFront To QueueBack - 1)
End Sub
```

Unfortunately, Visual Basic does not allow the Preserve keyword in a ReDim statement if you change the array's lower bound. Even if Visual Basic could perform this operation, the queue would "walk" through memory. Each time you added and removed an item from the queue, the array's bounds would increase. If you passed enough items through the queue, the bounds would eventually become too large to manage.

For these reasons, when you need to resize the array, you must first move the data to the beginning of the array. That may create enough unused entries near the end of the array that you will no longer need to resize it. Otherwise you can use the ReDim statement to make the array larger or smaller.

As is the case with lists, you can improve performance by adding more than one new item whenever you enlarge the array. You can also save time by shrinking the array only when it contains a large number of unused entries.

In a simple list or stack, you add items to one end of the array and remove them from the same end. If the list stays roughly the same size, you might not have to resize it too often. On the other hand, because you add items at one end of a queue and remove them from the other, you must occasionally rearrange a queue, even if its total size stays the same.

```
Const WANT_FREE_PERCENT = .1     ' Try for 10% free space.
Const MIN_FREE = 10              ' Min free space when resizing.
Global Queue() As String         ' The queue array.
Global QueueMax As Integer       ' Largest index in the array.
Global QueueFront As Integer     ' The next item to be removed.
Global QueueBack As Integer      ' Where the next new item goes.
Global ResizeWhen As Integer     ' Resize if QueueFront >= this.
```

```
' <During initialization the program should set QueueMax = -1 to
' indicate that no memory has ever been allocated for the array.>

Sub EnterQueue(value As String)
    If QueueBack > QueueMax Then ResizeQueue
    Queue(QueueBack) = value
    QueueBack = QueueBack + 1
End Sub


Sub LeaveQueue(value As String)
    value = Queue(QueueFront)
    QueueFront = QueueFront + 1
    If QueueFront > ResizeWhen Then ResizeQueue
End Sub


Sub ResizeQueue()
Dim want_free As Integer
Dim i As Integer
    ' Move the entries to the beginning of the array.
    For i = QueueFront To QueueBack - 1
        Queue(i - QueueFront) = Queue(i)
    Next i
    QueueBack = QueueBack - QueueFront
    QueueFront = 0

    ' Resize the array.
    want_free = WANT_FREE_PERCENT * (QueueBack - QueueFront)
    If want_free < MIN_FREE Then want_free = MIN_FREE
    Max = QueueBack + want_free - 1
    ReDim Preserve Queue(0 To Max)

    ' We will resize the array when QueueFront > ResizeWhen.
    ResizeWhen = want_free
End Sub
```

Example program ArrayQ uses this method to implement a simple queue. Enter a string, and click the Enter button to add a new item to the end of the queue. Click the Leave button to remove the top item from the queue.

As you run the program, notice that the queue requires resizing when you add and remove items from the queue, even if the total queue size does not change much. In fact, the queue will resize, even if you repeatedly add and remove a single item.

Keep in mind that each time the queue is resized, the items in use are first moved to the beginning of the array. This makes resizing array-based queues more time-consuming than resizing the linked lists and stacks described earlier.

Example program ArrayQ2 is similar to program ArrayQ except that it uses an ArrayQueue class to manage its queue.

Circular Queues

The queues described in the previous section require occasional rearrangement, even if the total queue size does not change much. The queue will require rearrangement, even if you repeatedly add and remove a single item.

If you know in advance how large a queue might need to be, you can avoid all this reorganizing by creating a *circular queue*. The idea is to treat the queue's array as if it wraps around to form a circle. You treat the last item in the array as if it comes just before the first item. Figure 3.2 shows a circular queue.

A program can use variable QueueFront to hold the index of the item that has been in the queue the longest. It can use variable QueueBack to hold the index of the position in the queue array where the next item should be added.

Unlike in the previous implementation, when the program updates QueueFront and QueueBack, it should use the Mod operator to make the indexes stay within the bounds of the array. For example, the following code adds an item to the queue:

```
Queue(QueueBack) = value
QueueBack = (QueueBack + 1) Mod QueueSize
```

Figure 3.3 shows the process of adding a new item to a circular queue that can hold four entries. Here the item C is added at the position indicated by QueueBack. QueueBack is then advanced to point to the next entry in the array.

Similarly, when a program removes an item from the queue, it should update QueueFront with code like this:

```
value = Queue(QueueFront)
QueueFront = (QueueFront + 1) Mod QueueSize
```

Figure 3.2 A circular queue.

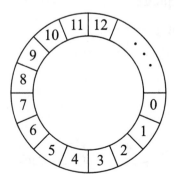

Figure 3.3 Adding an item to a circular queue.

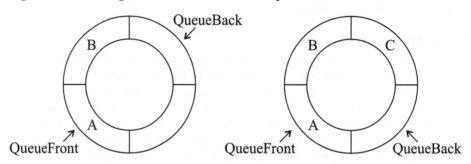

Figure 3.4 shows the process of removing an item from a circular queue. The first item, in this case the item A, is removed from the front of the queue and QueueFront is updated so that it indicates the next item in the array.

Telling the difference between a full queue and an empty one can be a little tricky with circular queues. In both cases QueueBottom will equal QueueTop. Figure 3.5 shows two circular queues, one empty and one full.

An easy way to solve this problem is to keep track of the number of items in the queue using a separate variable NumInQueue. This count tells if there are any items to remove from the queue and if there is room in the queue to add new items.

The following code uses all of these techniques to manage a circular queue.

```
Global Queue() As String       ' The queue array.
Global QueueSize As Integer    ' Largest index in queue.
Global QueueFront As Integer   ' The next item to be removed.
Global QueueBack As Integer    ' Where the next new item goes.
Global NumInQueue As Integer   ' # items in the queue.
```

Figure 3.4 Removing an item from a circular queue.

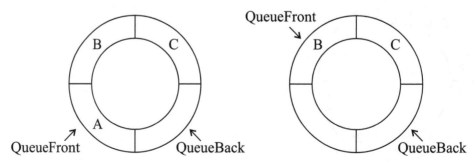

Figure 3.5 Empty and full circular queues.

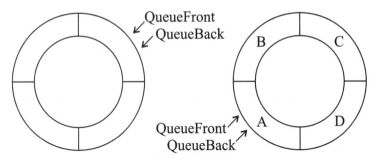

```
Sub NewCircularQueue(num_items As Integer)
    QueueSize = num_items
    ReDim Queue(0 To QueueSize - 1)
End Sub

Sub EnterQueue(value As String)
    ' If the queue is full, just exit.
    ' In a real application we would take more action.
    If NumInQueue >= QueueSize Then Exit Sub
    Queue(QueueBack) = value
    QueueBack = (QueueBack + 1) Mod QueueSize
    NumInQueue = NumInQueue + 1
End Sub

Sub LeaveQueue (value As String)
    ' If the queue is empty, just exit.
    ' In a real application we would take more action.
    If NumInQueue <= 0 Then Exit Sub
    value = Queue (QueueFront)
    QueueFront = (QueueFront + 1) Mod QueueSize
    NumInQueue = NumInQueue - 1
End Sub
```

As is the case with array-based lists, you can resize this array if the queue fills completely or if the array contains too much unused space. Resizing a circular queue, however, is more difficult than resizing an array-based list or stack.

When you resize the array, the list of items currently in the queue may wrap around the end of the array. If you simply enlarge the array, the newly inserted items will be at the end of the array so that they will fall into the middle of the list. Figure 3.6 shows what would happen if you enlarged the array in this way.

Figure 3.6 Incorrectly enlarging a circular queue.

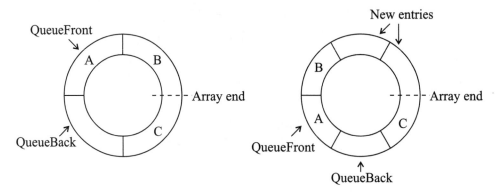

Similar problems occur if you simply shrink the array. If the items wrap past the end of the array, you will lose the items at the end of the array that are near the front of the queue.

To avoid these difficulties, you must reorganize the array before you resize it. The easiest way to do this is to use a temporary array. Copy the queue's items into the temporary array in their correct order, resize the queue array, and then copy the items from the temporary array back into the resized queue array.

```
Private Sub EnterQueue(value As String)
    If NumInQueue >= QueueSize Then ResizeQueue
    Queue(QueueBack) = value
    QueueBack = (QueueBack + 1) Mod QueueSize
    NumInQueue = NumInQueue + 1
End Sub

Private Sub LeaveQueue(value As String)
    If NumInQueue <= 0 Then Exit Sub
    value = Queue(QueueFront)
    QueueFront = (QueueFront + 1) Mod QueueSize
    NumInQueue = NumInQueue - 1
    If NumInQueue < ShrinkWhen Then ResizeQueue
End Sub

Sub ResizeQueue()
Dim temp() As String
Dim want_free As Integer
Dim i As Integer
```

```
    ' Copy items into temporary array.
    ReDim temp(0 To NumInQueue - 1)
    For i = 0 To NumInQueue - 1
        temp(i) = Queue((i + QueueFront) Mod QueueSize)
    Next i

    ' Resize the array
    want_free = WANT_FREE_PERCENT * NumInQueue
    If want_free < MIN_FREE Then want_free = MIN_FREE
    QueueSize = NumInQueue + want_free
    ReDim Queue(0 To QueueSize - 1)
    For i = 0 To NumInQueue - 1
        Queue(i) = temp(i)
    Next i
    QueueFront = 0
    QueueBack = NumInQueue

    ' We will shrink the array when NumInQueue < ShrinkWhen.
    ShrinkWhen = QueueSize - 2 * want_free

    ' Don't resize tiny queues. This can get us in trouble
    ' with "ReDim temp(0 To NumInQueue - 1)" above and
    ' just plain looks silly!
    If ShrinkWhen < 3 Then ShrinkWhen = 0
End Sub
```

Example program CircleQ demonstrates this technique for implementing a circular queue. Enter a string, and click the Enter button to add a new item to the queue. Click the Leave button to remove the top item from the queue. The program will resize its queue array when necessary.

Example program CircleQ2 is similar to program CircleQ except it uses a CircleQueue class to manage its queue.

Remember that each time the program resizes the queue, it copies the items into a temporary array, resizes the queue, and then copies the items back. The extra recopying steps make resizing circular queues slower than resizing linked lists and stacks. Even array-based queues, which require extra work to resize, do not take this much effort.

On the other hand, if the total number of items in the queue does not change much, you will not need to resize a circular queue very often. If you set the resizing parameters correctly, you may never need to resize the array. Even if you need to resize occasionally, the reduced frequency of resizing will make up for the extra work.

Linked List-Based Queues

A completely different approach to implementing queues is to use doubly linked lists. You can use sentinels to keep track of the top and bottom of the list. Add new items to the queue just before the bottom sentinel, and remove items leaving the queue from just after the top sentinel. Figure 3.7 shows a doubly linked list used as a queue.

It is easy to add and remove items from a doubly linked list, so you will never need complicated resizing algorithms. This method also has the advantage that it is a bit more intuitive than the circular array queue. It has the drawback that it requires extra memory to hold the linked list's NextCell and PrevCell pointers. This makes linked list queues a bit less space efficient than circular queues.

Example program LinkedQ manages a queue using a doubly linked list. Enter a string, and click the Enter button to add the new item to the bottom of the queue. Click the Leave button to remove the top item from the queue.

Example program LinkedQ2 is similar to program LinkedQ except it uses a LinkedListQueue class to manage its queue.

Collections as Queues

Visual Basic collections provide an extremely simple form of queue. A program can use a collection's Add method to add an item at the end of the queue. It can use the Remove method with the parameter 1 to remove the first item from the queue. The following code manages a collection-based queue.

```
Dim Queue As New Collection

Private Sub EnterQueue(value As String)
    Queue.Add value
End Sub

Private Function LeaveQueue() As String
    LeaveQueue = Queue.Item(1)
    Queue.Remove 1
End Function
```

Figure 3.7 A linked list queue.

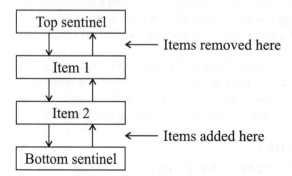

Even though this code is extremely simple, collections are not really intended to be used as queues. They provide other features, such as item keys, and managing these other features makes them slower than other queue implementations. Collection-based queues are so simple, however, that they are a reasonable choice for short queues in applications where performance is not an issue.

Example program CollectQ demonstrates a collection-based queue.

Priority Queues

Each item in a *priority queue* has an associated priority. When the program needs to remove an item from the queue, it selects the item with the highest priority. It does not matter how the items in a priority queue are stored, as long as the program can always find the highest priority item when it is needed.

Some operating systems use priority queues for job scheduling. In the UNIX operating system, each process can have a different priority. When the computer is ready to run, it selects the highest priority process that is ready to execute. Lower priority processes must wait until all of the higher processes have finished or are blocked, waiting for some external event like a data read on a disk drive.

Air traffic control also uses a priority queue concept. Planes that are trying to land and are running out of fuel have top priority. Other planes trying to land have second priority. Planes on the ground have third priority because they are in a safer position than planes in the air. Over time, some of the priorities might change because planes trying to land will eventually run low on fuel.

One simple way to build a priority queue is to keep all the items in a list. When you need to remove an item from the queue, you can search the list to see which item has the highest priority. To add an item to the queue, you place the new item at the top of the list. Using this method, it takes one step to add a new item to the queue. If the queue holds N items, it takes O(N) steps to locate and remove the highest priority item from the queue.

A slightly better scheme is to use a linked list and keep the items sorted in order of decreasing priority. The PriorityCell class for the list might use the following declarations.

```
Public Priority As Integer        ' The item's priority.
Public NextCell As PriorityCell   ' The pointer to the next item.
Public Value As String            ' Whatever data the program needs.
```

To add an item to the queue, search through the list until you find the position where the new item belongs and insert it at that position. To make it easier to find the item's correct position, you can use top and bottom sentinels with appropriate priorities. For example, if the items will have priorities between 0 and 100, you could give the top sentinel priority 101 and the bottom sentinel priority -1. Any real priorities will fall between these values.

Figure 3.8 shows a priority queue implemented using a linked list.

Figure 3.8 A linked list priority queue.

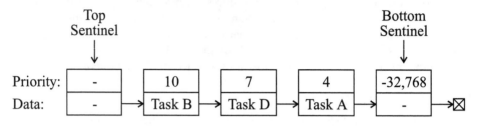

The following code fragment shows the heart of this search routine.

```
Dim cell As PriorityCell
Dim nxt As PriorityCell

    ' See where the new entry belongs in the list.
    cell = TopSentinel
    nxt = cell.NextCell
    Do While cell.Priority > new_priority
        cell = nxt
        nxt = cell.NextCell
    Loop

    ' Insert the item after cell in the list.
        :
```

To remove the highest priority item from the list, you simply remove the item after the top sentinel. Because the list is kept sorted in priority order, the top item always has the highest priority.

Adding a new item to this queue takes an average of N / 2 steps. Sometimes the new item will go near the top of the list, and sometimes it will go near the bottom, but on average it will fall somewhere in the middle. The previous simple list-based priority queue required O(1) step to insert a new item into the queue and O(N) steps to remove the highest priority items from the queue. The sorted linked list version requires O(N) steps to add an item to the queue and O(1) step to remove the top item. Both versions require O(N) steps for one of these operations, but the sorted linked list queue needs only N / 2 steps on the average.

Example program PriList uses a sorted linked list to manage a priority queue. You can fill in priority and data values and use the Enter button to add a new item to the priority queue. Click the Leave button to remove the highest priority item from the queue.

Example program PriList2 is similar to program PriList except it uses a LinkedPriorityQueue class to manage its queue.

With some extra work, you can build a priority queue where insertion and deletion both take O(log(N)) steps. For very large queues, the added speed is worth the extra effort. This sort of priority queue uses the *heap* data structure used by the sorting algorithm heapsort. Heaps and heap-based priority queues are discussed in more detail in Chapter 9, "Sorting."

Multi-Headed Queues

Another interesting type of queue is the *multi-headed queue*. Items enter the queue at the rear as usual, but the queue has more than one *front end* or *head*. The program may remove items from any of the heads.

An everyday example of a multi-headed queue is the customer service counter at a bank. All of the customers stand in a single line, but they are served by several tellers. The next available teller serves the customer at the front of the line. This sort of queue seems fair because the tellers serve customers in their order of arrival. It is also efficient because all of the tellers stay busy as long as any customers wait in the queue.

Compare this sort of queue to the multiple single-headed queues used in a grocery store. Here people are not necessarily served in arrival order. One person in a slow line may wait longer than someone who arrived later but got in a faster line. The cashiers may not always be busy, either, because one line could empty completely while people wait in other lines.

Generally, multi-headed queues are more efficient than multiple single-headed queues. The latter are used in grocery stores because shopping carts take up a lot of space. A multi-headed queue would force customers to stand in a single line that would take up a lot of room. When a cashier was available, the customer at the front of the line would need to maneuver a bulky shopping cart across the front of the store to the cashier. This could be difficult. In a bank, on the other hand, the customers do not have large shopping carts to push around, so it is easy for them to stand in a single line.

Some airport check-in counters have a combination of both situations. Their customers have large amounts of baggage to push around, but the airline still uses a multi-headed queue. They are willing to give up the extra space needed to create a large single line for their customers.

It is easy to build a multi-headed queue using a normal single-headed queue. Store the items representing customers or whatever in a normal single-headed queue. When an agent (teller, cashier, etc.) becomes available, remove the first item from the front of the queue and assign it to that agent.

A Queue Simulation

Suppose you are in charge of designing a check-in counter for a new airline terminal and you want to compare a single multi-headed queue to multiple single-headed queues. You would need some sort of model of customer behavior. For this example, you might make the following assumptions:

- Each customer requires between two and five minutes at the counter.
- When customers arrive in multiple single-headed queues, they enter the queue that is currently shortest.
- Customers arrive at roughly a constant rate.

Example program HeadedQ runs a simulation to model this situation. You can modify a number of simulation parameters, including the following:

- Number of customers arriving per hour
- Minimum and maximum time needed by customers
- Number of clerks available
- Milliseconds the program pauses between simulation steps

When you run the simulation, the program shows you the elapsed simulated time, the average and maximum amounts of time customers have to wait for service, and the percentage of time the clerks are busy.

As you experiment with different parameters, you will notice several interesting things. First, the multi-headed queue gives lower average and maximum waiting times for the customers. It also keeps the clerks slightly busier than the single-headed queue.

Both kinds of queue have a threshold beyond which customer waiting times increase dramatically. Suppose you indicate that customers need between 2 and 10 minutes each, or 6 minutes on average. If you specify 60 customers per hour, then the clerks must provide about 6 * 60 = 360 minutes of service per hour to satisfy all of the customers. Because each clerk can provide 60 minutes of service per hour, the program needs 6 clerks to satisfy the customers.

If you run program HeadedQ with those parameters, you will find that the queues do quite well. The multi-headed queue has an average wait time of only a few minutes. If you add another clerk so there are a total of 7 clerks, the average and maximum wait times decrease dramatically. The average wait for the multi-headed queue drops to about a tenth of a minute.

On the other hand, if you decrease the number of clerks to 5, the average and maximum waiting times show a large increase. The times also increase over time. The longer the simulation runs, the longer the waits become.

Table 3.1 Waiting Times in Minutes in Single- and Multiple-Headed Queues

Clerks	Multi-Headed Queue		Single-Headed Queue	
	Avg Time	Max Time	Avg Time	Max Time
5	11.37	20	12.62	20
6	1.58	5	3.93	13
7	0.11	2	0.54	6

Figure 3.9 Program HeadedQ.

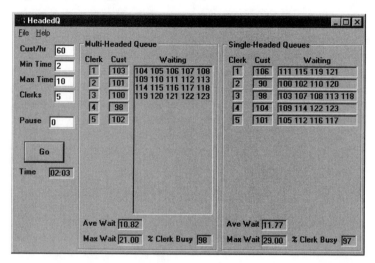

Table 3.1 shows the average and maximum wait times for the 2 different kinds of queues. Here the program ran for 3 simulated hours and assumed 60 customers per hour requiring between 2 and 10 minutes each.

The multi-headed queue also seems more fair than the single-headed queues because customers are served in arrival order. Figure 3.9 shows the HeadedQ program after it has run for slightly more than two simulated hours. In the multi-headed queue, customer 104 is next in line. All the customers who arrived before customer 104 have already been, or are currently being, served. In the single-headed queue, customer 106 is being served. Customers 100, 102, 103, and 105 are still waiting even though they arrived before customer 106.

Summary

Different stack and queue implementations offer different features. Array-based stacks and circular queues are simple and efficient, particularly if you know in advance how large a stack or queue will need to be. Linked lists provide more flexibility if the size must change frequently.

Stacks and queues based on Visual Basic collections are not as efficient as array-based implementations, but they are extremely simple. For small data structures where performance is not critical, a collection may be adequate. After you test an application, you can reimplement the stack or queue code if collections are too slow.

4

This chapter describes array data structures. Using Visual Basic, you can easily build arrays of standard or user-defined data types. If you initially declare an array without bounds, you can even redimension it later using the ReDim statement. These features make Visual Basic's arrays very useful.

Some programs use specialized types of arrays that are not directly supported by Visual Basic. These include triangular arrays, irregular arrays, and sparse arrays. This chapter explains how you can use flexible array structures that can greatly reduce your program's memory usage.

Triangular Arrays

Some programs need values for only half the entries in a two-dimensional array. For example, suppose you have a map with 10 cities on it numbered from 0 to 9. You can use an array to make an *adjacency matrix* indicating whether there is a highway between any pair of cities. The A(I, J) entry is True if there is a highway between city I and city J.

In this case, half of the array would contain duplicated data because A(I, J) = A(J, I). Also A(I, I) would be meaningless because you do not need to take a highway from city I to itself. The only entries you really need in this array are the A(I, J) in the lower left corner, where I > J. Alternatively, you could use the entries in the upper right corner. Because these entries form a triangle, this sort of array is called a *triangular array*.

Figure 4.1 shows a triangular array. Entries with meaningful data are indicated by Xs. Entries that are meaningful but duplicated by other entries are left blank. The meaningless diagonal entries A(I, I) are indicated by dashes.

For a small array, the space wasted by using a normal two-dimensional array to hold this data is not too important. If the map holds many cities, the wasted space can be large. For N cities there will be N * (N – 1) / 2 duplicated entries and N entries like A(I, I) that are not meaningful. If the map contains 1000 cities, the array will hold more than half a million unnecessary entries.

You can avoid wasting this space by creating a one-dimensional array B and then packing the meaningful entries of array A into array B. Place the entries in

Figure 4.1 A triangular array.

-				
X	-			
X	X	-		
X	X	X	-	
X	X	X	X	-

array B one row at a time, as shown in Figure 4.2. Notice that the array indexes are numbered starting from 0. This makes the equations that follow a little simpler.

To make this triangular array representation easier to use, you can write functions to translate between the indexing schemes used by arrays A and B. The equation for converting from A(I, J) to B(X) is:

```
X = I * (I - 1) / 2 + J          ' For I > J.
```

For example, if you plug in I = 2 and J = 1, you get X = 2 * (2 – 1) / 2 + 1 = 2. This means that A(2, 1) maps into position 2 in the B array as shown in Figure 4.2. Remember the arrays are numbered starting with zero.

This equation holds only when I > J. The values for the other entries in the array A are not stored in array B because they are redundant or not meaningful. If you need to compute the value of A(I, J) where I < J, you should instead calculate the value of A(J, I).

The equations for converting back from B(X) to A(I, J) are:

```
I = Int((1 + Sqr(1 + 8 * X)) / 2)
J = X - I * (I - 1) / 2
```

Figure 4.2 Packing a triangular array into a one-dimensional array.

Array A:

A(1, 0)			
A(2, 0)	A(2, 1)		
A(3, 0)	A(3, 1)	A(3, 2)	
A(4, 0)	A(4, 1)	A(4, 2)	A(4, 3)

Array B:

A(1, 0)	A(2, 0)	A(2, 1)	A(3, 0)	A(3, 1)	A(3, 2)	...

Plugging X = 4 into these equations gives I = Int((1 + Sqr(1 + 8 * 4)) / 2) = 3 and J = 4 – 3 * (3 – 1) / 2 = 1. This means entry B(4) maps into position A(3, 1). This also agrees with Figure 4.2.

These equations are not easy to compute. They require several multiplications and divisions, and even a square root. If a program must execute these functions very frequently, it will pay a slight penalty in execution speed. This is an example of a space versus time trade-off. Packing a triangular array into a one-dimensional array saves memory. Storing the data in a two-dimensional array takes more memory but is faster.

Using the equations above you can write Visual Basic subroutines to translate between the coordinates of the two arrays:

```
Private Sub AtoB(ByVal I As Integer, ByVal J As Integer, X As Integer)
Dim tmp As Integer

    If I = J Then          ' This entry is not meaningful.
        X = -1
        Exit Sub
    ElseIf I < J Then      ' Switch I and J so I > J.
        tmp = I
        I = J
        J = tmp
    End If
    X = I * (I - 1) / 2 + J
End Sub

Private Sub BtoA(ByVal X As Integer, I As Integer, J As Integer)
    I = Int((1 + Sqr(1 + 8 * X)) / 2)
    J = X - I * (I - 1) / 2
End Sub
```

Example program Triang uses these subroutines to demonstrate triangular arrays. If you click the "A to B" button, the program labels the entries in array A and copies the labels into the corresponding array B entries. If you click the "B to A" button, the program labels the entries in array B and then copies the labels into array A.

Example program TriangC uses a TriangularArray class to manage a triangular array. When the program starts, it loads a TriangularArray object with strings representing the array entries. It then retrieves and displays the array's entries.

Diagonal Entries

Some programs use triangular arrays that include the diagonal entries A(I, I). In this case you need to make only three changes to the index translation routines. The translation subroutine AtoB should not reject cases where I = J. It should also add 1 to I before calculating the index in array B.

```
Private Sub AtoB(ByVal I As Integer, ByVal J As Integer, X As Integer)
Dim tmp As Integer

    If I < J Then       ' Switch I and J so I > J.
        tmp = I
        I = J
        J = tmp
    End If
    I = I + 1
    X = I * (I - 1) / 2 + J
End Sub
```

The translation subroutine BtoA should subtract 1 from I just before returning.

```
Private Sub BtoA(ByVal X As Integer, I As Integer, J As Integer)
    I = Int((1 + Sqr(1 + 8 * X)) / 2)
    J = X - I * (I - 1) / 2
    I = I - 1
End Sub
```

Example program Triang2 is identical to program Triang except it uses these new functions to manipulate the diagonal entries in array A. Example program TriangC2 is similar to program TriangC except it uses a TriangularArray class that includes entries along the diagonal.

Irregular Arrays

Some programs need an array with an irregular size and shape. A two-dimensional array might need six items in the first row, three in the second, four in the third, and so forth. One example where this would be useful is in storing a number of polygons, each of which consists of a different number of points. The array should look like the picture shown in Figure 4.3.

Arrays in Visual Basic cannot have ragged edges like this. A program could use an array large enough to hold every row, but that would leave many entries in the array unused. For the example shown in Figure 4.3, the array would be declared using Dim Polygons(1 To 3, 1 To 6), and four entries would remain unused.

There are several other ways you can store irregular arrays.

Figure 4.3 An irregular array.

Polygon 1	(2, 5)	(3, 6)	(4, 6)	(5, 5)	(4, 4)	(4, 5)
Polygon 2	(1, 1)	(4, 1)	(2, 3)			
Polygon 3	(2, 2)	(4, 3)	(5, 4)	(1, 4)		

Forward Star

One way to avoid wasting space is to pack the data into a one-dimensional array B. Unlike triangular arrays, irregular arrays do not come with formulas for calculating how items map between the arrays. To handle this problem, you can create another array A that holds the offsets of each row in the one-dimensional array B.

To make it easier to locate the points in array B that correspond to each row, you can add a sentinel entry at the end of the array A that points *just beyond* the last item in array B. Then the points that make up polygon I are in array B at positions A(I) through A(I + 1) − 1. For example, a program can list the entries that make up row I using the following code:

```
For J = A(I) To A(I + 1) - 1
    ' List entry B(J).
       :
Next J
```

This method is called *forward star*. Figure 4.4 shows the forward star representation of the irregular array shown in Figure 4.3. In this figure the sentinel has been shaded so that it is easy to see.

You can easily generalize this method to form irregular arrays of higher dimensions. You might use three-dimensional forward star to store a set of pictures, each with a different number of polygons, each consisting of many points.

Figure 4.5 shows a schematic picture of a three-dimensional forward star data structure. The two sentinels are shaded so that they are easy to see. The sentinels point one position beyond the end of the real data in the following array.

These forward star representations require very little unused storage. The only "wasted" space is contained in the entries for the sentinels.

Listing the points that make up a polygon is fast and easy using a forward star data structure. Saving and loading forward star data in files is also easy. On the other hand, updating arrays in a forward star format is quite difficult. Suppose you want to add a new point to the first polygon in Figure 4.4. You would need to shift all the entries to the right of the new point one position to make room for the new entry. Then you would need to add one to all the entries that came after the first in array A to account for the new point. Finally, you

---

Figure 4.4 The forward star representation of an irregular array.

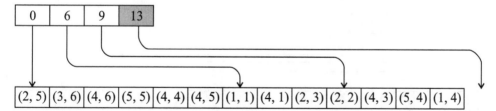

Figure 4.5 Three-dimensional forward star.

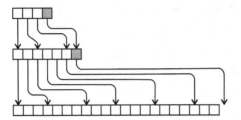

would insert the new item. Similar problems occur when you remove a point from the first polygon.

Figure 4.6 shows the forward star representation from Figure 4.4 after one point has been added to the first polygon. The entries that were updated are shaded. As the picture shows, almost every item in both arrays has been modified.

Irregular Linked Lists

Another method for creating irregular arrays is to use linked lists. Each cell contains a pointer to the next cell at its level of the hierarchy, plus a pointer to the list of cells below it in the hierarchy. A polygon cell, for example, would contain a pointer to the next polygon and a pointer to its first point cell.

The following code shows variable declarations for classes you could use to build a linked list of pictures, each containing a linked list of polygons, each containing a linked list of points.

In the PictureCell class:

```
Dim NextPicture As PictureCell    ' The next picture.
Dim FirstPolygon As PolygonCell   ' The first polygon in this picture.
```

In the PolygonCell class:

```
Dim NextPolygon As PolygonCell    ' The next polygon in this picture.
Dim FirstPoint As PointCell       ' The first point in this polygon.
```

In the PointCell class:

Figure 4.6 Adding a point in forward star.

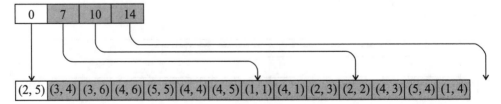

```
Dim NextPoint As PointCell    ' The next point in this polygon.
Dim X As Single               ' The point's coordinates.
Dim Y As Single
```

Using these linked techniques it is easy to add and remove pictures, polygons, or points from any position in the data structure.

Example program Poly, shown in Figure 4.7, uses this approach. The program allows you to create any number of drawing forms. Within each of these, you can use the left mouse button to draw a polygon. Each time you click the left mouse button, the program adds a new point to the polygon. Click the right mouse button to finish the polygon.

Each of the forms used by program Poly contains a linked list of polygons. Each polygon contains a linked list of points. When you close a form, the form's reference to the polygon list is destroyed. That reduces the reference count of the top polygon cell to zero. It is destroyed, so its references to the next polygon and its first point are also destroyed. Those cells' reference counts are reduced to zero, so they are destroyed. The destruction of each polygon or point cell leads to the destruction of the next. The process continues until all the polygons and points are destroyed.

Sparse Arrays

Many applications call for large arrays that contain only a few nonzero elements. A connectivity matrix for an airline, for example, might contain a 1 in position $A(I, J)$ if there is a flight between city I and city J. Many airlines service hundreds of cities, but the number of flights they actually run is much smaller than the N^2 possible combinations. Figure 4.8 shows a small airline flight map, in which the airline has flights between only 11 of the 100 possible pairs of cities.

Figure 4.7 Program Poly.

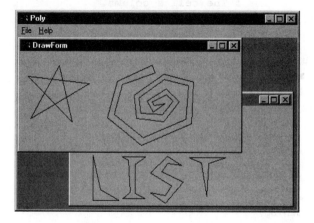

Figure 4.8 An airline flight map.

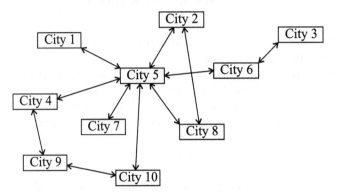

You could build the connectivity matrix for this example using a 10 by 10 array, but the array would be mostly empty. You can avoid wasting this space by using pointers to build a sparse array. Each cell contains pointers to the next item in its row and column in the array. This allows the program to locate any item within the array and to traverse the cells along any row or any column. Depending on the application, you might also find reverse pointers useful. Figure 4.9 shows the sparse connectivity matrix corresponding to the flight map shown in Figure 4.8.

To build a sparse array in Visual Basic, create a class to represent the nonblank array entries. In this case, each cell represents an airline connection between two cities. To represent the connection, the class should contain variables giving the indexes of the cities it connects. These indexes essentially give the row and column numbers for the cell. Each cell should also contain pointers to the next cell in its row and column.

The following code shows the variables declared by the ConnectionCell class.

```
Public FromCity As Integer        ' The cell's row.
Public ToCity As Integer          ' The cell's column.
Public NextInRow As ConnectionCell
Public NextInCol As ConnectionCell
```

The rows and columns in this array are basically linked lists. As is often the case with linked lists, it is easier to deal with the lists if they have sentinels. You can create arrays to contain the row and column sentinels. For example, RowHead(I) should contain the sentinel for row I. You could use the following code to traverse row I in the array.

```
Private Sub PrintRow(I As Integer)
Dim cell As ConnectionCell

    Set cell = RowHead(I).Next        ' The first real entry.
    Do While Not (cell Is Nothing)
```

Figure 4.9 A sparse connectivity matrix.

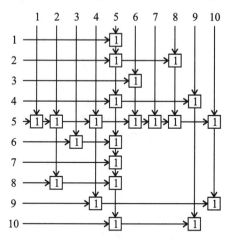

```
            Print Format$(cell.FromCity) & " -> " & Format$(cell.ToCity)
            Set cell = cell.NextInRow
        Loop
End Sub
```

Array Indexing

Normal array indexing like A(I, J) will not work on this sort of structure. You can make indexing easier by writing subroutines that set and get the values in the array. If the array represents a matrix, you might also want subroutines to add, multiply, and perform other matrix operations.

A special value NoValue represents an empty array entry. The routine that gets array entries should return NoValue when it is called to retrieve the value of an entry not contained in the array. Similarly, the routine that sets values should remove a cell from the array if its value is set to NoValue.

The particular value that NoValue should have depends on the nature of the application. For an airline connectivity matrix, empty entries might have the value False. Then you can set A(I, J) to True if there is a connection between cities I and J.

The SparseArray class defines the Value property get procedure to return the value of an entry in the array. The routine starts at the first cell in the indicated row and moves through the row's linked list of cells. If it finds a cell with column value equal to the target column, the procedure has found the required cell. Because the cells are kept in order within the row list, the routine can stop looking if it ever finds a cell with column value larger than the target column.

```
Property Get Value(r As Integer, c As Integer) As Variant
Dim cell As SparseArrayCell
```

```
Value = NoValue ' Assume we will not find it.
If r < 1 Or c < 1 Or _
    r > NumRows Or c > NumCols _
        Then Exit Property

Set cell = RowHead(r).NextInRow      ' Skip sentinel.
Do
    If cell Is Nothing Then Exit Property  ' Not found.
    If cell.Col > c Then Exit Property     ' Not found.
    If cell.Col = c Then Exit Do           ' Found.
    Set cell = cell.NextInRow
Loop

    Value = cell.Data
End Property
```

The Value property let procedure assigns a new value to a cell. If the new value equals NoValue, the routine calls RemoveEntry to delete the entry from the array. Otherwise, it searches through the target row to see where the new entry belongs. If the entry already exists, the procedure updates its value. Otherwise, it creates a new cell and adds it to the row list. It then adds the new cell at the correct position in the appropriate column list.

```
Property Let Value(r As Integer, c As Integer, new_value As Variant)
Dim i As Integer
Dim found_it As Boolean
Dim cell As SparseArrayCell
Dim nxt As SparseArrayCell
Dim new_cell As SparseArrayCell

    ' If value = NoValue, remove the entry from the array.
    If new_value = NoValue Then
        RemoveEntry r, c
        Exit Property
    End If

    ' Make more rows if needed.
    If r > NumRows Then
        ReDim Preserve RowHead(1 To r)

        ' Initialize a sentinel for each new row.
        For i = NumRows + 1 To r
            Set RowHead(i) = New SparseArrayCell
        Next i
        NumRows = r
```

```
End If

' Make more columns if needed.
If c > NumCols Then
    ReDim Preserve ColHead(1 To c)

    ' Initialize a sentinel for each new row.
    For i = NumCols + 1 To c
        Set ColHead(i) = New SparseArrayCell
    Next i
    NumCols = c
End If

' Try to locate the cell in question.
Set cell = RowHead(r)
Set nxt = cell.NextInRow
Do
    If nxt Is Nothing Then Exit Do
    If nxt.Col >= c Then Exit Do
    Set cell = nxt
    Set nxt = cell.NextInRow
Loop

' See if we found it.
If nxt Is Nothing Then
    found_it = False
Else
    found_it = (nxt.Col = c)
End If

' If we did not find the cell, make a new one.
If Not found_it Then
    Set new_cell = New SparseArrayCell

    ' Place the cell in the row.
    Set new_cell.NextInRow = nxt
    Set cell.NextInRow = new_cell

    ' Place the cell in the column list.
    Set cell = ColHead(c)
    Set nxt = cell.NextInCol
    Do
        If nxt Is Nothing Then Exit Do
        If nxt.Col >= c Then Exit Do
```

```
            Set cell = nxt
            Set nxt = cell.NextInRow
        Loop

        Set new_cell.NextInCol = nxt
        Set cell.NextInCol = new_cell
        new_cell.Row = r
        new_cell.Col = c

        ' We will put the value in the nxt cell.
        Set nxt = new_cell
    End If

    ' Set the value
    nxt.Data = new_value
End Property
```

Example program Sparse, shown in Figure 4.10, uses the SparseArray and SparseArrayCell classes to manage a sparse array. Using the program, you can set and fetch array entries. NoValue is zero for this program, so if you set the value of an entry to zero, the program removes the entry from the array.

Very Sparse Arrays

Some arrays contain so few nonblank entries that many rows and columns are completely empty. In that case, it is better to store row and column headers in linked lists rather than in arrays. That allows the program to omit empty rows and columns completely. Row and column headers point to the linked lists of row and column elements. Figure 4.11 shows a 100 by 100 array that contains only 7 nonempty entries.

Figure 4.10 Program Sparse.

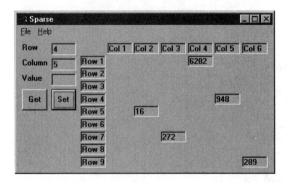

Figure 4.11 A very sparse array.

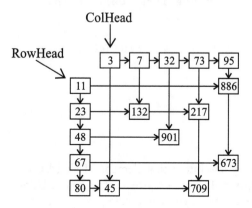

Modifying the previous code to handle this sort of array is fairly straightforward. Most of the code remains the same, and you can use the same SparseArrayCell class for the array entries. Instead of using arrays to store the row and column sentinels, however, you store the sentinels in their own linked lists.

Objects of the HeaderCell class represent the row and column linked lists. This class declares variables to hold the number of the row or column it represents, the sentinel that starts the linked list of row or column entries, and the HeaderCell representing the next row or column header.

```
Public Number As Integer          ' The number of the row or
                                  ' column.
Public Sentinel As SparseArrayCell ' The sentinel for the row or
                                  ' column.
Public NextHeader As HeaderCell   ' The next row or column.
```

To access row I, for example, you first look through the linked list of row HeaderCells until you find the one representing row I. You then proceed down row I as before.

```
Private Sub PrintRow(r As Integer)
Dim row As HeaderCell
Dim cell As SparseArrayCell

    ' Find the correct row header.
    Set row = RowHead.NextHeader      ' The first row list.
    Do
        If row Is Nothing Then Exit Sub ' No such row.
        If row.Number > r Then Exit Sub ' No such row.
        If row.Number = r Then Exit Do  ' Found it.
        Set row = row.NextHeader
    Loop
```

```
' Display the cells in the row.
Set cell = row.Sentinel.NextInRow    ' The first cell in the
                                     ' row.
Do While Not (cell Is Nothing)
    Print Format$(cell.FromCity) & " -> " & Format$(cell.ToCity)
    Set cell = cell.NextInRow
Loop
End Sub
```

Summary

Some programs use arrays that contain very few interesting elements. Using Visual Basic's normal arrays to store mostly empty cells would waste a lot of space. Using triangular, irregular, sparse, and very sparse arrays, you can create powerful array representations that require far less space.

RECURSION

Recursion is a powerful programming technique that allows you to break a problem into smaller and smaller pieces until the pieces are small enough to handle easily.

After you have gained some experience with recursion, you will find it all around you. In fact, many programmers who have recently mastered recursion get carried away and begin applying it in situations where it is unnecessary and even harmful.

The first sections of this chapter discuss factorials, Fibonacci numbers, and greatest common divisors. These provide good examples of bad uses of recursion—nonrecursive versions of these programs are much more efficient. These examples are interesting and easy to understand, however, so they are worth discussing.

Next, the chapter examines some examples where recursion is more appropriate. The Hilbert and Sierpinski curves use recursion properly and efficiently.

The final sections in this chapter explain why factorials, Fibonacci numbers, and greatest common divisors are better without recursion. These sections explain when you should avoid recursion, and they show ways to eliminate recursion when necessary.

What Is Recursion?

Recursion occurs when a function or subroutine calls itself. A recursive routine can call itself *directly* like this:

```
Function Factorial(num As Long) As Long
    Factorial = num * Factorial(num - 1)
End Function
```

A recursive routine can also call itself *indirectly* by calling a second subroutine that calls the first:

```
Private Sub Ping(num As Integer)
    Pong(num - 1)
End Sub
```

```
Private Sub Pong(num As Integer)
    Ping(num / 2)
End Sub
```

Recursion is useful for solving problems that naturally break into smaller instances of the same problem. You can think of the tree shown on the left in Figure 5.1, for example, as a "trunk" with two smaller trees attached. This leads to a naturally recursive procedure for drawing trees:

```
Private Sub DrawTree()
    Draw a "trunk"
    Draw a smaller tree rotated -45 degrees
    Draw a smaller tree rotated 45 degrees
End Sub
```

Even though recursion can make some problems easier to understand, people do not naturally think recursively. People tend to break big tasks into smaller tasks that can be performed one at a time in order until all are finished. To paint a fence, you might start at the left side and work your way to the right until you are done. You probably do not think in terms of recursively painting the left half of the fence and then recursively painting the right half.

To think recursively you need to break tasks into large subtasks, which you can then recursively break into smaller subtasks. At some point the subtasks become small enough to handle directly. When the subtasks are complete, the larger tasks they make up are also complete. When all of the subtasks are complete, the original task is finished.

Recursive Factorials

The factorial of a number N is written N! (pronounced "N factorial"). The value of 0! is defined to be 1. Other values are defined by:

$$N! = N * (N - 1) * (N - 2) * \ldots * 2 * 1$$

As mentioned in Chapter 1, "Fundamental Concepts," this function grows extremely quickly. Table 5.1 shows the first 10 values of the factorial function.

You can also define the factorial function recursively.

$$0! = 1$$
$$N! = N * (N - 1)! \text{ for } N > 0.$$

Figure 5.1 A tree made of two smaller trees.

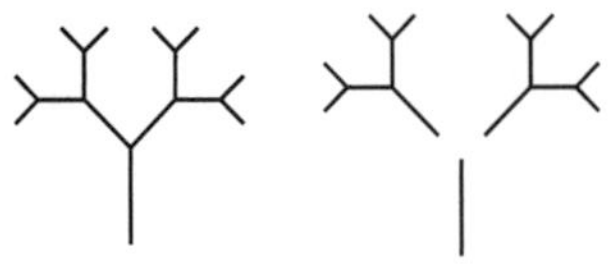

Table 5.1 Values of the Factorial Function

N	1	2	3	4	5	6	7	8	9	10
N!	1	2	6	24	120	720	5,040	40,320	362,880	3,628,800

It is easy to translate this definition into a recursive function.

```
Public Function Factorial(num As Integer) As Integer
    If num <= 0 Then
        Factorial = 1
    Else
        Factorial = num * Factorial(num - 1)
    End If
End Function
```

This function first checks to see if the number is less than or equal to 0. The factorial is not defined for numbers less than 0, but the function safeguards itself by checking for this condition anyway. If the function checked only to see if the number was equal to 0, it would enter an infinite recursion if the number was negative.

If the input value is less than or equal to 0, the function returns the value 1. Otherwise, the value of the function is the number times the factorial of the number minus 1.

Two things ensure that this recursive function eventually stops. First, on each subsequent call, the value of the parameter num is smaller. Second, the value of num is bounded below by 0. When the value of num reaches 0, the function ends the recursion. The condition, like num <= 0, that causes a recursion to end is called the *base case*, or the *stopping case*.

Whenever a program calls a subroutine, the system stores certain values in a stack similar to those described in Chapter 3, "Stacks and Queues." Because this stack is so important, it is called simply *the stack*. If a recursive function calls itself too many times, it may use up all of the stack space and crash with an "Out of stack space" error.

The number of times a function can call itself before using all the stack space depends on how much memory the computer has and how much data the program places on the stack. In one test, a program was able to recurse 452 times before it used up all the stack space. When the recursive function was modified to allocate 10 local integer variables each time it was called, it could recurse only 271 times.

Run Time Analysis

The factorial function takes only a single argument: the number for which it is to compute the factorial. Complexity analysis usually examines run time as a function of the *size* of the problem or the *number of inputs*. Because there is only one input in this case, that calculation could be a little strange.

For this reason algorithms that take a single parameter are usually evaluated in terms of the *number of bits required to store the input value* rather than the number of inputs. In some sense, this is the size of the input because it takes that many bits to store the input value. This, however, is not a very intuitive way to think about the problem. Also, in theory a computer could store the input N in $\log_2(N)$ bits, but in reality it probably stores N in some fixed number of bits. For example, all long integers are stored in 32 bits.

For these reasons this chapter analyzes this sort of algorithm in terms of the input's *value* rather than its *size*. If you want to rewrite the results in terms of the size of the input, you can do so using the fact that $N = 2^M$ where M is the number of bits needed to store N. If the run time of an algorithm is $O(N^2)$ in terms of the input value N, it is $O((2^M)^2) = O(2^{2*M}) = O((2^2)^M) = O(4^M)$ in terms of the input size M.

For this particular algorithm, the factorial function is called for N, N – 1, N – 2, and so on until the input parameter reaches 0 and the recursion ends. If the initial input is N, the function is called a total of N + 1 times, so its run time is $O(N)$. The run time is $O(2^M)$ in terms of the size of the input M.

$O(N)$ functions grow pretty slowly, so you might expect good performance from this algorithm. In fact, that is the case. The function runs into trouble only when it exhausts the stack by executing too many recursions or when the value of N! becomes too large to fit in an integer and the program generates an overflow error.

Because N! grows very quickly, overflow happens first unless you are using the stack heavily for other things. Using the integer data type, overflow occurs for 8! because 8! = 40,320 is larger than the largest possible integer, 32,767. To allow the program to compute approximate values for larger numbers, you can modify the function so it uses doubles instead of integers. Then the largest number for which the algorithm can compute N! is 170! ≈ 7.257E + 306.

Example program Facto demonstrates the recursive factorial function. Enter a number and click the Go button to make the program recursively compute factorials.

Recursive Greatest Common Divisor

The *greatest common divisor* (GCD) of two numbers is the largest integer that divides the two numbers evenly. The GCD of 12 and 9, for example, is 3 because 3 is the largest integer that divides both 12 and 9 with no remainder. Two numbers are *relatively prime* if their GCD is 1.

The eighteenth-century mathematician Euler discovered an interesting fact:

```
If A divides B evenly, GCD(A, B) = A.
Otherwise GCD(A, B) = GCD(B Mod A, A).
```

You can use this fact to compute GCDs quickly. For example:

```
GCD(9, 12)= GCD(12 Mod 9, 9)
         = GCD(3, 9)
         = 3
```

At each step the numbers being compared get smaller because 1 <= B Mod A < A if A does not divide B evenly. If the arguments continue to decrease, A will eventually reach the value 1. Because 1 evenly divides any number B, the recursion must stop. At some point A will divide B evenly, so the recursion will eventually stop.

Euler's discovery leads naturally to a simple recursive algorithm for computing GCDs.

```
Public Function GCD(A As Integer, B As Integer) As Integer
    If B Mod A = 0 Then         ' Does A divide B evenly?
        GCD = A                 ' Yes. We're done.
    Else
        GCD = GCD(B Mod A, A)   ' No. Recurse.
    End If
End Function
```

Run Time Analysis

To analyze the run time of this algorithm, you must determine how quickly A decreases. Because the function stops if A reaches the value 1, the rate at which A decreases gives an upper bound on how long the algorithm can run. It turns out that every second time the function GCD is called, the parameter A decreases by at least a factor of 1 / 2.

To see why, assume A < B. This is always true after the first call to GCD.

If B Mod A <= A / 2, the next call to GCD will have the first parameter reduced by at least a factor of 1 / 2, and the proof is done.

Suppose this is not the case. Suppose B Mod A > A / 2. The first recursive call to GCD will be GCD(B Mod A, A).

Plugging the values B Mod A and A into the function in place of A and B makes the second recursive call GCD(A Mod (B Mod A), B Mod A).

But we have assumed that B Mod A > A / 2. Then B Mod A will divide into A exactly once, leaving a remainder of A – (B Mod A). Because B Mod A is greater than A / 2, the value A – (B Mod A) must be less than A / 2. This shows that the first parameter in the second recursive call to GCD is smaller than A / 2, and the proof is done.

Now suppose N is the original value of the parameter A. After two calls to GCD, the value of parameter A will have been reduced to, at most, N / 2. After four calls, the value will be no more than (N / 2) / 2 = N / 4. After six calls, the value will be at most (N / 4) / 2 = N / 8. In general, after 2 * K calls to GCD, the value of parameter A will be at most $N / 2^K$.

Because the algorithm must stop when the value of the parameter A reaches 1, it can continue only until $N / 2^K = 1$. This happens when $N = 2^K$ or when $K = \log_2(N)$. Because the algorithm is running for 2 * K steps, this means the algorithm must stop after, at most, $2 * \log_2(N)$ steps. Ignoring the constant multiplier, this means that the algorithm runs in $O(\log(N))$ time.

This algorithm is typical of many recursive algorithms that run in O(log(N)) time. Each time it executes a certain fixed number of steps, in this case 2, it halves the problem size. More generally, if an algorithm decreases the problem size by a factor of at least 1 / D after every S steps, the problem will require S * log$_D$(N) steps.

Because you can ignore the constant multipliers and log bases in Big O notation, any algorithm that runs in S * log$_D$(N) time is an O(log(N)) algorithm. This does not necessarily mean you can completely ignore these constants when actually implementing an algorithm. An algorithm that reduces the problem size by a factor of 1 / 10 every step will probably be faster than an algorithm that reduces it by 1 / 2 every five steps. Still, they both have run times O(log(N)).

O(log(N)) algorithms are generally very fast, and the GCD algorithm is no exception. To find that the GCD of 1,736,751,235 and 2,135,723,523 is 71, for example, the function is called only 17 times. In fact, this algorithm can compute values for the largest possible long data type value 2,147,483,647 practically instantly. The Visual Basic Mod function cannot handle values larger than this, so that is the practical limit to this algorithm.

Example program GCD uses this algorithm to recursively compute greatest common divisors. Enter values for A and B and click the Go button, and the program will compute the GCD of the two numbers.

Recursive Fibonacci Numbers

You can define Fibonacci numbers recursively with the equations:

```
Fib(0) = 0
Fib(1) = 1
Fib(N) = Fib(N - 1) + Fib(N - 2)          for N > 1.
```

The third equation recursively uses the Fib function twice, once with input N – 1 and once with input N – 2. This makes it necessary to have two base cases for the recursion: Fib(0) = 0 and Fib(1) = 1. If you had only one, the recursion could slip past the base case and call itself recursively forever. For example, if you knew only that Fib(0) = 0, the computation of Fib(2) would look like this:

```
Fib(2) = Fib(1) + Fib(0)
       = [Fib(0) + Fib(-1)] + 0
       = 0 + [Fib(-2) + Fib(-3)]
       = [Fib(-3) + Fib(-4)] + [Fib(-4) + Fib(-5)]
       Etc.
```

You easily can translate this definition of Fibonacci numbers into a recursive function.

```
Public Function Fib(num As Integer) As Integer
    If num <= 1 Then
```

```
        Fib = num
    Else
        Fib = Fib(num - 1) + Fib(num - 2)
    End If
End Function
```

Run Time Analysis

The analysis of this algorithm is tricky. First, consider the number of times the algorithm reaches one of the base cases num <= 1. Let G(N) be the number of times the algorithm reaches a base case for input N. When N <= 1, the function reaches the base case once and requires no recursion.

If N > 1, the function recursively computes Fib(N – 1) and Fib(N – 2) and is then done. In the initial call to the function, the base case is not reached—it is reached only by other, recursive calls. The total number of times the base case is reached for input N is the number of times it is reached for input N – 1 plus the number of times it is reached for input N – 2. You can write these three facts as:

```
G(0) = 1
G(1) = 1
G(N) = G(N - 1) + G(N - 2)          for N > 1.
```

This recursive definition is very similar to the definition of the Fibonacci numbers. Table 5.2 shows some values for G(N) and Fib(N). It is easy to see from these numbers that G(N) = Fib(N + 1).

Next consider the number of times the algorithm reaches the recursive step. When N <= 1, the function does not reach this step. When N > 1, the function reaches this step once and then recursively computes Fib(N – 1) and Fib(N – 2). Let H(N) be the number of times the algorithm reaches the recursive step for input N. Then H(N) = 1 + H(N – 1) + H(N – 2). The defining equations for H(N) are:

```
H(0) = 0
H(1) = 0
H(N) = 1 + H(N - 1) + H(N - 2)          for N > 1.
```

Table 5.3 shows some values for Fib(N) and H(N). From these numbers you can see that H(N) = Fib(N + 1) – 1.

Table 5.2 Values of Fibonacci Numbers and G(N)

N	0	1	2	3	4	5	6	7	8
Fib(N)	0	1	1	2	3	5	8	13	21
G(N)	1	1	2	3	5	8	13	21	34

Table 5.3 Values of Fibonacci Numbers and H(N)

N	0	1	2	3	4	5	6	7	8
Fib(N)	0	1	1	2	3	5	8	13	21
H(N)	0	0	1	2	4	7	12	20	33

Combining the results for G(N) and H(N) gives the total run time for the algorithm:

```
Run time = G(N) + H(N)
         = Fib(N + 1) + Fib(N + 1) - 1
         = 2 * Fib(N + 1) - 1
```

Because Fib(N + 1) >= Fib(N) for all values of N, you know that:

```
Run time >= 2 * Fib(N) - 1
```

In Big O notation this simplifies to O(Fib(N)). It is interesting that this function is not only recursive, but that it also is used to compute its own run time.

To understand the speed at which the Fibonacci function grows, it helps to know that $Fib(M) > \emptyset^{M-2}$ for a certain constant $\emptyset$, which is roughly 1.6. This means that the run time is at least as big as the exponential function $O(\emptyset^M)$. Like other exponential functions, this function grows more quickly than polynomial functions and less quickly than factorial functions.

Because the run time function grows very quickly, this algorithm is quite slow for large inputs. In fact, the algorithm is so slow that it is impractical to compute values of Fib(N) for N much larger than 30. Table 5.4 shows the run times for this algorithm with different inputs on a 90 megahertz Pentium.

Example program Fibo uses this recursive algorithm to calculate Fibonacci numbers. Enter an integer and click the Go button to make the program compute Fibonacci numbers. Be sure to start with small numbers until you know how long your computer will take to make the computation.

Recursive Hilbert Curves

Hilbert curves are *self-similar* curves that are naturally defined recursively. Figure 5.2 shows Hilbert curves where the maximum depths of recursion are 1, 2, and 3.

Table 5.4 Fibonacci Program Run Times

M	20	22	24	26	28	30	32
Fib(M)	6,765	17,711	46,368	121,393	317,811	832,040	2,178,309
Time (secs)	0.17	0.44	1.21	2.97	7.80	20.33	51.90

Figure 5.2 Hilbert curves.

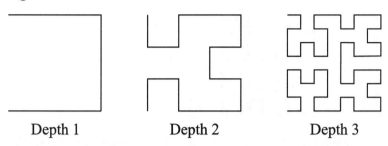

Depth 1   Depth 2   Depth 3

You create a Hilbert curve, or any other self-similar curve, by breaking up a large curve into smaller pieces. You then use the curve itself, properly sized and rotated, to build those pieces. You may break those pieces into smaller pieces and so on until the process reaches some desired depth of recursion. The depth of the curve is defined to be the greatest depth of recursion the routine reaches.

The Hilbert routine controls its recursion using a depth parameter. When the routine recursively calls itself, it decreases the depth parameter by 1. When the routine is called with depth 1, it draws the simple depth 1 curve shown on the left in Figure 5.2 and exits. This is the base case for the recursion.

For example, the Hilbert curve of depth 2 is made up of four Hilbert curves of depth 1. Similarly, a Hilbert curve of depth 3 is made up of four Hilbert curves of depth 2, each consisting of four Hilbert curves of depth 1. Figure 5.3 shows Hilbert curves of depths 2 and 3. The smaller curves making up the larger ones are drawn with bold lines.

The following code draws a depth 1 Hilbert curve:

```
Line -Step (Length, 0)
Line -Step (0, Length)
Line -Step (-Length, 0)
```

This code assumes that the current drawing position begins at the upper left corner of the drawing area and that Length is the desired length for each line segment.

You can sketch the method for drawing a Hilbert curve of greater depth as follows:

```
Private Sub Hilbert(Depth As Integer)
    If Depth = 1 Then
        Draw a depth 1 Hilbert curve
    Else
        Draw and connect the four curves Hilbert(Depth - 1)
    End If
End Sub
```

Figure 5.3 Hilbert curves made from smaller Hilbert curves.

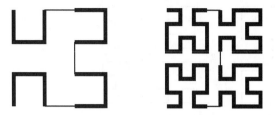

You must complicate this method slightly so the Hilbert routine can tell which direction it is heading and whether it is drawing clockwise or counter-clockwise. It needs to know this to decide which kinds of Hilbert curves to use.

You can give the routine this information by adding parameters Dx and Dy to indicate the direction of the first line in the curve. If the curve is of depth 1, the routine draws its first line as in Line –Step(Dx, Dy). If the curve has greater depth, the routine connects the first two smaller subcurves using Line –Step(Dx, Dy). In either case, the routine can use Dx and Dy to pick the direction in which it should draw the lines making up the curve.

The Visual Basic code for drawing Hilbert curves is short but tricky. You may need to step through it several times for curves of depth 1 and 2 to see exactly how Dx and Dy change to produce the different parts of the curve.

```
Private Sub Hilbert(depth As Integer, Dx As Single, Dy As Single)
    If depth > 1 Then Hilbert depth - 1, Dy, Dx
    HilbertPicture.Line -Step(Dx, Dy)
    If depth > 1 Then Hilbert depth - 1, Dx, Dy
    HilbertPicture.Line -Step(Dy, Dx)
    If depth > 1 Then Hilbert depth - 1, Dx, Dy
    HilbertPicture.Line -Step(-Dx, -Dy)
    If depth > 1 Then Hilbert depth - 1, -Dy, -Dx
End Sub
```

Run Time Analysis

To analyze this routine's run time, you must determine the number of times the Hilbert routine calls itself. Each time the routine recurses, it calls itself four times. If T(N) is the number of times the routine is executed when it is called for depth N, then:

```
T(1) = 1
T(N) = 1 + 4 * T(N - 1)          for N > 1.
```

If you expand the definition of T(N) a few times you get:

```
T(N) = 1 + 4 * T(N - 1)
     = 1 + 4 * (1 + 4 * T(N - 2))
```

```
= 1 + 4 + 16 * T(N - 2)
= 1 + 4 + 16 * (1 + 4 * T(N - 3))
= 1 + 4 + 16 + 64 * T(N - 3)
= ...
= 4⁰ + 4¹ + 4² + 4³ + ... + 4ᴷ * T(N - K)
```

Expanding this equation until you reach the base case $T(1) = 1$ gives:

$$T(N) = 4^0 + 4^1 + 4^2 + 4^3 + \ldots + 4^{N-1}$$

You can use the following mathematical formula to simplify this equation.

$$X^0 + X^1 + X^2 + X^3 + \ldots + X^M = (X^{M+1} - 1) / (X - 1)$$

Using this formula, the equation becomes:

$$T(N) = (4^{(N-1)+1} - 1) / (4 - 1)$$
$$= (4^N - 1) / 3$$

Ignoring the constants, this routine runs in time $O(4^N)$. Table 5.5 shows the first several values for the run time function. If you look closely at the numbers, you will see that they agree with the recursive definition.

This algorithm is typical of many recursive algorithms that run in $O(C^N)$ time for some constant C. Each time the Hilbert subroutine is called, it increases the problem size by a factor of 4. More generally, if an algorithm increases the problem size by a factor of at least C each time it executes a certain fixed number of steps, the algorithm will have $O(C^N)$ run time.

This is exactly the opposite of the GCD algorithm's behavior. The GCD routine decreases the problem size by a factor of at least 1 / 2 every second time it is called, so it has $O(\log(N))$ run time. The Hilbert curve routine increases the problem size by a factor of 4 each time it is called, so it has $O(4^N)$ run time.

The function $(4^N - 1) / 3$ is an exponential function that grows *very* quickly. In fact, this function grows so quickly that you might suspect that this is not a very efficient algorithm. This algorithm definitely takes a lot of time, but there are two reasons that this is not necessarily bad.

First, any other algorithm that draws Hilbert curves cannot be much faster. Hilbert curves contain a *lot* of line segments, and any algorithm that draws them all will take a long time. Each time the Hilbert routine is called, it draws three lines. Let $L(N)$ be the total number of lines drawn in a depth N Hilbert curve. Then $L(N) = 3 * T(N) = 4N - 1$, so $L(N)$ is also O(4N). Any algorithm that draws Hilbert curves must draw O(4N) lines, so it must execute O(4N) steps. There are other algorithms for drawing Hilbert curves, but they all take about as much time as this algorithm.

Table 5.5 Number of Recursive Calls to the Hilbert Subroutine

N	1	2	3	4	5	6	7	8	9
T(N)	1	5	21	85	341	1,365	5,461	21,845	87,381

The second fact that indicates this algorithm might not be too bad is that a depth 9 Hilbert curve contains so many lines it turns most computer monitors completely black. This is not surprising because this curve contains 262,143 line segments. This means you will probably never want to display a Hilbert curve of depth 9 or greater anyway. At some depth beyond 9 you would reach the limits of Visual Basic and your computer, but first you reach the limits of what you might reasonably want to display.

The conclusion is that Hilbert curves are just plain hard to draw. Drawing a quarter of a million lines is a lot of work, and it will take awhile no matter how clever your algorithm is.

Example program Hilbert, shown in Figure 5.4, uses this recursive algorithm to draw Hilbert curves. When you run the program, be sure to keep the depth of recursion small (under 6) until you have seen how long the program takes on your computer.

Recursive Sierpinski Curves

Like Hilbert curves, Sierpinski curves are self-similar curves that are naturally defined recursively. Figure 5.5 shows Sierpinski curves with depths 1, 2, and 3.

The Hilbert curve algorithm uses a single subroutine to draw Hilbert curves. Sierpinski curves are easier to draw using four separate routines that work together. These routines are named SierpA, SierpB, SierpC, and SierpD. The routines are indirectly recursive—each routine calls the others, which then call the first. They draw the top, left, bottom, and right portions of a Sierpinski curve, respectively.

Figure 5.6 shows how these routines work together to form a Sierpinski curve of depth 1. The subcurves are shown with arrows to indicate the direction in which they are drawn. Segments used to connect the four subcurves are drawn with dashed lines.

Figure 5.4 Program Hilbert.

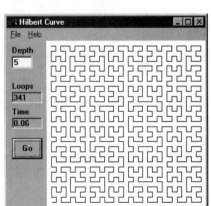

Figure 5.5 Sierpinski curves.

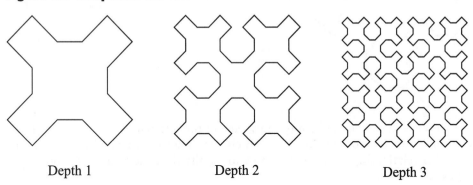

Depth 1   Depth 2   Depth 3

Each of the four basic curves is composed of a diagonal line segment, followed by a vertical or horizontal segment, followed by another diagonal line segment. When the depth of recursion is greater than 1, you must break each of these curves into smaller pieces. You do this by breaking each of the curves' two diagonal line segments into two subcurves.

For example, to break up a type A curve, break the first diagonal line segment into a type A curve followed by a type B curve. Then draw the horizontal line segment for the original type A curve unchanged. Finish by breaking the second diagonal line segment into a type D curve followed by a type A curve. Figure 5.7 shows how a depth 2 type A curve is built from depth 1 curves. The subcurves are drawn with bold lines so they are easy to see.

Figure 5.8 shows how a complete depth 2 Sierpinski curve is built from four depth 1 subcurves. Each of the subcurves is circled with dashed lines.

If you use arrows like ↗ and ↖ to indicate the types of lines that connect the subcurves (the thin lines in Figure 5.8), then you can list the recursive relationships among the four types of curves, as shown in Figure 5.9.

The routines that draw the Sierpinski subcurves are all very similar, so only one is shown here. The relationships shown in Figure 5.9 indicate the drawing

Figure 5.6 The parts of a Sierpinski curve.

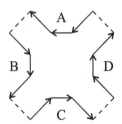

Figure 5.7 Breaking up a type A curve.

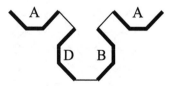

operations you should perform to draw each of the different types of curves. You can follow the relationships for a type A curve in the following code. You can use the other relationships to determine how to modify the code to draw the other types of curves.

```
Private Sub SierpA(Depth As Integer, Dist As Single)
    If Depth = 1 Then
        Line -Step(-Dist, Dist)
        Line -Step(-Dist, 0)
        Line -Step(-Dist, -Dist)
    Else
        SierpA Depth - 1, Dist
        Line -Step (-Dist, Dist)
        SierpB Depth - 1, Dist
        Line -Step(-Dist, 0)
        SierpD Depth - 1, Dist
        Line -Step(-Dist, -Dist)
        SierpA Depth - 1, Dist
```

Figure 5.8 A Sierpinski curve made from smaller Sierpinski curves.

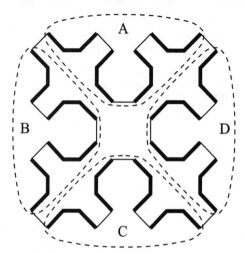

Figure 5.9 Recursive relationships among Sierpinski curves.

A: A $\swarrow$ B $\leftarrow$ D $\nwarrow$ A
B: B $\searrow$ C $\downarrow$ A $\swarrow$ B
C: C $\nearrow$ D $\rightarrow$ B $\searrow$ C
D: D $\nwarrow$ A $\uparrow$ C $\nearrow$ D

```
        End If
End Sub
```

In addition to routines that draw each of the four basic curves, you need a routine that uses the four of them to create the completed Sierpinski curve.

```
Sub Sierpinski (Depth As Integer, Dist As Single)
    SierpB Depth, Dist
    Line -Step(Dist, Dist)
    SierpC Depth, Dist
    Line -Step(Dist, -Dist)
    SierpD Depth, Dist
    Line -Step(-Dist, -Dist)
    SierpA Depth, Dist
    Line -Step(-Dist, Dist)
End Sub
```

Run Time Analysis

To analyze the run time of this algorithm, you must determine how many times each of the four curve drawing routines is called. Let $T(N)$ be the number of times any one of the four basic curve routines or the main Sierpinski routine is called when drawing a depth N curve.

When the depth of the curve is 1, each type of curve is drawn once. Adding one for the main Sierpinski routine gives $T(1) = 5$.

Each time one of the curve routines recurses, it calls itself or another of the routines four times. Because these routines are all pretty much the same, $T(N)$ is the same no matter which routine is called first. This makes sense because Sierpinski curves are symmetrical and contain the same number of each type of curve. The recursive equations for $T(N)$ are:

```
T(1) = 5
T(N) = 1 + 4 * T(N - 1)          for N > 1.
```

These equations are almost the same as the ones used to compute the run time for the Hilbert curve algorithm. The only difference is that $T(1) = 1$ for the Hilbert curve. Comparing a few values for these equations shows that $T_{Sierpinski}(N) = T_{Hilbert}(N + 1)$. The last section showed that $T_{Hilbert}(N) = (4^N - 1) / 3$ so $T_{Sierpinski}(N) = (4^{N+1} - 1) / 3$, which is also $O(4^N)$.

Like the Hilbert curve algorithm, this algorithm runs in $O(4^N)$ time, but that is not necessarily bad. The Sierpinski curve requires $O(4^N)$ lines, so no algorithm can draw a Sierpinski curve in less than $O(4^N)$ time.

The Sierpinski curve also completely fills most computer screens for depths of 9 or greater. At some depth beyond 9 you would reach the limits of Visual Basic and your computer, but you reach the limits of what you might reasonably want to display first.

Example program Sierp, shown in Figure 5.10, uses this recursive algorithm to draw Sierpinski curves. When you run the program, be sure to keep the depth of recursion small (under 6) until you know how long the program takes on your computer.

Dangers of Recursion

Recursion can be a powerful technique for decomposing large problems, but it has a few dangers. This section takes a look at some of these dangers and explains when recursion is appropriate and when it is not. The sections that follow explain techniques for removing recursion when it might cause problems.

Infinite Recursion

The most obvious danger of recursion is infinite recursion. If you do not build your algorithm properly, the function may slip past your base case and run forever. The easiest way to make this mistake is to forget the base case, as is done in the following bad version of the factorial function. Because the function does not test to see if the base case is reached, it will recursively call itself forever.

Figure 5.10 Program Sierp.

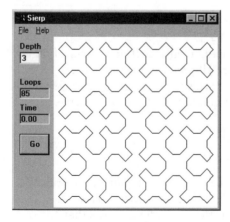

```
Private Function BadFactorial(num As Integer) As Integer
    BadFactorial = num * BadFactorial(num - 1)
End Function
```

A function will also recurse infinitely if its base case does not stop all of the possible paths of the recursion. In the following incorrect version of the factorial function, the function will recurse forever if the input is not an integer or if it is less than 0. These values are not valid inputs for the factorial function, so you could require that the program using this function check that the inputs are valid. It is better, however, for the function to protect itself.

```
Private Function BadFactorial2(num As Double) As Double
    If num = 0 Then
        BadFactorial2 = 1
    Else
        BadFactorial2 = num * BadFactorial2(num-1)
    End If
End Function
```

The following version of the Fibonacci function shows a trickier example. Here the base case stops only some paths of recursion. This function has the same problems with noninteger and negative values that BadFactorial2 has.

```
Private Function BadFib(num As Double) As Double
    If num = 0 Then
        BadFib = 0
    Else
        BadFib = BadFib(num - 1) + BadFib(num - 2)
    End If
End Function
```

A final problem related to infinite recursion is that "infinite" really only means "until you run out of stack space." Even correctly written recursive routines will sometimes run out of stack space and fail. The following function, which computes the sum $N + (N - 1) + ... + 2 + 1$, exhausts the computer's stack space for large values of N. The largest value of N that will work depends on your computer's configuration.

```
Private Function BigAdd(N As Double) As Double
    If N <= 1 Then
        BigAdd = 1
    Else
        BigAdd = N + BigAdd(N - 1)
    End If
End Function
```

Example program BigAdd demonstrates this algorithm. See how large an input you can give the program before it exhausts the stack on your computer.

Wasted Space

Wasted space is another danger of recursion. Each time your program executes a subroutine call, the computer allocates space for the variables local to the new procedure. If you have a complicated chain of recursive calls, the computer will spend a considerable amount of time and memory allocating and deallocating these variables during the recursion. Even if this does not cause the program to run out of stack space, the time spent managing the variables can be significant.

There are several ways you can minimize this overhead. First, do not use lots of unnecessary variables. Visual Basic will allocate space for these variables even if the subroutine does not use them. The following version of the BigAdd function runs out of stack space sooner than the previous version.

```
Private Function BigAdd (N As Double) As Double
Dim I1 As Integer
Dim I2 As Integer
Dim I3 As Integer
Dim I4 As Integer
Dim I5 As Integer

    If N <= 1 Then
        BigAdd = 1
    Else
        BigAdd = N + BigAdd(N - 1)
    End If
End Function
```

If you are not sure whether a variable is necessary, use the Option Explicit statement and comment out the variable's declaration. When you try to run the program, Visual Basic will complain if the variable is needed.

You can also reduce stack use by declaring variables globally. If you declare variables in the Declarations section of the module instead of in the subroutine, the computer will not need to allocate new memory each time the subroutine is called.

A better solution is to declare the variables within the routine using the Static keyword. Static variables are shared by all instances of the subroutine, so the computer does not need to allocate new copies each time the subroutine is called.

Logical Misuse

A more subtle danger of recursion is logical misuse. Here you use recursion when it is not the best way to do the job. The factorial, Fibonacci, GCD, and BigAdd functions presented earlier do not really need to be recursive. Better, nonrecursive versions of these functions are described a little later in this chapter.

In the cases of the factorial and GCD functions, the unnecessary recursion is mostly harmless. Both of these functions are quite fast, and they will execute for relatively large input values. Unless you have used up a lot of stack space in some other part of your program, these functions will not be limited by the size of the stack.

On the other hand, recursion destroys the Fibonacci algorithm. To compute Fib(N) the algorithm first computes Fib(N − 1) and Fib(N − 2). But to compute Fib(N − 1) it must compute Fib(N − 2) and Fib(N − 3). Here Fib(N − 2) is being computed twice.

The earlier analysis of this algorithm showed that Fib(1) and Fib(0) are computed a total of Fib(N + 1) times during the computation of Fib(N). Fib(30) = 832,040, so to compute Fib(29) you actually compute the same values for Fib(0) and Fib(1) a total of 832,040 times. The Fibonacci algorithm wastes a tremendous amount of time computing these intermediate values again and again.

The BigAdd function has a different problem. While it runs quite quickly, it enters a deep recursion and soon exhausts the stack space. The function could calculate values for much larger inputs if it did not exhaust the stack space first.

The factorial function has a similar problem. On input N both the BigAdd and factorial functions recurse to a depth of N function calls. The factorial function cannot accept inputs as large as the BigAdd function can. The value of 170! ≈ 7.257E + 306 is the largest value that fits in a double variable, so that is the largest value the function can compute. While the function is headed for deep recursion, it causes double precision overflow before it overflows the stack.

When to Use Recursion

This discussion may lead you to think that all recursion is bad. That is definitely not the case. Many algorithms are naturally recursive. Even though it is possible to rewrite any algorithm so it does not contain recursion, many are harder to understand, analyze, debug, and maintain when they are written nonrecursively.

The following sections present methods for removing recursion from any algorithm. Some of the resulting nonrecursive algorithms are still fairly easy to understand. The nonrecursive factorial, GCD, Fibonacci, and BigAdd functions are relatively straightforward.

On the other hand, the nonrecursive versions of the Hilbert and Sierpinski algorithms are quite complicated. They are harder to understand, will be more difficult to maintain, and even run a bit more slowly than the recursive versions. They are presented to show you techniques you could use to remove recursion from complicated algorithms, not because they are better than the recursive versions.

If an algorithm is naturally recursive, write it recursively. If all goes well, you will not encounter any of the problems described here. If you do run into some of these problems, you can rewrite the algorithm without recursion using the techniques presented in the following sections. Rewriting an algorithm is often easier than writing it nonrecursively in the first place.

Tail Recursion

Recall the functions presented earlier to compute factorials and greatest common divisors. Recall also the BigAdd function that exhausts the stack for relatively small inputs.

```
Private Function Factorial(num As Integer) As Integer
    If num <= 0 Then
        Factorial = 1
    Else
        Factorial = num * Factorial(num - 1)
    End If
End Function


Private Function GCD(A As Integer, B As Integer) As Integer
    If B Mod A = 0 Then
        GCD = A
    Else
        GCD = GCD(B Mod A, A)
    End If
End Function


Private Function BigAdd(N As Double) As Double
    If N <= 1 Then
        BigAdd = 1
    Else
        BigAdd = N + BigAdd(N - 1)
    End If
End Function
```

In all of these functions, the last thing before the end of the function is the recursive step. This sort or recursion at the end of a routine is called *tail recursion*, or *end recursion*.

Because nothing occurs in the routine after the recursive step, there is an easy way to remove the recursion. Instead of calling the function recursively, the routine resets its own parameters to match the ones it would normally pass into the recursive call. It then starts over from the beginning.

Consider this general recursive subroutine:

```
Private Sub Recurse(A As Integer)
    ' Do stuff here, calculate B, etc.
    Recurse B
End Sub
```

You can rewrite this routine without recursion as:

```
Private Sub NoRecurse(A As Integer)
    Do While (not done)
        ' Do stuff here, calculate B, etc.
        A = B
    Loop
End Sub
```

This process is called *tail recursion removal,* or *end recursion removal.* This process does not change the program's run time. The recursive steps have just been replaced with passes through a While loop.

Tail recursion removal does eliminate subroutine calls, however, and it may increase an algorithm's speed. More important, this method decreases the use of the stack. Algorithms like the BigAdd function that are limited by their depths of recursion will benefit greatly.

Some compilers remove tail recursion automatically. Visual Basic does not. Otherwise, the simple BigAdd function presented in the previous section would not exhaust the stack.

Using tail recursion removal, rewriting the factorial, GCD, and BigAdd functions nonrecursively is easy. These versions use the ByVal keyword to protect the values of their parameters for the calling routine.

```
Private Function Factorial(ByVal N As Integer) As Double
Dim value As Double

    value = 1#        ' This will be the value of the function.
    Do While N > 1
        value = value * N
        N = N - 1   ' Prepare the arguments for the "recursion."
    Loop
    Factorial = value
End Function


Private Function GCD(ByVal A As Double, ByVal B As Double) As Double
Dim B_Mod_A As Double

    B_Mod_A = B Mod A
    Do While B_Mod_A <> 0
        ' Prepare the arguments for the "recursion."
        B = A
        A = B_Mod_A
        B_Mod_A = B Mod A
    Loop
    GCD = A
End Function
```

```
Private Function BigAdd(ByVal N As Double) As Double
Dim value As Double

    value = 1#        ' This will be the value of the function.
    Do While N > 1
        value = value + N
        N = N - 1    ' Prepare the parameters for the "recursion."
    Loop
    BigAdd = value
End Function
```

For the factorial and GCD algorithms, there is little practical difference between the recursive and nonrecursive versions. Both are fast, and both can handle problems that are reasonably large.

For the BigAdd algorithm, however, there is a tremendous difference. The recursive version exhausts the stack for fairly small inputs. Because the nonrecursive version does not use up the stack, it should be able to compute values for N up to about 10^{154}. Beyond that point, the double data type will overflow. Of course, running the algorithm for 10^{154} steps will take a long time, so you may not want to try such a large example. Notice also that this function is the same as the value of the more easily calculated function N * (N + 1) / 2.

Example programs Facto2, GCD2, and BigAdd2 demonstrate these nonrecursive algorithms.

Nonrecursive Fibonacci Numbers

Unfortunately, the recursive algorithm for computing Fibonacci numbers does not contain only tail recursion. The algorithm uses two recursive calls to itself to calculate a value. The second call comes after the first finishes. Because the first call does not come at the very end of the function, it is not tail recursion, so it cannot be removed using tail recursion removal.

Perhaps this is just as well because the recursive Fibonacci algorithm is limited by the fact that it computes too many intermediate values rather than by its depth of recursion. Tail recursion removal decreases depth of recursion, but it does not change the algorithm's run time. Even if tail recursion removal applied to the Fibonacci algorithm, it would still be extremely slow.

The trouble with this algorithm is that it recomputes the same values many times. The values Fib(1) and Fib(0) are computed a total of Fib(N + 1) times when the algorithm computes Fib(N). To compute Fib(29) the algorithm computes the same values for Fib(0) and Fib(1) a total of 832,040 times.

Whenever an algorithm recomputes the same values many times, you should look for a way to avoid the duplicate computations. A straightforward and mechanical way to do this is to build a table of the calculated values. When you need an intermediate value, you can look it up in the table rather than recomputing it.

In this example you can build a table to store the values of the Fibonacci function Fib(N) for N less than 1477. For N >= 1477 the double precision variables used by the function overflow. The following code shows the Fibonacci function with this change.

```
Const MAX_FIB = 1476    ' The largest value we will compute.


Dim FibValues(0 To MAX_FIB) As Double

Private Function Fib(N As Integer) As Double
    ' Compute the value if it is not yet in the table.
    If FibValues(N) < 0 Then _
        FibValues(N) = Fib(N - 1) + Fib(N - 2)

    Fib = FibValues(N)
End Function
```

When the program begins, it should initialize each entry in the FibValues array to –1. It should then set the values of FibValues(0) to 0 and FibValues(1) to 1. These values establish the base case for the recursion.

When the function executes, it checks the array to see if it has already stored the value it needs. If not, it recursively calculates the value as before and stores the new value in the array for later use.

Example program Fibo2 uses this method for calculating Fibonacci numbers. The program can quickly compute Fib(N) for N up to 100 or 200. If you try to calculate Fib(1476), however, the program enters a chain of recursion 1476 levels deep that will probably exhaust your system's stack.

As Fibo2 computes new values, however, it fills the FibValues array. Those values allow the function to compute larger and larger values without using deep recursion. For example, if you ask the program to compute Fib(100), Fib(200), Fib(300), and so forth, you can eventually fill the FibValues array completely and compute the largest value possible, Fib(1476).

This process of slowly filling the FibValues array leads to a new method for computing Fibonacci numbers. When the program initializes the FibValues array, it can precompute all of the Fibonacci numbers.

```
Private Sub InitializeFibValues()
Dim i As Integer

    FibValues(0) = 0     ' Initialize the base cases.
    FibValues(1) = 1
    For i = 2 To MAX_FIB
        FibValues(i) = FibValues(i - 1) + FibValues(i - 2)
    Next I
End Sub
```

```
Private Function Fib(N As Integer) As Double
    Fib = FibValues(N)
End Function
```

This method takes a certain amount of time to create the lookup array. Once the array is ready, it takes only a single step to access a value in the array. Neither the initialization routine nor function Fib uses recursion, so neither will exhaust the stack space. Example program Fibo3 demonstrates this approach.

One more method for computing Fibonacci numbers is worth mentioning. The first recursive definition of the Fibonacci function uses a top-down approach. To get a value for Fib(N), the algorithm recursively computes Fib(N – 1) and Fib(N – 2) and adds them together.

Subroutine InitializeFibValues, on the other hand, works from the bottom up. It starts with the values of Fib(0) and Fib(1). It then uses smaller values to compute larger ones until the table is full.

You can use this same bottom-up strategy to compute the value of the Fibonacci function directly each time you need a value. This method takes longer than looking values up in an array, but it does not require the extra array memory. This is an example of a space versus time trade-off. Using extra space to store a table of values makes the algorithm faster.

```
Private Function Fib(N As Integer) As Double
Dim Fib_i_minus_1 As Double
Dim Fib_i_minus_2 As Double
Dim fib_i As Double
Dim i As Integer

    If N <= 1 Then
        Fib = N
    Else
        Fib_i_minus_2 = 0      ' Initially Fib(0)
        Fib_i_minus_1 = 1      ' Initially Fib(1)
        For i = 2 To N
            fib_i = Fib_i_minus_1 + Fib_i_minus_2
            Fib_i_minus_2 = Fib_i_minus_1
            Fib_i_minus_1 = fib_i
        Next i
        Fib = fib_i
    End If
End Function
```

This version takes O(N) steps to calculate Fib(N). This is more than the single step the previous version required, but it is much faster than the original O(Fib(N)) steps. On a 90 megahertz Pentium, the original recursive algorithm took almost 52 seconds to calculate Fib(32) = 2,178,309. The new algorithm takes no noticeable time to determine that Fib(1476) ≈ 1.31E + 308. Example program Fibo4 uses this method to compute Fibonacci numbers.

Avoiding More General Recursion

The factorial, GCD, and BigAdd functions can be simplified by tail recursion removal. The Fibonacci function can be simplified using a lookup table or by reformulating the problem in a bottom-up way.

Some recursive algorithms are so complicated that these methods are difficult or impossible. It would be hard to come up with nonrecursive algorithms for drawing Hilbert and Sierpinski curves from scratch. Other recursive algorithms are more complicated than those.

Earlier sections showed that any algorithm that draws Hilbert or Sierpinski curves must use $O(N^4)$ steps, so the original recursive implementations are pretty good. They are about as fast as possible and their depths of recursion are reasonable.

Still, you may come across other complicated algorithms that have large depths of recursion but do not yield to tail recursion removal. In that case, converting a recursive algorithm into a nonrecursive one is still possible.

The basic approach is to think about the way the computer performs recursion and then mimic the steps the computer follows. The new algorithm will perform the "recursion" instead of making the computer do all the work.

Because the new algorithm follows pretty much the same steps the computer follows, you might wonder if speed will increase. In Visual Basic it usually does not. The computer can perform the tasks it needs for recursion more quickly than you can mimic them. Handling these details yourself gives you more control over the allocation of local variables, however, and allows you to avoid great depth of recursion.

Normally when you make a subroutine call, the computer does three things. First, it saves any information it needs to resume execution when the subroutine returns. Second, it prepares for the call and transfers control to the subroutine. Third, when the called routine ends, the computer restores the information it saved in the first step and transfers control back to the appropriate point in the program. When you convert a recursive subroutine into a nonrecursive one, you perform these three steps yourself.

Consider the following generalized recursive subroutine:

```
Sub Subr(num)
    <code block 1>
    Subr(<parameters>)
    <code block 2>
End Sub
```

Because there is code after the recursive step, you cannot use tail recursion removal on this algorithm.

Begin by labeling the first lines in code blocks 1 and 2. You will use these labels to determine where to resume execution when a "recursion" returns. You will use the labels only to help understand what the algorithm is doing—they are not actually part of the Visual Basic code. In this example the labels would be:

```
        Sub Subr(num)
1           <code block 1>
            Subr(<parameters>)
2           <code block 2>
        End Sub
```

Use a special label "0" to indicate that a "recursion" is ending. Now you can rewrite the subroutine without recursion, like this:

```
Sub Subr(num)
Dim pc As Integer            ' Tells us where to resume execution.

    pc = 1     ' Start at the beginning.
    Do
        Select Case pc
            Case 1
                <code block 1>
                If (the base case has been reached) Then
                    ' Skip the recursion and go to code block 2.
                    pc = 2
                Else
                    ' Save variables needed after the recursion.
                    ' Save pc = 2. This is where we will resume
                    ' execution after the "recursion" returns.
                    ' Set variables needed by the recursive call.
                    ' For example, num = num - 1.
                        :
                    ' Go to code block 1 to start the recursion.
                    pc = 1
                End If
            Case 2        ' Execute code block 2
                <code block 2>
                pc = 0
            Case 0
                If (this is the last recursion) Then Exit Do
                ' Otherwise restore pc and other variables saved
                ' before the recursion.
                    :
        End Select
    Loop
End Sub
```

The variable pc, which stands for program counter, tells the routine what step it should execute next. For example, when pc = 1, the routine should execute code block 1.

When the routine reaches the base case, it does not recurse. Instead, it changes pc to 2 so it will continue execution with code block 2.

If the routine has not yet reached the base case, it prepares for "recursion." To do this, it saves the value of any local variables it will need later when the "recursion" ends. It also saves the value of pc for the code segment it should execute after the "recursion" returns. In this example, the routine executes code block 2 next, so it saves 2 as the next value for pc. The easiest way to save the values of the local variables and pc is to use stacks like the ones described in Chapter 3, "Stacks and Queues."

A concrete example should make this easier to understand. Consider a slightly rewritten version of the factorial function. It is rewritten here as a subroutine that returns its value through a variable, rather than as a function, to make things a little easier.

```
        Private Sub Factorial(num As Integer, value As Integer)
        Dim partial As Integer

1           If num <= 1 Then
                value = 1
            Else
                Factorial(num - 1, partial)
2               value = num * partial
            End If
        End Sub
```

After the routine returns from the recursion, it needs to know the original value of num so it can perform the multiplication value = num * partial. Because it needs access to the value of num after the recursion returns, it must save pc and num before starting the recursion.

The following routine saves these values in two array-based stacks. When preparing for recursion, it pushes num and pc onto the stacks. When a recursion finishes, it pops the most recently added values from the stacks. The following code shows a nonrecursive version of the factorial subroutine.

```
Private Sub Factorial(num As Integer, value As Integer)
ReDim num_stack(1 to 200) As Integer
ReDim pc_stack(1 to 200) As Integer
Dim stack_top As Integer            ' The top of the stack.
Dim pc As Integer

    pc = 1
    Do
        Select Case pc
```

```
        Case 1
            If num <= 1 Then        ' This is the base case.
                value = 1
                pc = 0              ' End this recursion.
            Else                    ' Recurse.
                ' Save num and the next pc.
                stack_top = stack_top + 1
                num_stack(stack_top) = num
                pc_stack(stack_top) = 2     ' Resume at 2.
                ' Start the recursion
                num = num - 1
                ' Transfer control back to the start.
                pc = 1
            End If
        Case 2
            ' value holds the result of the recently
            ' finished recursion. Multiply it by num.
            value = value * num
            ' "Return" from a "recursion."
            pc = 0
        Case 0
            ' End a "recursion."
            ' If the stacks are empty, we are done with the
            ' original call to the subroutine.
            If stack_top <= 0 Then Exit Do
            ' Otherwise restore local variables and pc.
            num = num_stack(stack_top)
            pc = pc_stack(stack_top)
            stack_top = stack_top - 1
        End Select
    Loop
End Sub
```

Like tail recursion removal, this technique mimics the behavior of the recursive algorithm. The routine has replaced each recursive call with an iteration in the While loop. Because the steps executed are the same, the overall run time of the algorithm is unchanged.

As is the case with tail recursion removal, this technique removes the need for the algorithm to recurse deeply, possibly exhausting the stack.

Nonrecursive Hilbert Curves

The factorial example in the previous section turned a simple but inefficient recursive factorial function into a complicated and inefficient nonrecursive subroutine. For the factorial function, a much better nonrecursive algorithm was presented earlier in the chapter.

Finding a simple nonrecursive version for more complicated algorithms can be difficult. The techniques of the previous section are useful when the algorithm is multiply recursive or calls itself indirectly.

For a more interesting example of, consider the recursive Hilbert curve algorithm.

```
Private Sub Hilbert(depth As Integer, Dx As Single, Dy As Single)
    If depth > 1 Then Hilbert depth - 1, Dy, Dx
    HilbertPicture.Line -Step(Dx, Dy)
    If depth > 1 Then Hilbert depth - 1, Dx, Dy
    HilbertPicture.Line -Step(Dy, Dx)
    If depth > 1 Then Hilbert depth - 1, Dx, Dy
    HilbertPicture.Line -Step(-Dx, -Dy)
    If depth > 1 Then Hilbert depth - 1, -Dy, -Dx
End Sub
```

The following code shows the numbering of the first lines in each code block between the recursive steps. These include the first line of the routine and any other places where you might have to resume execution after a "recursion" returns.

```
        Private Sub Hilbert(depth As Integer, Dx As Single, Dy As
Single)
1           If depth > 1 Then Hilbert depth - 1, Dy, Dx
2           HilbertPicture.Line -Step(Dx, Dy)
            If depth > 1 Then Hilbert depth - 1, Dx, Dy
3           HilbertPicture.Line -Step(Dy, Dx)
            If depth > 1 Then Hilbert depth - 1, Dx, Dy
4           HilbertPicture.Line -Step(-Dx, -Dy)
            If depth > 1 Then Hilbert depth - 1, -Dy, -Dx
        End Sub
```

Each time the nonrecursive routine begins a "recursion," it must save the values of the local variables Depth, Dx, and Dy, as well as the next value for pc. When it returns from a "recursion," it restores these values. To make these operations a little easier, you can write a pair of auxiliary routines to push and pop these values from a series of stacks.

```
Const STACK_SIZE = 20
Dim DepthStack(0 To STACK_SIZE)
Dim DxStack(0 To STACK_SIZE)
Dim DyStack(0 To STACK_SIZE)
Dim PCStack(0 To STACK_SIZE)
Dim TopOfStack As Integer
```

```
Private Sub SaveValues(Depth As Integer, Dx As Single, Dy As Single, _
        pc As Integer)
    TopOfStack = TopOfStack + 1
    DepthStack(TopOfStack) = Depth
    DxStack(TopOfStack) = Dx
    DyStack(TopOfStack) = Dy
    PCStack(TopOfStack) = pc
End Sub

Private Sub RestoreValues(Depth As Integer, Dx As Single, Dy As
Single, _
        pc As Integer)
    Depth = DepthStack(TopOfStack)
    Dx = DxStack(TopOfStack)
    Dy = DyStack(TopOfStack)
    pc = PCStack(TopOfStack)
    TopOfStack = TopOfStack - 1

End Sub
```

The following code shows the nonrecursive version of the Hilbert subroutine.

```
Private Sub Hilbert(Depth As Integer, Dx As Single, Dy As Single)
Dim pc As Integer
Dim tmp As Single

    pc = 1
    Do
        Select Case pc
            Case 1
                If Depth > 1 Then    ' Recurse.
                    ' Save the current values.
                    SaveValues Depth, Dx, Dy, 2
                    ' Prepare for the recursion.
                    Depth = Depth - 1
                    tmp = Dx
                    Dx = Dy
                    Dy = tmp
                    pc = 1  ' Go to start of recursive call.
                Else        ' Base case.
                    ' We have recursed deeply enough.
                    ' Continue with code block 2.
                    pc = 2
                End If
            Case 2
                HilbertPicture.Line -Step(Dx, Dy)
```

```
          If Depth > 1 Then ' Recurse.
              ' Save the current values.
              SaveValues Depth, Dx, Dy, 3
              ' Prepare for the recursion.
              Depth = Depth - 1
              ' Dx and Dy remain the same.
              pc = 1  ' Go to start of recursive call.
          Else      ' Base case.
              ' We have recursed deeply enough.
              ' Continue with code block 3.
              pc = 3
          End If
      Case 3
          HilbertPicture.Line -Step(Dy, Dx)
          If Depth > 1 Then ' Recurse.
              ' Save the current values.
              SaveValues Depth, Dx, Dy, 4
              ' Prepare for the recursion.
              Depth = Depth - 1
              ' Dx and Dy remain the same.
              pc = 1  ' Go to start of recursive call.
          Else      ' Base case.
              ' We have recursed deeply enough.
              ' Continue with code block 4.
              pc = 4
          End If
      Case 4
          HilbertPicture.Line -Step(-Dx, -Dy)
          If Depth > 1 Then        ' Recurse.
              ' Save the current values.
              SaveValues Depth, Dx, Dy, 0
              ' Prepare for the recursion.
              Depth = Depth - 1
              tmp = Dx
              Dx = -Dy
              Dy = -tmp
              pc = 1  ' Go to start of recursive call.
          Else        ' Base case.
              ' We have recursed deeply enough.
              ' This is the end of this recursive call.
              pc = 0
          End If
      Case 0  ' Return from recursion.
          If TopOfStack > 0 Then
              RestoreValues Depth, Dx, Dy, pc
```

```
            Else
                    'The stack is empty. We are done.
                    Exit Do
            End If
        End Select
    Loop
End Sub
```

The run time for this algorithm would be quite tricky to analyze directly. Because the techniques for converting recursive routines into nonrecursive ones do not change the algorithm's run time, this routine has the same $O(N^4)$ run time as the previous version.

Example program Hilbert2 demonstrates this nonrecursive algorithm for drawing Hilbert curves. Be sure to draw simple curves (depth under 6) until you know how long the program will take on your computer.

Nonrecursive Sierpinski Curves

The Sierpinski algorithm presented earlier is both multiply and indirectly recursive. Because the algorithm consists of four subroutines that call each other, you cannot number the important lines as you can with the Hilbert curve algorithm. You can deal with this problem by rewriting the algorithm a bit first.

The recursive version of this algorithm consists of four subroutines SierpA, SierpB, SierpC, and SierpD. Subroutine SierpA looks like this:

```
Private Sub SierpA(Depth As Integer, Dist As Single)
    If Depth = 1 Then
        Line -Step(-Dist, Dist)
        Line -Step(-Dist, 0)
        Line -Step(-Dist, -Dist)
    Else
        SierpA Depth - 1, Dist
        Line -Step(-Dist, Dist)
        SierpB Depth - 1, Dist
        Line -Step(-Dist, 0)
        SierpD Depth - 1, Dist
        Line -Step(-Dist, -Dist)
        SierpA Depth - 1, Dist
    End If
End Sub
```

The other three subroutines are similar. Combining these four routines into a single subroutine is not difficult.

```
Private Sub SierpAll(Depth As Integer, Dist As Single, Func As
Integer)
```

```
Select Case Func
      Case 1      '  SierpA
            <SierpA code>
      Case 2      '  SierpB
            <SierpB code>
      Case 3      '  SierpC
            <SierpC code>
      Case 4      '  SierpD
            <SierpD code>
   End Select
End Sub
```

The Func parameter tells the subroutine which piece of code to execute. You replace calls to the subroutines with calls to SierpAll using the appropriate value for Func. For example, you would replace a call to SierpA with a call to SierpAll where Func is set to 1. You would replace calls to SierpB, SierpC, and SierpD similarly.

The new routine is massively recursive, calling itself in 16 different places. This routine is much larger than the Hilbert subroutine, but otherwise it has a similar structure and you can apply the same techniques for making it nonrecursive.

You can use the first digit of the pc labels to indicate which general piece of code to execute. Number lines within the SierpA code 11, 12, 13, and so on. Number lines in the SierpB code 21, 22, 23, and so forth.

Now you can label the key lines of code within each section. For the SierpA code the key lines are:

```
      ' SierpA code
11    If Depth = 1 Then
            Line -Step(-Dist, Dist)
            Line -Step(-Dist, 0)
            Line -Step(-Dist, -Dist)
      Else
            SierpA Depth - 1, Dist
12          Line -Step(-Dist, Dist)
            SierpB Depth - 1, Dist
13          Line -Step(-Dist, 0)
            SierpD Depth - 1, Dist
14          Line -Step(-Dist, -Dist)
            SierpA Depth - 1, Dist
      End If
```

A typical "recursion" from the SierpA code into the SierpB code looks like this:

```
SaveValues Depth, 13      ' Resume at step 13 when done.
Depth = Depth - 1
pc = 21                   ' Transfer to the start of the SierpB code.
```

The label 0 is reserved to indicate a return from a "recursion." The following code shows the nonrecursive version of SierpAll. The code for the SierpB, SierpC, and SierpD code is similar to the code for SierpA, so it is omitted. You can find all the code on the CD-ROM.

```
Private Sub SierpAll(Depth As Integer, pc As Integer)
    Do
        Select Case pc
            ' *********
            ' * SierpA *
            ' *********
            Case 11
                If Depth <= 1 Then
                    SierpPicture.Line -Step(-Dist, Dist)
                    SierpPicture.Line -Step(-Dist, 0)
                    SierpPicture.Line -Step(-Dist, -Dist)
                    pc = 0
                Else
                    SaveValues Depth, 12        ' Run SierpA
                    Depth = Depth - 1
                    pc = 11
                End If
            Case 12
                SierpPicture.Line -Step(-Dist, Dist)
                SaveValues Depth, 13            ' Run SierpB
                Depth = Depth - 1
                pc = 21
            Case 13
                SierpPicture.Line -Step(-Dist, 0)
                SaveValues Depth, 14            ' Run SierpD
                Depth = Depth - 1
                pc = 41
            Case 14
                SierpPicture.Line -Step(-Dist, -Dist)
                SaveValues Depth, 0             ' Run SierpA
                Depth = Depth - 1
                pc = 11

            ' SierpB, SierpC, and SierpD code omitted.
                :


            ' ****************
            ' * End recursion *
            ' ****************
```

```
        Case 0
            If StackTop <= 0 Then Exit Do
            RestoreValues Depth, pc
    End Select
  Loop
End Sub
```

As is the case with the Hilbert curve algorithm, converting the Sierpinski curve algorithm into a nonrecursive format does not change the algorithm's run time. The new algorithm mimics the behavior of the recursive algorithm that runs in $O(N^4)$ time, so the new version also has $O(N^4)$ run time. It runs a little more slowly than the recursive version and is much more complicated.

The nonrecursive version would allow a much greater depth of recursion, but it is not practical to draw Sierpinski curves with depth greater than 8 or 9 anyway. These facts make the recursive algorithm the better algorithm.

Example program Sierp2 uses this nonrecursive algorithm to draw Sierpinski curves. Draw only simple curves (depth under 6) until you know how long the program will take on your computer.

Summary

You must watch for three main dangers in recursive algorithms:

Infinite recursion. Make sure your algorithm has a solid base case that stops all recursive paths.

Deep recursion. If the algorithm recurses too deeply, it will exhaust the stack. Minimize stack use by reducing the number of variables the routine allocates, allocating variables globally, or allocating variables statically. If the routine still exhausts the stack, rewrite the algorithm nonrecursively using tail recursion removal.

Inappropriate recursion. Usually this occurs when an algorithm like the recursive Fibonacci algorithm calculates the same intermediate values many times. If your program has this problem, try to rewrite the algorithm in a bottom-up way. If the algorithm does not lend itself to a bottom-up approach, create a lookup table of intermediate values.

Not all recursion is bad. Many problems are naturally recursive. In these cases, a recursive algorithm will be easier to understand, debug, and maintain than a nonrecursive one. The Hilbert and Sierpinski curve algorithms demonstrate appropriate recursion. Both are naturally recursive and are much easier to understand in their recursive forms. The recursive versions are even a little faster.

If you have an algorithm that is naturally recursive but you are not sure if the recursive version will cause problems, write it recursively and see. There may be no problem. If there is, it will probably be easier to translate the recursive algorithm into a nonrecursive one than to come up with the nonrecursive version from scratch.

TREES

6

Chapter 2, "Lists," explains ways to create dynamic, linked data structures like those shown in Figure 6.1. These kinds of data structures are called *graphs*. Chapter 12, "Network Algorithms," discusses graph and network algorithms in some detail. This chapter examines a special kind of graph called a *tree*.

This chapter first defines trees and explains some tree terminology. It then describes several methods for implementing different kinds of trees in Visual Basic.

The sections that follow examine tree traversal algorithms for trees stored using these different formats. The chapter finishes by discussing some specialized types of trees, including sorted trees, threaded trees, tries, and quadtrees.

Chapter 7, "Balanced Trees," and Chapter 8, "Decision Trees," explain two more advanced tree topics.

Figure 6.1 Graphs.

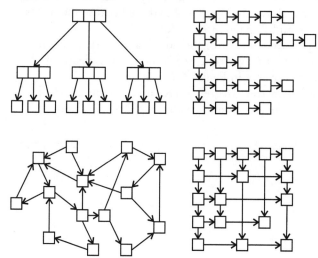

Definitions

You can define a tree recursively as:

*   An empty structure or

*   A *node,* called the *root* of the tree, connected to zero or more *subtrees*

Figure 6.2 shows a tree. Here the root node A is connected to three *subtrees* starting at nodes B, C, and D. Those nodes are connected to subtrees with roots E, F, and G, and those nodes are connected, in turn, to the subtrees with roots H, I, and J.

Tree terminology is a hodgepodge of terms borrowed from botany and genealogy. From botany come terms like *node* to describe where a branch might occur, *branch* to describe a link connecting two nodes, and *leaf* to describe a node that has no branches leaving it.

From genealogy come terms that describe relationships. When one node is directly above another, the upper node is called the *parent* and the lower node is called the *child.* The nodes along the path from a node upward to the root are that node's *ancestors.* For example, in Figure 6.2 the nodes E, B, and A are all ancestors of node I.

The nodes below another node in the tree are that node's *descendants.* The nodes E, H, I, and J in Figure 6.2 are all descendants of node B.

Occasionally people even refer to nodes that have the same parent as *sibling* (brother or sister) nodes.

There are also a few tree terms that do not come from botany or genealogy. An *internal node* is a node that is not a leaf. A node's *degree* is the number of children the node has. The degree of a tree is the largest degree of all of the nodes in the tree. The degree of the tree shown in Figure 6.2 is three because the nodes with the largest degree, nodes A and E, have three children.

The *depth* of a node is 1 plus the number of the node's ancestors. In Figure 6.2 node E has depth 3. The *depth* or *height* of a tree is the greatest depth of all of its nodes. The depth of the tree shown in Figure 6.2 is 4.

A degree 2 tree is called a *binary* tree. Degree 3 trees are sometimes called *ternary* trees. Beyond that, trees of degree N are usually called *N-ary* trees.

Figure 6.2 A tree.

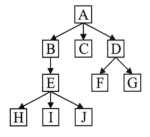

A degree 12 tree, for example, is called a 12-ary tree, not a "dodecadary" tree. Some people prefer to avoid odd terminology and simply say "tree of degree 12." Figure 6.3 illustrates some of these tree terms.

Tree Representations

Now that you know some basic tree terminology, you can think about ways to implement trees in Visual Basic. One approach is to create a different class for each type of node in the tree. To build the tree shown in Figure 6.3, you would define data structures for nodes that have zero, one, two, or three children. This approach would be rather inconvenient. In addition to managing four different classes, you would need to place some sort of indicators in the classes so you could tell what kind of nodes their children were. Algorithms that manipulate these trees would need to be able to work with all the different kinds of nodes.

Fat Nodes

A simpler solution is to define a single node type with enough child pointers to represent any of the nodes you need. I call this the fat node method because some nodes will be larger than they really need to be.

The tree shown in Figure 6.3 has degree 3. To build this tree using the fat node method, you would define a single class that contains pointers to three child nodes. The following code shows how the TernaryNode class might declare these pointers.

```
Public LeftChild As TernaryNode
Public MiddleChild As TernaryNode
Public RightChild As TernaryNode
```

Figure 6.3 Parts of a ternary (degree 3) tree.

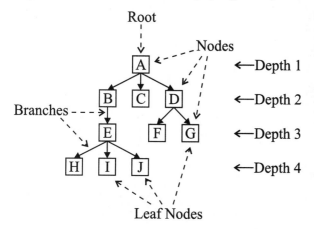

With this class you can build a tree using the nodes' Child entries to link the nodes together. The following code fragment builds the top two levels of the tree shown in Figure 6.3.

```
Dim A As New TernaryNode
Dim B As New TernaryNode
Dim C As New TernaryNode
Dim D As New TernaryNode
    :

    Set A.LeftChild = B
    Set A.MiddleChild = C
    Set A.LeftChild = D
        :
```

Example program Binary, shown in Figure 6.4, uses a fat node strategy to manage a binary tree. When you click on a node, the program enables the Add Left button if the node has no left child. It enables the Add Right button if the node has no right child. It enables the Remove button if the node is not the root node. If you click the Remove button, the program removes that node and all of its descendants.

Because this program allows you to create nodes with zero, one, or two children, it uses a fat node representation. You could easily extend this example for trees of higher degree.

Child Lists

If the degrees of the nodes in a tree vary greatly, the fat node strategy wastes a lot of space. To build the tree shown in Figure 6.5 using fat nodes, you would need

Figure 6.4 Program Binary.

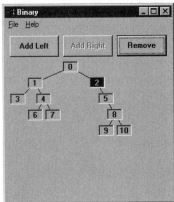

to give every node six child pointers, even though only one node actually needed all six of them. The tree's representation would require 72 child pointers, only 11 of which would actually be used.

Some programs add and remove nodes so node degrees change while the program is running. In this case, the fat node strategy will not work. You can represent these dynamic trees by keeping the nodes' children in lists. There are several strategies you might use for making the child lists. The most obvious approach is to give the node class a public array of child nodes, as in the following code. Then you could use array-based list techniques to manage the children.

```
Public Children() As TreeNode
Public NumChildren As Integer
```

Unfortunately, Visual Basic does not allow classes to include public arrays. You can work around this restriction by declaring the array private and then providing property procedures that manipulate the array members.

```
Private m_Children() As TreeNode
Private m_NumChildren As Integer

Property Get Children(Index As Integer) As TreeNode
    Set Children = m_Children(Index)
End Property

Property Get NumChildren() As Integer
    NumChildren = m_NumChildren
End Property
```

A second approach is to store child references in linked lists. Each node contains a pointer to its first child. It also contains a pointer to the next child at its level of the tree. Those links form a linked list of the node's siblings, so I call this

Figure 6.5 A tree with nodes of widely varying degree.

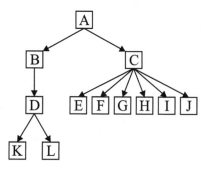

technique a *linked sibling* representation. See Chapter 2, "Lists," for more information about linked lists.

A third approach is to have the node class declare a public collection to contain its children.

```
Public Children As New Collection
```

This solution provides all of the conveniences given by collections. The program can easily add and remove items from the collection, assign keys to the child nodes, and use For Each statements to iterate over the child references.

Example program NAry, shown in Figure 6.6, uses a child collection to manage N-ary trees, much as program Binary manages binary trees. In this program, however, you can add as many children as you like to each node.

To avoid making the program's user interface more complicated than necessary, program NAry always adds new nodes at the end of the parent's child collection. You could modify the program to allow the insertion of children in the middle of a node's child collection, but the user interface would be more complicated.

Forward Star

The forward star representation introduced in Chapter 4, "Arrays," provides a compact array-based representation of trees, graphs, and networks. To store a tree using forward star, an array FirstLink holds the index of the first branch leaving each node. Another array, ToNode, gives the node to which the branch leads.

A sentinel entry at the end of the FirstLink array points just beyond the last entry in the ToNode array. This makes it easy to determine which branches leave each node. The branches leaving node I are those numbered FirstLink(I) through FirstLink(I + 1) − 1. You could use the following code to list the links leaving node I.

```
For link = FirstLink(I) To FirstLink(I + 1) - 1
    Print Format$(I) & " -> " & Format$(ToNode(link))
Next link
```

Figure 6.6 Program NAry.

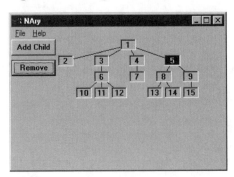

Figure 6.7 shows a tree and its forward star representation. The links out of node 3 (labeled D) are the links FirstLink(3) through FirstLink(4) − 1. FirstLink(3) = 9 and FirstLink(4) = 11, so these are the links numbered 9 and 10. The ToNode entries for these links are ToNode(9) = 10 and ToNode(10) = 11, so the children of node 3 are nodes 10 and 11. These are the nodes labeled K and L. This means the links leaving node D go to nodes K and L.

The forward star representation of a tree is compact and array-based. That makes it easy to read and write to files. The array operations used by forward star can also be faster than the operations required to use nodes containing public collections of children.

It is partly for these reasons that much of the literature about network algorithms uses a forward star representation. Many articles about shortest path calculations, for example, assume that the data is in a format similar to forward star. If you ever research these algorithms in journals like *Management Science* or *Operations Research,* you will need to understand forward star.

Using forward star, you can quickly find the links leaving a particular node. On the other hand, forward star is extremely difficult to modify. To add a new child to node A in Figure 6.7, you would have to update almost every entry in both the FirstLink and ToNode arrays. First, you would move every entry in the

Figure 6.7 A tree and its forward star representation.

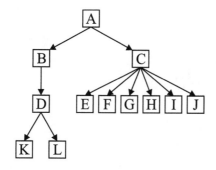

FirstLink:

Index	0	1	2	3	4	5	6	7	8	9	10	11	12
Label	A	B	C	D	E	F	G	H	I	J	K	L	
FirstLink	0	2	3	9	11	11	11	11	11	11	11	11	11

ToNode:

Index	0	1	2	3	4	5	6	7	8	9	10
ToNode	1	2	3	4	5	6	7	8	9	10	11

ToNode array one position to the right to make room for the new link. Next, you would insert the new ToNode entry, pointing to the new node. Finally, you would run through the FirstLink array, updating each entry so that it pointed to the new position of the corresponding ToNode entry. Because you moved all of the ToNode entries one position to the right to make room for the new link, you would need to add one to the affected FirstLink entries.

Figure 6.8 shows this tree after the new node has been added. The items that have been modified are shaded so they are easy to see.

Removing a node from the beginning of a tree's forward star representation is just as hard as adding one. If the node you are removing has children, the process becomes even more time consuming because you will need to remove the children as well.

The relative simplicity of a class with a public child collection makes that representation better if you need to modify the tree frequently. It is usually easier to understand and debug routines that modify that representation. On the other hand, forward star sometimes gives better performance for complicated tree algorithms. It is also a standard data structure discussed in the literature, so you need to be familiar with it if you want to do further research into tree and network algorithms.

Figure 6.8 Adding a node to forward star.

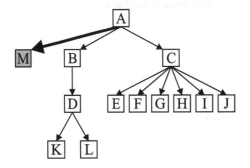

FirstLink:

Index	0	1	2	3	4	5	6	7	8	9	10	11	12	13
Label	A	B	C	D	E	F	G	H	I	J	K	L	M	
FirstLink	0	3	4	10	12	12	12	12	12	12	12	12	12	12

ToNode:

Index	0	1	2	3	4	5	6	7	8	9	10	11
ToNode	12	1	2	3	4	5	6	7	8	9	10	11

Example program FStar uses a forward star representation to manage a tree with nodes of varying degree. It is similar to program NAry except it uses forward star instead of child collections.

If you examine program Fstar's code, you will see how difficult it is to add and remove nodes. The following code shows how the program removes a node from the tree.

```
Sub FreeNodeAndChildren(ByVal parent As Integer, _
        ByVal link As Integer, ByVal node As Integer)

    ' Recursively remove the node's children.
    Do While FirstLink(node) < FirstLink(node + 1)
        FreeNodeAndChildren node, FirstLink(node), _
            ToNode(FirstLink(node))
    Loop

    ' Remove the link.
    RemoveLink parent, link

    ' Remove the node itself.
    RemoveNode node
End Sub

Sub RemoveLink(node As Integer, link As Integer)
Dim i As Integer

    ' Update FirstLink entries.
    For i = node + 1 To NumNodes
        FirstLink(i) = FirstLink(i) - 1
    Next i

    ' Shift ToNode array to fill in the link's spot.
    For i = link + 1 To NumLinks - 1
        ToNode(i - 1) = ToNode(i)
    Next i

    ' Remove the extra position in ToNode.
    NumLinks = NumLinks - 1
    If NumLinks > 0 Then ReDim Preserve ToNode(0 To NumLinks - 1)
End Sub

Sub RemoveNode(node As Integer)
Dim i As Integer
```

```
' Slide FirstLink entries over to fill in the vacated spot.
For i = node + 1 To NumNodes
    FirstLink(i - 1) = FirstLink(i)
Next i

' Slide NodeCaption entries over.
For i = node + 1 To NumNodes - 1
    NodeCaption(i - 1) = NodeCaption(i)
Next i

' Update ToNode entries pointing to nodes after this.
For i = 0 To NumLinks - 1
    If ToNode(i) >= node Then ToNode(i) = ToNode(i) - 1
Next i

' Remove the extra FirstLink entry.
NumNodes = NumNodes - 1
ReDim Preserve FirstLink(0 To NumNodes)

ReDim Preserve NodeCaption(0 To NumNodes - 1)
Unload FStarForm.NodeLabel(NumNodes)
End Sub
```

This is much more complicated than the corresponding code used by program NAry.

```
Public Function DeleteDescendant(target As NAryNode) As Boolean
Dim i As Integer
Dim child As NAryNode

    ' See if it's one of our children.
    For i = 1 To Children.Count
        If Children.Item(i) Is target Then
            Children.Remove i
            DeleteDescendant = True
            Exit Function
        End If
    Next i

    ' It's not one of our children. Recursively
    ' check the descendants.
    For Each child In Children
        If child.DeleteDescendant(target) Then
            DeleteDescendant = True
```

```
            Exit Function
        End If
    Next child
End Function
```

Complete Trees

A *complete tree* has as many nodes as it can hold at each level, except it may be missing some nodes on the bottom level. Any nodes present on the bottom level are pushed to the left. Each level in a ternary tree, for example, has exactly three children, except for the leaves and possibly one node on the level above the leaves. Figure 6.9 shows complete binary and ternary trees.

Complete trees have a number of important properties. First, they are the shortest trees that can hold a given number of nodes. The binary tree in Figure 6.9, for example, is as short as any other binary tree that holds six nodes. There are other binary trees of height 3 with six nodes, but there are none of height less than 3.

Second, if a complete tree of degree D contains N nodes, it will have $O(\log_D(N))$ height and $O(N)$ leaf nodes. These facts are important because many algorithms traverse trees from the top to the bottom or vice versa. An algorithm that does this once has $O(\log(N))$ run time.

A particularly useful property of complete trees is that they can be stored very compactly in arrays. If you number the nodes in the "natural" way, from top to bottom and left to right, you can place the tree entries in an array in this natural order. Figure 6.10 shows how to store a complete binary tree in an array.

The tree's root belongs in position 0. The children of node I belong in positions 2 * I + 1 and 2 * I + 2. For example, in Figure 6.10 the children of the node at position 1 (node B) are in positions 3 and 4 (nodes D and E).

It is easy to generalize this representation for complete trees of higher degree D. Again, the root node belongs in position 0. The children of node I belong in positions D * I + 1 through D * I + (I – 1). In a ternary tree, for instance, the children of a node at position 2 would be at positions 7, 8, and 9. Figure 6.11 shows a complete ternary tree and its array representation.

Figure 6.9 Complete trees.

  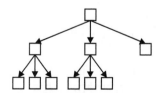

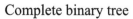
Complete binary tree   Complete ternary tree

Figure 6.10 Placing a complete binary tree in an array.

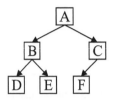

Index	0	1	2	3	4	5
Node	A	B	C	D	E	F

Accessing the children of a node using this array storage technique is fast and easy. This method is compact—it does not need extra storage for child collections or forward star sentinels. Saving and loading the tree from a file is a simple matter of reading and writing the tree's array. For these reasons this is clearly the best tree representation for programs that store data in complete trees.

Tree Traversal

Visiting each node in a tree is called *traversing* the tree. There are several possible orders in which you might want to visit the nodes in a binary tree. The three simplest, preorder, inorder, and postorder, have straightforward recursive algorithms. When the algorithm is considering any given node it should do the following.

Preorder:

1. Visit the node.
2. Recursively traverse the left subtree in preorder.
3. Recursively traverse the right subtree in preorder.

Figure 6.11 Placing a complete ternary tree in an array.

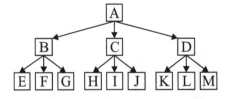

Index	0	1	2	3	4	5	6	7	8	9	10	11	12
ToNode	A	B	C	D	E	F	G	H	I	J	K	L	M

Inorder:

1. Recursively traverse the left subtree in inorder.
2. Visit the node.
3. Recursively traverse the right subtree in inorder.

Postorder:

1. Recursively traverse the left subtree in postorder.
2. Recursively traverse the right subtree in postorder.
3. Visit the node.

All three of these are *depth-first traversals*. The traversal begins by working its way deeply into the tree until it reaches the leaves. As the recursive subroutine calls return, the algorithm works its way back up through the tree, visiting paths that it skipped on the way down.

Depth-first traversals are useful in algorithms that must visit a leaf early. For example, the branch and bound algorithm described in Chapter 8, "Decision Trees," visits a leaf node as soon as possible. It uses the results it finds at the leaf to reduce the size of the search it makes through the rest of the tree.

A fourth method of visiting the nodes in a tree is *breadth-first traversal*. This method visits all the nodes at a given level of the tree before it visits any nodes on deeper levels. Algorithms that perform an exhaustive search of a tree often use breadth-first traversals. The label-setting shortest path algorithm described in Chapter 12, "Network Algorithms," is a breadth-first traversal of a shortest path tree within a network.

Figure 6.12 shows a small tree and the order in which the nodes are visited during preorder, inorder, postorder, and breadth-first traversals.

For trees of degree greater than 2, it still makes sense to define preorder, postorder, and breadth-first traversals. There is some ambiguity in defining inorder traversals because each node could be visited after one, two, or more of

Figure 6.12 Tree traversals.

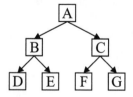

Preorder:	A B D E C F G
Inorder:	D B E A F C G
Postorder:	D E B F G C A
Breadth first:	A B C D E F G

its children. In a ternary tree, for example, a node might be visited after its first child was visited or after its second child was visited.

Details for traversing a tree depend on how it is stored. To traverse a tree stored using child collections, a program would use a slightly different algorithm than the one it would use to traverse a tree stored in forward star format.

Complete trees stored in arrays are particularly easy to traverse. The breadth-first traversal, which requires extra work for other tree representations, is trivial for array-based representations because the nodes are stored in breadth-first order. The following code shows the traversal algorithms for a complete binary tree.

```
Dim NodeLabel() As String        ' Stores the labels of the nodes.
Dim NumNodes As Integer

' Initialize the tree.
    :

Private Sub Preorder(node As Integer)
    Print NodeLabel(node)                         ' The node.
    If node * 2 + 1 <= NumNodes Then Preorder node * 2 + 1 ' Child 1.
    If node * 2 + 2 <= NumNodes Then Preorder node * 2 + 2 ' Child 2.
End Sub

Private Sub Inorder(node As Integer)
    If node * 2 + 1 <= NumNodes Then Inorder node * 2 + 1  ' Child 1.
    Print NodeLabel(node)                         ' The node.
    If node * 2 + 2 <= NumNodes Then Inorder node * 2 + 2  ' Child 2.
End Sub

Private Sub Postorder(node As Integer)
    If node * 2 + 1 <= NumNodes Then Postorder node * 2 + 1 ' Child 1.
    If node * 2 + 2 <= NumNodes Then Postorder node * 2 + 2 ' Child 2.
    Print NodeLabel(node)                         ' The node.
End Sub

Private Sub BreadthFirstPrint()
Dim i As Integer

    For i = 0 To NumNodes
        Print NodeLabel(i)
    Next i
End Sub
```

Example program Trav1 demonstrates preorder, inorder, postorder, and breadth-first traversals for array-based complete binary trees. Enter the height of the tree you want to traverse, and click the Create Tree button to create a full binary tree. Then click the Preorder, Inorder, Postorder, or Breadth-First buttons to see the tree's traversals. Figure 6.13 shows the program displaying the preorder traversal for a tree of depth 4.

The preorder and postorder traversals for trees stored in other representations are just as easy. The following code shows the preorder traversal routine for a tree stored in forward star format.

```
Private Sub PreorderPrint(node As Integer)
Dim link As Integer

    Print NodeLabel(node)
    For link = FirstLink(node) To FirstLink(node + 1) - 1
        PreorderPrint ToNode(link)
    Next link
End Sub
```

As mentioned earlier, it is hard to define inorder traversals for trees of degree greater than 2. If you do decide what an inorder traversal means, however, you would not have much trouble implementing it. The following code shows an inorder traversal routine that visits half of a node's children (rounding up), then visits the node itself, and then visits the remaining children.

```
Private Sub InorderPrint(node As Integer)
Dim mid_link As Integer
Dim link As Integer
```

Figure 6.13 Program Trav1 displaying a tree's preorder traversal.

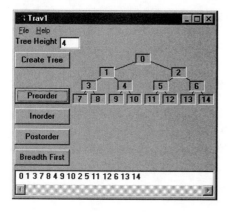

```
' Find the middle child.
mid_link = (FirstLink(node + 1) - 1 + FirstLink(node)) \ 2

' Visit the first group of children.
For link = FirstLink(node) To mid_link
    InorderPrint ToNode(link)
Next link

' Visit the node.
Print NodeLabel(node)

' Visit the second group of children.
For link = mid_link + 1 To FirstLink(node + 1) - 1
    InorderPrint ToNode(link)
Next link
End Sub
```

For complete trees stored in an array, the nodes just happen to be stored in breadth-first order. This makes breadth-first traversals easy for this kind of tree. For other tree representations, breadth-first traversals are a bit harder.

To traverse other kinds of trees, you can use a queue to store the nodes that must still be visited. Start by placing the root node in the queue. To visit a node, remove it from the front of the queue and add its children to the back. Repeat this process until the queue is empty. The following code shows a breadth-first traversal subroutine for a tree that uses nodes with child collections.

```
Dim Root As TreeNode
' Initialize the tree.
    :


Private Sub BreadthFirstPrint()
Dim queue As New Collection        ' A collection-based queue.
Dim node As TreeNode
Dim child As TreeNode

    ' Start with the root in the queue.
    queue.Add Root

    ' Repeatedly process the top item in
    ' the queue until the queue is empty.
    Do While queue.Count > 0
        node = queue.Item(1)
        queue.Remove 1
```

```
        ' Visit the node.
        Print NodeLabel(node)

        ' Add the node's children to the queue.
        For Each child In node.Children
            queue.Add child
        Next child
    Loop
End Sub
```

Example program Trav2 demonstrates tree traversal for trees using child collections. The program is a combination of program NAry, which manages N-ary trees, and program Trav1, which demonstrates tree traversals.

Select a node, and click the Add Child button to add a new child to the node. Select a node, and click Remove to remove the node and its descendants. Click the Preorder, Inorder, Postorder, or Breadth First buttons to see the corresponding tree traversals. Figure 6.14 shows program Trav2 displaying a postorder traversal.

Sorted Trees

Binary trees are often a natural way to store and manipulate information in computer programs. Because many computer operations are binary, they map naturally onto binary trees. For example, you can map the binary relationship "less than" onto a binary tree. If you use the tree's internal nodes to mean "the left child is less than the right child," you can use a binary tree to build and store a sorted list. Figure 6.15 shows a binary tree holding a sorted list containing the numbers 1, 2, 4, 6, 7, 9.

Figure 6.14 Program Trav2 displaying a tree's postorder traversal.

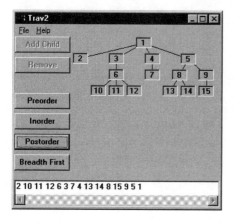

Figure 6.15 The sorted list: 1, 2, 4, 6, 7, 9.

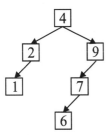

Adding Items

The algorithm for inserting a new item into this kind of tree is simple. Begin at the root node. As you examine each node, compare that node's value to the value of the new item. If the new value is less than or equal to the value at the node, continue down the left branch of the tree. If the new value is greater than the node's value, continue down the right branch. When you reach a leaf node, insert the item at that position.

To insert the value 8 in the tree shown in Figure 6.15, you begin at the root, which has value 4. Because 8 is greater than 4, you follow the right branch to node 9. Because 8 is less than 9, you then follow the left branch to node 7. Because 8 is greater than 7, you next try to follow the right branch again, but this node has no right child. This is where you insert the new item, giving the tree shown in Figure 6.16.

The following code adds a new value beneath a node in a sorted tree. The program begins the insertion at the root as in InsertItem Root, new_value.

```
Private Sub InsertItem(node As SortNode, new_value As Integer)
Dim child As SortNode

    If node Is Nothing Then
        ' We have reached a leaf.
        ' Insert the item here.
```

Figure 6.16 The sorted list: 1, 2, 4, 6, 7, 8, 9.

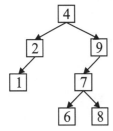

```
            Set node = New SortNode
            node.Value = new_value
            MaxBox = MaxBox + 1
            Load NodeLabel(MaxBox)
            Set node.Box = NodeLabel(MaxBox)
            With NodeLabel(MaxBox)
                .Caption = Format$(new_value)
                .Visible = True
            End With
        ElseIf new_value <= node.Value Then
            ' Branch left.
            Set child = node.LeftChild
            InsertItem child, new_value
            Set node.LeftChild = child
        Else
            ' Branch right.
            Set child = node.RightChild
            InsertItem child, new_value
            Set node.RightChild = child
        End If
End Sub
```

When this routine reaches the bottom of the tree, something fairly subtle occurs. In Visual Basic when you pass a parameter to a subroutine, that parameter is *passed by reference* unless you use the ByVal keyword. This means the subroutine works with the same copy of the parameter that the calling routine uses. If the subroutine modifies the value of the parameter, the value is changed for the calling routine as well.

When it recursively calls itself, subroutine InsertItem passes itself a pointer to a child in the tree. For example, in the following statements the routine passes a pointer to the node's right child as the node parameter to InsertItem. If the called routine modifies the value of the node parameter, the child pointer is automatically updated in the calling routine as well. The last line then sets the node's right child equal to the new value so the new node, if one was created, is added to the tree.

```
Set child = node.RightChild
InsertItem child, new_value
Set node.RightChild = child
```

Removing Items

Removing an item from a sorted tree is a bit trickier than inserting one. After an item is removed, the program may need to rearrange other nodes so the "less than" relationship still holds throughout the tree. There are several cases to consider.

Figure 6.17 Removing a node with one child.

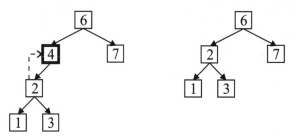

First, if the removed node has no children, you can just remove it from the tree. Because the node has no children, the ordering of the remaining nodes is not changed.

Second, if the removed node has one child, you can replace it with its child. The ordering of the node's descendants stays the same because those nodes are also descendants of the child. Figure 6.17 shows a tree from which node 4, which has only one child, is being removed.

If the removed node has two children, you cannot necessarily replace it with one of its children. If the node's children also have two children, there is no room for all the children at the removed node's location. The removed node has one extra child, and the child node you might like to replace it with has two children, so you would need to assign three children to the node in this location.

To solve this problem, you should replace the removed node with the right-most node to the left of it in the tree. In other words, move down the left branch out of the node being removed. Then move down right branches until you find a node with no right branch. That is the rightmost node to the left of the node you are removing. In the tree on the left in Figure 6.18, node 3 is the rightmost node to the left of node 4. You can replace node 4 with node 3 and preserve the tree's ordering.

One last detail remains if the replacement node has a left child. In that case, you can move this child into the position vacated by the replacement node and the tree will again be properly ordered. You know that the rightmost node does

Figure 6.18 Removing a node with two children.

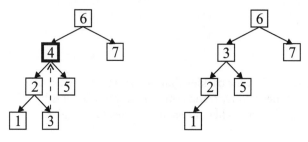

Figure 6.19 Removing a node when the replacement node has a child.

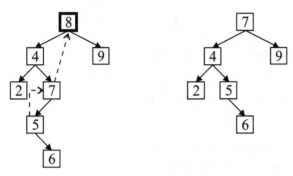

not have a right child; otherwise, it would not have been the rightmost node. That means you do not need to worry about the replacement node having two children.

Figure 6.19 shows this complicated situation. In this example, node 8 is being removed. The rightmost node to its left is node 7. Node 7 also has a child—node 5. To remove node 8 while preserving the tree's ordering, replace node 8 with node 7, and node 7 with node 5. Notice that node 7 gets completely new children while node 5 keeps its single child.

The following code removes a node from a sorted binary tree.

```
Private Sub DeleteItem(node As SortNode, target_value As Integer)
Dim target As SortNode
Dim child As SortNode

    ' If we did not find the item, say so.
    If node Is Nothing Then
        Beep
        MsgBox "Item " & Format$(target_value) & _
            " is not in the tree."
        Exit Sub
    End If

    If target_value < node.Value Then
        ' Continue down left subtree.
        Set child = node.LeftChild
        DeleteItem child, target_value
        Set node.LeftChild = child
    ElseIf target_value > node.Value Then
        ' Continue down right subtree.
        Set child = node.RightChild
        DeleteItem child, target_value
        Set node.RightChild = child
```

```
        Else
            ' This is the target.
            Set target = node
            If target.LeftChild Is Nothing Then
                ' Replace target with its right child.
                Set node = node.RightChild
            ElseIf target.RightChild Is Nothing Then
                ' Replace target with its left child.
                Set node = node.LeftChild
            Else
                ' Call ReplaceRightmost to replace
                ' target with the rightmost node
                ' to its left.
                Set child = node.LeftChild
                ReplaceRightmost node, child
                Set node.LeftChild = child
            End If
        End If
End Sub


Private Sub ReplaceRightmost(target As SortNode, repl As SortNode)
Dim old_repl As SortNode
Dim child As SortNode

    If Not (repl.RightChild Is Nothing) Then
        ' Move farther down to the right.
        Set child = repl.RightChild
        ReplaceRightmost target, child
        Set repl.RightChild = child
    Else
        ' We've reached the bottom.
        ' Remember what node repl is.
        Set old_repl = repl

        ' Replace repl with its left child.
        Set repl = repl.LeftChild

        ' Replace the target with repl.
        Set old_repl.LeftChild = target.LeftChild
        Set old_repl.RightChild = target.RightChild
        Set target = old_repl
    End If
End Sub
```

This algorithm uses the trick of passing parameters by reference into recursive subroutines in two places. First, subroutine DeleteItem uses this trick to make the target node's parent point to the replacement node. The following statement shows how subroutine DeleteItem is invoked.

```
Set child = node.LeftChild
DeleteItem child, target_value
Set node.LeftChild = child
```

When the routine finds the target node (node 8 in Figure 6.19), it receives the parent node's pointer to the target in the node parameter. By setting this parameter to the replacement node (node 7), DeleteItem sets the parent's child so it points to the new node.

The following statement shows how subroutine ReplaceRightmost recursively calls itself.

```
Set child = repl.RightChild
ReplaceRightmost target, child
Set repl.RightChild = child
```

When this routine finds the rightmost node to the left of the node being removed (node 7), the repl parameter holds the pointer from the parent to the rightmost node. When the routine sets the value of repl to repl.LeftChild, it automatically connects the rightmost node's parent to the rightmost node's left child (node 5).

Example program Treesort uses these routines to manage sorted binary trees. Enter an integer, and click the Add button to add an item to the tree. Enter an integer, and click Remove to remove that item from the tree. When you remove a node, the tree automatically rearranges itself to preserve the "less than" ordering.

Traversing Sorted Trees

A useful fact about sorted trees is that the inorder traversal visits the nodes in their sorted order. The inorder traversal of the tree shown in Figure 6.20, for instance, visits the nodes in the order 2-4-5-6-7-8-9.

Figure 6.20 Inorder traversal of a sorted tree: 2, 4, 5, 6, 7, 8, 9.

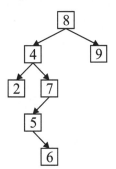

The fact that inorder traversals of sorted trees visit the items in sorted order leads to a simple sorting algorithm.

1.   Add the items to a sorted tree.

2.   Print the items using an inorder traversal.

This algorithm usually works quite well. If you add items to a tree in certain orders, however, the tree may become tall and thin. Figure 6.21 shows the sorted tree you get if you add items to it in the order 1, 6, 5, 2, 3, 4. Many other orders also produce tall, thin trees.

The taller a sorted tree becomes, the longer it takes to add new items at the bottom of the tree. In the worst case, after you add N items, the tree will have height O(N). The total time to insert all the items into the tree will be O(N²). Because it takes O(N) time to traverse the tree, the total time needed to sort the numbers using the tree would be O(N²) + O(N) = O(N²).

If the tree remains fairly short, it will have height O(log(N)). In that case it will take only O(log(N)) steps to insert an item in the tree. To insert all N items in the tree would require O(N * log(N)) steps. Then to sort the items using the tree would take time O(N * log(N)) + O(N) = O(N * log(N)).

This O(N * log(N)) time is much better than O(N²). For example, building a tall, thin tree containing 1000 items would take about 1 million steps. Building a short tree of height O(log(N)) would take only about 10,000 steps.

If the items are initially arranged randomly, the tree's shape will probably be somewhere between these two extremes. While it may have height slightly larger than log(N), it will not be too tall and thin, so the sorting algorithm will perform well.

Chapter 7, "Balanced Trees," describes ways you can rebalance trees so they do not grow tall and thin, no matter how the items are added. Those methods are

Figure 6.21 The tree obtained by adding items in the order: 1, 6, 5, 2, 3, 4.

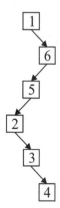

quite complicated, however, and they are really not worth applying to this tree-based sorting algorithm. Many of the sorting algorithms described in Chapter 9, "Sorting," provide better performance and are easier to implement.

Threaded Trees

Chapter 2, "Lists," explains how adding threads to a linked list makes listing the items in different orders easy. You can use the same idea to make visiting the nodes in a tree in different orders easy. For example, by placing threads in the leaf nodes in a binary tree, you can make inorder and reverse inorder traversal easier. If the tree is a sorted tree, these are the nodes' sorted and reversed sorted orders.

To create the threads, store pointers to the nodes' inorder predecessors and successors in unused child pointers. If a node has an unused left child pointer, store a thread in that position indicating the node's predecessor in the inorder traversal. If a node has an unused right child pointer, store a thread in that position indicating the node's successor in the inorder traversal. Because the threads are symmetric, with left child threads pointing to predecessors and right child threads pointing to successors, this kind of tree is called a *symmetrically threaded tree*. Figure 6.22 shows a symmetrically threaded tree with the threads drawn in dashed lines.

Because the threads occupy the positions of child pointers in the tree, you need a way to tell the difference between thread pointers and normal child pointers. The easiest way to do this is to add new Boolean variables HasLeftChild and HasRightChild to the nodes indicating whether they have left and right children.

To use the threads to find the predecessor of a node, examine the node's left child pointer. If the pointer is a thread, the thread indicates the node's predecessor. If the pointer has the value Nothing, this node is the first node in the tree, so it has no predecessor. Otherwise, follow the pointer to the node's left child. Then follow the descendants' right child pointers until you reach a node that has a thread instead of a right child. That node (not the one indicated by the thread) is the predecessor of the original node. This node is the rightmost node to the left of the original node in the tree. The following code shows how to find a node's predecessor in Visual Basic.

Figure 6.22 A symmetrically threaded tree.

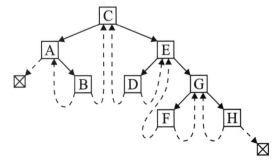

```
Private Function Predecessor(node As ThreadedNode) As ThreadedNode
Dim child As ThreadedNode

    If node.LeftChild Is Nothing Then
        'This is the first node in the inorder traversal.
        Set Predecessor = Nothing
    Else If node.HasLeftChild Then
        'This is a node pointer.
        'Find the rightmost node to the left.
        Set child = node.LeftChild
        Do While child.HasRightChild
            Set child = child.RightChild
        Loop
        Set Predecessor = child
    Else
        ' The thread points to the predecessor.
        Set Predecessor = node.LeftChild
    End If
End Function
```

Using the threads to locate the successor of a node is similar. If the node's right child pointer is a thread, the thread indicates the node's successor. If the pointer has the value Nothing, this node is the last node in the tree, so it has no successor. Otherwise follow the pointer to the node's right child. Then follow left child pointers until you reach a node with a thread for a left child pointer. That node is the successor of the original node. This node is the leftmost node to the right of the original node in the tree.

It is also convenient to have functions that locate the first and last nodes in the tree. To find the first node, simply follow the left child pointers down from the root until you reach a node with left child Nothing. To find the last node, follow the right child pointers down from the root until you reach a node with right child Nothing.

```
Private Function FirstNode() As ThreadedNode
Dim node As ThreadedNode

    Set node = Root
    Do While Not (node.LeftChild Is Nothing)
        Set node = node.LeftChild
    Loop
    Set FirstNode = node
End Function

Private Function LastNode() As ThreadedNode
Dim node As ThreadedNode
```

```
        Set node = Root
        Do While Not (node.RightChild Is Nothing)
            Set node = node.RightChild
        Loop
        Set FirstNode = node
End Function
```

Using these functions you can easily write routines that display the nodes in the tree in their forward and backward orders.

```
Private Sub Inorder()
Dim node As ThreadedNode

        ' Find the first node.
        Set node = FirstNode()

        ' Traverse the list.
        Do While Not (node Is Nothing)
            Print node.Value
            Set node = Successor(node)
        Loop
End Sub


Private Sub PrintReverseInorder()
Dim node As ThreadedNode

        ' Find the last node.
        Set node = LastNode

        ' Traverse the list.
        Do While Not (node Is Nothing)
            Print node.Value
            Set node = Predecessor(node)
        Loop
End Sub
```

The inorder printing routine presented earlier in the chapter uses recursion. These new routines use neither recursion nor the stack you might use to remove recursion.

Every child pointer in the tree contains either a link to a child or a thread to a predecessor or successor. Because each node has two child pointers, if there are N nodes in the tree there must be 2 * N links and threads. These traversal algorithms visit each link and thread in the tree once, so they require O(2 * N) = O(N) steps.

You can make these subroutines a bit faster if you keep track of the indexes of the first and last nodes in the tree. Then you do not need to search for the first or last node before listing the nodes in order. Because these algorithms visit all N nodes in the tree, the run time for the algorithms is still O(N), but they will be a little faster in practice.

Maintaining Threaded Trees

To maintain a threaded tree, you must be able to add nodes to and remove nodes from the tree while keeping the tree properly threaded.

Suppose you want to add a new node to the tree as the left child of node A. Because you are inserting the node in this position, the left child of node A must currently be unused as a child pointer; therefore it contains a thread. That thread points to the predecessor of node A. Because the new node will be the left child of node A, it will become node A's predecessor. Node A will be the new node's successor. The node that was the predecessor of node A now becomes the predecessor of the new node. Figure 6.23 shows the tree in Figure 6.22 after the new node X has been added as the left child of node H.

If you are keeping track of the index of the first and last nodes in the tree, you should check at this point whether the new node is the new first node in the tree. If the predecessor thread of the new node has the value Nothing, then it is the new first node.

Using all these facts, it is easy to write a routine to insert a new left child for a node. Inserting a right child is similar.

```
Private Sub AddLeftChild(parent As ThreadedNode, child As
ThreadedNode)
    ' The parent's predecessor becomes the new node's predecessor.
    Set child.LeftChild = parent.LeftChild
    child.HasLeftChild = False

    ' Insert the node.
    Set parent.LeftChild = child
```

Figure 6.23 Threaded tree with node X added.

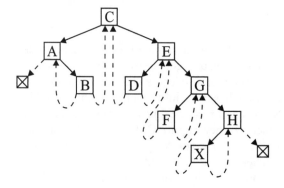

```
parent.HasLeftChild = True

' The parent is the new node's successor.
Set child.RightChild = parent
child.HasRightChild = False

' See if the new node is the first node in the tree.
If child.LeftChild Is Nothing Then Set FirstNode = child
End Sub
```

Before you can remove a node from the threaded tree, you should remove its descendants. Once the node has no children, removing it is easy.

Suppose the target node being removed is the left child of its parent. The target's left pointer is a thread indicating its predecessor in the tree. When the target is removed, that predecessor becomes the predecessor of the parent node. To remove the target, simply set the parent node's left child pointer to the target's left child pointer.

The target's right child pointer is a thread indicating its successor in the tree. Because the target is the left child of its parent, and because the target has no children, that thread indicates the parent node, so you can simply ignore it. Figure 6.24 shows the tree in Figure 6.23 after the node F has been removed. The method for removing a right child is similar.

```
Private Sub RemoveLeftChild(parent As ThreadedNode)
Dim target As ThreadedNode

    Set target = parent.LeftChild
    Set parent.LeftChild = target.LeftChild
End Sub
```

Figure 6.24 Threaded tree with node F removed.

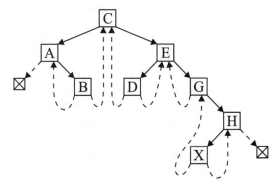

Quadtrees

A *quadtree* describes the spatial relationships between items within a physical area. For example, the area might be a map, and the items might be the locations of houses or businesses on the map.

Each node in a quadtree represents a part of the total area represented by the quadtree. Each nonleaf node has four children that represent the northwest, northeast, southeast, and southwest quadrants of the area represented by the node. A leaf node can store the items it contains in a collection or linked list. The following code shows the Declarations section for the QtreeNode class.

```
' The children.
Public NWchild As QtreeNode
Public NEchild As QtreeNode
Public SWchild As QtreeNode
Public SEchild As QtreeNode


' The items if it's a leaf.
Public Items As New Collection
```

The items stored in a quadtree can contain any sort of spatial data. They must contain position information the tree can use to locate the items. The following code shows the declaration section of a simple QtreeItem class that represents items located at point positions.

```
Public X As Single
Public Y As Single
```

To build a quadtree, place all the items in the root node. Then examine that node to see if it contains enough items to be worth subdividing. If it does, create four children for the node. Distribute the items among the four children according to the positions of the items within the four quadrants of the original area. Then recursively check the four children to see if they are worth subdividing. Continue subdividing the nodes until each leaf contains no more than some desired number of items.

Figure 6.25 shows a picture of several data items arranged in a quadtree. Each region has been subdivided until it contains no more than two items.

Quadtrees are useful for locating objects near specific locations. Suppose you have a program that draws a map with many locations on it. When the user clicks on the map, the program should find the location nearest to the point clicked. The program could search through the entire list of locations, checking each to see how close it is to the target point. If there are N locations, this is an O(N) algorithm.

A quadtree can make this operation much faster. Begin at the root node. Each time you examine a quadtree node, see which of the node's quadrants contains the point where the user clicked. Then move down the tree to the corresponding

Figure 6.25 A quadtree.

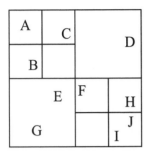 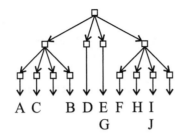

child node. If the user clicked in the upper right corner of the node's area, you would descend into the northeast child. Continue down the tree until you locate the leaf node that contains the point where the user clicked.

The QtreeNode's LocateLeaf function uses this method to find the leaf node that contains a given point. A program would invoke this function as in "Set the_leaf = Root.LocateLeaf(X, Y, Gxmin, Gxmax, Gymin, Gymax)" where Gxmin, Gxmax, Gymin, Gymax give the boundaries of the area represented by the tree.

```
Public Function LocateLeaf(X As Single, Y As Single, _
    xmin As Single, xmax As Single, ymin As Single, ymax As Single) _
    As QtreeNode

Dim xmid As Single
Dim ymid As Single
Dim node As QtreeNode

    If NWchild Is Nothing Then
        ' We have no children. It must be this node.
        Set LocateLeaf = Me
        Exit Function
    End If

    ' Search the appropriate child.
    xmid = (xmax + xmin) / 2
    ymid = (ymax + ymin) / 2
    If X <= xmid Then
        If Y <= ymid Then
            Set LocateLeaf = NWchild.LocateLeaf( _
                X, Y, xmin, xmid, ymin, ymid)
        Else
            Set LocateLeaf = SWchild.LocateLeaf( _
```

```
                    X, Y, xmin, xmid, ymid, ymax)
            End If
        Else
            If Y <= ymid Then
                Set LocateLeaf = NEchild.LocateLeaf( _
                    X, Y, xmid, xmax, ymin, ymid)
            Else
                Set LocateLeaf = SEchild.LocateLeaf( _
                    X, Y, xmid, xmax, ymid, ymax)
            End If
        End If
    End If
End Function
```

After deciding which leaf contains a point, examine the locations within that leaf to see which item is closest to the point. The NearPointInLeaf subroutine does this.

```
Public Sub NearPointInLeaf(X As Single, Y As Single, _
    best_item As QtreeItem, best_dist As Single, comparisons As Long)

Dim new_item As QtreeItem
Dim Dx As Single
Dim Dy As Single
Dim new_dist As Single

    ' Start with a terrible solution.
    best_dist = 10000000
    Set best_item = Nothing

    ' If there are no items in the leaf, stop now.
    If Items.Count < 1 Then Exit Sub

    For Each new_item In Items
        comparisons = comparisons + 1
        Dx = new_item.X - X
        Dy = new_item.Y - Y
        new_dist = Dx * Dx + Dy * Dy
        If best_dist > new_dist Then
            best_dist = new_dist
            Set best_item = new_item
        End If
    Next new_item
End Sub
```

The item found by NearPointInLeaf is usually the item the user was trying to select. If the point is close to the boundary between two leaf nodes, however, an item in another leaf node might be closer to the point clicked.

Suppose D_{min} is the distance from the user's selected point to the closest location found so far. If D_{min} is less than the distance from the user's point to the edge of its leaf node, you are done. The location is too far from the edge of the leaf for there to be a closer location in another leaf.

Otherwise start back at the root node and move into the tree, examining any quadtree nodes that are within distance D_{min} of the point clicked. If you find any items that are closer to the point, revise D_{min} and continue searching with the new value. When you finish checking the leaf nodes that are close to the point, you have found the correct item. Subroutine CheckNearbyLeaves uses these methods to complete the search.

```
Public Sub CheckNearbyLeaves(exclude As QtreeNode, _
    X As Single, Y As Single, best_item As QtreeItem, _
    best_dist As Single, comparisons As Long, _
    xmin As Single, xmax As Single, ymin As Single, ymax As Single)

Dim xmid As Single
Dim ymid As Single
Dim new_dist As Single
Dim new_item As QtreeItem

    ' If this is the leaf we are to exclude,
    ' do nothing.
    If Me Is exclude Then Exit Sub

    ' If this is a leaf node, check it out.
    If SWchild Is Nothing Then
        NearPointInLeaf X, Y, new_item, new_dist, comparisons
        If best_dist > new_dist Then
            best_dist = new_dist
            Set best_item = new_item
        End If
        Exit Sub
    End If

    ' See which children fall within best_dist
    ' of the point.
    xmid = (xmax + xmin) / 2
    ymid = (ymax + ymin) / 2
    If X - Sqr(best_dist) <= xmid Then
```

```
            ' The West children are eligible.
            If Y - Sqr(best_dist) <= ymid Then
                ' Check the NorthWest child.
                NWchild.CheckNearbyLeaves _
                    exclude, X, Y, best_item, _
                    best_dist, comparisons, _
                    xmin, xmid, ymin, ymid
            End If
            If Y + Sqr(best_dist) > ymid Then
                ' Check the SouthWest child.
                SWchild.CheckNearbyLeaves _
                    exclude, X, Y, best_item, _
                    best_dist, comparisons, _
                    xmin, xmid, ymid, ymax
            End If
        End If
        If X + Sqr(best_dist) > xmid Then
            ' The East children are eligible.
            If Y - Sqr(best_dist) <= ymid Then
                ' Check the NorthEast child.
                NEchild.CheckNearbyLeaves _
                    exclude, X, Y, best_item, _
                    best_dist, comparisons, _
                    xmid, xmax, ymin, ymid
            End If
            If Y + Sqr(best_dist) > ymid Then
                ' Check the SouthEast child.
                SEchild.CheckNearbyLeaves _
                    exclude, X, Y, best_item, _
                    best_dist, comparisons, _
                    xmid, xmax, ymid, ymax
            End If
        End If
End Sub
```

The FindPoint subroutine uses the LocateLeaf, NearPointInLeaf, and CheckNearbyLeaves subroutines provided by the QtreeNode class to quickly locate a point in a quadtree.

```
Function FindPoint(X As Single, Y As Single, comparisons As Long) _
    As QtreeItem

Dim leaf As QtreeNode
Dim best_item As QtreeItem
Dim best_dist As Single
```

```
' See what leaf the point is in.
Set leaf = Root.LocateLeaf( _
    X, Y, Gxmin, Gxmax, Gymin, Gymax)

' Find the closest point within the leaf.
leaf.NearPointInLeaf _
    X, Y, best_item, best_dist, comparisons

' Check nearby leaves.
Root.CheckNearbyLeaves _
    leaf, X, Y, best_item, best_dist, _
    comparisons, Gxmin, Gxmax, Gymin, Gymax

    Set FindPoint = best_item
End Function
```

Example program Qtree uses a quadtree. When the program begins, it asks how many data items it should create. It creates the items and draws them as points. Start with a small number of items (1000 or so) until you know how long it will take your computer to create the items.

Quadtrees are most interesting when the items are not evenly distributed, so this program selects the points using a *strange attractor* function from *chaos theory*. It selects the data points in a way that seems random, yet contains clusters that make the data interesting.

When you click on the form, program Qtree locates the item closest to the spot where you clicked. It highlights the item and displays the number of items it examined while locating the item.

Use the program's Options menu to tell the program whether it should use the quadtree or not. If you check the Use Quadtree option, the program displays the quadtree and uses it to locate items. If you do not check this option, the program does not display the quadtree and locates items by exhaustively searching them all.

The program examines far fewer items and is much faster when it uses the quadtree. If your computer is so fast that you do not notice this effect, run the program with 10,000 or 20,000 items. Even on a 90 megahertz Pentium, you should notice the difference.

Figure 6.26 shows program Qtree displaying 10,000 items. The small rectangle in the upper right shows the selected item. The label in the upper left indicates that the program examined only 40 of the 10,000 items before finding the one selected.

Modifying MAX_PER_NODE

An interesting experiment to perform with program Qtree is to modify the value of MAX_PER_NODE defined in the Declarations section of the QtreeNode class. This is the maximum number of items that will fit within a quadtree node before that node is subdivided. The program initially uses the value MAX_PER_NODE = 100.

Figure 6.26 Program Qtree.

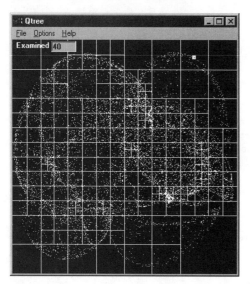

If you make this number small, like 10, each leaf node contains fewer data items, so the program will examine fewer items to locate the one closest to the spot you click. Locating items will be faster. On the other hand, the program will build far more quadtree nodes, so it will use a lot of memory.

Conversely, if you increase MAX_PER_NODE to 1000, the program will create fewer quadtree nodes. It will take a bit longer to locate items, but it will create a smaller quadtree that requires less memory.

This is an example of a time versus space trade-off. Using more quadtree nodes makes locating items faster but takes more memory. In this example, a value for MAX_PER_NODE around 100 gives a reasonable balance between speed and memory usage. You may need to experiment with MAX_PER_NODE to find the right balance for other applications.

Quadtree Pointer Faking

Program Qtree uses lots of classes and collections. Every internal quadtree node contains four references to its child nodes. Leaf nodes include a large collection holding the items within the node. All these objects and collections slow the program when it contains many items. Creating the objects is slow and takes lots of memory. If the program creates too many objects, it will begin paging and it will slow greatly.

Unfortunately, it is when the program contains many items that the benefits of quadtrees are greatest. To improve performance for large applications, you can use the pointer-faking techniques described in Chapter 2, "Lists."

Example program Qtree2 builds a quadtree using pointer faking. Nodes and items are allocated from arrays of user-defined data structures. For pointers, this program uses array indexes instead of object references. In one set of tests on a 90 megahertz Pentium, program Qtree took 25 seconds to build a quadtree containing 30,000 items. Program Qtree2 needed only 3 seconds to build the same tree.

Octtrees

An *octtree* is similar to a quadtree except it divides a three-dimensional volume instead of a two-dimensional area. While quadtree nodes contain four children, octtree nodes contain eight children, representing the eight octants that make up a three-dimensional volume. These octants are in the northwest top, northwest bottom, northeast top, northeast bottom, and so forth.

Octtrees are useful for managing objects spatially in three dimensions. A robot, for example, might use an octtree to keep track of nearby objects. A ray tracing program can use an octtree to quickly determine whether a ray passes near an object before it begins the slow process of calculating the exact intersection between the two.

You can build octtrees using techniques similar to those used to build quadtrees.

Summary

There are many ways to represent trees. Complete trees stored in arrays use the most efficient and compact representation. Child collections make tree management simple, but this sort of representation is relatively slow and uses a lot of memory. Forward star allows fast tree traversal and uses less memory than child collections, but it is very hard to modify. It is commonly used in network algorithms, however, so it is important to understand.

7

As a program works with an ordered tree, adding and removing nodes over time, the tree may become unbalanced. When that happens, algorithms that manipulate the tree become less efficient. If the tree becomes sufficiently unbalanced, it becomes little more than a complicated form of linked list, and the program using the tree may give very poor performance.

This chapter discusses techniques you can use to keep a tree balanced, even when items are added and removed over time. By keeping a tree balanced, you keep it efficient.

The chapter begins by describing what it means for a tree to be unbalanced and explaining how an unbalanced tree can ruin performance. Then it discusses AVL trees. In an AVL tree, the heights of the left and right subtrees at any node always differ by at most 1. By maintaining this property, you can keep the tree from becoming unbalanced.

Next the chapter describes B-trees and B+trees. These trees keep all of their leaves at the same depth. By ensuring that the number of branches in each node is within certain limits, these trees keep themselves balanced. B-trees and B+trees are commonly used in database programming. The final example program in this chapter uses a B+tree to implement a simple yet powerful database.

Balance

As mentioned in Chapter 6, "Trees," the shape of a sorted tree depends on the order in which you add items to it. Figure 7.1 shows two different trees created by adding the same items to trees in different orders.

Tall, thin trees like the one on the left in Figure 7.1 can have up to O(N) depth. Inserting or locating an item in such an unbalanced tree could take O(N) steps. Even if new items are placed randomly within the tree, on the average they will wind up at depth N / 2, which is still O(N).

Suppose you build a sorted binary tree containing 1000 nodes. If the tree is balanced, the height of the tree will be around $\log_2(1000)$, or about 10. Adding a new item to the tree will take only 10 steps. If the tree is tall and thin, it could

Figure 7.1 Trees built in different orders.

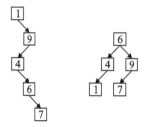

Order: 1 9 4 6 7   Order: 6 4 1 9 7

have height 1000. In this case, adding a new item at the bottom of the tree will take 1000 steps.

Now suppose you want to add 1000 more nodes to the tree. If the tree remains balanced, all 1000 nodes will fit on the next couple of levels of the tree. It will take only about 10 * 1000 = 10,000 steps to add the new items. If the tree continues to grow in an unbalanced fashion, each new item will make the tree grow taller. Adding the items will take around 1000 + 1001 +...+ 2000 = 1.5 million steps.

Although you cannot guarantee items will enter and leave a tree in a particular order, you can use techniques to keep a tree more or less balanced, no matter how items are added and removed.

AVL Trees

AVL trees were named after the Russian mathematicians Adelson-Velskii and Landis, who invented them. At every node in an AVL tree the heights of the left and right subtrees differ by at most 1. Figure 7.2 shows several AVL trees.

Even though an AVL tree may not be as short as a complete tree containing the same number of nodes, it still has depth O(log(N)). That means you can locate nodes within an AVL tree in time O(log(N)), which is relatively fast. It is not as obvious, but it is also possible to add or remove items from an AVL tree in O(log(N)) time while keeping the tree balanced.

Adding Nodes to an AVL Tree

Each time you add a node to an AVL tree, you must check to see if the AVL property is still satisfied. After adding a node, you can follow the node's ancestors back up toward the root, verifying that the subtrees at each ancestor have heights differing by at most 1. If you find a spot where this is not true, you can shuffle some of the nodes around to rebalance the subtrees while still keeping the tree properly ordered.

The routine that adds a new node to the tree recursively descends into the tree searching for the item's location. After inserting the new item, the recursive

Figure 7.2 AVL trees.

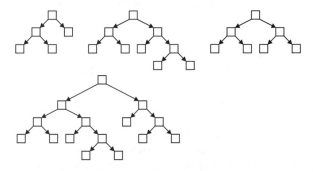

calls to the routine return and backtrack up the tree. As each call returns, the routine checks to see if the AVL property still holds at the higher level. This sort of backward recursion, where the routine performs an important action on the way out of a chain of recursive calls, is called *bottom-up* recursion.

As the routine returns up the tree, it also checks to see if the height of the subtree it is examining has changed. If the routine ever reaches a point where the height of its subtree has not changed, the heights of any subtrees farther up the tree cannot have changed either. In that case, the tree must once again be balanced, so the routine can stop checking.

For example, the tree on the left in Figure 7.3 is a properly balanced AVL tree. If you add a new item E to the tree, you get the tree shown in the middle. You then begin searching upward through the tree from the new node E. The tree is balanced at node E because the two subtrees at this node are both empty and have the same height: 0.

The tree is also balanced at node D. The left subtree at node D is empty, so it has height 0. The right subtree contains the single node E, so it has height 1. The heights of these subtrees differ by only 1, so the tree is balanced at node D.

The tree is not balanced at node C. The left subtree at node C has height 0 while the right subtree has height 2. You can rebalance the subtrees at this node as shown on the right in Figure 7.3. Here node D has replaced node C. The subtree rooted at node D now contains nodes C, D, and E and has height 2. Notice that the original subtree located at this position, which was rooted at node C, had

Figure 7.3 Adding a node to an AVL tree.

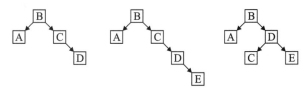

height 2 before the new node was added. Because the height of the subtree has not changed, the tree is now balanced at all nodes above node D.

AVL Tree Rotations

When you add a node to an AVL tree, there are four ways the tree can become unbalanced, depending on where the node was added. Each of these requires a different rebalancing. The rebalancing techniques are called right rotation, left rotation, left-right rotation, and right-left rotation. They are abbreviated R, L, LR, and RL.

Suppose you add a new node to an AVL tree and the tree is now unbalanced at node X, as shown in Figure 7.4. Node X and its two children are shown explicitly. The other parts of the tree are indicated by triangles because you will not need to look at them closely.

The new node may have been placed in any of the four subtrees drawn as triangles below node X. When you place the new node in one of these triangles, you must use the corresponding rotation to rebalance the tree. Keep in mind that the new node may not unbalance the tree, so sometimes no rebalancing is needed.

Right Rotation

First, suppose you added a new node to the R subtree in Figure 7.4. In that case you do not need to worry about the right two subtrees below node X, so you can group them together in a single triangle, as shown in Figure 7.5. The new node has been added to tree T_1, causing the subtree T_A rooted at node A to be at least two levels taller than subtree T_3.

In fact, because the tree was an AVL tree before you added the new node, T_A used to be at *most* one level taller than subtree T_3. You added only one node to the tree, so T_A must now be exactly two levels taller than subtree T_3.

You also know subtree T_1 is not more than one level taller than subtree T_2. Otherwise, node X would not be the lowest node in the tree with unbalanced subtrees. If T_1 were two levels taller than T_2, the tree would be unbalanced at node A.

Figure 7.4 The anatomy of an unbalanced AVL tree.

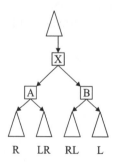

R   LR   RL   L

Figure 7.5 Adding a new node to the R subtree.

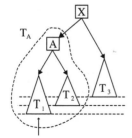

Node added here

You can rearrange the nodes using a right rotation, as shown in Figure 7.6. This is called a right rotation because the nodes A and X seem to have been rotated one position to the right.

Notice that this rotation preserves the "less than" ordering of the tree. An inorder traversal of either of these trees would visit the subtrees and nodes in the order T_1, A, T_2, X, T_3. Because the inorder traversals of both trees are the same, the orderings of the items within the trees are the same.

It is also important to note that the height of the subtree you are working with has remained the same. Before the new node was added, the height of the subtree was 2 plus the height of subtree T_2. After adding the node and applying the right rotation, the height of the subtree is still 2 plus the height of subtree T_2. Any parts of the tree that lie above node X must now be balanced, so you do not need to continue rebalancing the tree.

Left Rotation

A left rotation is similar to a right rotation. You use a left rotation to rebalance a tree when a new node is added to the L subtree shown in Figure 7.4. The AVL tree is shown before and after a left rotation in Figure 7.7.

Left-Right Rotation

When a node is added in the LR subtree shown in Figure 7.4, you must look one level deeper. Figure 7.8 shows the tree, assuming the new node was been added on

Figure 7.6 Right rotation.

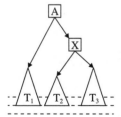

Figure 7.7 Before and after left rotation.

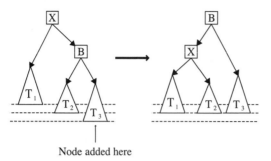

Node added here

the left side T_2 of the LR subtree. It could just as easily have been added to the right subtree T_3. In either case, the T_A and T_C subtrees still have the AVL property, but the T_X subtree does not.

Because the tree was an AVL tree before the node was added, T_A used to be at most one level taller than T_4. Only one node was added, so T_A has grown only one level taller. That means T_A must now be exactly two levels taller than T_4.

You also know that T_2 has height at most 1 greater than T_3. Otherwise T_C would not be balanced, and node X would not be the lowest node in the tree with unbalanced subtrees.

Also T_1 must reach the same depth as T_3. If it were shorter, T_A would be unbalanced, again contradicting the assumption that node X is the lowest node in the tree that has unbalanced subtrees. If T_1 reached a greater depth than T_3, then T_1 would reach a depth 2 greater than the depth reached by T_4. In that case, the tree would have been unbalanced before the new node was added.

All of this means that the bottoms of the trees are exactly as shown in Figure 7.8. Subtree T_2 reaches the greatest depth, T_1 and T_3 reach a depth one level above that, and T_4 reaches one level above T_1 and T_3.

Figure 7.8 Adding a new node to the LR subtree.

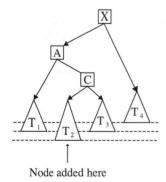

Node added here

Figure 7.9 Left-right rotation.

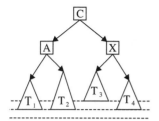

Using these facts you can rebalance the tree, as shown in Figure 7.9. This is called a left-right rotation because it looks as if nodes A and C were rotated one position to the left, and then nodes C and X were rotated one position to the right.

Like the other rotations, this rotation does not change the order of the items within the tree. The inorder traversal of the tree before and after the rotation visits the subtrees and nodes in the order: T_1, A, T_2, C, T_3, X, T_4.

The height of the subtree being rebalanced has also not changed. Before the new node was added, the height of the subtree was 2 plus the height of subtree T_1. After the tree is rebalanced, the height of the subtree is again 2 plus the height of subtree T_1. That means the rest of the tree is balanced, so you do not need to continue rebalancing other parts of the tree.

Right-Left Rotation

A right-left rotation is similar to a left-right rotation. Use a right-left rotation to rebalance the tree after adding a new node to the RL subtree in Figure 7.4. The AVL tree is shown before and after the right-left rotation in Figure 7.10.

Summary of Rotations

Figure 7.11 shows all the AVL tree rotations. Each preserves the tree's inorder traversal, and each leaves the height of the tree unchanged. After adding a new item and applying the appropriate rotation, the tree is once again balanced.

Adding Nodes in Visual Basic

Before considering how to remove AVL tree nodes, this section discusses some of the details of adding a node to an AVL tree in Visual Basic.

In addition to the usual LeftChild and RightChild fields, the AVLNode class contains a Balance field that indicates which subtree at the node is taller. Balance is -1 if the left subtree is taller, 1 if the right subtree is taller, and 0 if the two subtrees have the same height.

Figure 7.10 Before and after right-left rotation.

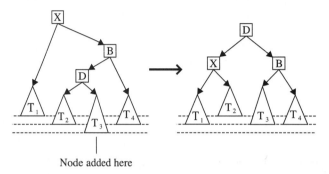

Node added here

```
Public LeftChild As AVLNode
Public RightChild As AVLNode
Public Balance As Integer
```

To make the program easier to read, you can use constants LEFT_HEAVY, RIGHT_HEAVY, and BALANCED to represent these values.

```
Global Const LEFT_HEAVY = -1
Global Const BALANCED = 0
Global Const RIGHT_HEAVY = 1
```

Subroutine InsertItem, shown shortly, recursively descends through the tree looking for the new item's location. When it reaches the bottom of the tree, the routine creates the new node and adds it to the tree.

InsertItem then uses bottom-up recursion to rebalance the tree. As the recursive calls return, the subroutine travels back up the tree. Each time it returns, InsertItem sets the parameter has_grown to be true if the subtree it is leaving has grown taller. In the instance of InsertItem that made the recursive call, the routine uses this parameter to determine whether the subtree it is examining is out of balance. If so, the routine applies the correct rotation to rebalance the subtree.

For example, suppose the subroutine is currently examining node X. Suppose it has just returned from visiting the right subtree beneath node X and that the parameter has_grown is true, indicating the right subtree grew taller. If the subtrees below node X previously had the same height, then the right subtree is now taller than the left. The tree is balanced at this point, but the subtree rooted at node X has also grown since its right subtree grew taller.

If the left subtree below node X was previously taller than the right, then the left and right subtrees are now the same height. The height of the subtree rooted at node X has not changed—it is still 1 plus the height of the left subtree. In this case InsertItem would reset variable has_grown to false, indicating that the tree is balanced.

Figure 7.11 Summary of AVL tree rotations.

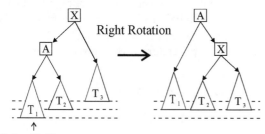

Right Rotation

Node added here

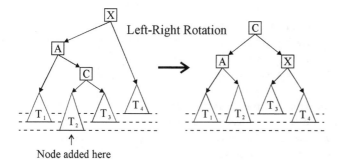

Left Rotation

Node added here

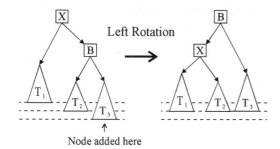

Left-Right Rotation

Node added here

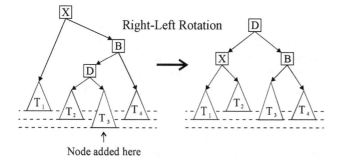

Right-Left Rotation

Node added here

Finally, if the right subtree below node X was previously taller than the left, the new node has unbalanced the tree at node X. InsertItem invokes subroutine RebalanceRightGrew to rebalance the tree. RebalanceRightGrew performs either a left or right-left rotation, depending on the exact situation.

Subroutine InsertItem follows a similar procedure if the new item was inserted into the left subtree.

```
Public Sub InsertItem(node As AVLNode, parent As AVLNode, _

    txt As String, has_grown As Boolean)
Dim child As AVLNode

    ' If this is the bottom of the tree, leave
    ' the parent pointing to the new node.
    If parent Is Nothing Then
        Set parent = node
        parent.Balance = BALANCED
        has_grown = True
        Exit Sub
    End If

    ' Continue down the left or right subtree.
    If txt <= parent.Box.Caption Then
        ' Insert the child in the left subtree.
        Set child = parent.LeftChild
        InsertItem node, child, txt, has_grown
        Set parent.LeftChild = child

        ' See if rebalancing is necessary. It will
        ' not be if the addition never unbalanced
        ' the tree or if we rebalanced the tree at
        ' a deeper level of recursion. In either
        ' case has_grown will be False.
        If Not has_grown Then Exit Sub

        If parent.Balance = RIGHT_HEAVY Then
            ' Was right heavy, now balanced. This
            ' subtree did not grow so the tree is
            ' balanced.
            parent.Balance = BALANCED
            has_grown = False
        ElseIf parent.Balance = BALANCED Then
            ' Was balanced, now left heavy. This
            ' subtree is still balanced but it
```

```
            ' grew so we need to continue checking
            ' up the tree.
            parent.Balance = LEFT_HEAVY
        Else
            ' Was left heavy, now left unbalanced.
            ' Perform a rotation to rebalance at
            ' this node.
            RebalanceLeftGrew parent
            has_grown = False
        End If   ' End checking this node's balance.
    Else
        ' Insert the child in the right subtree.
        Set child = parent.RightChild
        InsertItem node, child, txt, has_grown
        Set parent.RightChild = child

        ' See if rebalancing is necessary. It will
        ' not be if the addition never unbalanced
        ' the tree or if we rebalanced the tree at
        ' a deeper level of recursion. In either
        ' case has_grown will be False.
        If Not has_grown Then Exit Sub

        If parent.Balance = LEFT_HEAVY Then
            ' Was left heavy, now balanced. This
            ' subtree did not grow so the tree is
            ' balanced.
            parent.Balance = BALANCED
            has_grown = False
        ElseIf parent.Balance = BALANCED Then
            ' Was balanced, now right heavy. This
            ' subtree is still balanced but it
            ' grew so we need to continue checking
            ' up the tree.
            parent.Balance = RIGHT_HEAVY
        Else
            ' Was right heavy, now right unbalanced.
            ' Perform a rotation to rebalance at
            ' this node.
            RebalanceRightGrew parent
            has_grown = False
        End If   ' End checking this node's balance.
    End If   ' End if (down left) ... else (down right).
End Sub
```

```
Private Sub RebalanceRightGrew(parent As AVLNode)
Dim child As AVLNode
Dim grandchild As AVLNode

    Set child = parent.RightChild

    If child.Balance = RIGHT_HEAVY Then
        ' Perform a left rotation.
        Set parent.RightChild = child.LeftChild
        Set child.LeftChild = parent
        parent.Balance = BALANCED
        Set parent = child
    Else
        ' Perform a right-left rotation.
        Set grandchild = child.LeftChild
        Set child.LeftChild = grandchild.RightChild
        Set grandchild.RightChild = child
        Set parent.RightChild = grandchild.LeftChild
        Set grandchild.LeftChild = parent
        If grandchild.Balance = RIGHT_HEAVY Then
            parent.Balance = LEFT_HEAVY
        Else
            parent.Balance = BALANCED
        End If
        If grandchild.Balance = LEFT_HEAVY Then
            child.Balance = RIGHT_HEAVY
        Else
            child.Balance = BALANCED
        End If
        Set parent = grandchild
    End If    ' End if (right rotation)... else (double right rotation).
    parent.Balance = BALANCED
End Sub
```

Removing Nodes from an AVL Tree

In Chapter 6, "Trees," you saw that it is harder to remove an item from a sorted tree than it is to insert one. If the removed node has one child, you can replace it with that child and still preserve the tree's ordering. If the node has two children, you must replace it with the rightmost node to the left in the tree. If that node has a left child, you must also replace it with its left child.

Because AVL trees are a special type of sorted tree, you still need to perform these same steps. After you have finished, however, you must travel back up the tree to make sure it is still balanced. When you find a node where the AVL property does not hold, you must perform the appropriate rotations to rebalance the tree. While the rotations are the same ones used earlier for inserting a node in the tree, the cases you must look for are slightly different.

Left Rotation

Suppose you remove a node from the left subtree under node X. Suppose also that the right subtree is either evenly balanced or its right half has height 1 greater than its left half. Then the left rotation shown in Figure 7.12 will rebalance the tree at node X.

The bottom level of subtree T_2 in Figure 7.12 is shaded to indicate that the subtree T_B is either evenly balanced (T_2 and T_3 have the same height) or its right half is taller (T_3 is taller than T_2). In other words, the shaded level may or may not be part of subtree T_2.

If T_2 and T_3 have the same height, then the subtree T_X rooted at node X does not change in height when you remove the node. The height of T_X was and remains 2 plus the height of subtree T_2. Because the height does not change, the tree above this node is balanced.

If T_3 is taller than T_2, subtree T_X grows shorter by 1. In that case, the tree above node X may not be balanced, so you must continue up the tree checking to see if the AVL property holds for the ancestors of node X.

Right-Left Rotation

Suppose a node is taken from the left subtree under node X, but the left half of the right subtree is taller than the right half. Then you need to use a right-left rotation to rebalance the tree. Figure 7.13 shows this rotation.

Whether subtree T_2 or T_3 is taller, the right-left rotation will rebalance the subtree T_X. The rotation will also reduce the height of T_X by 1. That means the tree above node X may not be balanced, so you must continue up the tree, checking to see if the AVL property holds for the ancestors of node X.

Figure 7.12 Left rotation when removing a node.

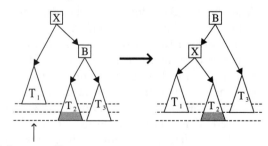

Node removed here

Figure 7.13 Right-left rotation when removing a node.

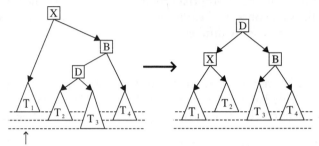

Node removed here

Other Rotations

The other rotations are similar to these. In these cases, the node being removed is in the right subtree below node X. All four of these rotations are the same as the rotations used to balance the tree after adding a node, with one exception.

When you add a new node to the tree, the first rotation you perform rebalances the subtree T_X without changing its height. That means the tree above T_X must still be balanced. When you use the rotations after removing a node from the tree, the rotation might reduce the height of the subtree T_X by 1. In that case, you cannot be sure the tree above node X is still balanced. You must continue up the tree, checking the AVL property at each node.

Removing Nodes in Visual Basic

Subroutine DeleteItem removes items from the tree. It recursively descends through the tree, looking for the item to be deleted. When it finds the target node, it removes the node. If the target has no children, the routine is done. If the node has a single child, it replaces the node with its child.

If the node has two children, DeleteItem calls routine ReplaceRightmost to replace the target node with the rightmost node to the target's left. ReplaceRightmost performs its duty much as it does in Chapter 6, "Trees," where it removes items from a normal (nonbalanced) sorted tree. The main difference occurs when the routine returns and recursively moves back up the tree. As it does so, ReplaceRightmost uses bottom-up recursion to make sure the tree is balanced at each node.

Each time a call returns, the calling instance of ReplaceRightmost invokes RebalanceRightShrunk to ensure that the tree is balanced at that point. Because ReplaceRightmost descended through the right branches, it always uses Rebalance-RightShrunk rather than RebalanceLeftShrunk to perform the rebalancing.

DeleteItem invoked the first call to ReplaceRightmost by sending it down the left branch beneath the node being removed. When that first call to Replace-Rightmost returns, DeleteItem uses RebalanceLeftShrunk to ensure the tree is balanced at that point.

After this, the recursive calls to DeleteItem return one at a time and work their way back up the tree. Like ReplaceRightmost, subroutine DeleteItem uses bottom-up recursion to verify that the tree is balanced. As each call to DeleteItem returns, the calling routine invokes RebalanceRightShrunk or RebalanceLeftShrunk, depending on which path it followed down into the tree.

RebalanceLeftShrunk is similar to RebalanceRightShrunk, so it is not shown in the following code.

```
Public Sub DeleteItem(node As AVLNode, txt As String, shrunk As
Boolean)
Dim child As AVLNode
Dim target As AVLNode

    If node Is Nothing Then
        Beep
        MsgBox "Item " & txt & " is not in the tree."
        shrunk = False
        Exit Sub
    End If

    If txt < node.Box.Caption Then
        Set child = node.LeftChild
        DeleteItem child, txt, shrunk
        Set node.LeftChild = child
        If shrunk Then RebalanceLeftShrunk node, shrunk
    ElseIf txt > node.Box.Caption Then
        Set child = node.RightChild
        DeleteItem child, txt, shrunk
        Set node.RightChild = child
        If shrunk Then RebalanceRightShrunk node, shrunk
    Else
        Set target = node
        If target.RightChild Is Nothing Then
            ' No children or left child only.
            Set node = target.LeftChild
            shrunk = True
        ElseIf target.LeftChild Is Nothing Then
            ' Right child only.
            Set node = target.RightChild
            shrunk = True
        Else
            ' Two children.
            Set child = target.LeftChild
            ReplaceRightmost child, shrunk, target
            Set target.LeftChild = child
```

```
                If shrunk Then RebalanceLeftShrunk node, shrunk
            End If
        End If
End Sub


Private Sub ReplaceRightmost(repl As AVLNode, shrunk As Boolean, _
        target As AVLNode)
Dim child As AVLNode

    If repl.RightChild Is Nothing Then
        target.Box.Caption = repl.Box.Caption
        Set target = repl
        Set repl = repl.LeftChild
        shrunk = True
    Else
        Set child = repl.RightChild
        ReplaceRightmost child, shrunk, target
        Set repl.RightChild = child
        If shrunk Then RebalanceRightShrunk repl, shrunk
    End If
End Sub


Private Sub RebalanceRightShrunk(node As AVLNode, shrunk As Boolean)
Dim child As AVLNode
Dim child_bal As Integer
Dim grandchild As AVLNode
Dim grandchild_bal As Integer

    If node.Balance = RIGHT_HEAVY Then
        ' Was Right heavy, now it is balanced.
        node.Balance = BALANCED
    ElseIf node.Balance = BALANCED Then
        ' Was balanced, now it is Left heavy.
        node.Balance = LEFT_HEAVY
        shrunk = False
    Else
        ' Was Left heavy, now unbalanced.
        Set child = node.LeftChild
        child_bal = child.Balance
        If child_bal <= 0 Then
            ' Right rotation.
            Set node.LeftChild = child.RightChild
            Set child.RightChild = node
```

```
            If child_bal = BALANCED Then
                node.Balance = LEFT_HEAVY
                child.Balance = RIGHT_HEAVY
                shrunk = False
            Else
                node.Balance = BALANCED
                child.Balance = BALANCED
            End If
            Set node = child
        Else
            ' Left-right rotation.
            Set grandchild = child.RightChild
            grandchild_bal = grandchild.Balance
            Set child.RightChild = grandchild.LeftChild
            Set grandchild.LeftChild = child
            Set node.LeftChild = grandchild.RightChild
            Set grandchild.RightChild = node
            If grandchild_bal = LEFT_HEAVY Then
                node.Balance = RIGHT_HEAVY
            Else
                node.Balance = BALANCED
            End If
            If grandchild_bal = RIGHT_HEAVY Then
                child.Balance = LEFT_HEAVY
            Else
                child.Balance = BALANCED
            End If
            Set node = grandchild
            grandchild.Balance = BALANCED
        End If
    End If
End Sub
```

Example program AVL manipulates an AVL tree. Enter a text value, and click the Add button to add an item to the tree. Enter a value, and click Remove to delete that item from the tree. Figure 7.14 shows program AVL.

B-trees

B-trees (pronounced "bee trees") are a different form of balanced tree, one that is a bit more intuitive than AVL trees. Each node in a B-tree can hold several data keys and several pointers to child nodes. Because each node holds several items, the nodes are often called *buckets*.

Figure 7.14 Program AVL.

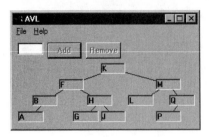

Between each pair of adjacent child pointers in a node is a key you can use to determine which branch to take when inserting or looking for an item. For example, in the tree shown in Figure 7.15, the root node contains two keys: G and R. To locate an item with value that comes before G, you look down the first branch. To find a value between G and R, you look down the second branch. To locate an item that comes after R, you look down the third branch.

A B-tree of *order* K has these properties:

- Each node holds at most 2 * K keys.

- Each node, except possibly the root, holds at least K keys.

- An internal node containing M keys has M + 1 children.

- All leaves are at the same level in the tree.

The B-tree in Figure 7.15 has order 2. Each node can hold up to four keys. Each node, except possibly the root, must hold at least two keys. For convenience, B-tree nodes usually can hold an even number of keys, so the order is a whole number.

Requiring that each node in a B-tree of order K contain between K and 2 * K keys keeps the tree balanced. Because each node must hold at least K keys, it must have at least K + 1 children so the tree cannot grow too tall and thin. A B-tree containing N nodes can have height at most $O(\log_{K+1}(N))$. This means searching the tree will be an $O(\log(N))$ operation. Although it is not obvious, inserting and removing items from a B-tree are also $O(\log(N))$ operations.

B-tree Performance

B-trees are particularly useful in large database applications. If the order of a B-tree is reasonably large, you will be able to locate any item in the tree after examining

Figure 7.15 A B-tree.

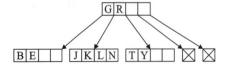

only a few nodes. For example, a B-tree of order 10 containing 1 million records can be at most $\log_{11}(1,000,000)$, or about six levels tall. You would need to examine at most six nodes before finding a particular item.

A balanced binary tree containing the same 1 million items would have height $\log_2(1,000,000)$, or about 20. These nodes, however, contain only one key value. To find an item in a binary tree, you would examine 20 nodes and 20 values. To find an item in a B-tree, you might need to examine 5 nodes and 100 keys.

The B-tree will be faster if it is easy to examine keys but relatively hard to examine nodes. For example, if the database is stored on a hard disk, reading data from the disk will be slow. Once the data is in memory, examining is quite fast.

Disk drives read data in large chunks, and it takes no longer to read an entire chunk of data than it takes to read a single byte. If a B-tree's nodes are not too large, it takes no longer to read a B-tree node from a disk than it takes to read a binary tree node. In that case, searching five nodes in a B-tree will require 5 slow disk accesses plus up to 100 fast memory accesses. Searching 20 nodes in a binary tree will require 20 slow disk accesses plus 20 fast memory accesses. The binary search is slower because the time spent on 15 extra disk accesses is much greater than the time saved by avoiding 80 memory accesses. Disk access issues are discussed more thoroughly later in this chapter.

Inserting Items in a B-tree

To insert a new item into a B-tree, locate the leaf node in which the new item should be placed. If that node contains fewer than 2 * K keys, there is room to add the new item to that node. Add the new item in its correct position so the items inside the node are in their proper order.

If the node already contains 2 * K items, there is no room for the new item. To make room, break the node into two new nodes. Counting the new item, there are 2 * K + 1 items to distribute between the two new nodes. Place K items in each node, keeping them in their proper order. Move the middle item up to the nodes' parent.

For example, suppose you want to insert the item Q into the B-tree shown in Figure 7.15. This new item belongs in the second leaf node, which is already full. To split the node, divide the items J, K, N, P, and Q between the two new nodes. Place the items J and K in the left node. Place P and Q in the right node. Then move the middle item, N, up to the nodes' parent. Figure 7.16 shows the new tree.

Dividing a node in two is called a *bucket split*. When a bucket split occurs, the parent node gains a new key and a new pointer. If the parent is already full,

Figure 7.16 B-tree after adding item Q.

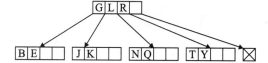

adding the new key and pointer will cause it to split as well. That, in turn, will require a new entry in the original node's grandparent. That may cause another bucket split, and so on up the tree. In the worst case, inserting an item causes a chain reaction that rises up the tree until the root node splits.

When a root split occurs, the B-tree grows taller. That is the only way a B-tree grows taller. This gives B-trees the strange property of always growing from the leaves toward the root.

Removing Items from a B-tree

In theory, removing an item from a B-tree is as simple as adding an item. In practice, the details are pretty complicated.

If the item being removed is not in a leaf node, you must replace it with another item so the tree maintains a proper ordering of the items. This is much like the case of removing an item from a sorted tree or from an AVL tree; you can handle it similarly. Replace the item with the rightmost item to its left in the tree. This rightmost item will always be in a leaf node. After you have replaced the item, you can treat the removal as if you had simply removed its replacement in the leaf node.

To remove an item from a leaf node, first slide the other items to the left if necessary to fill in the hole left behind. Remember that each node in a B-tree of order K must hold between K and 2 * K items. After you remove an item from a leaf node, the leaf may contain only K – 1 items.

In that case, you can try to borrow some items from one of the leaf's sibling nodes. You can then redistribute the items in the two nodes so they each have at least K items. In Figure 7.17 an item has been removed from the leftmost leaf in the tree, leaving that node with only one item. Redistributing items between the node and its right sibling gives both nodes at least two keys. Notice how the middle item J is moved up into the parent node.

When you try to rebalance nodes in this way, you may find the sibling node contains only K items. Between the target node and its sibling there are only 2 * K – 1 items, so there are not enough for the two nodes to share. In that case, all the items in both nodes can fit within a single node, so you can merge them. Remove the key that separates the two nodes from their parent. Place that item and the 2 * K – 1 items in the two nodes in the merged node. This process of

Figure 7.17 Rebalancing after removing an item.

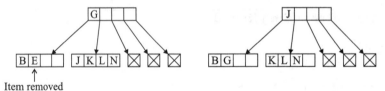

Item removed

Figure 7.18 Merging after removing an item.

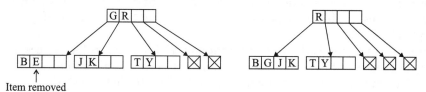

Item removed

merging two nodes is called a *bucket merge*, or *bucket join*. Figure 7.18 shows how to merge two nodes.

When you merge two nodes, you remove a key from the nodes' parent. The parent may then hold only K – 1 items. In that case, you must rebalance or merge it with one of its siblings. That, in turn, may cause the grandparent node to contain K – 1 items, and the whole process will start over again. In the worst case, the deletion will cause a chain reaction of bucket merges that reaches all the way to the root.

If you remove the last item from the root node, merge the root's two remaining children into a new root and shorten the tree by one level. The only way a B-tree grows shorter is when the children of the root node merge to form a new root.

Example program Btree allows you to manipulate a B-tree. Enter a text value, and click the Add button to add an item to the tree. Enter a value, and click Remove to remove an item from the tree. Figure 7.19 shows program Btree managing an order 2 B-tree.

B-tree Variations

There are several variations of B-trees, only a few of which are described here. *Top-down B-trees* manage the B-tree structure already described in a different

Figure 7.19 Program Btree.

way. By splitting full nodes whenever they are encountered, this variation is able to use more intuitive top-down recursion instead of bottom-up recursion when adding items. It also reduces the chances of having long cascades of bucket splits later.

The second variation is the *B+tree* (pronounced "bee plus tree"). B+trees store only data keys in internal nodes and store data records in leaf nodes. This allows B+trees to store more items in each bucket, so they are shorter than corresponding B-trees.

Top-Down B-trees

The subroutine that adds a new item to a B-tree first searches recursively through the tree to find the bucket where the item belongs. When it tries to insert the new item, the routine may need to split the bucket and move one of the node's items up to its parent.

As the routine returns from its recursive calls, the calling routine checks to see if the parent node must also split. If so, an item is passed up to its parent. Each time the routine returns from a recursive call, the calling routine must see if it should split the next ancestor node. Because these bucket splits occur as the routine is leaving its recursive subroutine calls, this is bottom-up recursion. B-trees managed in this way are sometimes called *bottom-up B-trees*.

An alternative strategy is to split any full nodes encountered on the way down. As the routine searches for a bucket to hold the new item, it splits any node it encounters that is already full. Each time it splits a node, it passes an item up to the parent. Because the routine has already split every full node it encountered on the way down, there is always room for the new item in the parent node.

When the routine reaches the leaf that should hold the item, the parent node is guaranteed to have room. If the program must split the leaf node, there is always room to pass the middle item up to the parent. Because this system works from the top down, this sort of B-tree is called a *top-down B-tree*.

This method causes bucket splits to occur sooner than they are absolutely necessary. A top-down B-tree splits a full node, even if its child nodes contain lots of unused space. By splitting nodes early, the top-down method causes the tree to hold more empty space than a bottom-up B-tree. On the other hand, by performing node splits early, this method reduces the chances of creating a long cascade of bucket splits.

Unfortunately, there is no top-down version for node merging. As the node removal routine descends down the tree, it cannot merge nodes that are half empty as it encounters them. It cannot know at that time whether two children of a node will be merged and an item removed from their parent. Because it cannot know if the parent will lose an item, it cannot tell if the parent should be merged with one of its siblings.

B+trees

B-trees are often used to store large records. A typical B-tree might hold employee records, each occupying several kilobytes of memory. The B-tree would arrange the records according to some key field such as employee name or ID number.

In that case, rearranging data items could be relatively slow. To merge two buckets, a program would need to move many records, each of which was quite large. Similarly, to split a bucket the program would need to move many large records.

To avoid moving large amounts of data, the program can store only record keys in the B-tree's internal nodes. The nodes also contain pointers to the actual data records stored elsewhere. Now when the program rearranges buckets, it needs to move only the record keys and pointers, not the entire records themselves. This type of B-tree is called a B+tree.

Keeping the items in the B+tree nodes small also allows the program to store more keys in each node. With the same node size, the program can increase the order of the tree and make it shorter.

For example, suppose you have an order 2 B-tree so each node has three to five children. To hold 1 million records, this tree would need to have height between $\log_5(1,000,000)$ and $\log_3(1,000,000)$, or between 9 and 13. To locate an item in this tree, a program might need to perform as many as 13 disk accesses.

Now suppose you store the same 1 million records in a B+tree using nodes of roughly the same size in bytes. Because a B+tree stores only keys in its nodes, this tree may be able to hold the keys for up to 20 records in each node. In that case, the tree would have between 11 and 21 children per node, so it would have height between $\log_{21}(1,000,000)$ and $\log_{11}(1,000,000)$, or between 5 and 6. To locate an item, the program would need to perform only six disk accesses to find the item's key, plus one additional disk access to retrieve the item itself.

Storing only pointers to the data within B+tree nodes also makes it easier to associate multiple keys with a set of records. In an employee record system, one B+tree could use last names as keys while another could use Social Security numbers. Both trees would contain pointers to the actual data records stored outside the trees.

Improving B-trees

This section discusses two techniques for improving the performance of B-trees and B+trees. The first technique allows you to rearrange items within a node and its siblings to avoid splitting a bucket. The second allows you to load or reload your data to add unused entries to the tree. This reduces the chances of bucket splits occurring later.

Rebalancing to Avoid Bucket Splits

When you add an item to a bucket that is full, the bucket splits. You can avoid the bucket split if you rebalance the node with one of its siblings. For example, adding a new item Q to the B-tree shown on the left in Figure 7.20 normally causes a bucket split. You can avoid this by rebalancing the node containing J, K, L, and N with its left sibling containing B and E. This gives the tree shown on the right in Figure 7.20.

This sort of rebalancing has a couple of advantages. By rebalancing the nodes, you have increased the usage of the buckets. There are now fewer unused tree entries, so you have decreased the amount of wasted memory.

More important, if you do not split the bucket you do not need to move an item up to the bucket's parent. That prevents a time-consuming cascade of bucket splits.

On the other hand, reducing the number of unused entries in the tree decreases the amount of wasted space, but it increases the chances of bucket splits in the future. Because there is less empty space, nodes are more likely to be full when a new node is added.

Initial Loading

Suppose you have a small customer database that contains 10 customer records. You could load the records into a B-tree so they filled each bucket completely, as shown in Figure 7.21. This tree contains little wasted space, but adding a new item to the tree immediately causes a bucket split. In fact, because every node is full, it will cause a cascade of bucket splits, reaching all the way to the root.

Instead of loading the tree densely, you could add some extra empty entries to each node, as shown in Figure 7.22. While this makes the tree a bit larger, it lets you add new items to the tree without immediately causing a long chain of bucket splits. After you use the tree for a while, the amount of free space might decrease to the point where bucket splits are likely. You could then rebuild the tree to add more empty space.

B-trees in real applications usually have larger orders than the trees shown here. Initially loading the tree with a small amount of empty space greatly reduces the need for rebalancing and bucket splits. For example, you might give 10 percent empty space to a B-tree of order 10 so each node has room for two new items. You could work with this tree for quite a while before causing any long chains of bucket splits.

This is an example of a space versus time trade-off. Adding empty space to the nodes makes the tree larger but reduces the chances of bucket splits.

Figure 7.20 Rebalancing to avoid a bucket split.

Figure 7.21 Loading a B-tree densely.

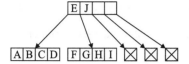

Disk Access Issues

B-trees and B+trees are particularly well suited for large database applications. A typical B+tree might hold hundreds of thousands or even millions of records. In that case, only a small fraction of the tree would fit in memory at any one time. Each time a program accesses a node, it needs to retrieve it from a hard disk. This section describes three issues that are particularly important when the data is stored on a hard disk: pointer faking, bucket size, and root caching.

Pointer Faking

Collections and object references are convenient for building trees in memory, but they are not useful for storing a tree on a hard disk. You cannot create an object reference to a record in a file.

Instead you can use pointer-faking techniques similar to those described in Chapter 2, "Lists." Rather than using object references to point to a tree node, you use the node's record number in the file. For example, suppose a B+tree of order 12 uses 80 byte keys. You could declare the node data structure using the following code.

```
Global Const ORDER = 12
Global Const KEYS_PER_NODE = 2 * ORDER

Type BtreeNode
    Key (1 to KEYS_PER_NODE) As String * 80     ' Keys.
    Child (0 To KEYS_PER_NODE) As Integer       ' Child pointers.
End Type
```

The Child array entries indicate the record number of the child nodes within the file. You open the B+tree data file for random access using records that matched the BtreeNode structure.

Figure 7.22 Loading a B-tree loosely.

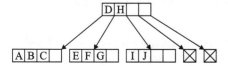

```
Dim node As BtreeNode
```

```
Open filename For Random As #filenum Len = Len(node)
```

Once the file is open, you can fetch a particular record using the Get statement.

```
Dim node As BtreeNode
```

```
' Fetch record number recnum.
Get #filenum, recnum, node
```

To make managing B+trees easier, you can store the B+tree nodes and the data records in separate files and use the same disk pointer-faking techniques to manage each.

When an object's reference count reaches 0, Visual Basic automatically destroys it. This makes managing data structures in memory simple. On the other hand, when a program no longer needs to use a record in a file, it cannot simply clear all of the references to that record. If it did, it would no longer be able to use that record, but the record would still take up space in the file.

The program must keep track of unused records so it can find and reuse them later. One easy way to do this is to keep a linked list of the unused records. When a record is no longer needed, it is added to the list. When the program needs a new record, it removes one from the list. If the program needs a new item and the list is empty, the program expands the file.

Selecting a Bucket Size

Disk drives read data in natural chunks. Most disk drives read data in blocks of 512 or 1024 bytes, or some other number of bytes that is a power of 2. It takes the disk no longer to read one of these blocks than it takes it to read a single byte.

You can take advantage of this fact by making buckets some multiple of the size your disk reads naturally. Then pack as many records or keys as possible into that size. For example, suppose you decide to make your buckets roughly 2048 bytes in size. If you are building a B+tree with 80 byte keys, you would be able to pack up to 24 keys plus their 25 pointers (assuming 4-byte-long integer pointers) into each bucket. You could then create an order 12 B+tree with buckets declared by the following code.

```
Global Const ORDER = 12
Global Const KEYS_PER_NODE = 2 * ORDER
Type BtreeNode
    Key(1 to KEYS_PER_NODE) As String * 80    ' Data key.
    Child(0 To KEYS_PER_NODE) As Integer       ' Child pointers.
End Type
```

To make Visual Basic read data as quickly as possible, a program should use the Get statement to read data one complete node at a time. If the program uses a

For loop to read the key and child data one item at a time, Visual Basic must access the disk separately for each item. This is much slower than reading the entire node's data all at once. In one test with a user-defined type that contained an array of 1000 items, it took almost 27 times as long to read the items one at a time as it took to read them all at once. The code below shows the good and bad ways to read the data for a node.

```
Dim i As Integer
Dim node As BtreeNode

    ' Get the data the slow way.
    For i = 1 To KEYS_PER_NODE
        Get #filenum, , node.Key(i)
    Next i
    For i = 0 To KEYS_PER_NODE
        Get #filenum, , node.Child(i)
    Next i

    ' Get the data the fast way.
    Get #filenum, , node
```

Node Caching

Every search through a B-tree starts at the root node. You can make searching faster if you always keep the root node loaded in memory. When you search for an item, you perform one less disk access. You still need to write the root node to disk any time it changes. Otherwise, if the program crashes after there has been a change, the B-tree will not be up to date.

You can also cache other B-tree nodes in memory. If you can keep all the children of the root node in memory, you will not need to read them from disk either. For a B-tree of order K, the root node will have between 1 and 2 * K keys and therefore will have between 2 and 2 * K + 1 children. That means you will have to cache up to 2 * K + 1 nodes.

A program can also cache nodes while traversing a B-tree. In a preorder traversal, for example, the program visits a node and then recursively visits its children. The program descends into one child. When it returns, it descends into the next. Each time it returns, the program must look at the parent node again to find the child to visit next. By caching the parent in memory, the program avoids the need to read it from disk again.

Recursion allows a program to automatically keep the nodes in memory without using a complicated caching scheme. Each call to the recursive traversal algorithm declares a local variable to hold the node while it is needed. When the recursive call returns, Visual Basic automatically frees this variable. The following code shows how you might implement this traversal algorithm in Visual Basic.

```
Private Sub PreorderPrint(node_index As Integer)
Dim i As Integer
Dim node As BtreeNode

    Get #filenum, node_index, node          ' Cache the node.
    Print node_index                        ' Visit this node.
    For i = 0 To KEYS_PER_NODE
        If node.Child(i) < 0 Then Exit For  ' Visit the children.
        PreorderPrint node.Child(i)         ' Visit this child.
    Next i
End Sub
```

A B+tree Database

Example program Bplus manages a B+tree database using two data files.
Custs.DAT contains customer data records. Custs.IDX holds the B+tree nodes.

Enter data in the Customer Record area, and click the Add button to add a
new item to the database. Enter a first name and a last name in the top part of
the form, and click Find to locate the corresponding record.

Figure 7.23 shows the program after finding the record for Rod Stephens.
The statistics at the bottom indicate that the data was found in record number
302 after only three disk accesses. The B+tree has height 3, holds 1303 data
records, and contains 118 buckets.

When you add a record or find an old one, program Bplus selects that record. If
you click the Remove button, the program removes the record from the database.

Figure 7.23 Program Bplus.

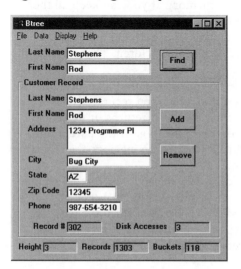

If you select the Display menu's Internal Nodes command, the program shows you the internal nodes in the tree. It displays the keys at each node indented to show the tree's internal structure.

The Display menu's Complete Tree command makes the program show the complete structure of the tree. Customer data is shown inside pointed brackets.

In addition to the usual name and address fields, the Bplus program's records also contain a NextGarbage field. The program uses NextGarbage to manage a linked list of the unused records in the file.

```
Type CustRecord
    LastName As String * 20
    FirstName As String * 20
    Address As String * 40
    City As String * 20
    State As String * 2
    Zip As String * 10
    Phone As String * 12
    NextGarbage As Long
End Type
```

```
' Size of the customer record.
Global Const CUST_SIZE = 20 + 20 + 40 + 20 + 2 + 10 + 12 + 4
```

The internal B+tree nodes contain keys used to locate customer data records. The key for a record will be the customer's last name padded with blanks to 20 characters, followed by a comma, followed by the customer's first name padded with blanks to 20 characters. For example, "Washington..........,George..............". This gives each key a total length of 41 characters.

Each internal node also stores pointers to child nodes in the tree. These pointers give the locations of customer data records in Custs.DAT. The nodes also include a variable NumKeys that indicates the number of keys in use.

This program reads and writes data in blocks of roughly 1024 bytes. If you assume K keys per bucket, each bucket will hold K keys of length 41 characters, K + 1 child pointers of length 4 bytes, and the 2 byte integer NumKeys. The buckets should be as large as possible while still fitting within 1024 bytes.

Solving the equation $41 * K + 4 * (K + 1) + 2 <= 1{,}024$ for K, you get $K <= 22.62$, so K should be 22. In this case the B+tree should have order 11 so it contains 22 keys per bucket. Each bucket occupies $41 * 22 + 4 * (22 + 1) + 2 = 996$ bytes. The following code shows how program Bplus defines its buckets.

```
Const KEY_SIZE = 41
Const ORDER = 11
Global Const KEYS_PER_NODE = 2 * ORDER
```

```
Type Bucket
    NumKeys As Integer
    Key(1 To KEYS_PER_NODE) As String * KEY_SIZE
    Child(0 To KEYS_PER_NODE) As Long
End Type
Global Const BUCKET_SIZE = 2 + _
    KEYS_PER_NODE * KEY_SIZE + _
    (KEYS_PER_NODE + 1) * 4
```

Program Bplus stores the B+tree buckets in file Custs.IDX. This file's first record contains header information that describes the current state of the B+tree. This includes the index of the root node, the current height of the tree, the index of the first garbage bucket in Custs.IDX, and the index of the first garbage data record in Custs.DAT.

To make reading and writing the header information easier, you can define another structure that has exactly the same size as the bucket structure but that contains the header information fields. The last field in the declaration is a string that fills this structure out so it has exactly the same size as the bucket structure.

```
Global Const HEADER_PADDING = BUCKET_SIZE - (7 * 4 + 2)

Type HeaderRecord
    NumBuckets As Long
    NumRecords As Long
    Root As Long
    NextTreeRecord As Long
    NextCustRecord As Long
    FirstTreeGarbage As Long
    FirstCustGarbage As Long
    Height As Integer
    Padding As String * HEADER_PADDING
End Type
```

When the program begins, it prompts you for a data directory. It then opens the B+tree data files Custs.DAT and Custs.IDX in that directory. If the files do not exist, the program creates them. Otherwise, it reads the tree's header information from Custs.IDX. It then reads the B+tree's root node and caches it in memory.

When the program descends into the tree to insert or delete an item, it caches the nodes it visits. As it recursively returns back up the tree, it may need these nodes again if there has been a bucket split, merge, or other node rearrangement. Because the program caches the nodes on the way down, they are available on the way back up.

Large bucket sizes make B+trees efficient, but it makes them harder to test manually. To make an order 11 B+tree grow to height 2, you would have to add 23 items to the database. To make it grow to height 3, you would need to add more than 250 additional items.

To make program Bplus easier to test, you might want to change the B+tree's order to 2. In file Bplus.BAS, comment out the line that sets the order to 11 and uncomment the line that makes the order 2.

```
'Const ORDER = 11
Const ORDER = 2
```

The Data menu's Create Data command allows you to create many data records quickly. Enter the number of records you want to create and the number the program should use to build the first item. The program then creates the records and inserts them into the B+tree. For example, if you tell the program to create 100 records starting from the value 200, the program creates entries for 200, 201, ... , 299 similar to this one:

```
FirstName:   First 0000200
LastName:    Last 0000200
Address:     Addr 0000200
City:        City 0000200
```

You can use these entries to experiment with a reasonably large B+tree.

Summary

Balanced trees allow a program to manipulate data efficiently. High-order B+trees are particularly useful for storing large databases on hard drives or other relatively slow storage devices. You can even use multiple B+trees to provide different indexes into the same large set of data.

Chapter 11, "Hashing," describes an alternative to balanced trees. Hashing allows even faster access to data under some circumstances, though it does not allow a program to perform such operations as listing records sequentially.

DECISION TREES

Many difficult real-world problems can be modeled using *decision trees*. Each node in the tree represents one step in the solution to the problem. Each branch in the tree represents a decision that leads to a more complete solution. Leaf nodes represent a complete solution. The goal is to find the "best" path through the tree from the root to a leaf while satisfying certain constraints. Exactly what the constraints are and what the "best" path means depends on the problem.

Decision trees are usually enormous. A decision tree for selecting a move in tic-tac-toe contains more than half a million nodes. Tic-tac-toe is a simple game, and many real-world problems are much more complicated. The corresponding decision trees may contain more nodes than there are atoms in the universe.

This chapter examines techniques you can use to search these huge trees. First, it examines *game trees*. Using tic-tac-toe as an example, it discusses ways to search game trees to find the best possible move.

The sections that follow describe ways to search more general decision trees. For the smallest trees, you can use *exhaustive searching* to examine every possible solution. For larger trees, *branch-and-bound techniques* allow you to find the best possible solution without searching the entire tree.

For even larger trees you must use a *heuristic*. The solution you find may not be the absolute best possible solution, but it should be good enough to be useful. Using heuristics, you can search practically any tree.

Finally, this chapter discusses several very difficult problems that you can try to solve using branch-and-bound and heuristic techniques. Many of these problems have important applications, and finding good solutions is critical.

Searching Game Trees

A strategy board game like chess, checkers, or tic-tac-toe can be modeled using a *game tree*. Each branch out of a node corresponds to a different move by one of the players. If a player has 30 possible moves at some point in the game, that node in the game tree will have 30 branches.

For example, in tic-tac-toe the root node corresponds to the initial, empty board position. The first player can place an X in any of the nine squares on the board. Corresponding to each of those nine moves is a branch leaving the root node. The nine nodes below these branches correspond to the nine different board positions where player X has chosen a square.

Once X has moved, O can pick any of the remaining eight squares. Corresponding to each of these moves is a branch leading out of the node representing the current board position. Figure 8.1 shows a small part of the tic-tac-toe game tree.

As you can see from Figure 8.1, the tic-tac-toe game tree grows extremely quickly. If the tree continued to grow like this, with each node in the tree having one less branch than its parent, the complete tree would have 9 * 8 * 7 ... * 1 = 362,880 leaves. There would be 362,880 paths through the tree corresponding to 362,880 possible games.

Actually, many of the possible nodes are missing from the tic-tac-toe game tree because they are forbidden by the rules of the game. In the first three moves, if X selects the upper left, upper center, and upper right squares, X wins and the game ends. The node representing this board position has no children because the game has ended. This game is shown in Figure 8.2.

Removing all the impossible nodes leaves about a quarter-million leaf nodes. This is still a pretty big tree, and searching it exhaustively still takes some time. For more complicated games like checkers, chess, or go, the game trees are enormous. If each player had only 16 options during each move in a chess game, the game tree would have more than 1 trillion nodes after each player had moved only five times. Some of the later sections in this chapter further explain searching these

Figure 8.1 Part of the tic-tac-toe game tree.

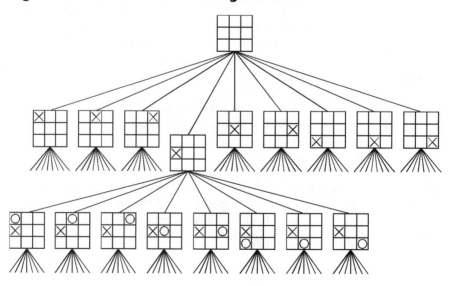

Figure 8.2 A game that ends early.

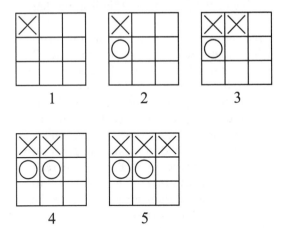

enormous game trees. The next section deals only with the relatively simple example of tic-tac-toe.

Minimax Searching

To begin searching a game tree, you need to be able to determine the *value* of a board position. In tic-tac-toe, X places a high value on board positions with three Xs in a row, because X wins those games. The O player places a low value on those board positions because player O loses those games.

For each player, you can assign one of four values to a particular board position. The value 4 means the board position will result in a win for this player. A value of 3 means it is not clear from the current board position who will eventually win. The value 2 means the board position will result in a draw (cat's game). Finally, the value 1 means the board position will result in a win for the other player.

To search the game tree exhaustively, you can use a *minimax* strategy. Here you try to *minimize* the *maximum* value your opponent can get from the current board position. You can do this by determining the maximum value the opponent can achieve for each of your possible moves. You then take the move that gives your opponent the smallest value.

Subroutine BoardValue shown later computes the value of a board position. This routine examines each possible move. For each move it recursively calls itself to see what the opponent's value for the new board position would be. It then selects the move that gives the opponent the smallest of those values.

To determine the value of a board position, BoardValue recursively calls itself until one of three things happens. First, it might find a position in which a player has won. In that case, it sets the value of the board position to 4, indicating that the player who just moved has won.

Second, BoardValue might find a position in which no player can move. The game is a draw, so the routine sets the value of the position to 2, indicating that the game is a tie.

Finally, the routine might reach a predetermined maximum depth of recursion. If it exceeds its allowed depth, BoardValue assigns the board position the value 3, indicating that it cannot tell who will win. The maximum depth of recursion stops the program from taking too long while searching the game tree. This is particularly important for more complicated games, like chess, where the program could search the game tree practically forever. The maximum depth can also set the program's skill level. The deeper into the tree the program can look, the better its moves will be.

Figure 8.3 shows a tic-tac-toe game tree near the end of a game. It is X's turn, and X has three possible moves. To select the best move for X, BoardValue recursively examines each of the three possible moves X can make. The first and third moves (the left and right branches in the tree) result in wins for player O, so those moves have value 4 for player O. The second possible move results in a draw, which has value 2 for player O. BoardValue picks the second move because it gives player O the smallest board value.

```
Private Sub BoardValue(best_move As Integer, best_value As Integer, _
    pl1 As Integer, pl2 As Integer, Depth As Integer)
Dim pl As Integer
Dim i As Integer
Dim good_i As Integer
```

Figure 8.3 The bottom of a game tree.

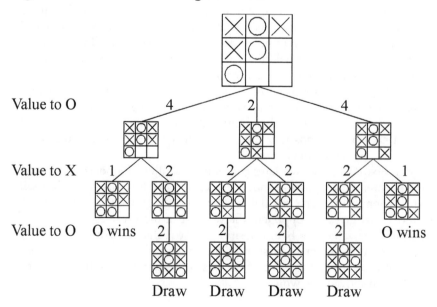

```
Dim good_value As Integer
Dim enemy_i As Integer
Dim enemy_value As Integer

    DoEvents        ' Don't be a CPU hog.

    ' If we are in too deep, we know nothing.
    If Depth >= SkillLevel Then
        best_value = VALUE_UNKNOWN
        Exit Sub
    End If

    ' If this board is finished, we know how we would do.
    pl = Winner()
    If pl <> PLAYER_NONE Then
        ' Convert the value for the winner pl
        ' into the value for player pl1.
        If pl = pl1 Then
            best_value = VALUE_WIN
        ElseIf pl = pl2 Then
            best_value = VALUE_LOSE
        Else
            best_value = VALUE_DRAW
        End If
        Exit Sub
    End If

    ' Try all the legal moves.
    good_i = -1
    good_value = VALUE_HIGH
    For i = 1 To NUM_SQUARES
        ' If the move is legal, try it.
        If Board(i) = PLAYER_NONE Then
            ' See what value this would give the opponent.
            If ShowTrials Then _
                MoveLabel.Caption = MoveLabel.Caption & Format$(i)

            ' Make the move.
            Board(i) = pl1
            BoardValue enemy_i, enemy_value, pl2, pl1, Depth + 1

            ' Unmake the move.
            Board(i) = PLAYER_NONE
            If ShowTrials Then _
```

```
        MoveLabel.Caption = Left$(MoveLabel.Caption, Depth)

        ' See if this is lower than the previous best.
        If enemy_value < good_value Then
            good_i = i
            good_value = enemy_value

            ' If we will win, things can get
            ' no better so take the move.
            If good_value <= VALUE_LOSE Then Exit For
        End If
    End If   ' End if Board(i) = PLAYER_NONE ...
Next i


    ' Translate the opponent's value into ours.
    If good_value = VALUE_WIN Then
        ' Opponent wins, we lose.
        best_value = VALUE_LOSE
    ElseIf enemy_value = VALUE_LOSE Then
        ' Opponent loses, we win.
        best_value = VALUE_WIN
    Else
        ' DRAW and UNKNOWN are the same for both players.
        best_value = good_value
    End If
    best_move = good_i
End Sub
```

Example program TicTac uses subroutine BoardValue to run a tic-tac-toe program. The bulk of the program manages interaction with the user. It draws the board, lets the user pick squares, sets options, and so forth.

The program's performance is much better if you do not activate the Options menu's Show Test Moves command. This option makes the program display each move it is considering. Constantly updating the display takes much longer than the actual game tree search.

Other commands in the Options menu allow you to play either X or O and to set the program's skill level (maximum depth of recursion). The first moves take much longer if the skill level is high.

Giving Up

Subroutine BoardValue has an interesting side effect. If the program finds two moves that are equally good, it takes the first one it finds. Usually this is fine, but it sometimes produces strange behavior. If the program can tell it will lose no matter what move it makes, it selects the first move it examines. Sometimes that move will seem silly to the human opponent. It may seem as if the computer has given up and is making a move at random. In a way that is true.

To see an example, run the TicTac program using skill level 3. Number the squares as shown in Figure 8.4. Begin by taking square 6. The program takes square 1. Take square 3, and the program takes square 9. Now when you take square 5 you threaten to win by taking either square 4 or square 7.

The computer can now search enough of the game tree to see that it will lose. In this situation, a human opponent would probably either move to block one of your possible wins or move to create two Os in a row and threaten a win. In a more complicated game like chess, a human opponent would try one of these strategies, hoping you do not yet see a way to force a win. You might make a mistake and give your opponent a chance.

The program, however, assumes you know as much as it does and that you also know you are about to win. Because no move will help it, the program picks the first move it examines, in this case square 2. This move seems silly because it does not block either of your possible wins and it does not threaten a win by the computer. It seems as if the computer has given up. This game is shown in Figure 8.5.

One way to prevent this behavior is to provide more distinctions between different board values. In the TicTac program, all losing board positions have the same value. You could give a position that loses in two moves a higher value than one that loses in one move. Then the program would select moves that would make the game continue as long as possible. You could also give a board position with two possible winning moves a higher score than a position with one winning move. Then the computer would move to block one of your possible wins.

Improving Game Tree Searching

If the only tool you had for searching game trees was minimax, searching large trees would be pretty hard. A game like chess is so complicated that a program could not hope to search more than a few levels of the tree. Fortunately, there are several tricks you can use for searching large game trees.

Precomputed Initial Moves and Responses

First, the program can store some initial moves chosen by game experts. You might decide that the tic-tac-toe program should take the center square if it moves first. That determines the first branch in the game tree, so the program can ignore

Figure 8.4 Tic-tac-toe board numbering.

1	2	3
4	5	6
7	8	9

Figure 8.5 Tic-tac-toe program giving up.

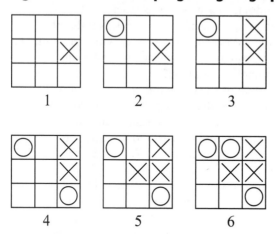

any paths that do not take this first branch. For tic-tac-toe this reduces the size of the tree by a factor of 1 / 9.

In fact, the program does not need to search the tree until its opponent has also made a move. Then both the computer and its opponent have selected branches, so the tree remaining is much smaller. It contains fewer than 7! = 5040 paths. By precomputing only one move, you reduce the size of the game tree from around a quarter-million paths to fewer than 5040.

Similarly, you can save responses to initial moves if the opponent moves first. The user has nine choices for a first move, so you need to store nine responses. Now the program does not need to search the game tree until the opponent moves twice and the computer moves once. Then the game tree holds fewer than 6! = 720 paths. By storing nine moves you reduce the size of the game tree enormously. This is an example of a space versus time trade-off. Using extra memory to store a few moves greatly reduces the time needed to search the game tree.

Example program TicTac2 uses 10 precomputed moves. Let the computer move first at skill level 9. Then do the same with program TicTac. You will see a tremendous difference in speed.

Commercial chess programs also begin with stored moves and responses commonly used by chess experts. These programs can make their first few moves extremely quickly. Once the game progresses beyond the stored responses, the program takes more time for each move.

Recognizing Important Patterns

Another way to improve game tree searches is to look for important patterns. When the program identifies one of these patterns, it can take specific action or it can alter the way in which it searches the tree.

During a chess game, players often arrange the pieces to protect each other. If the opponent captures a piece, the player can capture one of the opponent's pieces. Often that capture allows the opponent to capture another piece, and so forth. Sometimes the series of exchanges can involve quite a few pieces.

Some programs look for possible sequences of trades. If the program recognizes a trade, it temporarily breaks its limits on how far down the tree it can search so it can examine the sequence of trades to its end. This allows the computer to decide whether the exchange will be profitable. If the exchange takes place, the number of pieces remaining is also reduced, so searching the game tree becomes easier in the future.

Some chess programs also look for patterns such as castling moves, moves that threaten more than one of the opponent's pieces at the same time, moves that threaten the opponent's king or queen, and so forth.

Heuristics

In games more complicated than tic-tac-toe, it is almost never possible to search even a tiny fraction of the game tree. In these cases, you must use some sort of *heuristic* (pronounced "you-riss-tik"). A heuristic is an algorithm or rule of thumb that is likely, but not guaranteed, to produce a good result.

A common heuristic in chess is, "When ahead, trade mercilessly." If your opponent has lost more valuable pieces than you have, and if all else is equal, you should exchange pieces whenever possible as long as you do not lose on the deal. For example, if you can capture a knight but you will lose a knight in exchange, you should do so. By reducing the number of pieces remaining, you make the decision tree smaller and you make your relative strength advantage greater. This strategy does not guarantee that you will win the game, but it does improve your chances.

Another heuristic used in many strategy games is to assign different values to different parts of the board. In chess the squares nearest the center of the board are most valuable because pieces in those positions can attack a large part of the board. When the BoardValue subroutine calculates the value of a board position, it can give greater weight to pieces that hold these key squares.

Searching Other Decision Trees

Some of the techniques used to search game trees do not apply to more general decision trees. Many of these trees do not include a concept of players alternating moves, so minimax and precomputed moves make no sense. The following sections explain techniques you can use to search these other kinds of decision trees.

Branch and Bound

Branch and bound is a technique for *pruning* a decision tree so you do not need to consider all of the tree's branches. The general strategy is to keep track of bounds on the solutions discovered so far and on the solutions that are still possible. If you ever reach a point where the best solution so far is better than the best solution possible below a node, you can ignore all the paths below that node.

For example, suppose you have $100 million to spend and you can spend it on several possible investments. Each has a different cost and a different expected return. You must decide how to spend the money to get the greatest possible profit.

This sort of problem is called a *knapsack* problem. You have several items (investments) that you want to fit into a knapsack with a fixed size ($100 million). Each of the items has some cost (money) and a value (also money). You must find a selection of items that fits in the knapsack and gives the greatest possible total value.

You can model this problem using a decision tree. Each node in the tree represents a combination of items placed in the knapsack. Each branch represents the decision to put an item in the knapsack or to leave the item out. The left branch at the first node corresponds to spending money on the first investment. The right branch represents not paying for the first investment. Figure 8.6 shows a decision tree for four possible investments.

The decision tree for this problem is a complete binary tree of depth equal to the number of investments. Each leaf node corresponds to a complete selection of investments.

The size of this tree grows very quickly as the number of investments increases. For 10 possible investments, the tree holds $2^{10} = 1024$ leaf nodes. For 20 investments, the tree holds more than 1 million leaves. Searching every node in this tree is possible, but you do not have to add too many more investment choices to make the tree unreasonably large.

To use branch and bound, use an array to keep track of the items in the best solution you have found so far. Initialize the array so it does not contain any items. You can also use a variable to keep track of the value of this solution.

Figre 8.6 An investment decision tree.

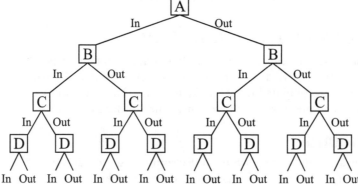

Initially this should be some small value so the first real solution considered will be an improvement.

While you search the decision tree, if you ever reach a point where the solution you are examining has no chance of improving enough to beat the current best solution, you can stop searching down that path in the tree. Also, if you ever reach a point where the selections cost more than $100 million, you can stop searching.

As a concrete example, suppose you can make any of the investments shown in Table 8.1. Figure 8.6 shows the corresponding decision tree. Some of these investment packages violate the problem's constraints. The leftmost path, for example, forces you to spend $178 million on all four choices.

Suppose you have started searching the tree shown in Figure 8.6. You have found that you could spend $97 million on options A and B for a profit of $23 million. This corresponds to the fourth leaf node from the left in Figure 8.6.

As you continue searching the tree, you come to the second node labeled C in Figure 8.6. This corresponds to investment packages that include option A, do not include option B, and may or may not include options C and D. At this point the package already costs $45 million for option A and produces a profit of $10 million.

The only remaining options are C and D. Together they can improve the solution by $12 million. The current solution has a value of $10 million, so the best possible solution below this node is worth at most $22 million. This is smaller than the $23 million solution you already found, so you do not need to continue down this path.

As the program moves through the tree, it does not need to continuously check to see if the partial solution it is considering is better than the best solution so far. If a partial solution is an improvement, the rightmost leaf node below that partial solution is also an improvement. That leaf represents the same combination of items as the partial solution with all other items excluded. This means the program needs to check for improved solutions only when it reaches a leaf node.

In fact, any leaf node the program reaches is *always* be an improved solution. If it were not, it would have been trimmed from the tree when the program considered the node's parent. At that point, moving to the leaf would reduce the total

Table 8.1 Possible Investments

Investment	Cost (Millions)	Profit (Millions)
A	45	10
B	52	13
C	46	8
D	35	4

value of the unassigned items to zero. If the value of the solution is not already larger than the best solution so far, the lower bound test stops the program from continuing to the leaf. Using this fact, the program can update the best solution whenever it reaches a leaf node.

The following code uses the upper- and lower-bound tests to implement the branch and bound algorithm.

```
' Total of unassigned profits.
Private unassigned_profit As Integer

Public NumItems As Integer
Public MaxItem As Integer

Type Item
    Cost As Integer
    Profit As Integer
End Type

Global Items() As Item
Global ToSpend As Integer
Global best_cost As Integer
Global best_profit As Integer

' True for the items in the best solution so far.
Public best_solution() As Boolean

' Solution we are testing.
Private test_solution() As Boolean
Private test_cost As Integer
Private test_profit As Integer

' Initialize variables and begin the search.
Public Sub Search(search_type As Integer)
Dim i As Integer

    ' Dimension the solution arrays.
    ReDim best_solution(0 To MaxItem)
    ReDim test_solution(0 To MaxItem)

    ' Initialize as if we are investing in nothing.
    NodesVisited = 0
    best_profit = 0
    best_cost = 0
    unassigned_profit = 0
```

```
        For i = 0 To MaxItem
            unassigned_profit = unassigned_profit + Items(i).Profit
        Next i
        test_profit = 0
        test_cost = 0

        ' Start the search with the item 0.
        BranchAndBound 0
End Sub

' Perform a branch and bound search starting with this item.
Public Sub BranchAndBound(item_num As Integer)
Dim i As Integer

        NodesVisited = NodesVisited + 1

        ' If this is a leaf node, it must be a better
        ' solution than we have so far or it would
        ' have been cut off earlier in the search.
        If item_num > MaxItem Then
            For i = 0 To MaxItem
                best_solution(i) = test_solution(i)
                best_profit = test_profit
                best_cost = test_cost
            Next i
            Exit Sub
        End If

        ' Otherwise descend down the child branches.
        ' First try including this item. Make sure it
        ' fits within the cost bound.
        If test_cost + Items(item_num).Cost <= ToSpend Then
            ' Add the item to the test solution.
            test_solution(item_num) = True
            test_cost = test_cost + Items(item_num).Cost
            test_profit = test_profit + Items(item_num).Profit
            unassigned_profit = unassigned_profit - Items(item_num).Profit

            ' Recursively see what the result might be.
            BranchAndBound item_num + 1

            ' Remove the item from the test solution.
            test_solution(item_num) = False
            test_cost = test_cost - Items(item_num).Cost
```

```
        test_profit = test_profit - Items(item_num).Profit
        unassigned_profit = unassigned_profit + Items(item_num).Profit
    End If


    ' Now try excluding the item. See if the
    ' remaining items have enough profit to make
    ' a path down this branch reach our lower bound.
    unassigned_profit = unassigned_profit - Items(item_num).Profit
    If test_profit + unassigned_profit > best_profit _
        Then BranchAndBound item_num + 1
    unassigned_profit = unassigned_profit + Items(item_num).Profit
End Sub
```

Example program BandB uses exhaustive search and branch-and-bound techniques to solve the knapsack problem. Enter maximum and minimum costs and values you want assigned to the items, as well as the number of items you want created. Then click the Randomize button to make the program generate the items.

Next use the option buttons at the bottom of the form to select either exhaustive search or branch and bound. When you click Go, the program uses the method you selected to find the best solution. The program displays the solution along with the number of nodes in the complete decision tree and the number of nodes the program actually visited. Figure 8.7 shows program BandB after solving a 20-item knapsack problem. Try small examples before you let the program run an exhaustive search on 20 items. A 90 megahertz Pentium can take 30 seconds or more to exhaustively search for a solution to the 20-item knapsack problem.

Branch-and-bound searches visit far fewer nodes than exhaustive searches. The decision tree for a 20-item knapsack problem contains 2,097,151 nodes. An exhaustive search will visit them all; branch and bound may visit only 1,500 or so.

Figure 8.7 Program BandB.

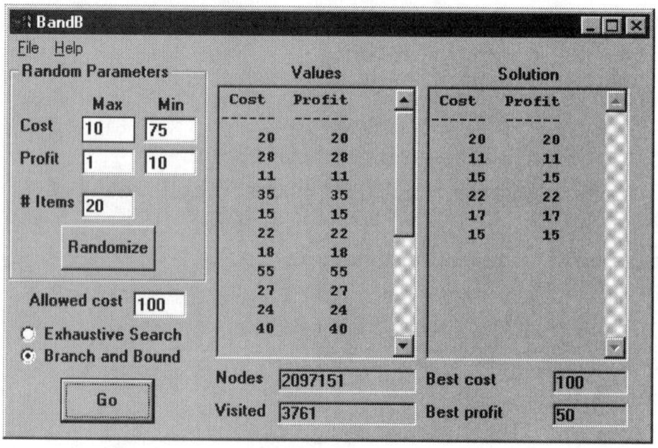

The number of nodes branch and bound visits depends on the exact data values. If the item costs are large, only a few items at a time will fit in a valid solution. Once several items are placed in the test solution, the remaining items are too expensive to consider, so much of the tree will be trimmed away.

On the other hand, if the items have small costs, many will fit in a valid solution, so the program must explore many valid combinations. Table 8.2 shows the number of nodes program BandB visited in a series of tests using different item costs. The program randomly generated 20 items, and the total allowed cost of the solution was 100.

Heuristics

Sometimes even branch-and-bound algorithms cannot search a decision tree completely. The decision tree for a 65-item knapsack problem holds more than $7 * 10^{19}$ nodes. If branch and bound visited only a tenth of 1 percent of those nodes, and if your computer could examine 1 million nodes per second, it would take you more than 2 million years to solve the problem. In problems where branch and bound is not fast enough, you can use a heuristic.

If the quality of the solution is not critical, the answer given by a heuristic may be good enough to be useful. In some cases, you may not know the input data with perfect accuracy. Then a good heuristic solution may be as valid as the theoretically "best" solution.

The previous example uses branch and bound to select investment opportunities. Investments are risky, however, and exact results are often not known ahead of time. You may not know the exact profit or even cost of some of the investments. In that case, an effective heuristic solution may be just as reliable as the best solution you can calculate exactly.

This section discusses heuristics that are useful for many difficult problems. Example program Heur demonstrates each of the heuristics. It also allows you to compare the heuristics to exhaustive search and branch and bound. Enter

Table 8.2 Nodes Visited by Exhaustive and Branch-and-Bound Searches

Average Item Cost	Exhaustive Search	Branch and Bound
60	2,097,151	203
50	2,097,151	520
40	2,097,151	1,322
30	2,097,151	4,269
20	2,097,151	13,286
10	2,097,151	40,589

information in the Parameters area to tell the program how to generate the test data. Select the algorithms you want to test, and click the Go button. The program displays the total cost and profit of the best solution found by each of the methods selected. It also ranks the solutions and displays the time required by each algorithm. Be sure to use branch and bound only on relatively small problems and exhaustive search only on the tiniest problems.

Figure 8.8 shows program Heur after solving a 20-item knapsack problem. The Fixed 1, Fixed 2, and No Changes 1 heuristics (all described shortly) gave the best heuristic solutions. Note that these solutions are not quite as good as the exact solution given by branch and bound.

Hill Climbing

A *hill-climbing* heuristic makes changes to the current solution to move as close as possible to the goal. The process is called hill climbing because it is like a lost hiker at night searching for the top of a mountain. Even if it is too dark to see far, the hiker can try to reach the mountain top by always moving uphill.

Of course, there is a chance the hiker will become stuck on a smaller hill and not make it all the way to the peak. This sort of problem can also occur when using hill-climbing heuristics. The algorithm may find a solution that seems good locally, but that is not the best solution possible.

In the knapsack problem, the goal is to pick a set of items with total cost no more than an allowed limit and with a large total value. A hill-climbing heuristic for this problem would select the item that gives the largest profit at each step. That moves the solution closer to the goal of selecting a large profit.

The program starts by adding the item with the largest profit to the solution. It then adds the item with the next largest profit that still fits within the remaining

Figure 8.8 Program Heur.

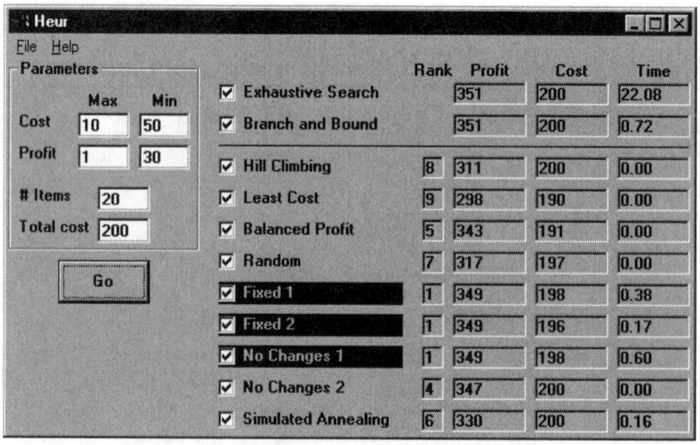

cost allowance. It continues adding the item with the next largest profit until no more items fit within the allowance.

For the investments shown in Table 8.3, the program first selects option A because it has the largest profit at $9 million. Next the program picks option C because it has the next largest profit at $8 million. At this point $93 million of the $100 million allowance is spent, and the program cannot afford any other options. The solution produced by the heuristic includes items A and C, has a cost of $93 million, and gives a profit of $17 million.

The hill-climbing heuristic fills the knapsack very quickly. If the items are initially sorted in order of decreasing profit, this is an O(N) algorithm. The program simply moves through the list, adding each item if there is room. Even if the list is not sorted, this is only an $O(N^2)$ algorithm. This is much better than the $O(2^N)$ steps required for an exhaustive search of every node in the tree. For 20 items, this heuristic uses around 400 steps, compared to a few thousand for branch and bound and more than 2 million for an exhaustive search.

```
Public Sub HillClimbing()
Dim i As Integer
Dim j As Integer
Dim big_value As Integer
Dim big_j As Integer

    ' Repeatedly pass through the list looking for
    ' the remaining item with the largest profit
    ' that will fit within the cost bounds.
    For i = 1 To NumItems
        big_value = 0
        big_j = -1
        For j = 1 To NumItems
            ' Make sure it is not already in the
            ' solution.
```

Table 8.3 Possible Investments

Investment	Cost	Return	Profit
A	63	72	9
B	35	42	7
C	30	38	8
D	27	34	7
E	23	26	3

```
        If (Not test_solution(j)) And _
            (test_cost + Items(j).Cost <= ToSpend) And _
            (big_value < Items(j).Profit) _
        Then
              big_value = Items(j).Profit
              big_j = j
        End If
    Next j


    ' Stop when we cannot find another item
    ' that fits.
    If big_j < 0 Then Exit For

    test_cost = test_cost + Items(big_j).Cost
    test_solution(big_j) = True
    test_profit = test_profit + Items(big_j).Profit
  Next i
End Sub
```

Least-Cost

A strategy that, in a sense, is the opposite of hill climbing is *least-cost*. Instead of moving the solution as far as possible toward the goal at each step, you move the *cost* of the solution as little as possible toward the constraint. In the knapsack example, you add the item with the lowest cost to the solution at each step.

This strategy will fit as many items as possible into the solution. If all items have roughly the same profit, this will be a good solution. If an expensive option has a large profit, this strategy may miss the option and not produce the best possible result.

For the investments shown in Table 8.3, a least-cost strategy starts by adding option E to the solution at a cost of $23 million. Next it selects D at $27 million, and then C at $30 million. At this point the algorithm has spent $80 million of the $100 million allowance, and it cannot afford any other investments.

This solution has a cost of $80 million and gives a profit of $18 million. This is $1 million better than the hill-climbing heuristic's solution, but least-cost does not always do better than hill climbing. Which gives the better solution depends on the exact data values.

The program structure for the least-cost heuristic is almost identical to that of the hill-climbing heuristic. The only difference is in selecting the next item to add to the test solution. The least-cost heuristic chooses the item that has the lowest cost; the hill-climbing method picks the item with the largest profit. Because the two methods are so similar, they have the same run time. If the items are properly sorted, both algorithms each run in $O(N)$ time. Even with the items arranged randomly, both can run in $O(N^2)$ time.

Because the Visual Basic code for the two heuristics is so similar, only the lines where the new item is selected are shown here.

```
If (Not test_solution(j)) And _
    (test_cost + Items(j).Cost <= ToSpend) And _
    (small_cost > Items(j).Cost) _
Then
    small_cost = Items(j).Cost
    small_j = j
End If
```

Balanced Profit

The hill-climbing strategy does not take into account the cost of the items being added to the solution. It selects items with large profits, even if they also have large costs. The least-cost strategy does not take into account the profit returned by an item. It selects items with small costs, even if they have small profits.

A *balanced profit* heuristic compares both the profit and cost of the items to decide which items to select. At each step the heuristic selects the item with the largest profit-to-cost ratio.

Table 8.4 shows the same data as Table 8.3 with an additional profit/cost column. The balanced profit strategy first picks option C because it has the highest profit/cost ratio at 0.27. Next it adds D to the solution with a ratio of 0.26, and B with a ratio of 0.20. At this point, the heuristic has spent $92 million of the $100 million and can fit no more items in the solution.

This solution has a cost of $92 million and gives a profit of $22 million. This is $4 million better than the least-cost solution and $5 million better than the hill-climbing solution. In this case, it is also the best possible solution and would be found by either exhaustive search or branch and bound. Balanced profit is still a heuristic, so it does not always find the best possible solution. It often finds better solutions than hill climbing and least-cost, but it does not always.

Table 8.4 Possible Investments with Profit/Cost Ratio

Investment	Cost	Return	Profit	Profit/Cost
A	63	72	9	0.14
B	35	42	7	0.20
C	30	38	8	0.27
D	27	34	7	0.26
E	23	26	3	0.13

In structure the balanced profit heuristic is almost identical to the hill-climbing and least-cost heuristics. The only difference is in the way the heuristic selects the next item to add to the solution.

```
If (Not test_solution(j)) And _
    (test_cost + Items(j).Cost <= ToSpend) And _
    (good_ratio < Items(j).Profit / CDbl (Items(j).Cost)) _
Then
    good_ratio = Items(j).Profit / CDbl (Items(j).Cost)
    good_j = j
End If
```

Random Searching

A *random search* is exactly what it sounds like. At each step the algorithm adds a randomly chosen item that fits within the cost bounds. This kind of search is also called a *Monte Carlo search* or a *Monte Carlo simulation*.

Because a randomly selected solution is unlikely to give the best possible solution, you must repeat the search many times to get a reasonable result. Even though it may seem that the odds of finding a good solution are small, this method sometimes produces surprisingly good results. Depending on the data values and the number of random solutions examined, this heuristic often does better than hill climbing or least-cost.

Random searching also has the advantage of being easy to understand and implement. Sometimes it is hard to decide how to create hill-climbing, least-cost, or balanced profit heuristics for a problem. It is always easy to generate solutions at random. Even for extremely complicated problems, random search provides an easy heuristic.

The RandomSearch subroutine in program Heur uses function AddToSolution to add a random item to the solution. This function returns the value True if it can find an item that fits within the cost allowance and False otherwise. RandomSearch calls AddToSolution until no more items fit within the allowance.

```
Public Sub RandomSearch()
Dim num_trials As Integer
Dim trial As Integer
Dim i As Integer

    ' Make several trials and keep the best.
    num_trials = NumItems    ' Use N trials.
    For trial = 1 To num_trials
        ' Make random selections until no more items fit.
        Do While AddToSolution()
            ' All the work is done by AddToSolution.
        Loop
```

```
    ' See if this solution is an improvement.
    If test_profit > best_profit Then
        best_profit = test_profit
        best_cost = test_cost
        For i = 1 To NumItems
            best_solution(i) = test_solution(i)
        Next i
    End If

    ' Reset the test solution for the next trial.
    test_profit = 0
    test_cost = 0
    For i = 1 To NumItems
        test_solution(i) = False
    Next i
    Next trial
End Sub


Private Function AddToSolution() As Boolean
Dim num_left As Integer
Dim j As Integer
Dim selection As Integer

    ' See how many items remain that will fit within
    ' the cost bound.
    num_left = 0
    For j = 1 To NumItems
        If (Not test_solution(j)) And _
            (test_cost + Items(j).Cost <= ToSpend) _
                Then num_left = num_left + 1
    Next j

    ' Stop when we cannot find another item that fits.
    If num_left < 1 Then
        AddToSolution = False
        Exit Function
    End If

    ' Pick one at random.
    selection = Int((num_left) * Rnd + 1)

    ' Find the randomly chosen item.
    For j = 1 To NumItems
        If (Not test_solution(j)) And _
```

```
                (test_cost + Items(j).Cost <= ToSpend) _
            Then
                    selection = selection - 1
                    If selection < 1 Then Exit For
            End If
        Next j

        test_profit = test_profit + Items(j).Profit
        test_cost = test_cost + Items(j).Cost
        test_solution(j) = True

        AddToSolution = True
End Function
```

Incremental Improvement

Another strategy is to start with a random solution and then make *incremental improvements*. Starting with a randomly generated solution, the program makes a random change. If the new solution is an improvement, the program makes the change permanent and continues testing other random changes. If the change does not improve the solution, the program discards it and tries again.

It is particularly easy to generate random changes for the knapsack problem. Given a test solution, the program simply picks an item in the solution at random and removes it from the current solution. It then randomly adds items back into the solution until no more fit. If the removed item has a very large cost, the program may be able to add more than one new item to the solution.

Like a random search, this heuristic is easy to understand and implement. It may be hard to design hill-climbing, least-cost, and balanced profit heuristics for a difficult problem, but it is usually easy to write an incremental improvement heuristic.

When to Stop

There are several good ways to decide when to stop making random changes. First, you can perform a fixed number of changes. For an N-item problem, you might make N or N^2 random changes before stopping.

In program Heur the MakeChangesFixed subroutine uses this approach. It makes a certain number of random changes to a number of different trial solutions.

```
Public Sub MakeChangesFixed(K As Integer, num_trials As Integer, _
    num_changes As Integer)
Dim trial As Integer
Dim change As Integer
Dim i As Integer
Dim removal As Integer
```

```
For trial = 1 To num_trials
    ' Find a random test solution to use as a
    ' starting point.
    Do While AddToSolution()
        ' All the work is done by AddToSolution.
    Loop

    ' Start with this as the trial solution.
    trial_profit = test_profit
    trial_cost = test_cost
    For i = 1 To NumItems
        trial_solution(i) = test_solution(i)
    Next i

    For change = 1 To num_changes
            ' Remove K random items.
        For removal = 1 To K
            RemoveFromSolution
        Next removal

        ' Add back as many random items as
        ' will fit.
        Do While AddToSolution()
            ' All the work is done by AddToSolution.
        Loop

        ' If this improves the trial, save it.
        ' Otherwise reset the trial to the
        ' previous value.
        If test_profit > trial_profit Then
                ' Save the improvement.
            trial_profit = test_profit
            trial_cost = test_cost
            For i = 1 To NumItems
                trial_solution(i) = test_solution(i)
            Next i
        Else
                ' Reset the trial.
            test_profit = trial_profit
            test_cost = trial_cost
            For i = 1 To NumItems
                test_solution(i) = trial_solution(i)
            Next i
        End If
```

```
        Next change

        ' If this trial is better than the best
        ' solution so far, save it.
        If trial_profit > best_profit Then
            best_profit = trial_profit
            best_cost = trial_cost
            For i = 1 To NumItems
                best_solution(i) = trial_solution(i)
            Next i
        End If

        ' Reset the test solution for the
        ' next trial.
        test_profit = 0
        test_cost = 0
        For i = 1 To NumItems
            test_solution(i) = False
        Next i
    Next trial
End Sub

Private Sub RemoveFromSolution()
Dim num_in_solution As Integer
Dim j As Integer
Dim selection As Integer

    ' See how many items are in the solution.
    num_in_solution = 0
    For j = 1 To NumItems
        If test_solution(j) Then num_in_solution = num_in_solution + 1
    Next j
    If num_in_solution < 1 Then Exit Sub

    ' Pick one at random.
    selection = Int((num_in_solution) * Rnd + 1)

    ' Find the randomly chosen item.
    For j = 1 To NumItems
        If test_solution(j) Then
            selection = selection - 1
            If selection < 1 Then Exit For
        End If
    Next j
```

```
' Remove the item from the solution.
test_profit = test_profit - Items(j).Profit
test_cost = test_cost - Items(j).Cost
test_solution(j) = False
End Sub
```

Another strategy is to make changes until there is no improvement for several consecutive changes. For an N-item problem, the program could make changes until it saw no improvement for N changes in a row.

In program Heur the MakeChangesNoChange subroutine follows this strategy. It runs trials until a certain number of consecutive trials show no improvement over the best solution it has found so far. For each trial it makes random changes to the trial solution until it finds no improvement in a certain number of random changes in a row.

```
Public Sub MakeChangesNoChange(K As Integer, max_bad_trials As
Integer, _
    max_non_changes As Integer)
Dim i As Integer
Dim removal As Integer
Dim bad_trials As Integer    ' # consecutive ineffective trials.
Dim non_changes As Integer   ' # consecutive ineffective-changes.

    ' Repeat trials until we have max_bad_trials
    ' runs in a row without an improvement.
    bad_trials = 0
    Do
        ' Find a random test solution to use as a
        ' starting point.
        Do While AddToSolution()
            ' All the work is done by AddToSolution.
        Loop

        ' Start with this as the trial solution.
        trial_profit = test_profit
        trial_cost = test_cost
        For i = 1 To NumItems
            trial_solution(i) = test_solution(i)
        Next i

        ' Repeat until we try max_non_changes in
        ' a row without an improvement.
        non_changes = 0
        Do While non_changes < max_non_changes
            ' Remove K random items.
```

```
For removal = 1 To K
    RemoveFromSolution
Next removal

' Add back as many random items as will fit.
Do While AddToSolution()
        ' All the work is done by
        ' AddToSolution.
Loop

' If this improves the trial, save it.
' Otherwise reset the trial to the
' previous value.
If test_profit > trial_profit Then
    ' Save the improvement.
    trial_profit = test_profit
    trial_cost = test_cost
    For i = 1 To NumItems
        trial_solution(i) = test_solution(i)
    Next i
    non_changes = 0 ' This was a good change.
Else
    ' Reset the trial.
    test_profit = trial_profit
    test_cost = trial_cost
    For i = 1 To NumItems
        test_solution(i) = trial_solution(i)
    Next i
    non_changes = non_changes + 1    ' Bad change.
End If
Loop    ' Continue trying random changes.

' If this trial is better than the best
' solution so far, save it.
If trial_profit > best_profit Then
    best_profit = trial_profit
    best_cost = trial_cost
    For i = 1 To NumItems
        best_solution(i) = trial_solution(i)
    Next i
    bad_trials = 0 ' This was a good trial.
Else
    bad_trials = bad_trials + 1 ' Bad trial.
```

```
    End If

    ' Reset the test solution for the
    ' next trial.
    test_profit = 0
    test_cost = 0
    For i = 1 To NumItems
        test_solution(i) = False
    Next i
    Loop While bad_trials < max_bad_trials
End Sub
```

Local Optima

If a program randomly replaces a single item in a test solution, it may find a solution that it cannot improve but that is also not the best possible solution. For example, consider the investments shown in Table 8.5.

Suppose the algorithm randomly selects items A and B for its initial solution. This solution has a cost of $90 million and a profit of $17 million.

If the program removes either A or B, the solution will still have a cost large enough that the program can add only one new item to the solution. Because items A and B have the largest profits, replacing them with one of the other items will decrease the total profit. Randomly removing one item from this solution will never result in an improvement.

The best solution contains items C, D, and E. It has a total cost of $98 million and a total profit of $18 million. To find this solution the algorithm would need to remove both items A and B from the solution at the same time and then add new items.

This kind of solution, where small changes cannot improve the solution, is called a *local optimum*. There are two ways to stop a program from becoming stuck in a local optimum so it can search for the *global optimum*.

Table 8.5 Possible Investments

Investment	Cost	Return	Profit
A	47	56	9
B	43	51	8
C	35	40	5
D	32	39	7
E	31	37	6

First, you can modify the program so that it removes more than one item when it makes its random changes. If the program removes two random items, it can find the correct solution to this example. For larger problems, however, removing two items may not be enough. The program may need to remove three, four, or even more items at a time.

An easier alternative is to run more trials starting with different initial solutions. Some of the starting solutions may lead to local optima, but one should allow the program to reach a global optimum.

Example program Heur demonstrates four incremental improvement strategies. Method "Fixed 1" makes N trials. During each trial it selects a random solution and tries to improve the solution 2 * N times by randomly removing a single item.

Method "Fixed 2" makes only one trial. It selects a random solution and tries to improve the solution 10 * N times by randomly removing two items.

Heuristic "No Changes 1" runs trials until it finds no improvements in N successive trials. During each trial the program selects a random solution and then tries to improve it by randomly removing one item until it finds no improvement during N consecutive changes.

Heuristic "No Changes 2" runs a single trial. It selects a random solution and tries to improve it by randomly removing two items until it finds no improvement during N successive changes.

The names and descriptions of the heuristics are summarized in Table 8.6.

Simulated Annealing

The method of *simulated annealing* was inspired by thermodynamics. When a metal is annealed, it is heated to a high temperature. While the metal is hot, the molecules in the metal move rapidly in relation to each other. If the metal cools slowly, the molecules start to line up to form crystals. These crystals are the minimum energy arrangements of the molecules they contain.

As the metal slowly cools, crystals that are adjacent to each other merge. The molecules in one crystal temporarily leave their minimum energy arrangement to line up with the molecules in the other crystal. The new larger crystal will have lower

Table 8.6 Incremental Improvement Strategies

Name	# Trials	# Changes	Items Removed per Change
Fixed 1	N	2 * N	1
Fixed 2	1	10 * N	2
No Changes 1	No improvement in N trials	No improvement in N changes	1
No Changes 2	1	No improvement in N changes	2

energy than the sum of the energies of the two smaller crystals. If the metal cools slowly enough, the crystals become huge. The final arrangement of molecules represents a very low energy state, and the metal is quite hard.

Starting from a high energy state, the molecules eventually reach a very low energy state. On the way to the final solution, they pass through many local minimums in energy. Every combination of crystals represents a local minimum. Only by temporarily raising the energy of the system can the crystals combine so the molecules fall into an even lower energy state.

The method of simulated annealing uses an analogous method to find the best solution to a problem. As the program works its way toward a solution, it may become stuck in a local optimum. To prevent this, the program occasionally makes a random change to the solution, even though the change does not immediately improve the result. This may allow the program to break free of a local optimum and find a better solution later. If the change does not lead to a better solution, the program will probably undo the change in a short time anyway.

To prevent the program from making these modifications forever, the algorithm changes the probability of making random changes over time. The probability of making one of these changes is given by $P = 1 / Exp(E / (k * T))$. Here E is the amount of "energy" being added to the system, k is a constant chosen to fit the problem, and T is a "temperature" variable.

Initially, T should be fairly large so $P = 1 / Exp(E / (k * T))$ is reasonably large. Otherwise, random changes will never occur. Over time the value of T should slowly shrink so the probability of random changes grows smaller. Once the simulation has reached the point where it cannot find any more changes that give an improvement, and T is small enough that random changes are rare, the algorithm can stop.

For a knapsack problem, the "energy" E is the amount by which the profit of the solution is decreased by the change. For instance, if you remove an item that has profit $10 million and replace it with an item having profit $7 million, the energy added to the system will be 3.

Notice that if E is large, the probability $P = 1 / Exp(E / (k * T))$ is small. This makes the chances of a large change occurring smaller than the chances of a small change occurring.

The simulated annealing algorithm in program Heur sets the constant k to the difference between the largest and smallest profits of the possible investment choices. It initially sets T to 0.75. Each time the program introduces a certain number of random changes, it multiplies T by 0.95 to make it smaller.

```
Public Sub AnnealTrial(K As Integer, max_non_changes As Integer, _
    max_back_slips As Integer)
Const TFACTOR = 0.95

Dim i As Integer
Dim non_changes As Integer
```

```
Dim t As Double
Dim max_profit As Integer
Dim min_profit As Integer
Dim doit As Boolean
Dim back_slips As Integer

    ' See what items have the largest and
    ' smallest profits.
    max_profit = Items(1).Profit
    min_profit = max_profit
    For i = 2 To NumItems
        If max_profit < Items(i).Profit Then max_profit =
Items(i).Profit
        If min_profit > Items(i).Profit Then min_profit =
Items(i).Profit
    Next i


    t = 0.75 * (max_profit - min_profit)
    back_slips = 0

    ' Find a random test solution to use as a
    ' starting point.
    Do While AddToSolution()
        ' All the work is done by AddToSolution.
    Loop

    ' Start with this as the trial solution.
    best_profit = test_profit
    best_cost = test_cost
    For i = 1 To NumItems
        best_solution(i) = test_solution(i)
    Next i

    ' Repeat until we try max_non_changes in a row
    ' without an improvement.
    non_changes = 0
    Do While non_changes < max_non_changes
        ' Remove a random item.
        For i = 1 To K
            RemoveFromSolution
        Next i

        ' Add back as many random items as will fit.
        Do While AddToSolution()
```

```
                    ' All the work is done by AddToSolution.
        Loop

        ' If this improves the trial, save it.
        ' Otherwise reset the trial to the previous
        ' value.
        If test_profit > best_profit Then
            doit = True
        ElseIf test_profit < best_profit Then
            doit = (Rnd < Exp((test_profit - best_profit) / t))
            back_slips = back_slips + 1
            If back_slips > max_back_slips Then
                back_slips = 0
                t = t * TFACTOR
            End If
        Else
            doit = False
        End If
        If doit Then
            ' Save the improvement.
            best_profit = test_profit
            best_cost = test_cost
            For i = 1 To NumItems
                best_solution(i) = test_solution(i)
            Next i
            non_changes = 0 ' This was a good change.
        Else
            ' Reset the trial.
            test_profit = best_profit
            test_cost = best_cost
            For i = 1 To NumItems
                test_solution(i) = best_solution(i)
            Next i
            non_changes = non_changes + 1 ' Bad change.
        End If
    Loop    ' Continue trying random changes.
End Sub
```

Comparing Heuristics

Different heuristics behave differently for different problems. For the knapsack problem, the balanced profit heuristic does quite well, considering how simple it is. Incremental improvement strategies usually do comparably, but they take much longer for large problems. For problems other than the knapsack problem, the best heuristic may be one of the others or it may be a heuristic not discussed here.

Heuristics are much faster than branch-and-bound searching. Some, like hill climbing, least-cost, and balanced profit, are extremely fast because they consider only one possible solution. These algorithms are so fast that it makes sense to run them all and take the best solution found by any of them. This still does not guarantee you will find the best solution possible, but it gives you some confidence that the solution is fairly good.

Other Hard Problems

Many problems other than the knapsack problem are extremely difficult to solve. Most have no known polynomial time solutions. In other words, there are no algorithms for solving these problems that run in $O(N^C)$ time for any constant C, not even $O(N^{1,000})$.

The following sections briefly describe a few of these problems. They also explain in general terms why each problem is difficult and how large the most straightforward decision tree for the problem might be. You may want to test the branch-and-bound and heuristic techniques on a few of them.

Satisfiability (SAT)

Given a logical statement like "(A And Not B) Or C," is there an assignment of true and false values to the variables A, B, and C that makes the statement true? In this example it is easy to see that the statement is true if A = true, B = false, and C = false. For more complicated statements involving hundreds of variables, it can be hard to tell whether there is a way to make the statement true.

Using a method similar to the one used to solve the knapsack problem, you can build a satisfiability decision tree. Each branch in the tree represents a decision to set a variable to either true or false. For example, the left branch leaving the root corresponds to setting the first variable's value to true.

If there are N variables in the logical statement, the decision tree is a binary tree of height N + 1. This tree has 2^N leaf nodes, each representing a different assignment of the values true and false to the variables.

In the knapsack problem you can use branch and bound to avoid searching much of the tree. An assignment of values for the satisfiability problem, however, makes the statement either true or false. It does not give you a partial solution you can use to trim paths out of the tree.

You also cannot use heuristics to find approximate solutions for the satisfiability problem. Any assignment of values produced by a heuristic will make the statement either true or false. There is no such thing as an approximate solution in logic.

With weakened branch-and-bound techniques and no useful heuristics, the satisfiability problem is generally quite difficult to solve. You can solve only extremely small satisfiability problems.

The Partition Problem

Given a collection of items with values X_1, X_2,..., X_N, is there a way to divide the items into two groups so the total value of the items in each group is the same? For example, if the items have values 3, 4, 5, and 6, you can divide them into the groups {3, 6} and {4, 5}, both having total value 9.

To model this problem as a tree, let the branches correspond to placing an item in one of the two groups. The left branch out of the root node corresponds to placing the first item in the first group. The right branch corresponds to placing the first item in the second group.

If there are N items, the decision tree is a binary tree of height N + 1. It contains 2^N leaf nodes and 2^{N+1} nodes altogether. Each leaf node corresponds to a complete assignment of the items into the two groups.

Branch-and-bound techniques do work with this problem. As you examine partial solutions in the tree, keep track of the amount by which the two groups of items differ. If you ever reach a branch where placing all of the remaining items in the smaller group cannot make that group at least as big as the larger, you do not need to continue down that branch of the tree.

As is the case for the satisfiability problem, you cannot generate approximate solutions for the partition problem. An assignment of items will create two groups that either do or do not have the same total values. This means that heuristics like the ones used for the knapsack problem will not help you find an even partition.

The partition problem can be generalized to: Given a collection of items with values X_1, X_2,..., X_N, in what way should they be divided into two groups so the total values of the groups are as close as possible?

This problem is more difficult to solve exactly than the partition problem. After all, if there were an easy way to solve this problem, you could use that method to solve the partition problem. You would simply find the groups that are closest in total value and see if their values are equal.

You can use a branch-and-bound technique similar to the one used in the partition problem to avoid searching the entire tree. You can also use heuristics to provide approximate solutions. One method would be to examine the items in decreasing order of value, placing the next item in the smaller of the two groups. It would also be easy to use random search, incremental improvement, or simulated annealing to find approximate solutions to this version of the problem.

The Hamiltonian Path Problem (HAM)

Given a network, a *Hamiltonian path* is a path that visits every node in the network exactly once and then returns to its starting point. Figure 8.9 shows a small network with a Hamiltonian path drawn in bold.

The Hamiltonian path problem is this: Given a network, does the network contain a Hamiltonian path?

Figure 8.9 A Hamiltonian path.

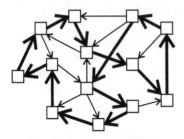

Because a Hamiltonian path visits every node in the network, you do not need to decide which nodes to visit. You need to determine only the order in which they should be visited to produce a Hamiltonian path.

To model this problem as a tree, let branches correspond to selecting the node to visit next. The root node has N branches corresponding to starting the path at each of the N nodes. The nodes beneath the root each have N – 1 branches, one for each of the remaining N – 1 nodes that you could visit next. Nodes in the next level of the tree have N – 2 branches, and so forth. The bottom of the tree contains N! leaf nodes corresponding to the N! possible orderings of the nodes. The tree holds a total of O(N!) nodes.

Every leaf corresponds to a Hamiltonian path, but some of the leaves may not be reachable for every network. If two nodes in the network are not connected, the branches in the tree that correspond to moving from one node to the other will be missing. That reduces the number of paths through the tree and thus the number of leaf nodes.

As is the case for the satisfiability and partition problems, you cannot generate partial or approximate solutions for Hamiltonian paths. Either a path is Hamiltonian or it is not. This means branch-and-bound techniques and heuristics will not help you locate a Hamiltonian path. To make matters worse, the Hamiltonian path decision tree contains O(N!) nodes. This is far more than the $O(2^N)$ nodes contained in the satisfiability and partition decision trees. For example, 2^{20} is roughly $1 * 10^6$ while 20! is about $2.4 * 10^{18}$—more than a million million times as large. Because this tree is so large, you will be able to search it for only the smallest Hamiltonian path problems.

The Traveling Salesman Problem (TSP)

The traveling salesman problem is closely related to the Hamiltonian path problem. The traveling salesman problem is this: What is the shortest Hamiltonian path through a network?

This problem has a similar relationship to the Hamiltonian path problem as the generalized partition problem has to the partition problem. The first problem asks if a solution exists. The second asks what the best approximate solution is. If there were an easy solution to the second problem, you could use it to find a solution to the first problem.

Typically, the traveling salesman problem arises only for networks that contain many Hamiltonian paths. In a common example, a salesman must visit several customer locations using the shortest possible route. In a normal street network, there are paths between any two points in the network, so any ordering of the customer locations gives a Hamiltonian path. The problem is to find the shortest.

Like the Hamiltonian path problem, the decision tree for this problem contains O(N!) nodes. Like the generalized partition problem, you can use branch-and-bound techniques to trim the tree and make finding a solution possible for problems of modest size.

There are also several good incremental improvement heuristics for the traveling salesman problem. The *2-opt* improvement strategy examines pairs of links within the path. The program checks whether there would be an improvement if the links were removed and replaced with two new links that keep the path connected. Figure 8.10 shows how the path would change if links X_1 and X_2 were replaced with links Y_1 and Y_2. Similar improvement strategies consider replacing three or even more links at one time.

Typically, you would repeat this sort of improvement many times or until you had tried all of the possible pairs of links in the path. Once you had improved the path as much as you could, you would save the results and start over again with a different randomly chosen initial path. By trying many different initial paths, you would have a good chance of finding a reasonably short path.

The Firehouse Problem

Given a network, a number F, and a distance D, is there a way to place F firehouses on nodes in the network in such a way that no node in the network is more than distance D away from the nearest firehouse?

You can model this problem with a decision tree where each branch determines where in the network a particular firehouse will be located. The root node will have N branches corresponding to placing the first firehouse at one of the network's

Figure 8.10 Improving a Hamiltonian path using 2-opt.

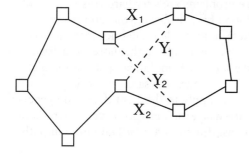

N nodes. Nodes at the next level of the tree will have N – 1 branches corresponding to placing the second firehouse at each of the remaining N – 1 nodes. If there are F firehouses, this tree will have height F and will contain $O(N^F)$ nodes. It will have N * (N – 1) *...* (N – F) leaf nodes corresponding to the possible locations where you could place the firehouses.

Like the satisfiability, partitioning, and Hamiltonian path problems, this problem asks a yes or no question. That means you cannot use partial or approximate solutions while examining the decision tree.

You may be able to use some sort of branch-and-bound technique if you can decide early on that certain firehouse placements will not lead to good solutions. For example, you gain nothing by placing a new firehouse between two other closely spaced firehouses. If all of the nodes within distance D of the new firehouse are already within distance D of another firehouse, you should place the new firehouse somewhere else. Making this sort of calculation is quite time-consuming, however, so the firehouse problem is still very difficult to solve.

Just as the partitioning and Hamiltonian path problems have generalizations, so does the firehouse problem. The generalized question is this: Given a network and a number F, at what nodes should you place F firehouses so the greatest distance between any node and a firehouse is minimized?

As was the case in the other generalized problems, you can use branch-and-bound techniques and heuristics to find partial and approximate solutions to this problem. That makes examining the decision tree a bit easier. While the decision tree is still enormous, you can at least find approximate solutions, even if they may not be the best solutions possible.

Summary of Hard Problems

While reading the previous sections, you may have noticed that many of these problems come in pairs. The first version of a problem asks, "Is there a solution of a certain quality to this problem?" The second, more general question asks, "What is the best solution to this problem?"

Both of the related problems use the same decision trees. In the first problem, you examine the decision tree until you find any solution. Because these problems do not have partial or approximate solutions, you generally cannot use branch and bound or heuristics to greatly reduce your work. Usually, only a few paths through the decision tree lead to a solution, so these problems are very hard to solve.

While solving the more generalized version of the problem, you can often use partial solutions to apply branch-and-bound techniques. This does not make it easier to find a solution to the problem, so it will not help in solving the more specialized problem. For example, it is harder to find the *shortest* Hamiltonian path through a network than it is to find *any* Hamiltonian path through the same network.

On the other hand, these questions usually apply to different data. You generally ask if a network *has* a Hamiltonian path when the network is very sparse and it is hard to tell if there is such a path. You ask for the *shortest* Hamiltonian path when the network is dense and there are many such paths. In that case, it is easy to find partial solutions, and branch-and-bound techniques may simplify the problem greatly.

Summary

You can use decision trees to model many difficult problems. Finding the best solution to the problem corresponds to finding the best path through the tree. Unfortunately, for many interesting problems the decision trees are huge, so you can search these trees exhaustively for only the smallest problems.

Branch-and-bound techniques allow you to prune many of the branches from some decision trees. This lets you solve much larger problems exactly.

For the largest problems, however, even branch and bound cannot help. In these cases, you must use heuristics to generate approximate solutions. Using techniques such as random search and incremental improvement, you may be able to find a good solution, though you may never know if it is the best solution possible.

SORTING

Sorting is one of the most heavily studied topics in computer algorithms for several reasons. First, sorting is a common task in many computer applications. Almost any list of data is more meaningful when it is sorted in some way. Frequently data must be sorted in several different ways.

Second, many sorting algorithms make interesting programming examples. They demonstrate important techniques such as partial ordering, recursion, merging of lists, and storing binary trees in an array.

Each sorting algorithm has different advantages and disadvantages. The performance of different algorithms depends on the data's type, number, initial arrangement, size, and values. It is important to understand several algorithms so you can pick the one that best fits a particular situation.

Finally, sorting is one of the few problems with exact theoretical performance bounds. It can be shown that any sorting algorithm that uses comparisons must take at least $O(N * \log(N))$ time. Several algorithms actually achieve this time, so you know they are optimal in the sense of Big O notation. There are even a few algorithms that use methods other than comparisons to achieve times faster than $O(N * \log(N))$.

General Considerations

This chapter describes several sorting algorithms that behave differently under different circumstances. For example, bubblesort is faster than quicksort when the items being sorted are already mostly in sorted order, but it is slower if the items are arranged randomly.

The peculiarities of each algorithm are described in the section that discusses the algorithm. Before discussing the specific algorithms, this chapter begins by discussing some issues that affect all sorting algorithms.

Index Tables

As a program sorts data items, it rearranges them in some kind of data structure. Depending on what the items are, this may be fast or slow. Moving an integer to a new position in an array is fast. Moving a user-defined data structure to a new position might be much slower. If the data structure is an employee record containing thousands of bytes of data, copying one data item to another may take quite some time.

One trick for improving performance while sorting large objects is to place the key data fields used for sorting in an *index table*. This table contains the keys for the records plus indexes into another array that stores the actual data. You can sort the index table without ever moving the large data records. For example, suppose you want to sort employee records defined by the following structure.

```
Type Employee
    ID As Integer
    LastName As String
    FirstName As String
    <lots more stuff>
        :
End Type
```

```
' Allocate the records.
Dim EmployeeData(1 To 10000)
```

To sort the employees by ID number, create an index table that contains the records' ID values and indexes. An entry's index tells which record in the EmployeeData array holds the corresponding data.

```
Type IdIndex
    ID As Integer
    Index As Integer
End Type
```

```
' The index table.
Dim IdIndexData(1 To 10000)
```

Initialize the index table so the first entry's index points to the first data record, the second points to the second data record, and so forth.

```
For i = 1 To 10000
    IdIndexData(i).ID = EmployeeData(i).ID
    IdIndexData(i).Index = i
Next i
```

Next, sort the index table by ID. When you finish, the Index field in each IdIndexData entry indicates the corresponding data record. For example, the first data record in the sorted list is EmployeeData(IdIndexData(1).Index). Figure 9.1 shows the relationship between the index and data records before and after sorting.

Figure 9.1 Sorting with an index table.

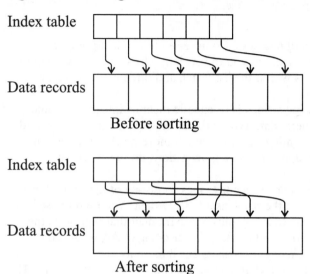

To sort the data in more than one order, create several different index tables and manage them separately. In this example, you might keep a separate index table ordering employees by last name. This is similar to the way threads can order lists in multiple ways, as described in Chapter 2, "Lists." When you add or remove a record, you must update each of the index tables separately.

Keep in mind that index tables take up extra memory. If you create an index table for every field in the data records, you will more than double the amount of memory used.

Key Combination and Compression

Sometimes a program can store and operate on a list's keys in a combined or compressed form. To sort a list of employees by their first and last names, a program could *combine* the two name fields by concatenating them into one key. This would make comparisons simpler and faster. Notice the differences between the following two code fragments that compare two employee records.

```
' Using separate keys:
If emp1.LastName > emp2.LastName Or _
    (emp1.LastName = emp2.LastName And _
        And emp1.FirstName > emp2.FirstName) Then
    DoSomething
```

```
' Using a combined key:
If emp1.CombinedName > emp2.CombinedName Then
    DoSomething
```

You can also sometimes *compress* keys. Compressed keys take up less space, making index tables smaller. This allows you to sort larger lists without running out of memory, makes moving items within the list faster, and often makes comparing the items faster as well.

One method for compressing strings is to encode them as integers or some other numeric data type. Numeric data types take up less space than strings, and the computer can compare two numeric values much more quickly than it can compare two strings. Of course, normal string operations do not work on numeric encodings.

For example, suppose you want to encode strings consisting of uppercase letters. You can think of each character in the string as a base 27 digit. You need to use base 27 because you need to represent 26 letters plus one extra digit that represents the end of a word. Without an end-of-word marker, the encoding of AA would come after the encoding of B because AA has two digits but B has only one.

The base 27 encoding of a three-character string is 27^2 * (first letter – A + 1) + 27 * (second letter – A + 1) + (third letter – A + 1). If the string has fewer than three characters, use 0 instead of (the letter – A + 1). For example, the encoding of FOX is:

```
27² * (F - A + 1) + 27 * (O - A + 1) + (X - A + 1) = 4803
```

The encoding of NO is:

```
27² * (N - A + 1) + 27 * (O - A + 1) + (0) = 10,611
```

Notice that 10,611 is greater than 4803. This makes sense because NO > FOX.

Using similar techniques you can encode strings of 6 uppercase letters in a long integer and strings with 10 letters in a double. The following two subroutines convert strings into doubles and back:

```
Const STRING_BASE = 27
Const ASC_A = 65          ' ASCII code for "A".
' Convert a string into a double encoding.
'
' full_len is the full length the string should have.
' We need it if the string is short (e.g. "AX" as a
' three character string).
Function StringToDbl (txt As String, full_len As Integer) As Double
Dim strlen As Integer
Dim i As Integer
Dim value As Double
Dim ch As String * 1
```

```
    strlen = Len(txt)
    If strlen > full_len Then strlen = full_len

    value = 0#
    For i = 1 To strlen
        ch = Mid$(txt, i, 1)
        value = value * STRING_BASE + Asc(ch) - ASC_A + 1
    Next i

    For i = strlen + 1 To full_len
        value = value * STRING_BASE
    Next i

    StringToDbl = value
End Function

' Turn a double string encoding back into a string.
Function DblToString (ByVal value As Double) As String
Dim strlen As Integer
Dim i As Integer
Dim txt As String
Dim power As Integer
Dim ch As Integer
Dim new_value As Double

    txt = ""
    Do While value > 0
        new_value = Int(value / STRING_BASE)
        ch = value - new_value * STRING_BASE
        If ch <> 0 Then txt = Chr$(ch + ASC_A - 1) + txt
        value = new_value
    Loop

    DblToString = txt
End Function
```

Example program Encode allows you to create a list of random strings and sort them using numeric encodings. The program uses all the encodings possible so you can compare the results. For example, if you tell the program to create strings of length 10, the program sorts the list using string and double encodings.

Table 9.1 shows the times required by program Encode to sort 2000 strings of different lengths on a 90 megahertz Pentium. Notice that the results are similar for each type of encoding. It takes about the same amount of time to sort 2000 doubles whether they represent 3-letter strings or 10-letter strings.

Table 9.1 Time in seconds to Sort 2,000 Strings Using Different Encodings

String length	3	6	10	11
String	5.99	6.10	6.09	6.15
Double	4.01	4.01	4.01	
Long	3.95	3.96		
Integer	3.79			

You can also encode strings containing characters other than capital letters. You could encode a string allowing uppercase letters and digits using a string base of 37 instead of 27. A maps to 1, B to 2, ... , Z to 26, 0 to 27, ... , and 9 to 36. The string AH7 would be encoded as $37^2 * 1 + 37 * 8 + 35 = 1700$.

Of course, with a larger string base, the longest string you could encode in an integer, long, or double data type is shorter. With a base of 37, you can encode 2 characters in an integer and 5 characters in a long, and you can still encode 10 characters in a double.

Example Programs

To make comparing different sorting algorithms easy, example program Sort demonstrates most of the algorithms described in this chapter. Sort allows you to specify the number of items to sort, the maximum value of the items, and whether the list should begin sorted, sorted backward, or randomly arranged. The program creates a list of random long integers and sorts it using the algorithm you select. Be sure to start with small lists until you know how long your computer will take. This is particularly important for the slower algorithms insertionsort, linked list insertionsort, selectionsort, and bubblesort.

Several of the algorithms move large chunks of memory all at once. For example, insertionsort moves items in a list so it can insert a new item in the middle. Using Visual Basic alone, a program must use a For loop to move the items. The following code shows how insertionsort moves the items List(j) through List(max_sorted) to make room for a new item in position List(j).

```
For k = max_sorted To j Step -1
    List(k + 1) = List(k)
Next k
List(j) = next_num
```

The Windows Application Programmer's Interface (API) includes two functions that make large memory moves like this much faster. Programs written in 16-bit Visual Basic 4 can use the hmemcpy function. Programs written in 32-bit Visual Basic 4 or Visual Basic 5 can use the RtlMoveMemory function. Both functions take as parameters the address to which the memory should be copied, the address from which it should be copied, and the number of bytes to copy. The following code shows how to declare these functions in a .BAS module:

```
#If Win16 Then
    Declare Sub MemCopy Lib "Kernel" Alias _
        "hmemcpy" (dest As Any, src As Any, _
        ByVal numbytes As Long)
#Else
    Declare Sub MemCopy Lib "kernel32" Alias _
        "RtlMoveMemory" (dest As Any, src As Any, _
        ByVal numbytes As Long)
#End If
```

The next code fragment shows how insertionsort can use these functions to copy memory. This code performs the same task as the For loop shown earlier, but it is much faster.

```
If max_sorted >= j Then _
    MemCopy List(j + 1), List(j), _
        Len(next_num) * (max_sorted - j + 1)
List(j) = next_num
```

Example program FastSort is similar to program Sort, but it uses MemCopy to make some of the algorithms faster. In FastSort the algorithms that use MemCopy are highlighted in blue.

Selectionsort

Selectionsort is a simple $O(N^2)$ algorithm. The idea is to search the list for the smallest item. Then swap that item with the one at the top of the list. Next find the smallest remaining item, and swap it with the second item. Continue swapping items until every item has been swapped to its final sorted position.

```
Public Sub Selectionsort(List() As Long, min As Long, max As Long)
Dim i As Long
Dim j As Long
Dim best_value As Long
Dim best_j As Long

    For i = min To max - 1
        ' Find the smallest remaining item.
        best_value = List(i)
        best_j = i
        For j = i + 1 To max
            If List(j) < best_value Then
```

```
            best_value = List(j)
            best_j = j
        End If
    Next j

    ' Swap it into position.
    List(best_j) = List(i)
    List(i) = best_value
  Next i
End Sub
```

While looking for the Ith smallest item, the algorithm must examine each of the N – I items that have not yet been swapped to their final positions. The algorithm takes time N + (N - 1) + (N - 2) +...+ 1, or $O(N^2)$ time.

Selectionsort performs quite well on random and sorted lists, but it does slightly worse when the list starts sorted backward. While it is looking for the smallest item in the list, selectionsort executes these lines of code:

```
If list(j) < best_value Then
    best_value = list(j)
    best_j = j
End If
```

If the list begins in reverse sorted order, the condition list(j) < best_value is true much of the time. During the first pass through the list, for example, it will be true for every item because each item is smaller than the one before. The algorithm will execute the lines of code within the If statement many times, and that slows the algorithm down slightly.

This is not the fastest algorithm described in this chapter, but it is extremely simple. Not only does that make it easy to implement and debug, it also makes selectionsort fast for small problems. Many of the other algorithms are so complicated they are slower at sorting very small lists.

Unsorting

Some programs need to perform the opposite of sorting. Given a list of items, the program needs to arrange them randomly. Randomizing a list is simple using an algorithm somewhat similar to selectionsort.

For each position in the list, the algorithm randomly selects an item to go in that position. It considers only the items that have not yet been placed in a previously considered position. It then swaps the selected item with the item that is currently in the position.

```
Public Sub Unsort(List() As Long, min As Long, max As Long)
Dim i As Long
Dim pos As Long
```

```
Dim tmp As Long

    For i = min To max - 1
        pos = Int((max - i + 1) * Rnd + i)
        tmp = List(pos)
        List(pos) = List(i)
        List(i) = tmp
    Next i
End Sub
```

Because this algorithm fills each position in the array once, it is an O(N) algorithm.

It is not too hard to show that the probability of any given item ending up in any position is 1 / N. Because any item could end up in any position with equal probability, the algorithm generates a truly random arrangement of the items.

This result depends on the fact that the random number generator is a good source of randomness. Visual Basic's Rnd function works reasonably well under most circumstances. You should be certain that your program uses the Randomize statement at some point to initialize Rnd. Otherwise, Rnd will produce the same series of "random" values every time you run the program.

Note that it does not matter to the algorithm how the items are initially arranged. If you have a program that must repeatedly randomize a list of items, it need not sort the items first.

Example program Unsort uses this algorithm to randomize a sorted list. Enter the number of items you want randomized, and click the Go button. The program displays the original sorted list of numbers and the randomized version.

Insertionsort

Insertionsort is another O(N²) algorithm. The idea is to build a new, sorted list by considering each item in the original list in turn. As the algorithm considers each item, it looks through the growing sorted list to see where the new item belongs. It then inserts the new item into its correct position in the list.

```
Public Sub Insertionsort(List() As Long, min As Long, max As Long)
Dim i As Long
Dim j As Long
Dim k As Long
Dim max_sorted As Long
Dim next_num As Long

    max_sorted = min - 1
    For i = min To max
        ' This is the number we are inserting.
        next_num = List(i)
```

```
    ' See where it belongs in the list.
    For j = min To max_sorted
        If List(j) >= next_num Then Exit For
    Next j

    ' Bump the bigger sorted numbers down to make
    ' room for the new number.
    For k = max_sorted To j Step -1
        List(k + 1) = List(k)
    Next k

    ' Insert the new number.
    List(j) = next_num

    ' Increment the count of the sorted items.
    max_sorted = max_sorted + 1
    Next i
End Sub
```

For each item in the original list, the algorithm might have to examine all the items that have been sorted. This will happen, for example, if the items were in sorted order in the original list. In that case, the algorithm places each new item at the end of the growing sorted list.

The total number of steps executed will be $1 + 2 + 3 + ... + (N - 1)$, which is $O(N^2)$. This is not very efficient compared to the theoretical $O(N * log(N))$ possible for algorithms that sort by comparisons. In fact, this algorithm is not even as fast as other $O(N^2)$ algorithms like selectionsort.

This insertionsort algorithm spends a great deal of time moving items so it can insert a new item in the middle of the sorted list. Using the MemCopy API function to do this makes the algorithm more than twice as fast.

The algorithm also spends a lot of time searching for the new item's correct position. Chapter 10, "Searching," describes several algorithms for searching sorted lists. Using the interpolation search algorithm described in Chapter 10 makes insertionsort much faster. Chapter 10 describes interpolation search in detail, so it is not explained here.

Program FastSort uses both of these techniques to improve insertionsort's performance. Using MemCopy and interpolation search, this version is more than 25 times faster than the previous version.

Insertion with Linked Lists

You can use a variation of insertionsort to sort items stored in a linked list instead of an array. The algorithm searches through the growing linked list for the position where the new item belongs. It then uses linked list operations to insert the new item.

```
Public Sub LinkInsertionSort(ListTop As ListCell)
Dim new_top As New ListCell
Dim old_top As ListCell
Dim cell As ListCell
Dim after_me As ListCell
Dim nxt As ListCell

    Set old_top = ListTop.NextCell
    Do While Not (old_top Is Nothing)
        Set cell = old_top
        Set old_top = old_top.NextCell

        ' See where cell belongs.
        Set after_me = new_top
        Do
            Set nxt = after_me.NextCell
            If nxt Is Nothing Then Exit Do
            If nxt.Value >= cell.Value Then Exit Do
            Set after_me = nxt
        Loop

        ' Insert after after_me.
        Set after_me.NextCell = cell
        Set cell.NextCell = nxt
    Loop
    Set ListTop.NextCell = new_top.NextCell
End Sub
```

As the algorithm considers each item, it might have to compare the item to every item in the sorted list. This makes the algorithm $O(N^2)$ in this worst case.

The best case for this algorithm occurs when the original list starts sorted in reverse order. Then each new item considered is smaller than the one before, so the algorithm places it at the beginning of the sorted list. The algorithm needs to compare the item to only one other, so in the best case the algorithm has $O(N)$ time.

In the average case, the algorithm will have to search about half way through the sorted list to find an item's correct location. The algorithm executes roughly $1 + 1 + 2 + 2 + ... + N/2$, or $O(N^2)$ steps.

The improved array-based insertionsort using MemCopy and interpolation search is much faster than the linked list version. The linked list version is better only if your program already stores the items in a linked list.

Insertion with linked lists has the advantage of moving only object pointers instead of complete data records. If the items are large data structures, it may be quicker to move pointers rather than to recopy whole records whenever an item must be moved.

Bubblesort

Bubblesort is an algorithm designed to sort lists that are already in mostly sorted order. If the list begins completely sorted, the algorithm runs in $O(N)$ time and is extremely fast. If some of the items are out of order, the algorithm runs more slowly. When the items start in random order, the algorithm runs in $O(N^2)$ time. For that reason it is extremely important to be certain the items are mostly in sorted order before using bubblesort.

Bubblesort scans through the list until it finds two adjacent items that are out of order. It swaps them and continues. The algorithm repeats this process until no more items are out of order.

In the example shown in Figure 9.2, the algorithm first finds that items 6 and 3 are out of order so it swaps them. During the next pass, the algorithm notices that items 5 and 3 are out of order, so it swaps them. In the next pass it swaps items 4 and 3. After one more pass through the array, the algorithm finds that there are no more items out of order, so it stops.

During bubblesort passes, you can follow an item that begins below its final position in the array, like item 3 in Figure 9.2. During each pass the item moves one position closer to its final correct position. The item moves toward the top of the array like a bubble moving toward the top of a glass of water. This bubbling effect is what gives bubblesort its name.

You can make several refinements to this algorithm. First, if you watch an item that begins above rather than below its correct position, you see a picture very different from Figure 9.2. In Figure 9.3 the algorithm first notices that item 6 and item 3 are out of order, so it swaps them. The algorithm then continues its pass through the array and notices that items 6 and 4 are now out of order, so it swaps them, too. The algorithm next swaps items 6 and 5, and item 6 is in its final correct position.

Figure 9.2 Bubbling an item up.

1	1	1	1
2	2	2	2
4	4	4	3
5	5	3	4
6	3	5	5
3	6	6	6
7	7	7	7
8	8	8	8

Figure 9.3 Bubbling an item down.

1	1
2	2
6	3
3	4
4	5
5	6
7	7
8	8

During downward passes through the array, items that need to move up move only one position. Items that need to move down, however, move many positions. You can use this fact to make the first refinement to the bubblesort algorithm. If you alternate downward and upward passes through the array, items will be able to move quickly both upward and downward.

During downward passes, the largest item that is out of order will be moved into its final position. During upward passes, the smallest item that is out of order will be moved into its final position. If there are M items out of order in the list, the algorithm will need at most M passes upward and downward through the array to put all the items in order. If there are N items in the list, the algorithm will need N steps per pass through the list. That makes the total run time for this algorithm O(M * N).

If the list is initially randomly arranged, a large fraction of the items will be out of order. The number M will be on the order of N, so the run time O(M * N) becomes $O(N^2)$.

The next refinement is to hold items in a temporary variable while they undergo multiple swaps. In the example shown in Figure 9.3, item 6 is swapped three times in a row. Instead of performing three separate swaps, the program can hold the value 6 in a temporary variable until it finds the item's new location. This can save the algorithm many steps when items are being moved long distances through the array.

One last refinement is in bounding the passes through the array. After a pass through the array, the last items swapped mark the last part of the array that could be out of order. In a downward pass, for example, the largest item that was out of order is moved to its final position. Because no larger items will need to be moved later, the algorithm can start its next upward pass at this position. It can also end downward passes here.

Similarly, when the algorithm makes an upward pass through the list, it can adjust the position in the list where it starts the next downward pass and ends future upward passes.

The Visual Basic implementation of bubblesort uses variables min and max to indicate the first and last items that might be out of order in the list. As the algorithm makes passes through the list, it updates these variables to indicate where the last swaps took place.

```
Public Sub Bubblesort(List() As Long, ByVal min As Long, ByVal max As Long)
Dim last_swap As Long
Dim i As Long
Dim j As Long
Dim tmp As Long

    ' Repeat until we are done.
    Do While min < max
        ' Bubble up.
        last_swap = min - 1
        ' For i = min + 1 To max.
        i = min + 1
        Do While i <= max
            ' Find a bubble.
            If List(i - 1) > List(i) Then
                ' See where to drop the bubble.
                tmp = List(i - 1)
                j = i
                Do
                    List(j - 1) = List(j)
                    j = j + 1
                    If j > max Then Exit Do
                Loop While List(j) < tmp
                List(j - 1) = tmp
                last_swap = j - 1
                i = j + 1
            Else
                i = i + 1
            End If
        Loop
        ' Update max.
        max = last_swap - 1

        ' Bubble down.
```

```
last_swap = max + 1
 ' For i = max - 1 To min Step -1.
i = max - 1
Do While i >= min
     ' Find a bubble.
    If List(i + 1) < List(i) Then
        ' See where to drop the bubble.
        tmp = List(i + 1)
        j = i
        Do
            List(j + 1) = List(j)
            j = j - 1
            If j < min Then Exit Do
        Loop While List(j) > tmp
        List(j + 1) = tmp
        last_swap = j + 1
        i = j - 1
    Else
        i = i - 1
    End If
Loop
 ' Update min.
min = last_swap + 1
    Loop
End Sub
```

To properly test bubblesort using program Sort, check the Sorted box in the Initial Ordering area. Enter a number of items in the # Unsorted field. When you click the Go button, the program creates a list, sorts it, and then swaps some random pairs of items to give the list some unsorted items. For example, if you enter 10 in the # Unsorted field, the program switches 5 pairs of numbers, so 10 items are out of order.

For the second enhancement to the original algorithm, the program holds an item in a temporary variable while moving it many positions. The process is even faster if the program uses the MemCopy API function. The bubblesort algorithm demonstrated by program FastSort uses MemCopy to sort items 50 to 75 times faster than the version used by program Sort.

Table 9.2 shows the times required by a 90 megahertz Pentium to bubblesort 2000 items where the original list was sorted in varying degrees. The table shows that bubblesort performs well only when the list begins mostly sorted. The quicksort algorithm described later in this chapter can sort the same list of 2000 items in about 0.12 seconds, no matter how the list is initially ordered. Bubblesort can beat this time only when the list is initially around 97 percent correctly sorted.

Table 9.2 Times to Bubblesort 2,000 Items

% Sorted	50	60	70	80	90	95	96	97	98	99	99.5
Time (seconds)	1.85	1.44	1.06	0.71	0.37	0.19	0.13	0.10	0.07	0.04	0.03

Despite the fact that bubblesort is slower than many other algorithms, it still has uses. Bubblesort is often fastest if the list being sorted begins in almost sorted order. If a program manages a list that is initially sorted and is modified incrementally, bubblesort may be the best choice.

Quicksort

Quicksort is a recursive algorithm that uses a divide-and-conquer technique. While the list of items to be sorted is at least a certain minimum size, quicksort divides it into two sublists. It then recursively calls itself to sort the two sublists.

The initial version of quicksort discussed here is quite simple. If the algorithm is called with a sublist containing zero or one item, the sublist is already sorted, so the subroutine ends.

Otherwise, the routine picks an item in the list to use as a dividing point to break the list into two smaller sublists. It moves items that are smaller than the dividing item into the first sublist. It places the other items in the second sublist. It then recursively calls itself to sort the two sublists.

```
Public Sub QuickSort(List() As Long, ByVal min As Integer, _
    ByVal max As Integer)
Dim med_value As Long
Dim hi As Integer
Dim lo As Integer

    ' If there is 1 (or 0) element, this sublist is done.
    If min >= max Then Exit Sub

    ' Pick a value to be the dividing value.
    med_value = list(min)
    lo = min
    hi = max
    Do
        ' Look down from hi for a value < med_value.
        Do While list(hi) >= med_value
            hi = hi - 1
            If hi <= lo Then Exit Do
        Loop
        If hi <= lo Then
```

```
                list(lo) = med_value
                Exit Do
           End If
            ' Swap the lo and hi values.
           list(lo) = list(hi)

            ' Look up from lo for a value >= med_value.
           lo = lo + 1
           Do While list(lo) < med_value
                lo = lo + 1
                If lo >= hi Then Exit Do
           Loop
           If lo >= hi Then
                lo = hi
                list(hi) = med_value
                Exit Do
           End If
            ' Swap the lo and hi values.
           list(hi) = list(lo)
     Loop

      ' Recursively sort the two sublists.
     QuickSort list(), min, lo - 1
     QuickSort list(), lo + 1, max
End Sub
```

There are a couple of important points worth mentioning about this version of the algorithm. First, the dividing item med_value is not included in either sublist. That means the two sublists together contain one less item than the original list. Because the total number of items considered grows smaller, the algorithm must eventually finish.

This algorithm uses the first item in its list as the dividing item. Ideally this value will belong somewhere in the middle of the list so the two sublists will be of about equal size. If the items are initially in sorted order, however, the item is the smallest item present. The algorithm will place no items in the first sublist and all of the items in the second sublist. The algorithm would take a path of execution like the one shown in Figure 9.4.

In this case, each call to the subroutine requires $O(N)$ steps to move all the items into the second sublist. Because the algorithm must recursively call itself a total of $N - 1$ times, the run time is $O(N^2)$, which is no improvement on the algorithms already examined. Even worse is the fact that the recursion is $N - 1$ levels deep. For large lists the great depth of recursion will exhaust the stack and crash the program.

There are many ways the program might select the dividing item. It could use the item currently in the middle of the list. This item would probably be a good

Figure 9.4 Quicksort on a sorted list.

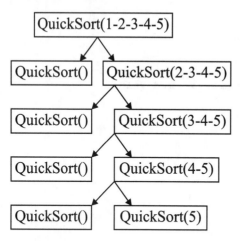

choice, but the program might be unlucky and the item could be one of the largest or smallest in the list. That would make one sublist much larger than the other and, if there were many unlucky choices, would give $O(N^2)$ performance and deep recursion.

Another strategy is to look through the list, compute the median of the values, and use that as the dividing value. This would work well, but it would require a lot of additional effort. An $O(N)$ pass through the list will not change the total theoretical run time, but it would hurt the overall performance.

A third strategy is to look at the first, last, and middle items and pick whichever value is between the other two. This method has the advantage of being quick because you need to look at only three items. The item selected is guaranteed not to be the absolute largest or smallest item in the list, and it will probably be somewhere near the middle.

A final strategy, and the one used by the Sort program, is to select the dividing item from the list randomly. The item selected will probably be a good choice. Even if it is not, the next time the algorithm divides the list it will probably make a better choice. The chance of the algorithm making a bad choice every time is extremely small.

An interesting fact about this method is that it turns "a small chance of bad run time always" into "always a small chance of bad run time." This rather confusing statement is explained in the following paragraphs.

With the earlier methods of selecting a dividing point, there is a small chance that the list will be arranged in a way that will produce $O(N^2)$ run time. While the odds of the list starting in such a bad arrangement are very small, if you did encounter such an arrangement, you would definitely experience $O(N^2)$ run time, no matter what. That is what "a small chance of bad run time always" means.

By selecting the dividing point randomly, the initial arrangement of the items makes no difference to the performance of the algorithm. There is a small chance of selecting a bad item, but the odds of selecting a bad item every time are extremely small. That is what "always a small chance of bad run time" means. No matter how the list is initially arranged, there is a very small chance that the algorithm will give $O(N^2)$ performance.

There is still one situation that gives all of these methods trouble. If there are very few *distinct* values in the list, the algorithm places many identical values in the same sublist each time it is called. If every item in the list has the value 1, for instance, the algorithm follows the sequence of execution shown in Figure 9.5. This sequence causes $O(N^2)$ performance and deep recursion.

The same sort of behavior occurs if there are many duplicates of more than one value. If a list of 10,000 items contains only values between 1 and 10, the algorithm will quickly divide the list into sublists that each contain only one value.

The easiest way to handle this problem is to ignore it. If you know the data does not have such an unusual distribution, there is no problem. If the data does cover only a small number of values, you should consider a different sorting algorithm. Countingsort and bucketsort, described later in this chapter, are extremely fast at sorting lists where the range of the data values is small.

You can make one final improvement to quicksort. Like many of the other more complicated algorithms described in this chapter, quicksort is not the fastest algorithm for sorting very small lists. Due to its simplicity, selectionsort is faster at sorting a dozen or so items.

You can improve the performance of quicksort by stopping recursion before the sublists are empty and using selectionsort to finish the job. Table 9.3 shows times required by a 90 megahertz Pentium to quicksort 20,000 items, stopping the

Figure 9.5 Quicksort on a list of ones.

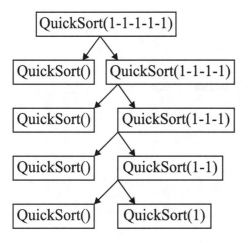

Table 9.3 Times to Quicksort 20,000 Items

Cutoff	1	5	10	15	20	25	30
Time (seconds)	1.97	1.70	1.59	1.54	1.60	1.70	1.76

recursion after the sublists reached a certain size. In this test the best cutoff value was 15 items.

The following code shows the revised quicksort algorithm.

```
Public Sub Quicksort(List() As Long, ByVal min As Long, ByVal max As
Long)
Dim med_value As Long
Dim hi As Long
Dim lo As Long
Dim i As Long

    ' If the list has no more than CutOff elements,
    ' finish it off with SelectionSort.
    If max - min < CutOff Then
        Selectionsort List(), min, max
        Exit Sub
    End If

    ' Pick the dividing value.
    i = Int((max - min + 1) * Rnd + min)
    med_value = List(i)

    ' Swap it to the front.
    List(i) = List(min)

    lo = min
    hi = max
    Do
        ' Look down from hi for a value < med_value.
        Do While List(hi) >= med_value
            hi = hi - 1
            If hi <= lo Then Exit Do
        Loop
        If hi <= lo Then
            List(lo) = med_value
            Exit Do
        End If
```

```
    ' Swap the lo and hi values.
    List(lo) = List(hi)

    ' Look up from lo for a value >= med_value.
    lo = lo + 1
    Do While List(lo) < med_value
        lo = lo + 1
        If lo >= hi Then Exit Do
    Loop
    If lo >= hi Then
        lo = hi
        List(hi) = med_value
        Exit Do
    End If

    ' Swap the lo and hi values.
    List(hi) = List(lo)
    Loop

    ' Sort the two sublists.
    Quicksort List(), min, lo - 1
    Quicksort List(), lo + 1, max
End Sub
```

Because it provides good performance under most circumstances, quicksort is the sorting algorithm of choice for many programmers.

Mergesort

Like quicksort, mergesort is a recursive algorithm. Also like quicksort, it divides the list to be sorted into two sublists and recursively sorts the sublists.

Mergesort divides its list in the middle to form two sublists of equal size. It then recursively sorts the sublists and merges the sorted sublists to form the completely sorted list.

While the merging step is easy to understand, it is also the most interesting part of the algorithm. The sublists are merged into a scratch array, and the result is copied back into the original list. Creating a scratch array can be a drawback, particularly if the list of items is large. If the scratch array is too big, it may cause the algorithm to page and may slow performance greatly. The scratch array also forces the algorithm to spend a lot of time copying items back and forth between the arrays.

As is the case with quicksort, you can make mergesort faster by stopping the recursion when sublists reach a certain minimum size. The algorithm can then use selectionsort to finish the job.

```
Public Sub Mergesort(List() As Long, Scratch() As Long, _
    ByVal min As Long, ByVal max As Long)
Dim middle As Long
Dim i1 As Long
Dim i2 As Long
Dim i3 As Long

    ' If the list has no more than CutOff elements,
    ' finish it off with SelectionSort.
If max - min < CutOff Then
    Selectionsort List(), min, max
    Exit Sub
End If

    ' Recursively sort the sublists.
middle = max \ 2 + min \ 2
Mergesort List(), Scratch(), min, middle
Mergesort List(), Scratch(), middle + 1, max

    ' Merge the sorted lists.
i1 = min            ' Index in list 1.
i2 = middle + 1 ' Index in list 2.
i3 = min            ' Index in merged list.
Do While i1 <= middle And i2 <= max
    If List(i1) <= List(i2) Then
        Scratch(i3) = List(i1)
        i1 = i1 + 1
    Else
        Scratch(i3) = List(i2)
        i2 = i2 + 1
    End If
    i3 = i3 + 1
Loop

    ' Empty out whichever list is not already empty.
Do While i1 <= middle
    Scratch(i3) = List(i1)
    i1 = i1 + 1
    i3 = i3 + 1
Loop
Do While i2 <= max
    Scratch(i3) = List(i2)
    i2 = i2 + 1
    i3 = i3 + 1
```

```
    Loop

    ' Move the merged list back into list.
    For i3 = min To max
        List(i3) = Scratch(i3)
    Next i3
End Sub
```

Mergesort spends a fair amount of time copying its scratch array into the original array. Program FastSort uses the MemCopy API function to make this operation a bit faster.

Even using MemCopy, mergesort is generally slightly slower than quicksort. In one test on a 90 megahertz Pentium, mergesort required 2.95 seconds to sort 30,000 items with values between 1 and 10,000. Quicksort needed only 2.44 seconds.

Mergesort has the advantage that its times remain the same for different data distributions and initial arrangements. Quicksort gives $O(N^2)$ performance and enters deep recursion if there are many duplicated values in the list. If the list is large, quicksort may exhaust the stack and crash. Because mergesort always divides the list into equal parts, it never enters deep recursion. For an N-item list, mergesort reaches only log(N) depth of recursion.

In another test using 30,000 items with values between 1 and 100, mergesort took the same time it took to sort items with values between 1 and 10,000: 2.95 seconds. Quicksort needed 15.82 seconds. With item values between 1 and 50, mergesort still took 2.95 seconds, while quicksort took 138.52 seconds.

Heapsort

Heapsort uses a special data structure called a *heap* to organize the items in a list. Heaps are also interesting in their own right and are useful for implementing priority queues.

This section begins by describing heaps and explaining how you can implement heaps in Visual Basic. It then shows how to use a heap to build an efficient priority queue. With the tools developed to manage heaps and priority queues, implementing heapsort is easy.

Heaps

A heap is a complete binary tree where each node is at least as large as its two children. This does not say anything about the relationship between the two children. While both must be smaller than their parent, either may be larger than the other. Figure 9.6 shows a small heap.

Because each node is at least as large as the two nodes below, the root node is always the largest node in the heap. This makes heaps a good data structure for implementing priority queues. Whenever you need the highest priority item in the queue, it is sitting at the top of the heap.

Figure 9.6 A heap.

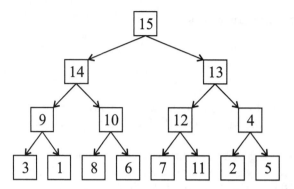

Because a heap is a complete binary tree, you can use techniques covered in Chapter 6, "Trees," to store the heap in an array. Place the root node at array position 1. Place the children of node I in positions 2 * I and 2 * I + 1. Figure 9.7 shows the heap in Figure 9.6 stored in an array.

To see how to build a heap, notice that a heap is made of smaller subheaps. The subtree starting at any node in a heap is also a heap. For example, in the heap shown in Figure 9.8, the subtree rooted at node 13 is also a heap.

Using this fact, you can build a heap from the bottom up. First, place the items in a tree, as shown in Figure 9.9. Then make heaps out of the little three-node subtrees at the bottom. Because there are only three nodes in these trees, this is simple. Compare the top node with its two child nodes. If either of the children is larger, swap it with the node on top. If both children are larger, swap the parent with the larger child. Repeat this step until all of the three-node subtrees at the bottom of the tree are heaps, as shown in Figure 9.10.

Now join little heaps to form larger heaps. In Figure 9.10 join the small heaps with tops 15 and 5 plus item 7 to form a larger heap. To join the two smaller heaps, compare the new top item 7 with each of its children. If one of the children is bigger than this item, swap the item with the larger child. In this case, 15 is larger than 7 and 4, so you should swap node 15 with node 7.

Because the right subtree starting with node 4 is not modified, that subtree is still a heap. The left subtree, however, has changed. To determine whether it is still a heap, compare its new top 7 to its children 13 and 12. Because 13 is larger than 7 and 12, you should swap the 7 and 13 nodes.

Figure 9.7 Array representation of a heap.

Index	1	2	3	4	5	6	7	8	9	10	11	12	13	14	15
Value	15	14	13	9	10	12	4	3	1	8	6	7	11	2	5

Figure 9.8 A heap is made up of subheaps.

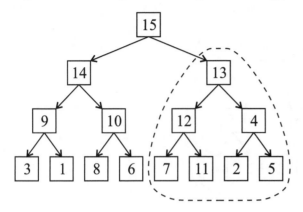

Figure 9.9 An unsorted list in a complete tree.

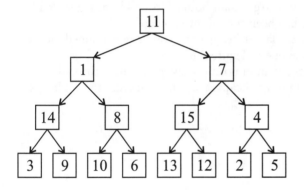

Figure 9.10 Two-level subtrees are heaps.

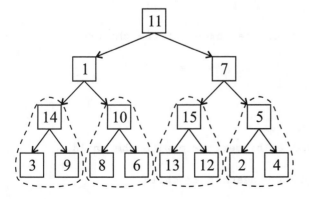

Figure 9.11 Combining subheaps into larger heaps.

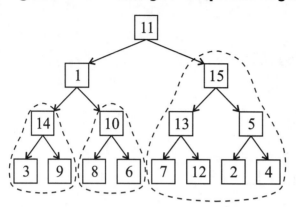

If the subtree was taller, you would continue pushing the 7 node down into the subtree. Eventually you would either hit the bottom of the tree, or you would reach a point where the 7 node was larger than both of its children. Figure 9.11 shows the tree after this subtree has been turned into a heap.

Continue joining heaps to form larger heaps until you have combined all the items into one large heap, like the one in Figure 9.6.

The following code pushes the item in position List(min) down through a heap. If the subtrees below List(min) are heaps, the routine merges the subheaps to form a larger heap.

```
Private Sub HeapPushDown(List() As Long, ByVal min As Long, _
    ByVal max As Long)
Dim tmp As Long
Dim j As Long

    tmp = List(min)
    Do
        j = 2 * min
        If j <= max Then
            ' Make j point to the larger of the children.
            If j < max Then
                If List(j + 1) > List(j) Then _
                    j = j + 1
            End If

            If List(j) > tmp Then
                ' A child is bigger. Swap with the child.
                List(min) = List(j)
                ' Push down beneath that child.
```

```
                        min = j
                Else
                        ' The parent is bigger. We're done.
                        Exit Do
                End If
        Else
                Exit Do
        End If
    Loop
    List(min) = tmp
End Sub
```

The complete algorithm for using HeapPushDown to create a heap out of a tree of items is remarkably simple.

```
Private Sub BuildHeap()
Dim i As Integer

    For i = (max + min) \ 2 To min Step -1
        HeapPushDown list(), i, max
    Next i
End Sub
```

Priority Queues

It is easy to manage a priority queue using the BuildHeap and HeapPushDown subroutines. If you use a heap as a priority queue, the item with the highest priority is always at the top. Finding the highest priority item is easy. When you remove this item, however, the rootless tree that remains is not a heap.

To turn the rootless tree back into a heap, take the last item (the rightmost item on the bottom level) and place it at the top of the heap. Then use the HeapPushDown routine to push the new root node item down into the tree until the tree is once again a heap. At this point, the priority queue is ready to output the next highest priority item.

```
Public Function Pop() As Long
    If NumInPQueue < 1 Then Exit Function

    ' Remove the top item.
    Pop = PQueue(1)

    ' Move the last item to the top.
    PQueue(1) = PQueue(NumInPQueue)
    NumInPQueue = NumInPQueue - 1

    ' Make it a heap again.
```

```
    HeapPushDown PQueue(), 1, NumInPQueue
End Function
```

To add a new item to the priority queue, enlarge the heap to make room for the new item. Place the new item in the empty position at the end of the array. The resulting tree may no longer be a heap.

To make the tree a heap again, compare the new item with its parent. If the new item is bigger, swap the two. You already know that the parent's other child is smaller than the parent, so you do not need to compare the new item to the other child. If the new item is larger than the parent, it is also larger than the other child.

Continue comparing the new item to its parent and moving it up through the tree until you find a parent that is already larger than the new item. At that point, the tree is once again a heap, and the priority queue is ready for business.

```
Private Sub HeapPushUp(List() As Long, ByVal max As Integer)
Dim tmp As Long
Dim j As Integer

    tmp = List(max)
    Do
        j = max \ 2
        If j < 1 Then Exit Do
        If List(j) < tmp Then
            List(max) = List(j)
            max = j
        Else
            Exit Do
        End If
    Loop
    List(max) = tmp
End Sub
```

The Push subroutine adds a new item to the tree and uses subroutine HeapPushUp to rebuild the heap.

```
Public Sub Push(value As Long)
    NumInPQueue = NumInPQueue + 1
    If NumInPQueue > PQueueSize Then ResizePQueue

    PQueue(NumInPQueue) = value
    HeapPushUp PQueue(), NumInPQueue
End Sub
```

Heap Analysis

When you first turn the list of items into a heap, you do so by building a lot of smaller heaps. For every internal node in the tree, you build a smaller heap rooted at that node. If the tree contains N items, there are O(N) internal nodes in the tree, so you end up building O(N) heaps.

As you build each heap, you might need to push the top item down the heap, possibly until it reaches a leaf node. The tallest heaps you build have height O(log(N)). Because you build O(N) heaps and the tallest requires at most O(log(N)) steps to build, you can build all of the heaps in O(N $*$ log(N)) time.

In fact, it does not take even that much time to build the heaps. Only a few of the heaps have height O(log(N)). Most are much shorter. Only one heap actually has height equal to log(N), and half have height only 2. If you add up all the steps needed to build all the heaps, you actually need at most O(N) steps.

To see why this is true, suppose the tree contains N nodes. Let H be the height of the tree. This is a complete binary tree, so H = log(N).

Now suppose you are building larger and larger heaps. You build a heap of height I for each internal node that is H − I levels from the root of the tree. There are 2^{H-I} such nodes, so in total you build 2^{H-I} heaps of height I.

To build these heaps, you might need to push the top item down until it reaches a leaf. It takes up to I steps to push the item down through a heap of height I. To build 2^{H-I} heaps in at most I steps each, the total number of steps spent building heaps of height I is I $* 2^{H-I}$.

Adding together all the steps spent building heaps of different sizes, you get $1 * 2^{H-1} + 2 * 2^{H-2} + 3 * 2^{H-3} + ... + (H-1) * 2^1$. Dividing out a factor of 2^H gives $2^H * (1 / 2 + 2 / 2^2 + 3 / 2^3 + ... + (H-1) / 2^{H-1})$.

It can be shown that $(1 / 2 + 2 / 2^2 + 3 / 2^3 + ... + (H-1) / 2^{H-1})$ is less than 2. Then the number of steps spent building all the heaps is less than $2^H * 2$. Because H is the height of the tree and equals log(N), the total number of steps is less than $2^{\log(N)} * 2 = N * 2$. That means it takes only O(N) steps to initially build a heap.

To remove an item from a priority queue, you move the last item to the top of the tree. You then push the item down until it reaches its final position and the tree is again a heap. Because the tree has height log(N), this process can take, at most, log(N) steps. That means you can remove an item from a heap-based priority queue in O(log(N)) steps.

When you add a new item to the heap, you place it at the bottom of the tree and push it toward the top until it comes to rest. Because the tree has height log(N), this can take, at most, log(N) steps. That means you can add a new item to a heap-based priority queue in O(log(N)) steps.

Another way to manage a priority queue is to use a sorted list. Using quicksort you can build the initial queue in O(N $*$ log(N)) time. When you remove or add an item, you can use bubblesort to put the list back in order in O(N) time.

These times are fast but not as fast as those given by a heap. Inserting or removing an item from a sorted list priority queue of 1 million items requires about 1 million steps. Inserting or removing an item from a comparable heap-based priority queue takes only 20 steps.

Example program Priority uses a heap to manage a priority queue. Enter a number and click the Add button to add the new item to the queue. Click the Leave button to remove the highest priority item from the queue.

The Heapsort Algorithm

Using the algorithms already described for manipulating heaps, the heapsort algorithm is straightforward. The idea is to build a priority queue and then remove each item from the queue one at a time in order.

To remove an item, the algorithm swaps it with the last item in the heap. This places the newly removed item in its proper final position at the end of the array. The algorithm then reduces its count of the number of items in the list, so it does not consider the last position again.

After swapping the largest item with the last item, the array is no longer a heap, because the new top item may be smaller than its children. The algorithm uses the HeapPushDown routine to push the new item to its proper position. The algorithm continues swapping items and rebuilding the heap until there are no items left.

```
Public Sub Heapsort(List() As Long, ByVal min As Long, ByVal max As
Long)
Dim i As Long
Dim tmp As Long

    ' Make a heap (except for the root node).
    For i = (max + min) \ 2 To min + 1 Step -1
        HeapPushDown List(), i, max
    Next i

    ' Repeatedly:
    '    1. HeapPushDown.
    '    2. Output the root.
    For i = max To min + 1 Step -1
        ' HeapPushDown.
        HeapPushDown List(), min, i

        ' Output the root.
        tmp = List(min)
        List(min) = List(i)
        List(i) = tmp
    Next i
End Sub
```

The earlier discussion of priority queues showed that initially building the heap takes O(N) steps. After that it takes O(log(N)) steps to rebuild the heap when an item is swapped into its final position. Heapsort does this N times, so it needs a total of O(N) * O(log(N)) = O(N * log(N)) steps to pull the sorted list out of the heap. The total run time for heapsort is O(N) + O(N * log(N)) = O(N * log(N)).

This is the same as the run time for mergesort and the average run time for quicksort. Like mergesort, heapsort does not depend on the values or distribution of the items being sorted. Quicksort has trouble with lists containing many duplicated values; mergesort and heapsort do not.

Even though heapsort is usually a little slower than mergesort, it does not require the temporary scratch space mergesort needs. Heapsort builds the initial heap and moves the items into sorted order within the original list array.

Countingsort

Countingsort is a specialized algorithm that works extremely well if the data items are integers with values that fall within a relatively small range. The algorithm is fast, for example, if all the values lie between 1 and 1000.

As long as the list meets these conditions, countingsort is incredibly fast. In one test on a 90 megahertz Pentium, quicksort sorted 100,000 items with values between 1 and 1000 in 24.44 seconds. To sort the same items, countingsort required only 0.88 seconds—1/27th as long.

Countingsort achieves its remarkable speed by not using comparisons to sort the items. Earlier this chapter mentioned that any sorting algorithm using comparisons must take at least $O(N * \log(N))$ time. By not using comparisons, countingsort is able to sort items in $O(N)$ time.

Countingsort starts by creating an array to count the items with each data value. If item values range from min_value to max_value, the algorithm creates a Counts array with lower bound min_value and upper bound max_value. If the program reuses an array from a previous run, it must initialize the values to zero. If there are M item values, the array holds M entries, so this is an $O(M)$ step.

Next, the algorithm counts the occurrences of each value in the list. It examines each item and increments the value of the corresponding Counts entry. For example, if an item's value is 37, the program increases Counts(37) by 1. The algorithm examines each item once during this process, so this step takes $O(N)$ time.

```
For i = min To max
    Counts(List(i)) = counts(List(i)) + 1
Next i
```

Finally, the algorithm runs through the Counts array, placing the appropriate number of items with each value in the sorted array. For each value i between min_value and max_value, it places Counts(i) items with value i in the array. Because this step places one entry in each position in the array, it takes $O(N)$ steps.

```
new_index = min
For i = min_value To max_value
    For j = 1 To Counts(i)
        sorted_list(new_index) = i
        new_index = new_index + 1
    Next j
Next i
```

The complete algorithm takes $O(M) + O(N) + O(N) = O(M + N)$ steps. If M is small compared to N, this is extremely fast. If $M < N$, for example, $O(M + N) = O(N)$, which is quite fast. If $N = 100,000$ and $M = 1000$, then $M + N = 101,000$, while $N * \log(N) = 1.6$ million. The steps taken by countingsort are also quite simple compared to those taken by quicksort. These facts combine to make countingsort incredibly quick.

On the other hand, if M is larger than $O(N * \log(N))$, then $O(M + N)$ will be larger than $O(N * \log(N))$. In that case countingsort may be slower than $O(N * \log(N))$ algorithms like quicksort. In one test quicksort took 0.054 seconds to sort 1000 items with values between 1 and 500,000, while countingsort needed 1.76 seconds.

Countingsort relies on the fact that the data values are integers, so the algorithm cannot easily sort noninteger data. In Visual Basic you cannot create an array with bounds AAA to ZZZ.

The section "Key Combination and Compression" earlier in this chapter shows how to encode noninteger data using integers. If you can encode your data as integers or long integers, you can still use countingsort.

Bucketsort

Like countingsort, bucketsort does not use comparisons to sort items. It uses the item values to divide the items into buckets. It then sorts the buckets recursively. When the buckets are small enough, the algorithm stops and uses a simpler algorithm like selectionsort to finish sorting.

In a sense, this algorithm is similar to quicksort. Quicksort divides the items into two sublists and recursively sorts the sublists. Bucketsort does the same thing except it divides the list into many buckets instead of just two sublists.

To divide the list into buckets, the algorithm assumes that the data values are evenly distributed, and it divides the items evenly among the buckets. For example, suppose the data items have values ranging from 1 to 100 and the algorithm is using 10 buckets. The algorithm places items with values 1–10 in the first bucket, items with values 11–20 in the second bucket, and so forth. Figure 9.12 shows a list of 10 items with values between 1 and 100 placed in 10 buckets.

If the items are evenly distributed, each bucket receives roughly the same number of items. If there are N items in the list and the algorithm uses N buckets, each

Figure 9.12 Placing items in buckets.

Unsorted list	1	74	38	72	63	100	89	57	7	31

Bucket number	1	2	3	4	5	6	7	8	9	10
Bucket	1 7		38 31			57	63	74 72	89		100

bucket receives only one or two items. The program can sort the one or two items in a constant number of steps, so the total run time for the algorithm is O(N).

In practice, data values are usually not distributed perfectly evenly. Some buckets receive more items and some receive fewer. If the distribution is at all close to uniform, however, each bucket receives only a small number of items.

Even if there is a clump in the data so that one bucket receives many items, the items within the bucket will probably be evenly distributed. When the algorithm recursively sorts this large bucket, the items will be divided evenly among the new buckets. The items will be handled easily in the second round of the algorithm.

One case that causes trouble occurs when the list contains few distinct values. If every item has the same value, for example, bucketsort puts them all in the same bucket. If the algorithm does not detect this, it will recursively put them all in the same bucket again and again, causing runaway recursion and using up all of the stack space.

Linked List Bucketsort

You can implement bucketsort in Visual Basic in several ways. First, you can make the buckets linked lists. This makes it easy to move items from one bucket to another as the algorithm progresses.

This method can be troublesome if the items are originally stored in an array. In that case, you need to move the items from the array into the linked list and back into the array when you are done sorting. It also requires extra memory for the linked list. The following code shows the linked list bucketsort algorithm.

```
Public Sub LinkBucketSort(ListTop As ListCell)
Dim count As Long
Dim min_value As Long
Dim max_value As Long
Dim Value As Long
Dim item As ListCell
Dim nxt As ListCell
Dim bucket() As New ListCell
Dim value_scale As Double
Dim bucket_num As Long
Dim i As Long

    Set item = ListTop.NextCell
    If item Is Nothing Then Exit Sub

    ' Count the items and find the min and max values.
    count = 1
    min_value = item.Value
    max_value = min_value
    Set item = item.NextCell
```

```
Do While Not (item Is Nothing)
    count = count + 1
    Value = item.Value
    If min_value > Value Then min_value = Value
    If max_value < Value Then max_value = Value
    Set item = item.NextCell
Loop

' If min_value = max_value, there is only one
' value so the list is sorted.
If min_value = max_value Then Exit Sub

' If the list has no more than CutOff elements,
' finish it off with LinkInsertionSort.
If count <= CutOff Then
    LinkInsertionSort ListTop
    Exit Sub
End If

' Allocate the empty buckets.
ReDim bucket(1 To count)

value_scale = _
    CDbl(count - 1) / _
    CDbl(max_value - min_value)

' Move the items into the buckets.
Set item = ListTop.NextCell
Do While Not (item Is Nothing)
    Set nxt = item.NextCell
    Value = item.Value
    If Value = max_value Then
        bucket_num = count
    Else
        bucket_num = _
            Int((Value - min_value) * _
                value_scale) + 1
    End If
    Set item.NextCell = bucket(bucket_num).NextCell
    Set bucket(bucket_num).NextCell = item
    Set item = nxt
Loop
```

```
' Recursively sort the buckets that hold more
' than one item.
For i = 1 To count
    If Not (bucket(i).NextCell Is Nothing) Then _
        LinkBucketSort bucket(i)
Next i


' Merge the sorted lists.
Set ListTop.NextCell = bucket(count).NextCell
For i = count - 1 To 1 Step -1
    Set item = bucket(i).NextCell
    If Not (item Is Nothing) Then
        Do While Not (item.NextCell Is Nothing)
            Set item = item.NextCell
        Loop
        Set item.NextCell = ListTop.NextCell
        Set ListTop.NextCell = bucket(i).NextCell
    End If
Next i
End Sub
```

This version of bucketsort is much faster than linked list insertionsort. In a test on a 90 megahertz Pentium, insertionsort took 6.65 seconds to sort 2000 items; bucketsort took 1.32 seconds. For longer lists the $O(N^2)$ performance of insertionsort makes the difference even greater.

Array-Based Bucketsort

You can also implement bucketsort in an array using concepts similar to those used by countingsort. Each time the algorithm is invoked, it first counts the items that belong in each bucket. It uses the counts to compute offsets in a temporary scratch array. The algorithm then uses the offsets to place the items in their correct positions within the array. Finally, it recursively sorts the buckets and moves the sorted data back into the original array.

```
Public Sub ArrayBucketSort(List() As Long, Scratch() As Long, _
    min As Long, max As Long, NumBuckets As Long)
Dim counts() As Long
Dim offsets() As Long

Dim i As Long
Dim Value As Long
Dim min_value As Long
Dim max_value As Long
Dim value_scale As Double
Dim bucket_num As Long
```

```
Dim next_spot As Long
Dim num_in_bucket As Long

    ' If the list has no more than CutOff elements,
    ' finish it off with SelectionSort.
    If max - min + 1 < CutOff Then
        Selectionsort List(), min, max
        Exit Sub
    End If

    ' Find the min and max values.
    min_value = List(min)
    max_value = min_value
    For i = min + 1 To max
        Value = List(i)
        If min_value > Value Then min_value = Value
        If max_value < Value Then max_value = Value
    Next i

    ' If min_value = max_value, there is only one
    ' value so the list is sorted.
    If min_value = max_value Then Exit Sub

    ' Create the empty bucket counts array.
    ReDim counts(1 To NumBuckets)

    value_scale = _
        CDbl(NumBuckets - 1) / _
        CDbl(max_value - min_value)

    ' Create bucket counts.
    For i = min To max
        If List(i) = max_value Then
            bucket_num = NumBuckets
        Else
            bucket_num = _
                Int((List(i) - min_value) * _
                    value_scale) + 1
        End If
        counts(bucket_num) = counts(bucket_num) + 1
    Next i

    ' Turn the counts into offsets.
```

```
ReDim offsets(1 To NumBuckets)
next_spot = min
For i = 1 To NumBuckets
    offsets(i) = next_spot
    next_spot = next_spot + counts(i)
Next i

' Place the values in their buckets.
For i = min To max
    If List(i) = max_value Then
        bucket_num = NumBuckets
    Else
        bucket_num = _
            Int((List(i) - min_value) * _
                value_scale) + 1
    End If
    Scratch(offsets(bucket_num)) = List(i)
    offsets(bucket_num) = offsets(bucket_num) + 1
Next i

' Recursively sort the buckets that hold
' more than one item.
next_spot = min
For i = 1 To NumBuckets
    If counts(i) > 1 Then ArrayBucketSort _
        Scratch(), List(), next_spot, _
        next_spot + counts(i) - 1, counts(i)
    next_spot = next_spot + counts(i)
Next i

' Copy the scratch array back into the list.
For i = min To max
    List(i) = Scratch(i)
Next i
End Sub
```

Due to the overhead required to manage linked lists, this version of bucketsort is much faster than the linked list version. Using the pointer faking techniques described in Chapter 2, "Lists," however, you can improve the performance of the linked list version until the two are roughly equivalent.

You can make the new version faster using the MemCopy API function to copy entries from the scratch array back into the original list. This enhanced version is demonstrated by program FastSort.

Summary

Table 9.4 shows the advantages and disadvantages of the sorting algorithms described in this chapter. Taking these into account, here are some rules you can use to help you select a sorting algorithm.

The guidelines in the following list and the information in Table 9.4 can help you pick the algorithm that will give you the best possible performance:

- If you just want to implement some algorithm quickly, use quicksort and switch algorithms later if necessary.
- If your list is more than 99 percent sorted already, use bubblesort.
- If you have a very small list (under 100 items or so), use selectionsort.

Table 9.4 Advantages and Disadvantages of Sorting Algorithms

Algorithm	Advantages	Disadvantages
Insertionsort	Very simple Fast for small lists	Very slow for large lists
Linked List Insertionsort	Simple Fast for small lists Moves pointers, not data	Slow for large lists
Selectionsort	Very simple Fast for small lists	Slow for large lists
Bubblesort	Fast for lists that are almost sorted	Very slow for all other lists
Quicksort	Fast for large lists	Trouble if there are lots of duplicate values
Mergesort	Fast for large lists	Requires scratch space Not as fast as quicksort
Heapsort	Fast for large lists No scratch space required	Not as fast as mergesort
Countingsort	Very fast when value range is small	Slower when value range > log(N) Requires extra memory Only works with integer data
Bucketsort	Very fast with evenly distributed data Handles data spread over wide ranges Handles non-integer data	Slower than countingsort

- If your program stores the values in a linked list, use linked list bucketsort.
- If the items in your list range over a small number of integer values (up to several thousand), use countingsort.
- If the values vary over a wide range or are not integers, use array-based bucketsort.
- If you cannot spare the extra memory required by bucketsort, use Quicksort.

If you understand your data and a variety of different sorting algorithms, you can select the algorithm that best fits your needs.

SEARCHING

10

After you sort a list of items, you might want to locate a particular item in the list. This chapter describes several algorithms for locating items in sorted lists. The chapter begins by briefly discussing exhaustive searching. Although not as fast as the other algorithms, exhaustive searching is very simple. That makes it easy to program and debug. Its simplicity also makes exhaustive searching faster than other algorithms for very small lists.

Next, the chapter describes binary searching. A binary search repeatedly subdivides the list to locate an item and for larger lists is much faster than an exhaustive search. The idea behind binary searching is simple, but the implementation is a little tricky.

The chapter then discusses interpolation searching. Like a binary search, an interpolation search repeatedly subdivides the list to locate an item. Using interpolation, this algorithm makes a reasonable guess about where the target item should lie, so it is much faster than binary search for evenly distributed lists.

Finally, the chapter discusses hunt and search methods. These techniques sometimes make searching for several items faster.

Example Programs

Example program Search demonstrates all the algorithms described in this chapter. Enter the number of items the list should contain. Click the Make List button, and the program creates an array-based list where each item is between 0 and 5 greater than the previous item. The program displays the value of the largest item in the list so you know what values you might find.

After you create the list, use the check boxes to select the algorithms you want to use. Enter a target value and click the Search button to make the program locate the value using the algorithms you selected. Because the items are not all consecutive, you may need to search for several different values before you find one that is in the list.

The program also lets you specify the number of times it should repeat each search. Some of the algorithms are very fast, so you may need to use many repetitions if you want to compare their speeds.

Figure 10.1 shows program Search after locating an item with the value 250,000. The item was in position 99,802 in a list of 100,000 items. To find the item, the exhaustive search algorithm examined 99,802 list entries. Binary search examined 16 entries, and interpolation search examined just 3.

Exhaustive Search

To perform an *exhaustive* or *linear* search, start at the beginning of the list and examine every item until you find the target item.

```
Private Function LinearSearch(target As Long) As Long
Dim i As Long

    For i = 1 To NumItems
        If List(i) = target Then Exit For
    Next i

    If i > NumItems Then
        Search = 0      ' Not found.
    Else
        Search = i      ' Found.
    End If
End Function
```

Because it examines each item in order, this algorithm locates items near the front of the list more quickly than items near the rear. The worst case for this algorithm occurs when the item is near the end of the list or is not present at all. In these cases, the algorithm must search all the items in the list, so it has O(N) worst case behavior.

Figure 10.1 Program Search.

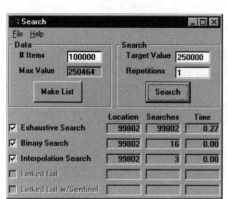

If the item is in the list, the algorithm must examine N / 2 entries on the average before it finds the target item. This gives the algorithm an average behavior of O(N).

Even though this O(N) behavior is not particularly fast, the algorithm is simple enough that it is quite fast in practice. For small lists, the algorithm gives adequate performance.

Searching Sorted Lists

If a list is sorted, you can modify the exhaustive searching algorithm to get slightly better performance. As the algorithm searches the list, if it ever finds an item that has value greater than the target value, the algorithm can stop. Because it has passed the position where the target item would belong if it were in the list, the item must not be present.

For example, suppose you are searching for the value 12 and you come to the value 17. You have passed the position where 12 would be, so you know the value 12 is not in the list. The following code shows the improved exhaustive search algorithm.

```
Public Function LinearSearch(target As Long) As Long
Dim i As Long

    For i = 1 To NumItems
        If List(i) >= target Then Exit For
    Next i

    If i > NumItems Then
        LinearSearch = 0      ' Not found.
    ElseIf List(i) <> target Then
        LinearSearch = 0      ' Not found.
    Else
        LinearSearch = i      ' Found.
    End If
End Function
```

This modification makes the algorithm faster when the target item is not in the list. The previous version of this function needed to search all the way to the end of the list if the target item was not present. The new version will stop as soon as it finds an item greater than the target item.

If the target item is randomly positioned between the smallest and largest items in the list, the algorithm will require an average of N / 2 steps to determine that the item is not there. The run time is still O(N), but the performance in practice is faster. Example program Search uses this version of the algorithm.

Searching Linked Lists

Exhaustive searching is the only way to search a linked list. Because you have access to items only through their NextCell pointers, you must start at the beginning of the list and step through the items one at a time until you find the one you seek.

As is the case with exhaustive search in an array, if the list is sorted, you can stop searching when you find an item that has value greater than the target value. Once you have passed the position where the target item would be if it were in the list, you know the item is not there.

```
Public Function LListSearch(target As Long) As SearchCell
Dim cell As SearchCell

    Set cell = ListTop.NextCell
    Do While Not (cell Is Nothing)
        If cell.Value >= target Then Exit Do
        Set cell = cell.NextCell
    Loop

    If Not (cell Is Nothing) Then
        If cell.Value = target Then
            Set LListSearch = cell      ' Found it.
        End If
    End If
End Function
```

Example program Search uses this algorithm to locate items within a linked list. The overhead involved in managing object pointers makes this algorithm slower than the array-based exhaustive search. Note that program Search will build linked lists only if the list contains 10,000 or fewer items.

You can make one more change to the linked list search algorithm to make it a little faster. If you keep a pointer to the bottom of the list, you can add a new cell at the end of the list that contains the target value. This item is called a *sentinel*, and it serves a purpose similar to that of the sentinels used in the lists built in Chapter 2, "Lists." It allows the program to treat a special case as if it were not special.

In this case, adding the sentinel to the end of the list ensures that the algorithm will eventually find the target item. The program cannot run off the end of the list, so it need not check the condition Not (cell Is Nothing) each time the While loop executes.

```
Public Function SentinelSearch(target As Long) As SearchCell
Dim cell As SearchCell
Dim sentinel As New SearchCell

    ' Initialize the sentinel.
    sentinel.Value = target
    Set ListBottom.NextCell = sentinel

    ' Find the target.
```

```
Set cell = ListTop.NextCell
Do While cell.Value < target
    Set cell = cell.NextCell
Loop

' See if we found it.
If Not ((cell Is sentinel) Or _
    (cell.Value <> target)) _
Then
    Set SentinelSearch = cell    ' Found it.
End If

' Remove the sentinel.
Set ListBottom.NextCell = Nothing
End Function
```

Even though this may seem like a small change, the Not (cell Is Nothing) test is contained in a frequently executed loop. For large lists this loop is executed many times, and the savings accumulate. In Visual Basic, this linked list search runs about 20 percent faster than the previous version. Program Search demonstrates both versions of the linked list search algorithms so you can compare the two.

Some algorithms use threads through linked lists to improve searching. For example, pointers within the list cells could organize the cells into a binary tree. Searching for an item using the tree would take $O(\log(N))$ time if the tree is properly balanced. This sort of data structure is not a simple list, so it is not discussed further here. For more information on trees, see Chapter 6, "Trees," and Chapter 7, "Balanced Trees."

Binary Search

As is mentioned in the previous sections, an exhaustive search is very fast for small lists. For larger lists, binary search is much faster. The binary search algorithm examines the item in the middle of the list and compares it to the target item. If the target item is smaller, the algorithm continues searching the first half of the list. If the target item is larger than the middle item, the algorithm searches the second half of the list. Figure 10.2 shows this process graphically.

Although this algorithm is naturally recursive, it is fairly easy to write without recursion. Because it is easy to understand either way, the algorithm is written nonrecursively here to save the expense of making a lot of function calls.

The general idea behind the algorithm is simple, but the details are a little tricky. The program must keep careful track of the portion of the array that might contain the target item. Otherwise, the algorithm may miss the target.

The algorithm uses two variables, min and max, to keep track of the minimum and maximum indexes of the array entries that could contain the target item.

───────────────────────────────

Figure 10.2 Binary search for the value 44.

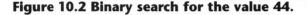
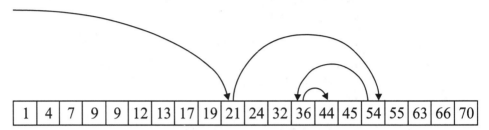

1	4	7	9	9	12	13	17	19	21	24	32	36	44	45	54	55	63	66	70

While the algorithm runs, the target will always have an index between min and max. In other words, min <= target index <= max.

During each pass, the algorithm sets middle = (min + max) / 2 and examines the item with index middle. If the middle item has the same value as the target item, the algorithm has found the target and is done.

If the target item is smaller than the middle item, the algorithm sets max to middle – 1 and continues searching. Because the range of indexes that might contain the target item is now min to middle – 1, the program searches the first half of the list.

If the target item is larger than the middle item, the program sets min to middle + 1 and continues searching. The range of indexes that might hold the target item is now middle + 1 to max, so the program searches the second half of the list.

Eventually the program will either find the item or min will be raised and max lowered until min is greater than max. The program adjusts min and max so the index of the target item is always between them. Because there are no more indexes between min and max at this point, the item must not be in the list.

The following code shows how program Search performs binary search.

```
Public Function BinarySearch(target As Long) As Long
Dim min As Long
Dim max As Long
Dim middle As Long

    ' During the search the target's index will be
    ' between Min and Max: Min <= target index <= Max.
    min = 1
    max = NumItems
    Do While min <= max
        middle = (max + min) / 2
        If target = List(middle) Then       ' We have found it!
            BinarySearch = middle
            Exit Function
        ElseIf target < List(middle) Then ' Search the left half.
            max = middle - 1
```

```
        Else                          ' Search the right half.
            min = middle + 1
        End If
    Loop

    ' If we get here the target is not in the list.
    BinarySearch = 0
End Function
```

At each step, this algorithm cuts the number of items that still might contain the target item in half. For a list of size N, the algorithm needs at most O(log(N)) steps to locate any given item or to decide that it is not contained in the list. This makes binary search much faster than exhaustive search. To exhaustively search a list of 1 million items would take an average of 500,000 steps. The binary search algorithm would need at most log(1,000,000), or 20, steps.

Interpolation Search

Binary search is a great improvement over exhaustive search because it eliminates large portions of the list without actually examining all the eliminated values. If you know that the values are fairly evenly distributed, you can use interpolation to eliminate even more values at each step.

Interpolation is the process of using known values to guess where an unknown value lies. In this case, you use the indexes of known values in the list to guess what index the target value should have.

For example, suppose you had the same list of values shown in Figure 10.2. This list contains 20 items with values between 1 and 70. Now suppose you wanted to locate the item in this list with value 44. The value 44 is 64 percent of the way between the values 1 and 70. If you assume the values are evenly distributed, you would expect the target item to be about 64 percent of the way through the list at index 13.

If the position chosen by the interpolation is incorrect, the search compares the target value to the value at the chosen position. If the target value is smaller, the search continues to locate the target in the first part of the list. If the target value is larger, the search continues to locate the target in the second part of the list. Figure 10.3 shows an interpolation search graphically.

A binary search subdivides the list by examining the item in the middle of the list. An interpolation search subdivides the list by examining an item that should be close to the target item in the list. The program selects the dividing point by interpolation using the following code.

```
middle = min + (target - List(min)) * _

    ((max - min) / (List(max) - List(min)))
```

Figure 10.3 Interpolation search for the value 44.

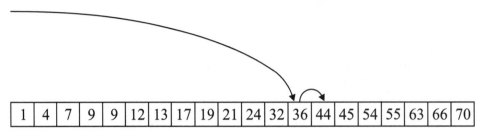

| 1 | 4 | 7 | 9 | 9 | 12 | 13 | 17 | 19 | 21 | 24 | 32 | 36 | 44 | 45 | 54 | 55 | 63 | 66 | 70 |

This statement places middle between min and max in a way that reflects where the target value lies between List(min) and List(max). If the target is close to List(min), the "target − List(min)" term is close to 0. Then the complete statement is close to middle = min + 0, so the value of middle is near min. This makes sense. You would expect the item to have an index near min if its value is close to List(min).

Similarly, if the target is close to List(max), the "target − List(min)" term is about the same as the "List(max) − List(min)" term. These two terms cancel out and the statement is approximately middle = min + (max − min). This simplifies to middle = max and also makes sense. You would expect the item to have an index near max if its value is close to List(max).

Once the program has computed middle, it compares the item at that position to the target item much as it would during a binary search. If the item matches the target, it has found the target item and is done. If the target is smaller than this middle item, the program sets max to middle − 1 and continues searching the smaller items in the list. If the target is larger than the middle item, the program sets min to middle + 1 and continues searching the larger items in the list.

Notice that the statement that calculates the new value for middle divides by (List(max) − List(min)). If List(min) and List(max) have the same value, this statement tries to divide by 0 and the program crashes. This can happen if the list has two identical values in it. Because the algorithm keeps min <= target index <= max, this problem can also occur if min is raised and max is lowered until min = max.

To handle this problem, the program checks whether List(min) and List(max) are the same before performing the division. If they are, there is only a single distinct value left that must be considered. The program can simply check that value to see if it matches the target.

One other detail is that the value calculated for middle is sometimes not between min and max. The simplest case where this occurs is when the target is outside the range of values in the list. Suppose you are looking for the value 300 in the list 100, 150, 200. The first time the program calculates middle min = 1 and max = 3. Then middle = 1 + (300 − List(1)) * (3 − 1) / (List(3) − List(1)) = 1 + (300 − 100) * 2 / (200 − 100) = 5. The index 5 is not only outside the range min <= target index <= max, but it is also outside the array bounds. If the program tries to access List(5), it will crash with a "Subscript out of range" error.

A similar problem can occur if the values between min and max are very unevenly distributed. Suppose you want to locate the value 100 in the list 0, 1, 2, 199, 200. The first time the program calculates middle, it finds middle = 1 + (100 – 0) * (5 – 1) / (200 – 0) = 3. It then compares List(3) to the target 100. Because List(3) = 2, which is less than 100, it sets min = middle + 1, so min = 4.

When the program next calculates middle, it finds middle = 4 + (100 – 199) * (5 – 4) / (200 – 199) = –98. The value –98 is outside the range min <= target index <= max and is also far outside the array bounds.

If you look closely at the calculation of middle, you will see that there are two ways in which the new value might be smaller than min or greater than max. First, suppose middle is less than min.

```
min + (target - List(min)) * ((max - min) / (List(max) - List(min)) <
min
```

Subtracting min from both sides gives:

```
(target - List(min)) * ((max - min) / (List(max) - List(min)) < 0
```

Because max >= min, the (max – min) term must be greater than 0. Because List(max) >= List(min), the (List(max) – List(min) term must also be greater than 0. Then the only way the entire value can be less than 0 is if the (target – List(min)) term is less than 0. That means the target value is less than List(min). In that case, the target item cannot be in the list, because all of the list entries smaller than List(min) have already been eliminated.

Now suppose middle is larger than max.

```
min + (target - List(min)) * ((max - min) / (List(max) - List(min)) >
max
```

Subtracting min from both sides gives:

```
(target - List(min)) * (max - min) / (List(max) - List(min)) > max -
min
```

Multiplying both sides by (List(max) – List(min)) / (max – min) makes this become:

```
target - List(min) > List(max) - List(min)
```

Finally, by adding List(min) to both sides you get:

```
target > List(max)
```

That means the target value is greater than List(max). In that case, the target item cannot be in the list, because all the list entries larger than List(max) have already been eliminated.

Putting these results together, the only way the new value for middle can be outside the range min to max is if the target value is outside the range List(min) to List(max). The algorithm can use this fact whenever it calculates a new value for middle. It first checks to see if the new value is between min and max. If it is not, the target item is not in the list and the algorithm is done.

The following code shows how program Search performs interpolation search.

```
Public Function InterpSearch(target As Long) As Long
Dim min As Long
Dim max As Long
Dim middle As Long

    min = 1
    max = NumItems
    Do While min <= max
        ' Prevent division by zero.
        If List(min) = List(max) Then
            ' This must be the item (if it's in the list).
            If List(min) = target Then
                InterpSearch = min
            Else
                InterpSearch = 0
            End If
            Exit Function
        End If

        ' Compute the dividing point.
        middle = min + (target - List(min)) * _
            ((max - min) / (List(max) - List(min)))

        ' Make sure we stay in bounds.
        If middle < min Or middle > max Then
            ' It's not in the list.
            InterpSearch = 0
            Exit Function
        End If

        If target = List(middle) Then          ' We found it.
            InterpSearch = middle
            Exit Function
        ElseIf target < List(middle) Then      ' Search the left half.
            max = middle - 1
        Else                                   ' Search the right half.
            min = middle + 1
```

```
        End If
    Loop

    ' If we got to this point, the item is not in the list.
    InterpSearch = 0
End Function
```

Binary search is very fast, but interpolation search is much faster. In one set of tests, binary search took more than 7 times as long to locate values in a list of 100,000 items. The difference would have been even greater had the data been stored on a hard disk or other relatively slow device. Even though interpolation search spends more time calculating than binary search does, the reduced number of disk accesses would have saved far more time.

String Data

If the data items in a list are strings, you have a couple of options. The easiest thing to do is use a binary search. Binary search compares items to each other directly, so it can easily handle string data.

Interpolation search, on the other hand, uses the items' numeric data values to compute the index where the target item should be. If the items are strings, the algorithm cannot use the data values directly to compute the target item's location.

If the strings are short enough, you can encode them as integers, long integers, or doubles using the techniques described in the section "Key Combination and Compression" in Chapter 9, "Sorting." Once you have encoded the strings, you can use interpolation search to locate items within the list.

If the strings are too long to encode as doubles, you can still use the string values for interpolation. Begin by finding the first character at which List(min) and List(max) differ. Encode the next three characters of each string and the corresponding three characters of the target value using the techniques from Chapter 9, "Sorting." Then use those values for the interpolation.

For example, suppose you are searching for the string TARGET in the list TABULATE, TANTRUM, TARGET, TATTERED, TAXATION. When min = 1 and max = 5, you examine the values TABULATE and THEATER. These values first differ at the second character, so you consider the three characters starting with character 2. These are ABU for List(1), AXA for List(5), and ARG for the target string.

The encodings of these strings are 804, 1378, and 1222, respectively. Plugging these values into the calculation of middle in the interpolation search algorithm gives:

```
middle = min + (target - List(min)) * ((max - min) / (List(max) -
List(min)))
        = 1 + (1222 - 804) * ((5 - 1) / (1378 - 804))
        = 2.91
```

This rounds to 3, so the next value for middle is 3. This happens to be the location of TARGET in the list, so the search ends.

Hunting and Searching

If you know your program needs to locate many items within a list and you suspect that each item will be close to the previous one, a hunting technique can make the search faster. Instead of starting the search by considering the entire list, you can use the value from the previous search to begin searching close to the target's correct position.

Binary Hunt and Search

To begin a binary hunt, compare the target value from the previous search to the new target value. If the new target value is smaller, begin hunting to the left. If the new target is larger, begin hunting to the right.

To hunt to the left, set min and max both equal to the index returned by the previous search. Then set min equal to min − 1 and compare the target value to List(min). If the target is smaller than List(min), set max = min and min = min − 2, and try again. If the target is still smaller, set max = min and min = min − 4. If that fails, set max = min and min = min − 8, and so forth. Continue setting max equal to min and subtracting the next power of 2 from min until you find a value for min where List(min) is less than the target.

Be sure you do not run off the end of the array with min smaller than the lower array bound. If you reach a point where min is smaller, set min equal to the lower array bound. If List(min) is still larger than the target item, the target is not in the list. Figure 10.4 shows a hunt to the left from the previous target value 44, looking for the new target 17.

A hunt to the right is similar to a hunt to the left. Start by setting min and max both equal to the index returned by the previous search. Then set min = max and max = max + 1, min = max and max = max + 2, min = max and max = max + 4, and so forth until you come to a point where List(max) is greater than the target. Once again, be sure you do not run past the end of the array.

Once you have finished the hunt phase, you will know that the target has index between min and max. You can then use a normal binary search to find the target's exact location.

Figure 10.4 A binary hunt for the value 17 from the value 44.

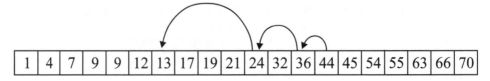

| 1 | 4 | 7 | 9 | 9 | 12 | 13 | 17 | 19 | 21 | 24 | 32 | 36 | 44 | 45 | 54 | 55 | 63 | 66 | 70 |

If the new target is close to the old target, a hunt will quickly find the correct values for min and max. If the indexes of the new and old targets are P positions apart, the hunt will take roughly log(P) steps to find the new values for min and max.

Suppose you started a normal binary search for the target without a hunt phase. It would take that search about log(NumItems) – log(P) steps to narrow the search down to the point where min and max were within P positions of each other. That means a hunt and search will be faster than a normal binary search if log(P) < log(NumItems) – log(P). Adding log(P) to both sides of this equation gives 2 * log(P) < log(NumItems). If you exponentiate both sides, you get $2^{2*\log(P)} < 2^{\log(NumItems)}$ or $(2^{\log(P)})^2 <$ NumItems. This simplifies to $P^2 <$ NumItems.

This shows that a hunt and search will be faster if you are fairly certain that the distance between two consecutive searches will be less than the square root of the number of items in the list. If consecutive searches will be for targets that are farther apart, you will be better off using a normal binary search.

Interpolative Hunt and Search

You can build on the techniques of the previous section to perform a hunt using interpolation. Begin as before by comparing the target value from the previous search to the new target value. If the new target value is smaller, begin a hunt to the left. If the new target is larger, begin a hunt to the right.

To hunt to the left, you would now use interpolation to guess where the value is between the previous target and List(1). But this is the same as a normal interpolation search where min = 1 and max is the index returned by the previous search. After a single step, the hunt phase is over, and you can proceed with a normal interpolation search.

A hunt to the right is similar. Simply set max = NumItems and min to the index returned by the previous search. Then continue with a normal interpolation search.

Figure 10.5 shows an interpolation search starting from the previous target value 44, looking for the new target 17.

If the data values are fairly evenly distributed, interpolation search always picks a value near the target in its first step or in any later step. That means starting from a previous value does not improve the algorithm too much. In its first step, without using the result of the previous search, interpolation search will probably pick an index close to the target's true location anyway.

Figure 10.5 Interpolation search for the value 17 from the value 44.

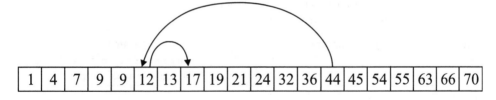

| 1 | 4 | 7 | 9 | 9 | 12 | 13 | 17 | 19 | 21 | 24 | 32 | 36 | 44 | 45 | 54 | 55 | 63 | 66 | 70 |

On the other hand, using the previous target value may help protect against unevenness in the data. If you know the new target's value is close to the old target's value, an interpolation starting from the previous search's value will have to give a value near the old target's location. This means using the old target as a starting point may provide some benefit.

The previous search's result also bounds the new target's location a little more tightly than the range 1 to NumItems, so the algorithm might save a step or two. This is especially important if the list is stored on a hard disk or other slow device where every disk access counts. If you can save the results of the previous search in memory, you can at least compare the new target to the previous target without an extra disk access.

Summary

If your items are stored in a linked list, use exhaustive search. If possible, use a bottom sentinel to make the search faster.

If you need to occasionally search a list containing a dozen or so items, use an exhaustive search. This will be easier to debug and maintain than a more complicated search technique, and it will provide adequate performance.

If you need to search a larger list, use an interpolation search. As long as the data values are fairly evenly distributed, interpolation search will give you the best performance. If your list is on a hard disk or other slow storage device, the difference between interpolation search and other search techniques may be quite large.

If the data values are strings, try to encode them as integers, longs, or doubles. Then you can use an interpolation search to locate items. If the data values are too long to fit in doubles, it may be easiest to use a binary search. Table 10.1 summarizes the advantages and disadvantages of each of the different search techniques.

Using binary search or interpolation search, you can locate items within a huge list extremely quickly. If data values are evenly distributed, interpolation search allows you to locate an item in a list containing millions of items in only a few steps.

Table 10.1 Advantages and Disadvantages of Search Techniques

Technique	Advantages	Disadvantages
Exhaustive	Simple Fast for small lists	Slow for large lists
Binary	Fast for large lists Not dependent on data distribution Easily handles string data	More complicated
Interpolation	Very fast for large lists	Very complicated Data must be evenly distributed Difficult to handle string data

Such a large list is still difficult to manage if you need to make changes to it. Inserting or removing an item from a sorted list requires O(N) time. If the item is at the beginning of the list, this could be quite time-consuming, especially if the list is stored on a slow storage device.

If you need to add and remove items from a large list, you should consider using a different data structure. Chapter 7, "Balanced Trees," discusses data structures that allow you to add and remove items in only O(log(N)) time.

Chapter 11, "Hashing," explains techniques for adding and locating items even more quickly. To achieve this speed, these methods require extra storage space. Hash tables also do not provide information about the ordering of the data. You can add, locate, and remove items from a hash table, but you cannot easily list the items in the table in order.

If your list will never change, a sorted list using interpolation search gives excellent performance. If you need to add and remove items from the list, you may want to consider using a hash table. If you also need to list the items in order or move forward and backward through the list, balanced trees provide both speed and flexibility. After you decide which operations you must perform, you can pick the algorithm that best suits your needs.

HASHING

Chapter 10, "Searching," describes interpolation search. That algorithm uses interpolation to quickly locate an item within a list. By comparing a target value with values at known locations, the algorithm can guess the position where the target item should be. It essentially creates a function that maps the target value to the index where the item should lie. If the first guess is wrong, the algorithm uses the function again to make a new guess. It continues making guesses until it finds the target item.

Hashing uses a similar concept to map items into a *hash table*. Using the value of a target item, a hashing algorithm uses some sort of function to decide where in the table the item should lie.

For example, suppose you need to store several records that have unique keys with values between 1 and 100. You could create an array of records with 100 entries and initialize the keys of each entry to 0. To add a new record to the array, you simply copy its data into the corresponding position. To add a record with key value 37, you copy the record into the 37th position in the array. To locate a record with a particular key, you examine the corresponding array entry. To remove a record you simply reset the corresponding array entry's key value to 0. Using this scheme you can add, locate, and remove items from the array in a single step.

Unfortunately, in real applications the key values do not always fit in nice ranges like 1 to 100. Usually, the possible key values span a very wide range. An employee database might use Social Security number as a key. There are 1 billion possible values for nine-digit numbers like Social Security numbers. In theory you could allocate an array with one entry for every possible nine-digit number; in reality you probably do not have enough memory or disk space. If each employee record required 1 kilobyte of memory, the array would occupy 1 terabyte (1 million megabytes) of memory. Even if you could allocate this much storage, this scheme would be quite wasteful. Unless your company hired more than 10 million employees, the array would always be more than 99 percent empty.

To work around these problems, hashing schemes map a potentially large number of possible keys into a relatively small hash table. If your company employs 700 workers, you might allocate a hash table with 1000 entries. The hashing scheme maps the 700 employee records into the 1000 positions in the table. The hashing function might map records into entries according to the first three digits of the employees' Social Security numbers. An employee with Social Security number 123-45-6789 would map to table position 123.

Of course, if there are more possible key values than there are table entries, some key values must map to the same position in the hash table. For example, the values 123-45-6789 and 123-99-9999 both map to table position 123. If there are 1 billion possible Social Security numbers and if you have only 1000 positions in the table, on the average 1 million records must map to each table position.

To handle this potential problem, a hashing scheme must have a *collision resolution policy* that tells what to do when a key maps to a position that is already occupied by another record. The following sections discuss several different methods for handling collisions.

All the methods discussed follow a similar approach to collision resolution. They first map a record's key to a position in the hash table. If that position is already occupied, they map the key to a new position. If that position is also occupied, they remap the key again until the algorithm finally locates an empty table position. The sequence of positions examined while locating or inserting an item in a hash table is called a *probe sequence*.

To summarize, you need three things to implement hashing:

- A data structure (hash table) to hold the data

- A hashing function to map key values into table entries

- A collision resolution policy that tells what to do when keys map to the same position

The sections that follow describe several different data structures you can use for hashing. Each has a corresponding hashing function and one or more possible collision resolution policies. As is the case with most computer algorithms, each method has its strengths and weaknesses. The final section in the chapter summarizes these so you can pick the best hashing technique for your situation.

Chaining

One method for collision resolution is to store records that map to the same table position in linked lists. To add a new record to the table, you use a hash function to pick the linked list that should hold it. You then add the record to that list.

Figure 11.1 shows an example of chaining in a hash table that contains 10 entries. The hashing function maps a key K into array position K Mod 10. Each position in the array contains a pointer to the first item in a linked list. To add an item to the table, you add it to the appropriate list.

To initially create the hash table in Visual Basic, use the ReDim statement to allocate sentinels for the tops of the lists. If you want NumLists linked lists in the hash table, dimension the ListTops array with the statement ReDim ListTops(0 To NumLists – 1). Initially each list is empty, so each sentinel's NextCell pointer

Figure 11.1 Chaining.

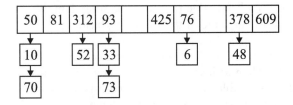

should have the value Nothing. When you use the ReDim statement to resize the sentinel array, Visual Basic automatically initializes all of the NextCell values to Nothing.

To locate an item with key K in the hash table, compute K Mod NumLists. This gives the index of the sentinel of the linked list in which the item may lie. Then look through that list until you find the item or you reach the end of the list.

```
Global Const HASH_FOUND = 0
Global Const HASH_NOT_FOUND = 1
Global Const HASH_INSERTED = 2


Private Function LocateItemUnsorted(Value As Long) As Integer
Dim cell As ChainCell

    ' Get the top of the linked list.
    Set cell = m_ListTops(Value Mod NumLists).NextCell
    Do While Not (cell Is Nothing)
        If cell.Value = Value Then Exit Do
        Set cell = cell.NextCell
    Loop

    If cell Is Nothing Then
        LocateItemUnsorted = HASH_NOT_FOUND
    Else
        LocateItemUnsorted = HASH_FOUND
    End If
End Function
```

Functions to add and remove items from the linked lists are similar to the functions described in Chapter 2, "Lists."

Advantages and Disadvantages of Chaining

One advantage of this method is that chaining hash tables never become full. It is always easy to insert or locate items, even if there are many items in the table. In some of the hashing techniques described in later sections, performance drops drastically when the table is almost full.

It is also easy to remove items from a hash table that uses chaining. Simply remove the item's cell from its linked list. In some of the following hashing schemes, removing items is difficult or impossible.

One disadvantage of chaining is that, unless the number of linked lists is relatively large, the chains can grow long. Then to insert or locate an item, you must search down a fairly long chain. If a hash table contains 10 linked lists and you add 1000 items to the table, the linked lists will have an average length of 100. Whenever you need to locate an item in the table, you might have to search through 100 or more cells.

One way you can make the search a little faster is to keep the linked lists in sorted order. Then you can use the techniques presented in Chapter 10, "Searching," to search for items in a sorted linked list. This allows you to stop searching for a target value if you encounter an item with a value larger than the target. On the average, you will need to search only half of a linked list before you either find the item or can conclude that it is not present.

```
Private Function LocateItemSorted(Value As Long) As Integer
Dim cell As ChainCell

    ' Get the top of the linked list.
    Set cell = m_ListTops(Value Mod NumLists).NextCell
    Do While Not (cell Is Nothing)
        If cell.Value >= Value Then Exit Do
        Set cell = cell.NextCell
    Loop

    If cell Is Nothing Then
        LocateItemSorted = HASH_NOT_FOUND
    ElseIf cell.Value = Value Then
        LocateItemSorted = HASH_FOUND
    Else
        LocateItemSorted = HASH_NOT_FOUND
    End If
End Function
```

Keeping the lists sorted makes searches a little faster, but it does not address the real problem. The chains are long because the table is too full. A better though more time-consuming solution is to create a larger hash table and rehash the items into the new table so the new linked lists are smaller. This can be a lot of work, particularly if the lists are stored on a hard disk or other slow device rather than in memory.

Example program Chain implements a hash table with chaining. Enter the number of lists you want in the Table Creation area on the form. Check the Sort

Lists box if you want the program to use sorted chains. Then click the Create Table button to create the hash table. You can enter new values in this section and click Create Table at any time to create a new hash table.

Because hash tables are often most interesting when they contain lots of items, program Chain allows you to create many random items at the same time. Enter the number of items you want to create and the maximum value those items should have in the Random Items area. Click the Create Items button, and the program adds the random items to the hash table.

Finally, enter a value in the Search area. If you click the Add button, the program inserts the item in the hash table if it is not already there. If you click the Find button, the program locates the item in the table.

After finishing an add or find operation, the program displays the status of the operation at the bottom of the form. The program tells whether the operation succeeded and shows the number of items the program examined during the operation.

The status label also tells you the current average length of a successful probe sequence (when the item is in the table) and an unsuccessful probe sequence (when the item is not in the table). The program calculates this average by searching for every number between 1 and the largest number currently in the hash table, then computing the average probe sequence length.

Figure 11.2 shows program Chain after it has successfully located the item 414.

Buckets

Another way to handle collisions is to allocate a number of buckets, each of which can hold several data items. To add an item to the table, you map the item into a bucket and then insert the item in that bucket. If the bucket is full, you use an overflow policy to deal with the new item.

Figure 11.2 Program Chain.

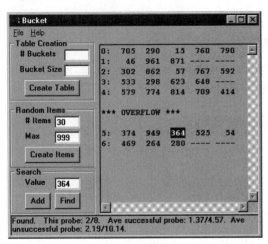

Probably the simplest overflow policy is to place all overflowed items into overflow buckets at the end of the array of "normal" buckets. This makes it easy to extend the hash table when necessary. When you need more overflow buckets, you simply redimension the array of buckets to make it larger and create new overflow buckets at the end.

For example, to add a new item K to a hash table containing five buckets, first try to place it in bucket number K Mod 5. If that bucket is full, place it in an overflow bucket.

To locate an item K in the table, calculate K Mod 5 to see where the item belongs. Then search that bucket. If the item does not appear in the bucket and the bucket is not full, then the item is not present in the hash table. If the item does not appear in the bucket and the bucket is full, search the overflow buckets.

Figure 11.3 shows five buckets numbered 0 through 4 and one overflow bucket. Each bucket can hold five items. In this example, the following items have been added to the hash table in this order: 50, 13, 10, 72, 25, 46, 68, 30, 99, 85, 93, 65, 70. When items 65 and 70 were added, their buckets were already full, so they were placed in the first overflow bucket.

To implement a bucket hashing scheme in Visual Basic, you can use a two-dimensional array to hold the buckets. If you want NumBuckets buckets that can each hold BucketSize entries, allocate the buckets with the statement ReDim TheBuckets(0 To BucketSize – 1, 0 To NumBuckets – 1). The second dimension is the one that indicates the bucket number. It may seem more natural to use the first dimension to hold the bucket number, but you may need to change the number of buckets later to add overflow buckets. Visual Basic's ReDim statement allows you to change only the last dimension in an array, so the bucket number must come last.

To locate an item K, calculate the bucket number K Mod NumBuckets. Then search that bucket until you find the item, an empty bucket entry, or the end of the bucket. If you find the item, you are done. If you find an unused entry, you know the item is not in the hash table and you are also done. If you search the entire bucket and do not find the item or an unused entry, search the overflow buckets.

Figure 11.3 Hashing with buckets.

Buckets

0	1	2	3	4		Overflow
50	46	72	13	99		65
10			68			70
25			93			
30						
85						

```
Public Function LocateItem(Value As Long, _
    bucket_probes As Integer, item_probes As Integer) As Integer
Dim bucket As Integer
Dim pos As Integer

    bucket_probes = 1
    item_probes = 0

    ' See what bucket it belongs in.
    bucket = (Value Mod NumBuckets)

    ' Look for the item or an unused position.
    For pos = 0 To BucketSize - 1
        item_probes = item_probes + 1
        If Buckets(pos, bucket).Value = UNUSED Then
            LocateItem = HASH_NOT_FOUND ' Not here.
            Exit Function
        End If
        If Buckets(pos, bucket).Value = Value Then
            LocateItem = HASH_FOUND        ' We found it.
            Exit Function
        End If
    Next pos

    ' Check the overflow buckets.
    For bucket = NumBuckets To MaxOverflow
        bucket_probes = bucket_probes + 1
        For pos = 0 To BucketSize - 1
            item_probes = item_probes + 1
            If Buckets(pos, bucket).Value = UNUSED Then
                LocateItem = HASH_NOT_FOUND ' Not here.
                Exit Function
            End If
            If Buckets(pos, bucket).Value = Value Then
                LocateItem = HASH_FOUND        ' We found it.
                Exit Function
            End If
        Next pos
    Next bucket

    ' If we still haven't found it, it's not here.
    LocateItem = HASH_NOT_FOUND
End Function
```

Example program Bucket demonstrates this scheme. This program is very similar to program Chain except it uses hashing with buckets instead of chaining. When this program reports probe lengths, it gives the number of buckets it examined followed by the number of items it examined within the buckets. Figure 11.4 shows the program after it successfully located item 661 in the first overflow bucket. In this example, the program examined nine items in two buckets.

Hash Tables on Disk

Most storage devices, like tape drives, floppy drives, and hard disks, can retrieve large chunks of data a block at a time. Usually this block is 512 or 1024 bytes long. It takes the device no more time to read one of these blocks of data than it takes it to read a single byte.

If you have a large hash table stored on a hard disk, you can use this fact to improve performance. Accessing data on a disk takes much longer than accessing it in memory. If you load all of the items in a bucket at once, you may be able to read them all in a single disk access. Once the items are loaded into memory, you can examine them much more quickly than you could if you had to read them one at a time from the disk.

If you use a For loop to read each item from the disk one at a time, Visual Basic will need to access the disk separately for each item. On the other hand, if you use a Get statement to read the entire bucket at once, Visual Basic can read the data one bucket at a time. This may require only a single disk access, so it will be much faster.

You can create a user-defined type containing an array of items to represent a bucket. Because you cannot redimension an array within a user-defined type at run time, you must decide how many items will be in the bucket ahead of time. This gives you a little less flexibility than you had before in sizing the buckets.

```
Global Const ITEMS_PER_BUCKET = 10    ' Items per bucket.
Global Const MAX_ITEM = 9             ' ITEMS_PER_BUCKET - 1.

Type ItemType
    Value As Long
End Type
Global Const ITEM_SIZE = 4            ' Size of this type.

Type BucketType
    Item(0 To MAX_ITEM) As ItemType
End Type
Global Const BUCKET_SIZE = ITEMS_PER_BUCKET * ITEM_SIZE
```

Before you read data from the hash file, open the data file in Random mode.

```
Open filename For Random As #DataFile Len = BUCKET_SIZE
```

Figure 11.4 Program Bucket.

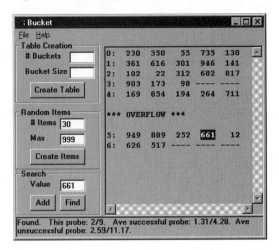

For convenience you can write functions to read and write buckets. These functions read and write data from the global variable TheBucket that holds the data for a single bucket. Once you have loaded the data into this variable, you can search the items within the bucket in memory.

Because random access files start numbering records at 1, not 0, these functions must add 1 to the hash table's bucket number before reading data from the file. The hash table's bucket number 0, for example, is stored in file record number 1.

```
Private Sub GetBucket(num As Integer)
    Get #DataFile, num + 1, TheBucket
End Sub

Private Sub PutBucket(num As Integer)
    Put #DataFile, num + 1, TheBucket
End Sub
```

Using functions GetBucket and PutBucket, you can rewrite the hash table search routine to read records from a file.

```
Public Function LocateItem(Value As Long, _
    bucket_probes As Integer, item_probes As Integer) As Integer
Dim bucket As Integer
Dim pos As Integer

    item_probes = 0
```

```
' See what bucket it belongs in.
GetBucket Value Mod NumBuckets
bucket_probes = 1

' Look for the item or an unused position.
For pos = 0 To MAX_ITEM
    item_probes = item_probes + 1
    If TheBucket.Item(pos).Value = UNUSED Then
        LocateItem = HASH_NOT_FOUND ' Not here.
        Exit Function
    End If
    If TheBucket.Item(pos).Value = Value Then
        LocateItem = HASH_FOUND        ' We found it.
        Exit Function
    End If
Next pos

' Check the overflow buckets.
For bucket = NumBuckets To MaxOverflow
    ' Get the next overflow bucket.
    GetBucket bucket
    bucket_probes = bucket_probes + 1

    For pos = 0 To MAX_ITEM
        item_probes = item_probes + 1
        If TheBucket.Item(pos).Value = UNUSED Then
            LocateItem = HASH_NOT_FOUND ' Not here.
            Exit Function
        End If
        If TheBucket.Item(pos).Value = Value Then
            LocateItem = HASH_FOUND        ' We found it.
            Exit Function
        End If
    Next pos
Next bucket

' If we still haven't found it, it's not here.
LocateItem = HASH_NOT_FOUND
End Function
```

Example program Bucket2 is similar to program Bucket except it stores its buckets on disk. It also does not compute and display average probe sequence lengths because those calculations would require many disk accesses and would slow the program greatly.

Because bucket accesses occur on disk and item accesses occur in memory, the number of buckets accessed is much more important in determining the program's run time than the total number of items examined. You can use program Bucket to compare the average number of bucket and item probes when searching for items.

Each bucket in program Bucket2 can hold up to 10 items. This makes it easy for you to fill the buckets until they overflow. In a real program, you should try to fit as many items as possible into a bucket while keeping the bucket size a multiple of your disk drive's natural block size.

For example, you might decide to read and write data in blocks of 1024 bytes. If your data items have a size of 44 bytes, you can fit 23 data items into one bucket while keeping the bucket size under 1024 bytes.

```
Global Const ITEMS_PER_BUCKET = 23    ' Items per bucket.
Global Const MAX_ITEM = 22            ' ITEMS_PER_BUCKET - 1.


Type ItemType
    LastName As String * 20           ' 20 bytes.
    FirstName As String * 20          ' 20 bytes.
    EmployeeId As Long                ' 4 bytes (this is the key).
End Type
Global Const ITEM_SIZE = 44           ' Size of this type.


Type BucketType
    Item(0 To MaxItem) As ItemType
End Type
Global Const BUCKET_SIZE = ITEMS_PER_BUCKET * ITEM_SIZE
```

Putting more items in each bucket allows you to read more data in a single disk access. It also allows the table to hold more items before you need to use overflow buckets. Accessing overflow buckets requires extra disk accesses, so you should avoid using them whenever possible.

On the other hand, if the buckets are large they may contain a lot of unused entries. If the data items are not evenly distributed among the buckets, some buckets may overflow and others may be nearly empty. A different arrangement with a larger number of smaller buckets might reduce this problem. Even though some data items will still overflow and some buckets will be nearly empty, the nearly empty buckets will be smaller, so they will not contain as many unused entries.

Figure 11.5 shows two bucket arrangements holding the same data. The arrangement on the top uses 5 buckets containing 5 items each. It holds all of the data with no overflow buckets and 12 unused item entries. The arrangement on the bottom uses 10 buckets containing 2 items each. It holds the items with 1 overflow bucket and contains only 9 unused item entries.

Figure 11.5 Two different bucket arrangements.

Buckets

0	1	2	3	4
50	46	72	18	
10		57	68	
25			93	
35			28	
65			73	

Buckets

0	1	2	3	4	5	6	7	8	9	Overflow
50		72	93		25	46	57	18		28
10			73		35			68		65

This is an example of a space versus time trade-off. In the first arrangement, all the items are located in normal (nonoverflow) buckets so that you can locate them all quickly. The second arrangement saves space but places some of the items in overflow buckets that take longer to access.

Bucket Chaining

A slightly different way to manage full buckets is to chain them to overflow buckets. Each full bucket gets its own set of overflow buckets rather than having all overflow buckets shared. When you search for an item in a full bucket, you do not need to examine any items that have overflowed from other buckets. If there has been a lot of overflow, this can save quite a bit of time.

Figure 11.6 shows the same data in two different hashing schemes. In the top arrangement, items that overflow are added to common overflow buckets. To locate the items 32 or 30, you must access three buckets. First, you examine the bucket in which the item normally belongs. The item is not there, so you then examine the first overflow bucket. The item is not there either, so you must examine the second overflow bucket. There you finally find the item.

In the bottom arrangement, full buckets are linked to their own overflow buckets. In this arrangement, you can locate every item after accessing, at most, two buckets. As before, you start by examining the bucket where the item normally belongs. If you do not find the item there, you examine that bucket's linked list of overflow buckets. In this example, you need to check only one overflow bucket to find the item.

If the hash table contains many items in its overflow buckets, chaining the overflow buckets may save a lot of time. Suppose you have a moderately large

Figure 11.6 Linked overflow buckets.

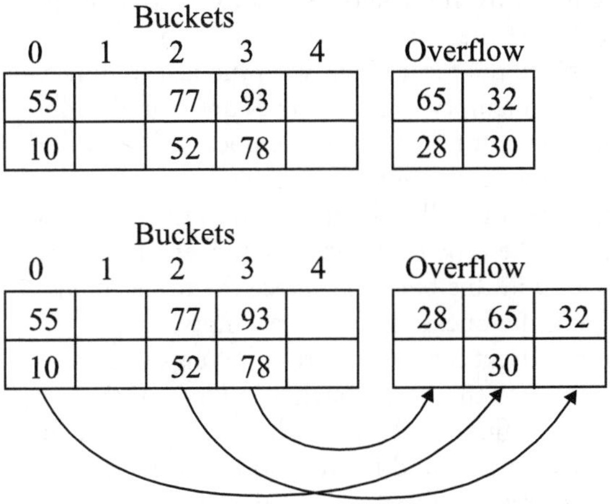

hash table containing 1000 buckets holding 10 items each. Suppose also that you have 1000 items in overflow buckets. To hold all of those overflow items, you would need 100 overflow buckets. To locate one of the last items in the overflow buckets you would have to examine 101 buckets.

Even worse, suppose you wanted to locate an item K that is not in the table but that maps to a full bucket. You would need to search all 100 overflow buckets before you learned that the item was not in the table. If your program often searches for items that are not in the table, it will spend a huge amount of time looking through the overflow buckets.

If you chain overflow buckets, and if the key values are reasonably distributed, you will be able to locate items much more quickly. If the largest number of items that have overflowed out of any single bucket is 10, each bucket will have at most 1 overflow bucket. In that case, you can locate any item or determine that an item is not in the table by examining, at most, 2 buckets.

On the other hand, if the hash table is just a little too full, many buckets may have overflow buckets containing only 1 or 2 items. To continue this example, suppose 11 items mapped into each bucket. Because each bucket holds only 10 items, every normal bucket would need an overflow bucket. In this case, you would need 1000 overflow buckets, each containing a single item. Between them all, these overflow buckets would contain 900 unused entries.

This is another example of a space versus time trade-off. Chaining buckets allows you to add and locate items more quickly, but it may also fill the hash table with unused space. Of course, you could probably avoid the problem completely by creating a new, larger hash table and rehashing all the table entries.

Removing Items

Although it is not as easy to remove items from buckets as it is to remove them from chains, it is still possible. First, locate the item you want to remove in the hash table. If its bucket is not full, replace the target item with the last item in the bucket. This will ensure that all of the nonempty bucket entries are stored at the front of the bucket. Later, when you search for an item in the bucket, if you find an unused item you can conclude that the item is not in the table.

If the bucket containing the target item is full, you must search the overflow buckets to find an item that can replace the target item in this bucket. If none of the items in the overflow buckets belong in this bucket, replace the target item with the last item in the bucket, leaving the bucket's last entry empty.

Otherwise, if there is an item in the overflow buckets that belongs in this bucket, move the chosen overflow item into the target bucket in place of the target item. That will leave a hole in the overflow bucket, but that is easy to fix. Just take the last item from the last overflow bucket and move it to fill in the hole.

Figure 11.7 illustrates the process of removing an item from a full bucket. First, item 24 is removed from bucket 0. Because bucket 0 was full, you must look for an item in the overflow buckets that you can move into bucket 0. In this case, bucket 0 holds all of the even items, so any even item in the overflow buckets will do. The first even item in the overflow buckets is item 14, so you can replace item 24 in bucket 0 with item 14.

That leaves a hole in the third position in the first overflow bucket. Fill in the hole by replacing item 14 with the last item in the last overflow bucket, in this case item 79. At this point the hash table is again ready for use.

An alternative method for removing an item is to mark the item as having been removed but to leave it in its bucket. To locate items in that bucket, you should ignore removed items. Later, when you are adding a new item to that bucket, you can reuse the removed item's position.

Marking an item as removed is faster and easier than actually removing it from the hash table, but eventually the table may become full of unused entries. If

---

Figure 11.7 Removing an item from a bucket.

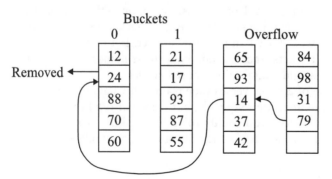

you add a bunch of items to the hash table and then remove most of them in first-in-first-out order, the buckets will become "bottom heavy." Most of the real data will be in the bottom of the buckets and in the overflow buckets. Adding new items to the table will be easy, but you will waste a fair amount of time skipping removed entries when you search for an item.

As a compromise, when you remove an item from a bucket, you can move the last item in the bucket into the emptied position and then mark the last item in the bucket as removed. Then when you search a bucket, you can stop looking through that bucket if you encounter an item that has been marked as removed. You would then search the overflow buckets if there are any.

Advantages and Disadvantages of Buckets

Adding or locating an item in a hash table with buckets is relatively fast, even when the table is completely full. In fact, a hash table using buckets will usually be faster than a hash table using chaining (chaining from the previous section, not bucket chaining). If the hash table is stored on a hard disk, a bucket scheme can read an entire bucket of data in one disk access. With chaining, the next item in a chain may not be anywhere near the previous one on the disk. You would need one disk access every time you needed to examine an item.

Removing an item from a table using buckets is harder than removing an item from a table using chaining. To remove an item from a bucket that is full, you may need to examine all the overflow buckets to find a suitable replacement item.

A final advantage to a hash table that uses buckets is that it is easy to extend the table when it becomes full. When all the overflow buckets are full, you simply redimension the bucket array and create a new overflow bucket at the end.

If you extend the table in this way too many times, a large fraction of the data will be stored in the overflow buckets. Then to find or insert an item, you must examine many buckets, and performance will suffer. In that case, it may be better to create a new hash table with more initial buckets and rehash the items than to expand the overfull table.

Open Addressing

Sometimes the data items you need to store are too big to fit conveniently in buckets. If you need a list of 1000 items, each occupying 1Mb of disk space, it would be difficult to use buckets that could hold more than one or two items. If the buckets only hold one or two items, you must examine many buckets to add or locate an item.

In open addressing you use a hashing function to map data items directly into positions in an array. For example, you could use an array with dimensions 0 to 99 for a hash table. Then for a hashing function you could map the key value K to array position K Mod 100. You would insert the value 1723 in the table at position 23. Later, if you wanted to locate item 1723, you would look for it at position 23.

Different open addressing schemes use different methods for generating probe sequences. The following sections examine three of the more important methods: linear probing, quadratic probing, and pseudo-random probing.

Linear Probing

When you map a new item into an array position that is already in use, you can simply look through the array from that point until you come to an unoccupied position. This collision resolution policy is called *linear probing* because you search through the table in a linear fashion.

Consider again the example where you have an array dimensioned 0 to 99 and the hashing function maps K to position K Mod 100. To insert the item 1723, you first examine array position 23. If that position is full, you try position 24. If it is also in use, you try positions 25, 26, 27, and so on until you find an empty position.

To insert a new item into a hash table, you follow that item's probe sequence until you find an unused entry. To locate an item in the table, you follow the item's probe sequence until you find the item or you find an unused entry. If you find an unused entry first, you know the item is not in the hash table.

You could write a combined hashing and probing function as:

```
Hash(K, P) = (K + P) Mod 100        where P = 0, 1, 2, ...
```

Here P is the number of the item in the probe sequence for K. In other words, to hash item K you try Hash(K, 0), Hash(K, 1), Hash(K, 2), ... until you find an empty position.

You can generalize this idea to build a table of size N using an array dimensioned from 0 to N − 1. The hashing function is:

```
Hash(K, P) = (K + P) Mod N        where P = 0, 1, 2, ...
```

The following code shows how you can locate an item using linear probing in Visual Basic.

```
Public Function LocateItem(Value As Long, pos As Integer, _
    probes As Integer) As Integer
Dim new_value As Long

    probes = 1
    pos = (Value Mod m_NumEntries)
    Do
        new_value = m_HashTable(pos)

        ' We found it.
        If new_value = Value Then
            LocateItem = HASH_FOUND
```

```
        Exit Function
    End If


    ' The item's not here.
    If new_value = UNUSED Or probes >= NumEntries Then
        LocateItem = HASH_NOT_FOUND
        pos = -1
        Exit Function
    End If


    pos = (pos + 1) Mod NumEntries
    probes = probes + 1
  Loop
End Function
```

Example program Linear demonstrates open addressing with linear probing. By filling in the Table Size field and clicking the Create Table button, you can create hash tables of different sizes. You can then enter the value of an item and click the Add or Find button to insert or locate the item in the table.

To add several random values to the table all at once, enter the number of items you want to add and the maximum value they should have in the Random Items area. Then click the Create Items button to make the program add the items to the table.

After the program completes each operation, it displays the status of the operation (whether it succeeded or not) and the length of the probe sequence it just followed. It also displays the average lengths of a successful and an unsuccessful probe sequence. The program computes the average probe sequence lengths by searching for every value between 1 and the largest value in the table at that time.

Table 11.1 shows the average lengths of successful and unsuccessful probe sequences produced by program Linear for a table with 100 entries and items in the range 1 to 999. The table shows that the algorithm's performance degrades as the table becomes full. Whether the performance is acceptable to you depends on how you use the table. If a program spends most of its time searching for values that are in the table, performance will be reasonably good, even when the table is quite full. If a program often searches for values that are not in the table, performance will be poor if the table is too full.

As a rule, hashing provides reasonable performance without too much wasted space when the table is 50 to 75 percent full. If the table is more than 75 percent full, performance suffers. If the table is less than 50 percent full, it occupies more space than it really needs. This makes open addressing a good example of a space versus time trade-off. By making a hash table larger, you can decrease the time needed to insert and locate items.

Table 11.1 Lengths of Successful and Unsuccessful Probe Sequences

Entries Used	Successful	Unsuccessful
10	1.10	1.12
20	1.15	1.26
30	1.20	1.50
40	1.35	1.83
50	1.92	2.64
60	2.03	3.35
70	2.61	5.17
80	3.41	8.00
90	3.81	10.74
100	6.51	100.00

Primary Clustering

Linear probing has an unfortunate *primary clustering* property. After you insert many items into the table, the items tend to cluster together to form large groups. When you add more items, the new items tend to collide with the clusters. Then you need to search past the cluster before you find an empty position in the table.

To see how clusters form, suppose you begin with an empty hash table that can hold N entries. If you pick a number at random and insert it into the table, there will be a 1 / N chance that the item will end up in any given position P in the table.

When you insert a second randomly chosen item, there is a 1 / N chance that the item maps to the same position P. This collision forces you to put the item in position P + 1. There is also a 1 / N chance that the item maps directly to position P + 1 and a 1 / N chance that it maps to position P – 1. In all three of these cases, the new item ends up next to the previously inserted item. There is a total chance of 3 / N that the new item winds up next to the previous one, starting a small cluster. These odds are slightly greater than the 1 / N odds that the item ends up in any other particular position.

Once a cluster starts to grow, the chance of subsequent items landing on or next to the cluster increases. When a cluster contains two items, there is a 4 / N chance that the next item will add to the cluster. When it contains four items, there is a 6 / N chance that the cluster will grow, and so forth.

Worse still, once a cluster starts to grow, it continues to grow until it bumps into an adjacent cluster. The two clusters join to form an even larger cluster that grows even faster, meets other clusters, and forms still larger clusters.

Ideally if a hash table is half full, the items in the table will occupy every other array position. Then there is a 50 percent chance that the algorithm immediately finds an empty position for the next item added. There is also a 50 percent chance that it would find an empty position after examining only two table positions. The average probe sequence length is 0.5 * 1 + 0.5 * 2 = 1.5.

In the worst case, all of the items in the table will be grouped together in one giant cluster. There is still a 50 percent chance that the algorithm immediately finds an empty position for the next item added. When it does not find an empty position, however, the algorithm takes a much longer time to find an open position. If the item lands on the first position in the cluster, the algorithm must search past all the entries in the cluster to find an open position. On average, it takes much longer to insert an item in this arrangement than it does if the items are evenly spaced throughout the hash table.

In practice, the amount of clustering will be somewhere between these extremes. You can use program Linear to see the clustering effect. Run the program and build a hash table with 100 entries. Then randomly add 50 items with values up to 999. You will notice that several clusters have formed. In one test 38 of the 50 items were part of clusters. If you add another 25 items to the table, most of the items will be part of clusters. In another test 70 of the 75 items were grouped in clusters.

Ordered Linear Probing

When you perform an exhaustive search of a sorted list, you can stop whenever you find an item with value greater than the value you are seeking. Because you have passed the position where the target item would be if it were in the list, the item must not be present.

You can use a similar idea when searching a hash table. Suppose you can arrange the items in the hash table so the values along every probe sequence are arranged in increasing order. Then as you follow a probe sequence looking for an item, you can stop if you ever find an item greater than the target value. In that case, you have passed the position where the item belongs, so you know it is not in the table.

```
Public Function LocateItem(Value As Long, pos As Integer, _
    probes As Integer) As Integer
Dim new_value As Long

    probes = 1
    pos = (Value Mod m_NumEntries)
    Do
        new_value = m_HashTable(pos)

        ' The item's not here.
        If new_value = UNUSED Or probes > NumEntries Then
```

```
            LocateItem = HASH_NOT_FOUND
            pos = -1
            Exit Function
        End If


        ' We found it or it's not here.
        If new_value >= Value Then Exit Do

        pos = (pos + 1) Mod NumEntries
        probes = probes + 1
    Loop

    If Value = new_value Then
        LocateItem = HASH_FOUND
    Else
        LocateItem = HASH_NOT_FOUND
    End If
End Function
```

For this method to work, you must arrange the items in the hash table so that you encounter them in increasing order whenever you follow a probe sequence. There is a fairly simple method for inserting items that guarantees this arrangement.

When you insert a new item into the table, follow its probe sequence. If you find an empty position, insert the item at that position and you are done. If you come to an item with value larger than the new item, swap the two items. Then follow the probe sequence for the larger item to find a new location for it in the table. As you search for a new position for the larger item, you may come to another item that is larger still. Swap those items and go on to find a new location for the new, even larger item. Continue this process, possibly swapping several items, until you eventually find an empty position to hold the item you are currently placing.

```
Public Function InsertItem(ByVal Value As Long, pos As Integer, _
    probes As Integer) As Integer
Dim new_value As Long
Dim status As Integer

    ' See if the table is full.
    If m_NumUnused < 1 Then
        ' See if we can find the item.
        status = LocateItem(Value, pos, probes)
        If status = HASH_FOUND Then
            InsertItem = HASH_FOUND
        Else
```

```
            InsertItem = HASH_TABLE_FULL
            pos = -1
        End If
        Exit Function
    End If

    probes = 1
    pos = (Value Mod m_NumEntries)
    Do
        new_value = m_HashTable(pos)

        ' If we found the value, we're done.
        If new_value = Value Then
            InsertItem = HASH_FOUND
            Exit Function
        End If

        ' If the entry is unused, this is where it
        ' belongs.
        If new_value = UNUSED Then
            m_HashTable(pos) = Value
            InsertItem = HASH_INSERTED
            m_NumUnused = m_NumUnused - 1
            Exit Function
        End If

        ' If the table entry is larger than the
        ' value, swap them and continue.
        If new_value > Value Then
            m_HashTable(pos) = Value
            Value = new_value
        End If

        pos = (pos + 1) Mod NumEntries
        probes = probes + 1
    Loop
End Function
```

Example program Ordered demonstrates open addressing with ordered linear probing. It is identical to program Linear except it uses an ordered hash table.

Table 11.2 shows average probe sequence lengths of successful and unsuccessful searches using linear and ordered linear probing. The average lengths of successful searches are similar for the two methods. For unsuccessful searches, however, ordered probing is significantly faster. The difference is particularly noticeable when the hash table is more than about 70 percent full.

Table 11.2 Lengths of Searches Using Linear and Ordered Linear Probing

Entries Used	Linear Successful	Linear Unsuccessful	Ordered Successful	Ordered Unsuccessful
10	1.10	1.12	1.10	1.04
20	1.15	1.26	1.10	1.09
30	1.20	1.50	1.23	1.13
40	1.35	1.83	1.38	1.23
50	1.92	2.64	1.36	1.35
60	2.03	3.35	1.53	1.56
70	2.61	5.17	1.64	1.76
80	3.41	8.00	2.04	2.18
90	3.81	10.74	3.42	3.88
100	6.51	100.00	6.16	6.20

Both methods require roughly the same number of steps to insert a new item. To add item K to the table, each method starts at position (K Mod NumEntries) and moves through the hash table until it finds an empty position. During ordered hashing you may need to swap the item you are inserting with others in its probe sequence. If the items are large records, this may be quite time-consuming, particularly if the records are stored on a disk or other slow storage device.

Ordered linear probing is definitely a better choice if you expect your program to make many unsuccessful searches. If your program will usually search for items that are in the hash table or if the items in the table are large and difficult to move, you may get better performance using unordered linear probing.

Quadratic Probing

One way to reduce primary clustering is to use a hashing function like this one:

```
Hash(K, P) = (K + P²) Mod N        where P = 0, 1, 2, ...
```

Suppose, while inserting an item into a hash table, you map the item into a cluster of other items. If the item maps to a position near the beginning of the cluster, you will have several more collisions before you find an empty position for the item. As the parameter P in the probe function grows, the value of this function changes quickly. That means the final position where you place the item will probably not be adjacent to the cluster.

Figure 11.8 shows a hash table containing a large cluster of items. It also shows the probe sequences that result when you try to insert two different items into positions occupied by the cluster. Both of these probe sequences end in a final position that is not adjacent to the cluster, so the cluster does not grow when you insert these items.

The following code shows how to locate an item using quadratic probing.

```
Public Function LocateItem(Value As Long, pos As Integer, _
    probes As Integer) As Integer
Dim new_value As Long

    probes = 1
    pos = (Value Mod m_NumEntries)
    Do
        new_value = m_HashTable(pos)

        ' We found it.
        If new_value = Value Then
            LocateItem = HASH_FOUND
            Exit Function
        End If

        ' The item's not here.
        If new_value = UNUSED Or probes >= NumEntries Then
            LocateItem = HASH_NOT_FOUND
            pos = -1
            Exit Function
        End If

        pos = (Value + probes * probes) Mod NumEntries
        probes = probes + 1
    Loop
End Function
```

Example program Quad demonstrates open addressing with quadratic probing. It is similar to program Linear except it uses quadratic rather than linear probing.

Table 11.3 shows average probe sequence lengths produced by programs Linear and Quad for a hash table with 100 entries and items ranging in value from 1 to 999. Quadratic probing generally gives better results.

Figure 11.8 Quadratic probing.

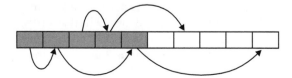

Table 11.3 Lengths of Searches Using Linear and Quadratic Probing

Entries Used	Linear Successful	Linear Unsuccessful	Quadratic Successful	Quadratic Unsuccessful
10	1.10	1.12	1.00	1.11
20	1.15	1.26	1.10	1.21
30	1.20	1.50	1.33	1.44
40	1.35	1.83	1.77	1.75
50	1.92	2.64	1.80	2.14
60	2.03	3.35	1.88	2.67
70	2.61	5.17	2.09	3.43
80	3.41	8.00	2.30	5.05
90	3.81	10.74	2.77	15.03
100	6.51	100.00	3.79	101.00

Quadratic probing does have some disadvantages. Because of the way the probe sequence is generated, you cannot guarantee that it will visit every item in the table. That means you may sometimes be unable to insert an item, even though the table is not completely full.

For example, consider a small hash table that holds only six entries. The probe sequence for the number 3 is:

```
3
3 +  1² =    4 = 4 (Mod 6)
3 +  2² =    7 = 1 (Mod 6)
3 +  3² =   12 = 0 (Mod 6)
3 +  4² =   19 = 1 (Mod 6)
3 +  5² =   28 = 4 (Mod 6)
3 +  6² =   39 = 3 (Mod 6)
3 +  7² =   52 = 4 (Mod 6)
3 +  8² =   67 = 1 (Mod 6)
3 +  9² =   84 = 0 (Mod 6)
3 + 10² =  103 = 1 (Mod 6)
Etc.
```

This probe sequence visits the positions 1 and 4 twice each before visiting the position 3, and it never visits positions 2 and 5. To see this effect, create a six-entry hash table using program Quad. Then add the items 1, 3, 4, 6, and 9 in that order. The program will tell you that the table is full, even though there are two unused entries. The probe sequence for the item 9 does not visit positions 2 and 5, so the program cannot insert the new item in the table.

It can be shown that a quadratic probe sequence will visit at least N / 2 of the table entries if the size of the table N is prime. While this guarantees some level of performance, it may still become a problem when the table is almost full. Because performance drops when the table is almost full anyway, you are probably better off enlarging the hash table rather than worrying about not being able to find the last empty entries.

A more subtle problem with quadratic probing is that, while it eliminates primary clustering, it allows a similar problem called *secondary clustering*. If two items initially hash to the same location, they follow the same probe sequence. If many items initially map to the same table location, they form a secondary cluster that is spread out within the hash table. When a new item with the same initial value appears, it must follow a long probe sequence before it gets past the other items in the secondary cluster.

Figure 11.9 shows a hash table that can hold 10 entries. The table contains the items 2, 12, 22, and 32, all of which map initially to position 2. If you try to add the item 42 to the table, you must follow a long probe sequence that visits each of these other items' positions before finding an empty spot.

Pseudo-Random Probing

Clustering occurs when items that map into a cluster join the cluster. Secondary clustering occurs when items that initially collide at the same location follow the same probe sequence to form a secondary cluster spread through the hash table. You can eliminate both of these effects if you can make different items follow different probe sequences, even if they initially map to the same position.

One way to do this is to use a pseudo-random number generator to provide the probe sequence. To compute the probe sequence of an item, use the item's value to initialize the random number generator. Then use the successive numbers produced by the generator to build the probe sequence. This is called *pseudo-random probing*.

Later, when you want to locate an item in the hash table, reinitialize the random number generator using the item's value. The generator will then produce the same sequence of numbers you used to insert the item into the table. Using these numbers you can recreate the original probe sequence and find the item.

If your random number generator is good, different item values will produce different random numbers and therefore different probe sequences. Even if two

Figure 11.9 Secondary clustering.

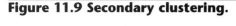

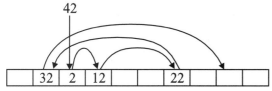

	32	2	12			22			

item values initially map to the same position, the next positions in their probe sequences will probably be different. In this case, your hash table will not suffer from clustering or secondary clustering.

You can initialize Visual Basic's random number generator using a seed value with the following code.

```
Rnd -1
Randomize seed_value
```

The Rnd statement will generate the same sequence of numbers every time it is initialized with the same seed value.

The following code shows how you can locate an item using pseudo-random probing.

```
Public Function LocateItem(Value As Long, pos As Integer, _
    probes As Integer) As Integer
Dim new_value As Long

    ' Initialize the random number generator.
    Rnd -1
    Randomize Value

    probes = 1
    pos = Int(Rnd * m_NumEntries)
    Do
        new_value = m_HashTable(pos)

        ' We found it.
        If new_value = Value Then
            LocateItem = HASH_FOUND
            Exit Function
        End If

        ' The item's not here.
        If new_value = UNUSED Or probes > NumEntries Then
            LocateItem = HASH_NOT_FOUND
            pos = -1
            Exit Function
        End If

        pos = Int(Rnd * m_NumEntries)
        probes = probes + 1
    Loop
End Function
```

Example program Rand demonstrates open addressing with pseudo-random probing. It is the same as programs Linear and Quad except it uses pseudo-random rather than linear or quadratic probing.

Table 11.4 shows approximate average probe sequence lengths produced by programs Quad and Rand for a hash table with 100 entries and items ranging from 1 to 999. Pseudo-random probing generally gives the best results, though the difference between quadratic and pseudo-random probing is not as great as the difference between linear and quadratic probing.

Pseudo-random probing also has its drawbacks. Because the probe sequence is chosen pseudo-randomly, you cannot be certain how quickly the algorithm will visit every item in the table. If the table is small compared to the number of possible pseudo-random values, there is a chance that the probe sequence will visit the same value repeatedly before it visits other values in the table. It is also possible that a probe sequence will completely miss a table entry so it will be unable to insert an item even when the table has room.

As is the case with quadratic probing, these effects cause trouble only when the table is mostly full. At that point, enlarging the table provides a much greater performance improvement than worrying about finding the last unused table entries.

Table 11.4 Lengths of Searches Using Quadratic and Pseudo-Random Probing

Entries Used	Quadratic Successful	Quadratic Unsuccessful	Pseudo-Random Successful	Pseudo-Random Unsuccessful
10	1.00	1.11	1.00	1.10
20	1.10	1.21	1.15	1.24
30	1.33	1.44	1.13	1.41
40	1.77	1.75	1.23	1.63
50	1.80	2.14	1.36	1.91
60	1.88	2.67	1.47	2.37
70	2.09	3.43	1.70	3.17
80	2.30	5.05	1.90	4.70
90	2.77	15.03	2.30	9.69
100	3.79	101.00	3.79	101.00

Removing Items

Removing items from a hash table that uses open addressing is not as easy as removing items from a table that uses chains or buckets. You cannot simply remove an item from the table, because that item may lie in the probe sequence for some other item.

Suppose item A is in the probe sequence for item B. If you remove A from the table, you will no longer be able to find item B. When you search for B, you will find the empty position left by the removal of item A, so you will incorrectly conclude that item B is not in the table.

Instead of removing the item from the hash table, you can mark it as removed. If you later find a position marked as removed while you are adding a new item to the table, you can reuse that position. If you encounter a marked item while you are searching for another item, ignore the removed item and continue following the probe sequence.

After you have marked many items as removed, the hash table may become full of garbage. When you search for items, you will spend a great deal of time skipping over these removed items. Eventually you may want to rehash the table to reclaim the unused space.

Rehashing

To free removed entries in a hash table, you can rehash the table in place. For this algorithm to work, you must have some way to tell whether an item has already been rehashed. The easiest way to do this is to assume that the items are user-defined structures that contain a Rehashed field.

```
Type ItemType
    Value As Long
    Rehashed As Boolean
End Type
```

Begin by initializing all the Rehashed fields to false. Then pass through the table looking for entries that are not marked as removed and that have not yet been rehashed.

When you find such an item, remove it from the table and rehash it. Follow the normal probe sequence for the item. If you come to an entry that is empty or marked as removed, deposit the item there, mark it as rehashed, and continue looking for other items that have not yet been rehashed.

While rehashing an item, if you find an item that is already marked as rehashed, continue following the item's probe sequence.

If you come to an item that has not yet been rehashed, swap the two items, mark the position as rehashed, and start the process over to rehash the new item.

Resizing Hash Tables

If a hash table becomes too full, performance drops dramatically. In that case, you might want to enlarge the table to improve performance and make room for more entries. Conversely if a hash table contains very few entries, you might want to make it smaller to free some memory. Using techniques similar to those used to rehash a table in place, you can expand or shrink a hash table.

To expand a hash table, first make its table array larger using a ReDim Preserve statement. Then rehash the table allowing items to hash into the newly created space at the end of the table. When you are finished, the table will be ready for use.

To reduce the size of a hash table, first decide how many entries you want the smaller table array to hold. Then rehash the table, allowing items to hash only into the reduced part of the table. When you have finished rehashing all the items, resize the array using the ReDim Preserve statement to make it smaller.

The following code shows how to rehash a table that uses linear probing. The code to rehash a table that uses quadratic or pseudo-random probing is similar.

```
Public Sub Rehash()
Dim i As Integer
Dim pos As Integer
Dim probes As Integer
Dim Value As Long
Dim new_value As Long

    ' Mark all items as not rehashed.
    For i = 0 To NumEntries - 1
        m_HashTable(i).Rehashed = False
    Next i

    ' Look for unrehashed items.
    For i = 0 To NumEntries - 1
        If Not m_HashTable(i).Rehashed Then
            Value = m_HashTable(i).Value
            m_HashTable(i).Value = UNUSED

            If Value <> DELETED And Value <> UNUSED Then
                ' Follow this item's probe sequence
                ' until we find an empty, deleted,
                ' or unrehashed item.
                probes = 0
                Do
                    pos = (Value + probes) Mod NumEntries
                    new_value = m_HashTable(pos).Value

                    ' If empty or deleted, place
                    ' the item here.
                    If new_value = UNUSED Or _
```

```
                        new_value = DELETED _
            Then
                    m_HashTable(pos).Value = Value
                    m_HashTable(pos).Rehashed = True
                    Exit Do
            End If

            ' If not rehashed, swap and
            ' continue.
            If Not m_HashTable(pos).Rehashed Then
                    m_HashTable(pos).Value = Value
                    m_HashTable(pos).Rehashed = True
                    Value = new_value
                    probes = 0
            Else
                    probes = probes + 1
            End If
                Loop
            End If
        End If
    Next i
End Sub
```

Example program Rehash uses open addressing with linear probing. It is similar to program Linear, but it also allows you to mark objects as removed and to rehash the table.

Summary

The different kinds of hash tables described in this chapter each have their strengths and weaknesses.

Hash tables that use chaining or buckets are easy to enlarge and allow easy removal of items. Buckets can also take advantage of disk behavior by loading many data items with a single disk access. Both of these methods, however, are slower than open addressing techniques.

Linear probing is simple and allows you to insert and locate items in the hash table fairly quickly. Ordered linear probing allows you to determine that an item is not in the table more quickly than does unordered linear probing. On the other hand, adding items to the table using ordered linear probing is more difficult.

Quadratic probing prevents clustering that affects linear probing, so it gives better performance. Pseudo-random probing avoids clustering and secondary clustering so it gives better performance still.

Table 11.5 shows a summary of the advantages and disadvantages of the various hashing methods.

Table 11.5 Advantages and Disadvantages of Hashing Methods

Method	Advantages	Disadvantages
Chaining	Easy to enlarge Easy to remove items Contains no unused entries	Slows when lists grow long
Buckets	Easy to enlarge Easy to remove items Works naturally on disks	Slow when there are many overflow buckets Contains unused entries
Bucket Chaining	Easy to enlarge Easy to remove items Works naturally on disks	Contains more unused entries
Linear Probing	Fast access	Hard to enlarge Hard to remove items Contains unused entries
Ordered Linear Probing	Fast access Short unsuccessful probes	Hard to enlarge Hard to remove items Takes longer to insert items Contains unused entries
Quadratic Probing	Faster access	Hard to enlarge Hard to remove items Contains unused entries
Pseudo-Random Probing	Fastest access	Hard to enlarge Hard to remove items Contains unused entries

Which hashing technique is best for a given application depends on the data and the ways in which the data will be used. The different schemes offer different tradeoffs in size, speed, and ease of modification. Table 11.5 can help you pick the algorithm that best meets your needs.

NETWORK ALGORITHMS

Chapter 6, "Trees," and Chapter 7, "Balanced Trees," discuss tree algorithms. This chapter covers the more general topic of networks. Networks play important roles in many applications. You can use them to model network-like objects such as streets, telephone facilities, power lines, water pipes, sewers, storm drains, airline connections, and railroad lines. You can also use networks in less obvious ways to solve problems such as districting, critical path scheduling, crew scheduling, and work assignment.

Definitions

Like a tree, a *network* or *graph* is a set of *nodes* connected by a set of *edges* or *links*. Unlike a tree, a network has no concept of parent or child nodes.

The links in a network may each have an associated direction, in which case the network is called a *directed network*. Each link may also have an associated *cost*. In a street network, for example, the cost might be the time it takes to drive across the section of road represented by the link. In a telephone network, the cost might be the amount of electrical loss across the cable represented by the link. Figure 12.1 shows a small directed network where numbers next to the links show the links' costs.

A *path* between nodes A and B is a series of links that connects the two nodes. If there is at most one link between any two nodes in the network, a path can be described uniquely by listing the nodes along the path. Because that is usually easier to visualize, paths are described in this way if possible. In Figure 12.1, the path containing the nodes B, E, F, G, E, and D is a path connecting nodes B and D.

A *cycle* is a path that connects a node to itself. The path E, F, G, E in Figure 12.1 is a cycle. A path is *simple* if it contains no cycles. The path B, E, F, G, E, D is not simple because it contains the cycle E, F, G, E.

If there is any path between two nodes, then there must be a simple path between the two nodes. You can find this path by removing any cycles from the original path. For example, if you replace the cycle E, F, G, E with the node E in the nonsimple path B, E, F, G, E, D, you get the simple path B, E, D connecting nodes B and D.

Figure 12.1 A directed network with link costs.

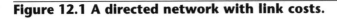

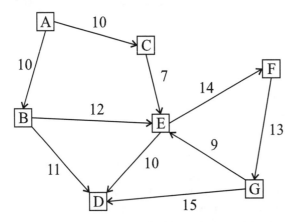

A network is *connected* if there is at least one path from every node in the network to every other node. In a directed network, it is not always obvious whether the network is connected. In Figure 12.2, the network on the left is connected. The network on the right is not because there is no path from node E to node C.

Network Representations

Chapter 6, "Trees," described several representations for trees. Most of those representations are useful for manipulating networks as well. For example, the fat node, child list (neighbor list for networks), and forward star representations can all be used to store networks. See Chapter 6 for an explanation of these representations.

Which network representation is best depends on the application. A fat node representation works well if each node in the network is connected to a limited number of edges. A neighbor list strategy provides more flexibility than a fat node

Figure 12.2 Connected (left) and disconnected (right) networks.

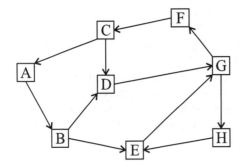
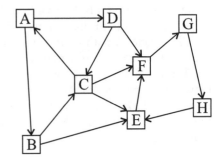

approach. Forward star representations, while harder to modify than the others, provide better performance.

In addition to these options, several explicit link variations can make certain types of networks easier to manage. These representations use one class to represent nodes and another class to represent links. The link class makes it easier to work with link properties such as costs.

For example, a directed network with link costs might use the following node class definition.

```
Public Id Integer         ' The node's Id.
Public Links As Collection   ' Links leading to neighbors.
```

The network would use this link class definition.

```
Public ToNode As NetworkNode ' The node at the other end of the link.
Public Cost As Integer       ' The link's cost.
```

Using these definitions, a program could find the least costly link out of a node using the following code.

```
Dim link As NetworkLink
Dim best_link As NetworkLink
Dim best_cost As Integer

    best_cost = 32767
    For Each link In node.Links
        If link.cost < best_cost Then
            Set best_link = link
            best_cost = link.cost
        End If
    Next link
```

The node and link classes are often extended for the convenience of particular algorithms. For example, a Marked flag is often added to the node class. When the program visits a node, it sets Marked to true so it will later know that it has already visited the node.

A program managing an undirected network might use a slightly different representation. The node class is the same as before, but the link class includes a reference to both of the nodes at its end points.

```
Public Node1 As NetworkNode  ' One of the link's nodes.
Public Node2 As NetworkNode  ' The other node.
Public Cost As Integer       ' The link's cost.
```

For an undirected network, the previous representation would use two objects to represent each link—one for each of the link's directions. In the new version, each link is represented by a single object. This representation is fairly easy to understand, so it is the representation used throughout the rest of this chapter.

Using this representation, example program NetEdit allows you to manage undirected networks with link costs. The File menu allows you to open and save networks in files. The commands in the Edit menu allow you to add and remove nodes and links. Program NetEdit is shown in Figure 12.3.

The OldSrc\Ch12 directory contains network programs that use the forward star representation. These programs are a bit harder to understand, but they are generally faster. They are not explained in the text, but they use techniques similar to those demonstrated by the Visual Basic 4.0 versions. For example, programs Src\Ch12\PathS and OldSrc\Ch12\PathS both calculate shortest paths using the label setting algorithm described later. The main difference is that the first program uses collections and classes while the second uses pointer faking and forward star.

Managing Nodes and Links

The root of a tree is unique: It is the only node in a tree that has no parent. From the root node you can follow child pointers to locate all the other nodes in the tree. This makes the root a convenient handle for the tree. If you store a pointer to the root node in a variable, you can later access all the nodes in the tree.

Networks do not always contain a node in such a unique position. In a disconnected network, there may not be a way to follow links from one node to all of the others.

For this reason, network programs often keep a complete list of all the nodes in the network. A program may also keep a list of all the links. These lists make it easy to act on all the links or nodes in the network. For example, if a program stores pointers to the nodes and links in the Nodes and Links collections, it can use the following method to draw the network.

```
Dim node As NetworkNode
Dim link As NetworkLink
```

Figure 12.3 Program NetEdit.

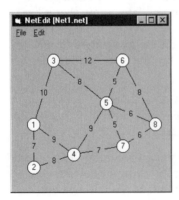

```
For Each link in Links
     ' Draw the link.
        :
Next link

For Each node in Nodes
     ' Draw the node.
        :
Next node
```

The NetEdit program uses Nodes and Links collections to draw networks in this way.

Network Traversals

Traversing a network is similar to traversing a tree. You can traverse a network using either a depth-first or breadth-first traversal. Depth-first traversals are generally similar to preorder traversals in trees, though you could also define postorder and even inorder traversals for a network.

The algorithm for performing a preorder traversal for a binary tree described in Chapter 6, "Trees," is:

1. Visit the node.

2. Recursively traverse the left subtree in preorder.

3. Recursively traverse the right subtree in preorder.

In a tree there is a parent-child relationship between nodes that are connected. Because the algorithm starts at the root and always works downward through the child nodes, it will never visit a node twice.

On the other hand, in a network nodes are not necessarily linked in a top-down manner. If you try to implement this preorder traversal algorithm in a network, you may stumble into a cycle and enter an infinite loop.

To prevent this, when the algorithm reaches a node it should mark the node as visited. When the algorithm searches neighboring nodes, it visits only the nodes that are not yet marked. When the algorithm finishes, all the nodes in the network will be marked as visited (if the network is connected). The preorder network traversal algorithm is:

1. Mark the node.

2. Visit the node.

3. Recursively traverse the node's neighbors that are not yet marked.

In Visual Basic you can add a Marked flag to the NetworkNode class.

```
Public Id As Long
```

```
Public Marked As Boolean
Public Links As Collection
```

The NetworkNode class can include a public subroutine for traversing the network starting at the node. A node's PreorderPrint routine visits all the nodes that have not yet been visited that can be reached from the node. If the network is connected, the resulting traversal will visit every node in the network.

```
Public Sub PreorderPrint()
Dim link As NetworkLink
Dim node As NetworkNode

    ' Mark this node as visited.
    Marked = True

    ' Visit the unmarked neighbors.
    For Each link In Links
        ' See which node is the neighbor.
        If link.Node1 Is Me Then
            Set node = link.Node2
        Else
            Set node = link.Node1
        End If

        ' See if we should visit the neighbor.
        If Not node.Marked Then node.PreorderPrint
    Next link
End Sub
```

Because this subroutine does not visit any node twice, the collection of links traversed does not contain any cycles. That makes this collection a tree.

If the network is connected, the tree will reach every node in the network. Because the tree spans every node in the network, it is called a *spanning tree*. Figure 12.4 shows a small network with a spanning tree rooted at node A drawn in bold lines.

You can use a similar node marking technique to convert the breadth-first tree traversal algorithm into a network algorithm. The tree traversal algorithm begins by placing the tree's root node in a queue. It then removes the first node from the queue, visits it, and places its children at the end of the queue. It repeats this process until the queue is empty.

In the network traversal algorithm, you must make certain that a node is not placed in the queue if it has been visited before or if it is currently in the queue. To do this, mark each node as you place it in the queue. The network version of the algorithm is:

1. Mark the first node (this will be the root of the spanning tree) and add it to the end of the queue.

Figure 12.4 A spanning tree.

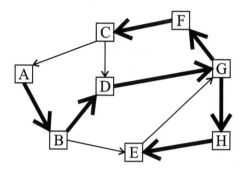

2. Repeat until the queue is empty:
   a. Remove the first node from the queue and visit it.
   b. For each of the node's neighbors that are not yet marked, mark the neighbor and add it to the end of the queue.

The following subroutine prints a list of network nodes in breadth-first order.

```
Public Sub BreadthFirstPrint(root As NetworkNode)
Dim queue As New Collection
Dim node As NetworkNode
Dim neighbor As NetworkNode
Dim link As NetworkLink

    ' Put the root in the queue.
    root.Marked = True
    queue.Add root

    ' Repeatedly process the top item in the queue until
    ' the queue is empty.
    Do While queue.Count > 0
        ' Get the next node from the queue.
        Set node = queue.Item(1)
        queue.Remove 1

        ' Visit the node.
        Print node.Id

        ' Add the node's unmarked neighbors to the queue.
        For Each link In node.Links
            ' See which node is the neighbor.
            If link.Node1 Is Me Then
                Set neighbor = link.Node2
```

```
        Else
            Set neighbor = link.Node1
        End If

        ' See if we should visit the neighbor.
        If Not neighbor.Marked Then queue.Add neighbor
    Next link
  Loop
End Sub
```

Minimal Spanning Trees

Given a network with link costs, a *minimal spanning tree* is a spanning tree where the total cost of all the links in the tree is as small as possible. You can use a minimal spanning tree to pick the least costly way to connect all the nodes in a network.

For example, suppose you need to design a telephone network connecting six cities. You could build a trunk between every pair of the cities, but that would be needlessly expensive. A less costly solution would be to connect the cities along the links contained in a minimal spanning tree. Figure 12.5 shows six cities with a possible trunk drawn between each pair of cities. A minimal spanning tree is drawn in bold.

Notice that a network may contain more than one minimal spanning tree. Figure 12.6 shows two pictures of one network with two different minimal spanning trees drawn in bold. The total cost of both of these trees is 32.

There is a simple algorithm for finding a minimal spanning tree for a network. Start by placing any node in the spanning tree. Then find the least costly link that connects a node in the tree to a node that is not yet in the tree. Add that link and

---

Figure 12.5 Telephone trunks connecting six cities.

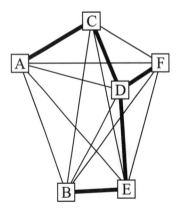

Figure 12.6 Two different minimal spanning trees for the same network.

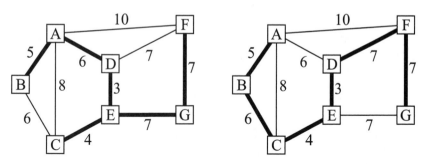

the corresponding node to the tree. Repeat this procedure until you have added all the nodes to the tree.

In a way, this algorithm is similar to the hill climbing heuristic described in Chapter 8, "Decision Trees." At each step both algorithms modify the solution to improve it as much as possible. At each step the spanning tree algorithm selects the smallest link that adds a new node to the tree. Unlike the hill climbing heuristic, which does not always find an optimal solution, this algorithm is guaranteed to find a minimal spanning tree.

Algorithms like this, which reach globally optimal solutions by making locally optimal decisions, are called *greedy algorithms*. You can think of greedy algorithms as hill climbing algorithms that are not heuristics—they are guaranteed to find the best solution possible.

The minimal spanning tree algorithm uses a collection named "candidates" to store the links that might be added to the spanning tree. Initially the algorithm places the links out of the root node in the candidate list.

It then searches the list for the link with the smallest cost. To make this search as fast as possible, a program could use a priority queue like those described in Chapter 9, "Sorting," with the links ordered by cost. Alternatively, to keep things as simple as possible, the program can store the candidate list in a collection.

If the node at the other end of that link is not already in the spanning tree, the program adds it and the link. It then adds the links leaving the new node to the candidate list so they will be considered.

The algorithm uses a Used flag in the link class to indicate whether a link has been in the candidate list before. Once a link has been on the list, it need not be added to the list again.

It is possible that the candidate list will empty completely before all the nodes have been added to the spanning tree. In that case, the network is not connected. There is no path from the root node to all the other nodes in the network.

```
Private Sub FindSpanningTree(root As SpanNode)
Dim candidates As New Collection
```

```
Dim to_node As SpanNode
Dim link As SpanLink
Dim i As Integer
Dim best_i As Integer
Dim best_cost As Integer
Dim best_to_node As SpanNode

    If root Is Nothing Then Exit Sub

    ' Reset all nodes' Marked flags and all links'
    ' Used and InSpanningTree flags.
    ResetSpanningTree

    ' Start with the root in the spanning tree.
    root.Marked = True
    Set best_to_node = root

    Do
        ' Add the latest node's links to the
        ' candidate list.
        For Each link In best_to_node.Links
            If Not link.Used Then
                candidates.Add link
                link.Used = True
            End If
        Next link

        ' Find the shortest link in the candidate
        ' list that leads to a node not yet in the
        ' tree.
        best_i = 0
        best_cost = INFINITY
        i = 1
        Do While i <= candidates.Count
            Set link = candidates(i)
            If link.Node1.Marked Then
                Set to_node = link.Node2
            Else
                Set to_node = link.Node1
            End If
            If to_node.Marked Then
                    ' The link connects two nodes that
                    ' are both already in the tree.
                    ' Remove it from the candidate list.
```

```
                candidates.Remove i
        Else
            If link.Cost < best_cost Then
                best_i = i
                best_cost = link.Cost
                Set best_to_node = to_node
            End If
            i = i + 1
        End If
    Loop


    ' If there were no useable links, we've
    ' done the best we can.
    If best_i < 1 Then Exit Do

    ' Add the best link and to_node to the tree.
    Set link = candidates(best_i)
    link.InSpanningTree = True
    candidates.Remove best_i

    best_to_node.Marked = True
    Loop

    GotSpanningTree = True

    ' Redraw the network.
    DrawNetwork
End Sub
```

This algorithm examines each link at most once. As each link is examined, it is added and then later removed from the candidate list. If the candidate list is stored as a heap-based priority queue, it takes $O(\log(N))$ time to add or remove an item from the queue where N is the number of links in the network. In that case, the total run time for the algorithm is $O(N * \log(N))$.

If the candidate list is stored in a collection as in the previous code, it takes $O(N)$ time to locate the least costly link in the list. That makes the total run time for the algorithm $O(N^2)$. If N is relatively small, this performance is reasonable. If the number of links in the network is large, you should store the candidate list in a priority queue instead of a collection.

Example program Span uses this algorithm to find minimal spanning trees. The program is similar to program NetEdit. It lets you load, edit, and save network files. When you are not adding or removing a node or link, you can click on a node to make the program find and display a minimal spanning tree rooted at that node. Figure 12.7 shows program Span displaying a minimal spanning tree rooted at node 9.

Figure 12.7 Program Span.

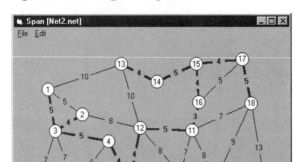

Shortest Paths

The types of shortest path algorithms discussed in the following sections find all the shortest paths from a single point to every other point in the network, assuming the network is connected. The collection of links used by all of the shortest paths forms a *shortest path tree.*

Figure 12.8 shows a network where the shortest path tree rooted at node A is drawn in bold. This tree shows the shortest path from node A to every other node in the network. The shortest path from node A to node F, for example, follows the path A, C, E, F.

Most shortest path algorithms start with an empty shortest path tree and then add links one at a time to the tree until the tree is complete. These algorithms can be divided into two categories according to how they select the next link to add to the growing shortest path tree.

Label setting algorithms always select a link that is guaranteed to be part of the final shortest path tree. This is similar to the way the minimal spanning tree algorithm works. Once a link has been added to the tree, it will not be removed later.

Label correcting algorithms add links that may or may not be part of the final shortest path tree. As the algorithm progresses, it may discover that a different link should have been added instead of one that is already in the tree. In that case, the algorithm replaces the old link with the new one and continues. Replacing a link in the tree may make new paths possible that were not possible before. To check for these paths, the algorithm must reexamine any paths it previously added to the tree using the link that was removed.

Figure 12.8 A shortest path tree.

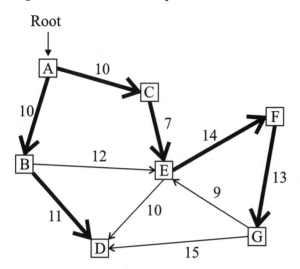

The label setting and the label correcting algorithms described in the following sections use similar classes to represent nodes and links. The node class includes a Dist field that indicates the distance from the root to the node in the growing shortest path tree. In a label setting algorithm, Dist is correct once a node has been added to the tree and it will not be changed later. In a label correcting algorithm, Dist may be revised later when the algorithm replaces a link with a different one.

The node class also includes a NodeStatus field to indicate whether the node is currently in the shortest path tree, in a candidate list, or neither. The InLink field gives the link that leads to the node in the shortest path tree.

```
Public Id As Integer
Public X As Single
Public Y As Single
Public Links As Collection
Public Dist As Integer          ' Distance from root of path tree.
Public NodeStatus As Integer    ' Path tree status.
Public InLink As PathSLink      ' The link into the node.
```

Using the InLink fields, a program can list the nodes in the path from the root to node I in reverse order using the following code.

```
Dim node As PathSNode

    Set node = I
    Do
        ' List the node.
```

```
Print node.Id
If node Is Root Then Exit Do

' Go to the next node up the tree.
If node.InLink.Node1 Is node Then
    Set node = node.InLink.Node2
Else
    Set node = node.InLink.Node1
End If
Loop
```

The algorithm's link class includes an InPathTree field that indicates whether the link is part of the shortest path tree.

```
Public Node1 As PathSNode
Public Node2 As PathSNode
Public Cost As Integer
Public InPathTree As Boolean
```

Both label setting and label correcting algorithms use a candidate list to keep track of links that might be added to the shortest path tree. The algorithms differ in the ways they manage the candidate list. Label setting algorithms always select a candidate that is guaranteed to be part of the shortest path tree. The label correcting algorithm described here selects whatever item is at the top of the candidate list.

Label Setting

This algorithm begins by setting the root node's Dist value to 0 and by placing the root node in the candidate list. It sets the node's NodeStatus value to NOW_IN_LIST to indicate that it is currently in the candidate list.

It then searches the list for the node with the smallest Dist value. Initially that will be the root node because it is the only node in the list.

The algorithm removes the selected node from the candidate list. It sets the node's NodeStatus entry to the value WAS_IN_LIST to indicate that the node is now a permanent part of the shortest path tree. Its Dist and InLink fields have their correct final values. For the root node, InLink is Nothing and Dist is zero.

Next, the algorithm examines each of the links leaving the selected node. If the neighbor node at the other end of a link has never been on the candidate list before, the algorithm adds the neighbor to the list. It sets the neighbor's NodeStatus value to NOW_IN_LIST. It sets the neighbor's Dist value to the distance from the root node to the selected node plus the cost of the link. Finally, it sets the neighbor's InLink value to indicate the link connecting it to the selected node.

As the algorithm examines the links leaving the selected node, if a neighbor node has NodeStatus value NOW_IN_LIST, it is already in the candidate list. The algorithm compares the neighbor's current Dist value to see if the new path via the selected node would be shorter. If so, it updates the neighbor's InLink and Dist entries and leaves it in the candidate list.

The algorithm repeats this process, removing nodes from the candidate list, examining their neighbors, and adding neighbors to the candidate list, until the list is empty.

Figure 12.9 shows a partial shortest path tree. At this point the algorithm has considered nodes A and B, has removed them from the candidate list, and has examined their links. It has added nodes A and B to the shortest path tree, and the candidate list now contains nodes C, D, and E. The bold arrows in Figure 12.9 indicate the InLink values at this point. For example, the InLink value for node E currently connects nodes E and B.

Next the algorithm searches the candidate list for the node with the smallest Dist value. At this point, the Dist values of C, D, and E are currently 10, 21, and 22, respectively, so the algorithm selects node C. It removes node C from the candidate list and sets the node's NodeStatus value to WAS_IN_LIST. Now node C is part of the shortest path tree and its Dist and InLink entries have their correct final values.

The algorithm then examines the links leaving node C. The only link leaving node C goes to node E. Node E is currently in the candidate list, so the algorithm does not add it to the list again.

The current shortest path from the root to node E is the path A, B, E, with a total cost of 22. But the path A, C, E has a cost of only 17. This is lower than the current cost of 22, so the algorithm updates the InLink value for node E and sets node E's Dist entry to 17.

Figure 12.9 A partial shortest path tree.

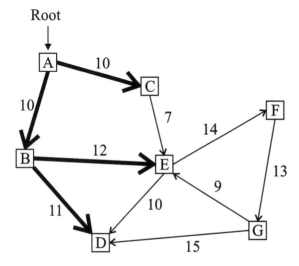

```
Private Sub FindPathTree(root As PathSNode)
Dim candidates As New Collection
Dim i As Integer
Dim best_i As Integer
Dim best_dist As Integer
Dim new_dist As Integer
Dim node As PathSNode
Dim to_node As PathSNode
Dim link As PathSLink

    If root Is Nothing Then Exit Sub

    ' Reset all nodes' Marked and NodeStatus values,
    ' and all links' Used and InPathTree flags.
    ResetPathTree

    ' Start with the root in the shortest path tree.
    root.Dist = 0
    Set root.InLink = Nothing
    candidates.Add root

    Do While candidates.Count > 0
        ' Find the candidate closest to the root.
        best_dist = INFINITY
        For i = 1 To candidates.Count
            new_dist = candidates(i).Dist
            If new_dist < best_dist Then
                best_i = i
                best_dist = new_dist
            End If
        Next i

        ' Add this node to the shortest path tree.
        Set node = candidates(best_i)
        candidates.Remove best_i
        node.NodeStatus = WAS_IN_LIST

        ' Examine the node's neighbors.
        For Each link In node.Links
            If node Is link.Node1 Then
                Set to_node = link.Node2
            Else
                Set to_node = link.Node1
            End If
```

```
         If to_node.NodeStatus = NOT_IN_LIST Then
             ' The node has not been in the
             ' candidate list. Add it.
             candidates.Add to_node
             to_node.NodeStatus = NOW_IN_LIST
             to_node.Dist = best_dist + link.Cost
             Set to_node.InLink = link
         ElseIf to_node.NodeStatus = NOW_IN_LIST Then
             ' The node is in the candidate
             ' list. Update its Dist and inlink
             ' values if necessary.
             new_dist = best_dist + link.Cost
             If new_dist < to_node.Dist Then
                 to_node.Dist = new_dist
                 Set to_node.InLink = link
             End If
         End If
     Next link
 Loop

 GotPathTree = True

 ' Mark the inlinks so they are easy to draw.
 For Each node In Nodes
     If Not (node.InLink Is Nothing) Then _
         node.InLink.InPathTree = True
 Next node

 ' Redraw the network.
 DrawNetwork
End Sub
```

It is important that the algorithm update the InLink and Dist entries only for nodes with NodeStatus NOW_IN_LIST. For many networks there will be no improvement possible for a node unless it is in the candidate list. If the network contains a cycle of negative total length, however, the algorithm will find that it can improve the distances to some nodes that are already in the shortest path tree. This will connect two branches of the shortest path tree so that it will no longer be a tree.

Figure 12.10 shows a network with a negative cost cycle and the shortest path "tree" that would result if the algorithm updated the costs of nodes already in the tree.

Example program PathS uses this label setting algorithm to compute shortest paths. It is similar to programs NetEdit and Span. If you are not adding or

Figure 12.10 Incorrect shortest path "tree" for a network with a negative cost cycle.

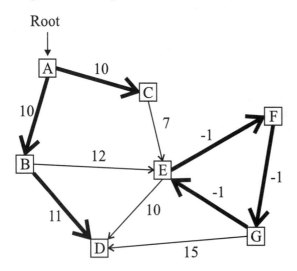

removing a node or link, you can click on a node to make the program find and display a shortest path tree rooted at that node. Figure 12.11 shows program PathS displaying a shortest path tree rooted at node 3.

Label Setting Variations

The main bottleneck in this algorithm is in locating the node in the candidate list that has the smallest Dist value. Several variations of this algorithm use different data structures for storing the candidate list. For example, you could store the candidate list as a sorted linked list. Using this method it would take only a single

Figure 12.11 A shortest path tree rooted at node 3.

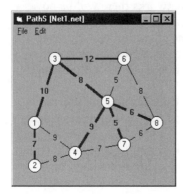

step to find the next node to add to the shortest path tree. The list would always be sorted, so the node at the top would always be the one to add.

This would make finding the correct node in the list easier, but it would also make adding a node to the list harder. Instead of placing the node at the beginning of the list, you would need to add it at the appropriate position in the list.

You would also sometimes need to move nodes around in the list. If, by adding a node to the shortest path tree, you reduced the best distance to another node that was already in the list, you would need to move that node closer to the top of the list.

The previous algorithm and this new variation represent two extremes for managing the candidate list. The first stores the list in a totally unordered way and spends a lot of time looking for nodes in the list. The second spends a lot of effort maintaining a sorted linked list but can select nodes very quickly. Other variations use intermediate strategies.

For example, you could store the candidate list in a heap-based priority queue. Then you could easily select the next node from the top of the heap. Adding a new node to the heap and rearranging the heap would be faster than performing the same operations on a sorted linked list. Other strategies use clever arrangements of buckets to keep the best candidates easy to find.

Some of these variations are quite complicated. The extra complication often makes these algorithms slower than simpler algorithms for small networks. For very large networks or networks where each node has a very large number of links, these algorithms may be worth the extra complication.

Label Correcting

Like the label setting algorithm, this algorithm begins by setting the root node's Dist value to 0 and by placing the root node in the candidate list. It initializes the Dist values of the other nodes to infinity. It then selects the first node in the candidate list to add to the shortest path tree.

Next, the algorithm examines each of the neighbors of the selected node. It checks whether the distance from the root to the selected node plus the cost of the link is less than the neighbor's current Dist value. If it is, the algorithm updates the neighbor's Dist and InLink entries so the best path to the neighbor goes through the selected node. If the neighbor is not already in the candidate list, the algorithm also adds it. Notice that this algorithm does not check whether the item has been on the list before. If there is improvement in the path from the root to the neighbor, it is always added to the candidate list.

The algorithm continues removing nodes from the candidate list, examining their neighbors, and adding neighbors to the candidate list until the list is empty.

If you compare the label setting and label correcting algorithms carefully, you will find that they are very similar. The only difference is in how each selects a node from the candidate list to add to the shortest path tree.

The label setting algorithm always picks a link that is guaranteed to belong in the shortest path tree. Once it removes a node from the candidate list, that node has been permanently added to the tree and will not be placed in the candidate list again.

The label correcting algorithm always selects the first node from the candidate list. That node may not always be the best choice. The node's Dist and InLink entries may not hold the best possible values. In that case, the algorithm will eventually examine a node in the candidate list that gives a better path to the node than the one originally chosen. The algorithm then updates the incorrect node's Dist and InLink entries, and it places the updated node back in the candidate list.

The algorithm may be able to use the new path to form other paths that it might have missed earlier. By placing the updated node back in the candidate list, the algorithm ensures it will consider the node again and find any such paths.

```
Private Sub FindPathTree(root As PathCNode)
Dim candidates As New Collection
Dim node_dist As Integer
Dim new_dist As Integer
Dim node As PathCNode
Dim to_node As PathCNode
Dim link As PathCLink

    If root Is Nothing Then Exit Sub

    ' Reset all nodes' Marked and NodeStatus values,
    ' and all links' Used and InPathTree flags.
    ResetPathTree

    ' Start with the root in the shortest path tree.
    root.Dist = 0
    Set root.InLink = Nothing
    root.NodeStatus = NOW_IN_LIST
    candidates.Add root

    Do While candidates.Count > 0
        ' Add a node to the shortest path tree.
        Set node = candidates(1)
        candidates.Remove 1
        node_dist = node.Dist
        node.NodeStatus = NOT_IN_LIST

        ' Examine the node's neighbors.
        For Each link In node.Links
            If node Is link.Node1 Then
                Set to_node = link.Node2
            Else
```

```
            Set to_node = link.Node1
        End If


        ' See if there is an improved path
        ' using this node.
        new_dist = node_dist + link.Cost
        If to_node.Dist > new_dist Then
            ' It's better. Update the Dist and
            ' InLink values.
            Set to_node.InLink = link
            to_node.Dist = new_dist

            ' Add it to the candidate list if
            ' is not already there.
            If to_node.NodeStatus = NOT_IN_LIST Then
                candidates.Add to_node
                to_node.NodeStatus = NOW_IN_LIST
            End If
        End If
    Next link
Loop


' Mark the inlinks so they are easy to draw.
For Each node In Nodes
    If Not (node.InLink Is Nothing) Then _
        node.InLink.InPathTree = True
Next node


' Redraw the network.
DrawNetwork
End Sub
```

Unlike the label setting algorithm, this algorithm cannot handle networks that contain negative cost cycles. If it finds such a cycle, the algorithm enters an infinite loop following the links in the cycle. Each time it passes through the cycle, it can reduce the distances to the nodes it is examining. As it reduces their distances, it places the nodes back in the candidate list so it can update other paths. When it examines the nodes again, it reduces their distances further. This process continues until the distances to these nodes underflow with values less than −32,768 if the program uses integers for its calculations. If you know that your network contains negative cycles, the easiest thing to do is to use label setting instead of label correcting.

Example program PathC uses this label correcting algorithm to compute shortest paths. It is similar to program PathS except it uses label correcting instead of label setting.

Label Correcting Variations

This label correcting algorithm can select a node from the candidate list very quickly. It can also add a node to the list in only one or two steps. The trouble with this algorithm is that, when it selects a node from the candidate list, it may not make a very good choice. If the algorithm selects a node before that node's Dist and InLink fields reach their final values, it must correct the fields later and place the node back in the candidate list. The more often the algorithm places nodes back in the candidate list, the longer it takes.

Variations on this algorithm try to improve the quality of the node selections without creating a lot of additional work. One technique that works well in practice is to add nodes to both the front and back of the candidate list. If a node has never been on the candidate list before, the algorithm adds it at the back of the list as usual. If the node has previously been on the candidate list but is not now, the algorithm adds it at the front of the list. This makes the algorithm revisit that node quite soon, probably the next time it selects a node.

The idea behind this approach is that, if the algorithm has made a mistake, it should fix the mistake as soon as possible. If the mistake is left uncorrected, the algorithm may use the incorrect information to build long, false paths that must be corrected later. By reexamining the node quickly, the algorithm may be able to reduce the number of incorrect paths it needs to rebuild. In the best case, if the node's neighbors are still in the candidate list, reexamining this node before examining its neighbors prevents any incorrect paths from starting.

Other Shortest Path Problems

The previous shortest path algorithms compute all of the shortest paths from a single root node to all of the other nodes in the network. There are many other types of shortest path problems. This section examines three: point-to-point shortest paths, all pairs shortest paths, and shortest paths with turn penalties.

Point-to-Point Shortest Path

In some applications, you may want to find the shortest path between two points, but you may not care about all of the other shortest paths stored in a complete shortest path tree. One easy way you can find a point-to-point shortest path is to compute the complete shortest path tree using either a label setting or label correcting algorithm. Then use the shortest path tree to find the shortest path between the two points.

Another method is to use a label setting algorithm that stops when it finds a path to the destination node. A label setting algorithm never adds to the shortest path tree links that do not belong there. When it adds the destination node to the shortest path tree, the algorithm has found a correct shortest path. In the algorithm described earlier, this occurs when the algorithm removes the destination node from the candidate list.

The only change you need to make in the label setting algorithm comes right after the algorithm has found the node in the candidate list with the smallest Dist value. Before removing the node from the candidate list, the algorithm should check whether the node is the destination node. If so, the shortest path tree already holds a correct path from the start node to the destination node so the algorithm can stop early.

```
' Find the candidate closest to the root.
    :


' See if this is the destination node.
If node = destination Then Exit Do


' Add this node to the shortest path tree.
    :
```

In practice if the two points are far apart in the network, this algorithm will usually take longer than computing the entire shortest path tree. Checking for the destination node each time the loop executes makes the algorithm slower. On the other hand, if the nodes are close together in the network, this algorithm may be much faster than building a complete shortest path tree.

For some networks, like street networks, you may be able to guess how far apart the two points are and then decide which version of the algorithm to use for those points. If your network contains all the streets in southern California and the 2 points are 10 miles apart, you should use the version that stops when it removes the destination from the candidate list. If the points are 100 miles apart, it will probably be faster to compute the entire shortest path tree.

All Pairs Shortest Paths

Some applications may require you to quickly find the shortest path between any pair of nodes in the network. If the application requires you to compute a large fraction of the possible N^2 paths, it may be faster to precompute all of the possible shortest paths rather than finding each as you need it.

You can store the shortest paths using two two-dimensional arrays, Dists and InLinks. Dists(I, J) holds the shortest distance from node I to node J. InLinks(I, J) holds the link that leads to node J in the shortest path from node I to node J. These values are similar to the Dist and InLink values stored in the node class in the previous algorithms.

One way to find the shortest path information is to build the shortest path tree rooted at each node in the network using one of the previous algorithms. Then save the results in the Dists and InLinks arrays.

Another method for computing all of the shortest paths successively constructs paths through the network using more and more nodes. First, the algorithm finds all the shortest paths that use only the first node plus the end nodes in the path. In other words, for nodes J and K the algorithm finds the shortest path between nodes J and K that uses only node number 1 plus nodes J and K, if any such paths exist.

Next, the algorithm finds all the shortest paths that use only the first two nodes. It then builds paths using the first three nodes, the first four nodes, and so forth until it has built all the shortest paths using all the nodes. At this point, because the shortest paths can use any node, the algorithm has found all the shortest paths in the network.

Notice that the shortest path from node J to node K, using only the first I nodes, includes the node I only if $Dist(J, K) > Dist(J, I) + Dist(I, K)$. Otherwise, the shortest path will be whatever path was shortest using only the first $I - 1$ nodes. That means when the algorithm adds the node I into consideration, it needs to check only whether $Dist(J, K) > Dist(J, I) + Dist(I, K)$. If so, the algorithm updates the shortest path from node J to node K. Otherwise, the old shortest path between these two nodes is still the shortest.

Turn Penalties

Some networks, particularly street networks, are more useful if you add turn penalties and turn prohibitions. In a street network, a car must slow down before it turns. It may also take longer to turn left than to turn right or to go straight. At some intersections certain turns may be illegal or impossible due to a center median. You can handle these details by adding turn penalties to the network.

Few Turn Penalties

Often only a few key turn penalties are important. You might like to prevent illegal or impossible turns and place turn penalties on a few key intersections, without placing turn penalties on every intersection in the network. In that case, you can break each node that should have turn penalties into subnodes that implicitly take the penalties into account.

Suppose you want to add a turn penalty for entering an intersection and turning left, and a different penalty for entering the intersection and turning right. Figure 12.12 shows an intersection where you might like to place these penalties. The numbers next to each link are the link's cost. You want to place penalties for entering node A along link L_1 and then leaving along the links L_2 or L_3.

To add turn penalties to node A, break the node into one subnode for each of the links leaving it. In this example, there are two links leaving node A, so you should break node A into two subnodes, A_1 and A_2. Replace the links leaving node A, with corresponding links leaving these subnodes. You can think of the subnodes as representing the action of entering node A and turning onto the corresponding link.

Next replace the link L_1 entering node A with links entering each of the subnodes. These links should have costs equal to the original cost of link L_1, plus any turn penalty you want to assign to the corresponding turn. Figure 12.13 shows

Figure 12.12 An intersection.

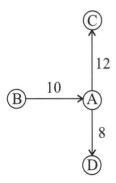

the intersection with turn penalties added. This figure shows a turn penalty of 5 for the left turn out of node A and a turn penalty of 2 for a right turn.

By placing turn penalty information directly in the network, you avoid the need to modify your shortest path algorithms. Those algorithms will correctly find shortest paths taking the turn penalties into account.

You still need to modify your programs slightly to deal with the fact that some nodes have been split into subnodes. Suppose you want to find the shortest path between nodes I and J, but node I has been split into subnodes. Assuming you are allowed to leave node I along any link, you can create a dummy node to use as the root node in the shortest path tree. Connect that node to each of the subnodes of node I using zero-cost links. Then when you build the shortest path tree rooted at the dummy node, you will have found all the shortest paths that use any of the subnodes. Figure 12.14 shows the intersection from Figure 12.13 connected to a dummy root node.

It is easier to deal with the case of finding a path to a node that has been split into subnodes. If you want to find the shortest path between nodes I and J and

Figure 12.13 An intersection with turn penalties.

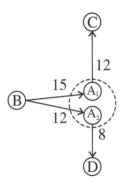

Figure 12.14 An intersection connected to a dummy root.

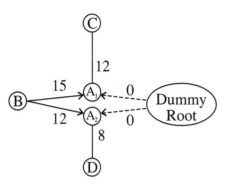

node J has been split into subnodes, first find the shortest path tree rooted at node I as usual. Then check each of the subnodes of node J to see which is closest to the tree's root. The path to that subnode is the shortest path to the original node J.

Many Turn Penalties

If you want to add turn penalties to most of the nodes in your network, the previous method is not very efficient. A better method is to create a completely new network to include the turn penalty information.

- For each link in the original network connecting nodes A and B, create a node AB in the new network.

- Create a link between two nodes if the corresponding links were connected in the original network. For example, suppose in the original network one link connects nodes A and B and another link connects nodes B and C. Then you should make a link in the new network connecting the node AB to the node BC.

- Set the cost of the new link to be the cost of the second link in the original network plus the turn penalty. In this example, the cost of the link from node AB to node BC should be the cost of the link connecting nodes B and C in the original network plus the turn penalty for moving from node A to B to C.

Figure 12.15 shows a small network and the corresponding new network representing the turn penalties. Left turns carry a penalty of 3, right turns carry a penalty of 2, and straight "turns" carry no penalty. For example, because the turn from node B to E to F in the original network is a left turn, the link between nodes BE and EF in the new network carries a turn penalty of 3. The cost of the link connecting nodes E and F in the original network is 3, so the total cost of the new link is $3 + 3 = 6$.

Figure 12.15 A network and corresponding turn penalty network.

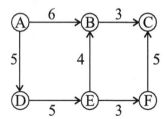

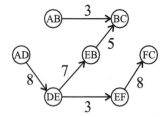

Now suppose you want to find the shortest path tree rooted at node D in the original network. To do this in the new network, create a dummy root node. Build links connecting that node to all the links that leave node D in the original network. Give these links the same costs as the corresponding links in the original network. Figure 12.16 shows the new network from Figure 12.15 with a dummy root node corresponding to node D. The shortest path tree through this network is drawn in bold lines.

To find the shortest path from node D to node C, examine all the nodes in the new network that correspond to links ending at node C. In this example, those are the nodes BC and FC. The node that is closest to the dummy root gives

Figure 12.16 Shortest path tree in a turn penalty network.

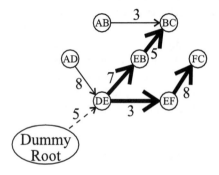

the shortest path to node C in the original network. The nodes in the shortest path in the new network correspond to the links in the shortest path in the original network.

In Figure 12.16, the best path goes from the dummy root node, to node DE, to node EF, to node FC and has a total cost of 16. This path corresponds to the path D, E, F, C in the original network. Adding one left turn penalty for the E, F, C turn, this path also has a cost of 16 in the original network.

Notice that you would not have found this path if you had built a shortest path tree in the original network. Without turn penalties the shortest path from node D to node C would be D, E, B, C with a total cost of 12. With turn penalties that path has a cost of 17.

Shortest Path Applications

Shortest path calculations are used in many applications. Finding the shortest route between two points in a street network is an obvious example. Many other applications use shortest paths through networks in less obvious ways. The following sections describe a few of these applications.

Districting

Suppose you have the map of a city that shows the locations of all fire stations. You might want to determine, for every point in the city, which is the closest fire station. At first glance, this might seem like a difficult problem. You might try computing the shortest path tree rooted at every node in the network to see which fire station was closest to each node. You might compute the shortest path tree rooted at each fire station and record how close each node is to each fire station. There is a much faster method.

Create a dummy root node and connect it with zero-cost links to each of the fire stations. Then find the shortest path tree rooted at this dummy node. For each point in the network, the shortest path from the root node to the point will pass through the fire station that is closest to that point. To find the fire station closest to a point, simply follow the shortest path from that point toward the root until it reaches one of the fire stations. By building a single shortest path tree, you can find the closest fire station to every point in the network.

Example program District uses this algorithm to divide a network into districts. Like PathC and other programs described in this chapter, it allows you to load, edit, and save undirected networks with link costs. When you are not adding or deleting nodes or links, you can select stations for districting. Click on nodes with the left mouse button to add a node to the list of stations. Click anywhere on the form with the right button to make the program divide the network into districts.

Figure 12.17 shows the program districting a network with three stations. The stations at nodes 3, 18, and 20 are shown with bold circles. The districting shortest path trees are drawn with bold lines.

Figure 12.17 Program District.

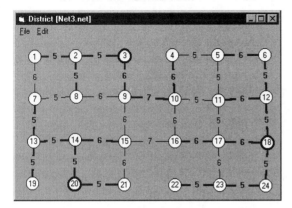

Critical Path Scheduling

In many projects, including large programming projects, certain tasks must be completed before certain others can begin. When building a house, for example, the land must be graded before the foundation is poured, the foundation must be dry before the framing can begin, the framing must be finished before the electrical, plumbing, and roofing work can start, and so forth.

Some of these tasks can be performed at the same time; others must happen one after another. The electrical and plumbing work, for example, can be done at the same time.

A *critical path* is one of the longest sequences of tasks that must occur to finish the project. Items that lie along a critical path are important because a slip in any of their schedules will change the completion time of the entire project. If the foundation is poured a week late, the house will be finished a week late. You can use a shortest path algorithm, modified to find longest paths, to identify the critical path tasks.

First, create a network that represents the scheduling relationships among the project tasks. Create a node for each task. Create a link between task I and task J if task I must be completed before task J can begin. Set the cost of the link between task I and task J equal to the length of time it will take to complete task I.

Next, create two dummy nodes, one to represent the start of the project and one to represent the completion. Create zero-cost links connecting the start node to every node in the project that has no links leading into it. These nodes correspond to tasks that can begin immediately without waiting for the completion of any other tasks.

Then create zero-cost dummy links connecting every node that has no links leaving it to the finish node. These nodes represent tasks for which no other task must wait. Once all of these tasks have been finished, the entire project is completed.

By finding the longest path between the start and finish nodes in this network, you can find a critical path for the project. The tasks along this path are the critical tasks.

Table 12.1 Sprinkler Installation Tasks

Task	Time	Must start after
A. Buy pipe	1 day	(nothing)
B. Dig trenches	2 days	(nothing)
C. Cut pipe	1 day	A
D. Install pipe	2 days	B, C
E. Bury pipe	1 day	D

For example, consider a simplified sprinkler installation project with five tasks. The tasks and their precedence relationships are shown in Table 12.1. The network for this installation project is shown in Figure 12.18.

In this simple example it is easy to see that the longest path through the network follows the sequence of tasks: dig trenches, install pipe, bury pipe. Those are the critical tasks, and if any of them is delayed, the project completion will be delayed.

The length of this critical path gives the expected completion time of the project. In this case, if all the tasks are completed on schedule, the project will take five days. This also assumes that tasks are performed at the same time whenever possible. For example, one person should dig trenches while another buys pipe.

In a larger project, like building a skyscraper or producing a movie, there may be thousands of tasks, and the critical paths may be much less obvious.

Crew Scheduling

Suppose you can hire any of several part-time contractors to answer your phone. Each has a certain number of available hours, and each costs a different amount per hour. You want to hire the least expensive combination of contractors who can answer your phone between 9:00 A.M. and 5:00 P.M. Table 12.2 lists the contractors' prices and hours of availability.

Figure 12.18 A sprinkler installation task network.

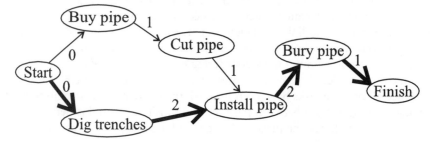

Table 12.2 Employee Availability and Costs

Contractor	Hours available	Cost per hour
A	9–11	$6.50
	12–3	
B	9–2	$6.75
C	2–5	$7.00
D	11–12	$6.25
E	9–12	$6.70
	3–5	

To build a corresponding network, create a node to represent each hour of the day. For each contractor, build links representing the hours that contractor is available. If a contractor is available between 9:00 and 11:00, make a link between the 9:00 node and the 11:00 node. Set the link's cost to the total cost for that contractor working during that period. If the contractor charges $6.50 per hour and the period is two hours long, the cost of the link is $13.00. Figure 12.19 shows the network corresponding to the data in Table 12.2.

The shortest path from the first node to the last node gives the least expensive combination of contractors. Each link in the path corresponds to a contractor working a particular time period. In this case, the shortest path from the 9:00 node to the 5:00 node passes through the 11:00, 12:00, and 3:00 nodes. The corresponding employment schedule is this: A works 9:00–11:00, D works 11:00–12:00, A works 12:00–3:00, and E works 3:00 to 5:00. The total cost of this work schedule is $52.15.

Figure 12.19 A crew scheduling network.

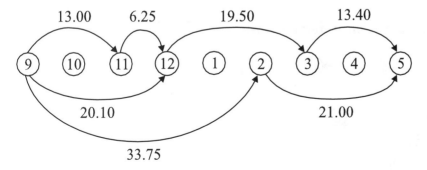

Maximum Flow

In many networks, links have *capacities* in addition to costs. Each link can carry a *flow* that is no greater than its capacity. For instance, the streets in a street network can carry only a certain number of cars per hour. If the number of cars on a link exceeds the link's capacity, the result is a traffic jam. A network with capacities on its links is called a *capacitated network*. Given a capacitated network, the maximum flow problem is to determine the largest flow possible through the network from a specific *source* node to a specific *sink* node.

Figure 12.20 shows a small capacitated network. The numbers next to the links in this network are the link capacities rather than the link costs. In this example, the maximum flow is 4 and can be produced by flowing two units along the path A, B, E, F and two units along the path A, C, D, F.

The algorithm described here starts with no flows on the links and then incrementally modifies the flows to improve the solution it has found so far. When it can make no more improvements, the algorithm is finished.

To find ways to increase the total flow, the algorithm examines the *residual capacities* of the links. The residual capacity of the link between nodes I and J is the maximum additional net flow that you could send from node I to node J using the link between I and J and the link between J and I. This net flow can include additional flow across the I–J link if that link has unused capacity. It can also include removing flow from the J–I link if that link is carrying flow.

For example, suppose there is a flow of 2 on the link connecting nodes A and C in Figure 12.20. Because that link has a capacity of 3, you could add an additional flow of 1 to that link so its residual capacity is 1. Even though the network shown in Figure 12.20 does not have a C–A link, there is a residual capacity for that link. In this example, because there is a flow of 2 units across the A–C link, you could remove up to two units of that flow. This would increase the net flow from node C to node A by 2, so the residual capacity of the C–A link is 2.

The network consisting of all the links with positive residual capacities is called the *residual network*. Figure 12.21 shows the network in Figure 12.20 with flows assigned to each link. For each link, the first number is the flow across the

---

Figure 12.20 A capacitated network.

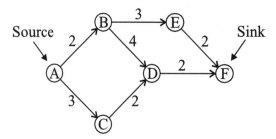

Figure 12.21 Network flows.

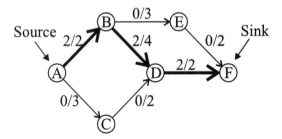

link, and the second is the link's capacity. The label "1 / 2," for example, means the link holds a flow of 1 and has capacity 2. The links carrying flows greater than 0 are shown in bold.

Figure 12.22 shows the residual network corresponding to the flows shown in Figure 12.21. Only the links that might actually have residual capacity have been drawn. For example, no links between nodes A and D have been drawn. The original network does not contain an A–D link or a D–A link, so those links will always have zero residual capacity.

A key fact about residual networks is that any path using links with residual capacities greater than 0 and that connects the source to the sink shows a way to increase the flow in the network. Because this path shows how to increase or augment the flow, this type of path is called an *augmenting path*. Figure 12.23 shows the residual network in Figure 12.22 with an augmenting path drawn in bold.

To update the solution using an augmenting path, find the smallest residual capacity along the path. Then adjust the flows along the path by this amount. In Figure 12.23, for example, the smallest residual capacity of any link along the augmenting path is 2. To update the flows in the network, you add a flow of 2 to any link I–J along the path. You also subtract a flow of 2 from any link J–I where the reversed I–J link is in the path.

Figure 12.22 Residual network.

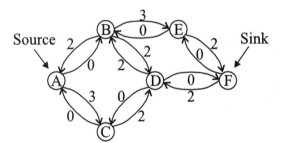

Figure 12.23 An augmenting path through a residual network.

Figure 12.23 An augmenting path through a residual network.

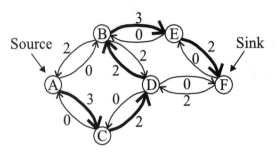

Rather than actually adjusting the flows and then rebuilding the residual network, it is easier to simply adjust the residual network. Then, when the algorithm is finished, you can use the result to compute the flows for the links in the original network.

To adjust the residual network in this example, follow the augmenting path. Subtract 2 from the residual capacity of any link I–J along the path and add 2 to the residual capacity of the corresponding link J–I. Figure 12.24 shows the updated residual network for this example.

When you can find no more augmenting paths, you can use the residual network to compute the flows for the original network. For each link between nodes I and J, if the residual flow between nodes I and J is less than the capacity of the link, then the flow should equal the capacity minus the residual flow. Otherwise the flow should be 0.

For instance, in Figure 12.24 the residual flow from node A to node C is 1 and the capacity of the A–C link is 3. Because 1 is less than 3, the flow across this link should be 3 – 1 = 2. Figure 12.25 shows the network flows corresponding to residual network in Figure 12.24.

So far the algorithm does not have a method for finding augmenting paths in the residual network. One method is similar to a label correcting shortest path algorithm. Start by placing the source node in a candidate list. Then, while the

Figure 12.24 Updated residual network.

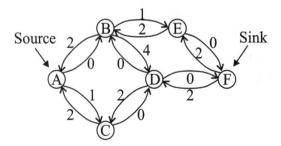

Figure 12.25 Maximum flows.

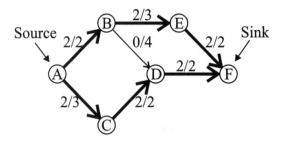

candidate list is not empty, remove an item from the list. Examine any neighboring nodes connected to the selected node by a link that has a remaining residual capacity greater than 0. If the neighbor has not yet been placed in the candidate list, add it to the list. Continue this process until the candidate list is empty.

There are two ways in which this method differs from a label correcting shortest path algorithm. First, this method does not follow links with residual capacity 0. The shortest path algorithm will examine any link, no matter what its cost.

Second, this algorithm examines each node, at most, once. The label correcting shortest path method will update a node and place it back in the candidate list if it later finds an improved path from the root to that node. In this algorithm you do not care how short the augmenting path is, so you do not need to update paths and place nodes back in the candidate list.

The following code shows how a program can compute maximum flows. This code is designed to work with undirected networks similar to the ones used by the example programs described in this chapter. When the algorithm is finished, it sets the cost of a link to the negative of the flow across the link if the link is used backward. In other words, if the network contains a link object representing the I–J link, and the algorithm determines that flow should occur across the J–I link, it sets the flow across the I–J link object to be the negative of the flow that should occur across the J–I link. This allows the program to determine the direction of flow using the existing node structures.

```
Private Sub FindMaxFlows()
Dim candidates As Collection

Dim Residual() As Integer
Dim num_nodes As Integer
Dim id1 As Integer
Dim id2 As Integer
Dim node As FlowNode
Dim to_node As FlowNode
Dim from_node As FlowNode
Dim link As FlowLink
```

```
Dim min_residual As Integer

    If SourceNode Is Nothing Or SinkNode Is Nothing _
        Then Exit Sub

    ' Dimension the Residual array.
    num_nodes = Nodes.Count
    ReDim Residual(1 To num_nodes, 1 To num_nodes)

    ' Initially the residual values are the same as the capacities.
    For Each node In Nodes
        id1 = node.Id
        For Each link In node.Links
            If link.Node1 Is node Then
                Set to_node = link.Node2
            Else
                Set to_node = link.Node1
            End If
            id2 = to_node.Id
            Residual(id1, id2) = link.Capacity
        Next link
    Next node

    ' Repeat until we can find no more augmenting paths.
    Do
        ' Find an augmenting path in the residual network.
        ' Reset the nodes' NodeStatus and InLink values.
        For Each node In Nodes
            node.NodeStatus = NOT_IN_LIST
            Set node.InLink = Nothing
        Next node

        ' Start with an empty candidate list.
        Set candidates = New Collection

        ' Put the source on the candidate list.
        candidates.Add SourceNode
        SourceNode.NodeStatus = NOW_IN_LIST

        ' Repeat until the candidate list is empty.
        Do While candidates.Count > 0
            Set node = candidates(1)
            candidates.Remove 1
            node.NodeStatus = WAS_IN_LIST
```

```
    id1 = node.Id

    ' Examine the links out of this node.
    For Each link In node.Links
        If link.Node1 Is node Then
            Set to_node = link.Node2
        Else
            Set to_node = link.Node1
        End If
        id2 = to_node.Id

        ' See if the residual > 0 and this
        ' node has never been on the list.
        If Residual(id1, id2) > 0 And _
            to_node.NodeStatus = NOT_IN_LIST _
        Then
            ' Add it to the list.
            candidates.Add to_node
            to_node.NodeStatus = NOW_IN_LIST
            Set to_node.InLink = link
        End If
    Next link

    ' Stop if the sink has been labeled.
    If Not (SinkNode.InLink Is Nothing) Then _
        Exit Do
Loop

' Stop if we found no augmenting path.
If SinkNode.InLink Is Nothing Then Exit Do

' Find the smallest residual along the augmenting path.
min_residual = INFINITY
Set node = SinkNode
Do
    If node Is SourceNode Then Exit Do
    id1 = node.Id

    Set link = node.InLink
    If link.Node1 Is node Then
        Set from_node = link.Node2
    Else
        Set from_node = link.Node1
    End If
```

```
        id2 = from_node.Id

        If min_residual > Residual(id2, id1) Then _
            min_residual = Residual(id2, id1)

        Set node = from_node
    Loop

    ' Update the residuals using the augmenting path.
    Set node = SinkNode
    Do
        If node Is SourceNode Then Exit Do
        id1 = node.Id

        Set link = node.InLink
        If link.Node1 Is node Then
            Set from_node = link.Node2
        Else
            Set from_node = link.Node1
        End If
        id2 = from_node.Id

        Residual(id2, id1) = Residual(id2, id1) _
            - min_residual
        Residual(id1, id2) = Residual(id1, id2) _
            + min_residual
        Set node = from_node
    Loop
Loop ' Repeat until there are no more augmenting paths.

' Calculate the flows from the residuals.
For Each link In Links
    id1 = link.Node1.Id
    id2 = link.Node2.Id
    If link.Capacity > Residual(id1, id2) Then
        link.Flow = link.Capacity - Residual(id1, id2)
    Else
        ' Negative to indicate backwards.
        link.Flow = Residual(id2, id1) - link.Capacity
    End If
Next link

' Find the total flow.
TotalFlow = 0
```

```
For Each link In SourceNode.Links
    TotalFlow = TotalFlow + link.Flow
Next link
End Sub
```

Example program Flow uses the augmenting path technique to compute maximal flows through a network. It is similar to the other programs described in this chapter. When you are not adding or removing a node or link, use the left mouse button to select the source node. Use the right mouse button to select the sink node. When you have selected a source and a sink, the program calculates and displays the maximum flows. Figure 12.26 shows the program displaying the flows for a small network.

Maximum Flow Applications

Maximum flow calculations are used in many applications. While maximal flows may be directly useful for some networks, they are most often used indirectly to calculate results that may seem at first to have little relation to network capacity.

Disjoint Paths

Redundancy is important in large communications networks. Given a network like the one shown in Figure 12.27, you might like to know how many disjoint paths there are between the source node and the sink node. If there are many paths between the two nodes that do not share a common link, there will still be a path between the nodes, even if several links in the network fail.

You can determine how many different paths there are using a maximum flow calculation. Create a network with nodes and links corresponding to those in the communications network. Set the capacity of each link to 1.

Next, perform a maximum flow calculation on the network. The maximum flow will be the same as the number of different paths from the source to the

---

Figure 12.26 Program Flow.

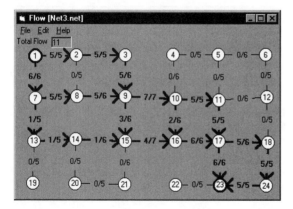

Figure 12.27 A communications network.

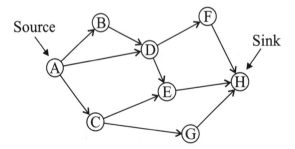

sink. Because each link can hold a flow of only 1, none of the paths used by the maximum flow calculation can share a common link.

A stricter definition of redundancy might require that the different paths share no links and no nodes. By modifying the previous network slightly, you can still use a maximum flow calculation to solve this problem.

Divide each node, except the source and sink nodes, into two subnodes connected by a single link with capacity 1. Connect the first subnode to all the links entering the original node. Connect all the links leaving the original node to the second subnode. Figure 12.28 shows the network in Figure 12.27 with the nodes divided in this way. Now find the maximal flow for this new network.

If a path used by the maximal flow calculation passes through a node, it must use the link that connects the two corresponding subnodes. Because that link has a capacity of 1, no two paths used by the maximum flow calculation can cross this connecting link, so no two paths can use the same node in the original network.

Work Assignment

Suppose you have a group of employees with certain skills. Suppose you also have a collection of jobs that require the attention of an employee who has a particular

Figure 12.28 A transformed communications network.

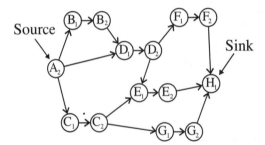

Figure 12.29 A work assignment network.

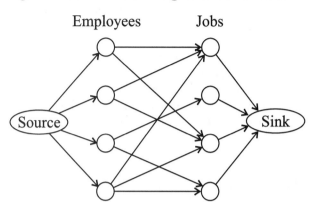

set of skills. The assignment problem is to match the employees to the jobs so each job is assigned to an employee who has the skills to work that job.

To convert this problem into a maximum flow calculation, create a network with two columns of nodes. In the left column, place one node to represent each employee. In the right column, place one node to represent each job.

Next, compare the skills of each employee with the skills needed to perform each job. Create links between each employee and every job that employee can work. Set the capacities of all these links to 1.

Create a source node and connect it to every employee with a link of capacity 1. Then create a sink node and connect every job to it, again using links of capacity 1. Figure 12.29 shows the assignment network for a four-person, four-job assignment problem.

Now find the maximum flow from the source node to the sink node. Each resulting unit of flow must pass through one employee node and one job node. That flow represents the assignment of that employee to that job.

Figure 12.30 Program Work.

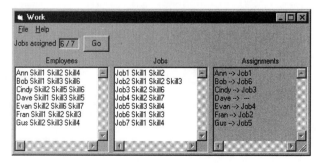

If the employees have the proper skills to work all the jobs, the maximum flow calculation will assign all the jobs. If it is not possible to work all the jobs, the maximum flow calculation will assign employees to jobs so that as many jobs as possible are worked.

Example program Work uses this algorithm to assign work to employees. Enter employee names followed by their skills in the left text box. Enter jobs followed by required skills in the middle text box. When you click the Go button, the program uses a maximum flow network to assign work to the employees. Figure 12.30 shows the program displaying a work assignment.

Summary

You can apply some network algorithms directly to network-like objects. For example, you can use shortest path algorithms to find the best route through a street network. You can use a minimal spanning tree to determine the least expensive way to build a communications network or to connect cities with railroad track.

Many other network algorithms are used in less obvious ways. For example, you can use shortest path algorithms for districting, critical path scheduling, or crew scheduling. You can use maximum flow algorithms to perform work assignment. These less obvious uses for network algorithms usually prove more challenging and more interesting.

OBJECT-ORIENTED TECHNIQUES

unctions and subroutines allow a programmer to break the logic of a large program into manageable pieces. Arrays and user-defined data structures allow a programmer to group data items in ways that make data management easier.

The classes introduced by Visual Basic 4 allow a programmer to group logic and data in new ways. A class lets you combine data and logic in a single object. This new method for managing program complexity allows you to view algorithms from a different perspective.

This chapter explains object-oriented issues raised by Visual Basic classes. It describes the advantages of object-oriented programming (OOP) and tells how you can benefit from them in Visual Basic. It then explains an assortment of useful object-oriented paradigms you can use to help manage complexity in your applications.

Benefits of OOP

The traditional benefits of object-oriented programming are encapsulation, polymorphism, and reuse. Visual Basic's classes provide these benefits in ways slightly different from other object-oriented languages. The following sections explain these benefits and outline how you can take advantage of them in Visual Basic.

Encapsulation

An object defined by a class encapsulates the data it contains. Other parts of a program can use the object to manipulate the data without understanding exactly how the data values are stored or modified. The object provides public subroutines, functions, and property procedures that allow the program to view and manipulate the data indirectly. Because this keeps the data abstract from the program's point of view, this is also called *data abstraction*.

Encapsulation allows your program to treat objects as black boxes. The program can use the objects' public methods to examine and modify values without needing to understand what happens inside the box.

Because the internal workings of the objects are hidden from the main program, the object's implementation can change without forcing changes to the main program. Changes to the object's internals occur only in the class module.

For example, suppose you have a FileDownload class that retrieves files from the Internet. The program passes a FileDownload object the location of the file and the object returns a string containing the file's contents. In this case, the program does not need to know how the object retrieves the file. It might fetch the file using a direct Internet connection or a dial-up connection. It might even load some of the files from a local disk cache. The program knows only that the object returns a string when it is passed a file location.

Maintaining Encapsulation

To maintain encapsulation, a class must not allow direct access to its data. If a variable is declared public within the class, other parts of the program can directly view and modify the data. Later, if the data representation changes, any parts of the program that interact directly with the data must also be changed. This removes one of the main benefits of encapsulation.

To provide simple access to data, a class should use property procedures. For example, the following procedures allow other parts of a program to view and modify a Temperature object's DegreesF value.

```
Private m_DegreesF As Single     ' Degrees Fahrenheit.

Public Property Get DegreesF() As Single
    DegreesF = m_DegreesF
End Property

Public Property Let DegreesF(new_DegreesF As Single)
    m_DegreesF = new_DegreesF
End Property
```

At this point there is little practical difference between these routines and declaring m_Degrees to be a public variable. They allow the class to be easily modified later, however. For example, suppose you decided to store temperature in degrees Kelvin instead of in degrees Fahrenheit. You could modify the class to use the new storage method without changing parts of the program that use the DegreesF property procedures. You could also add error checking code to ensure that the program does not give the object invalid values.

```
Private m_DegreesK As Single     ' Degrees Kelvin.

Public Property Get DegreesF() As Single
    DegreesF = (m_DegreesK - 273.15) * 1.8
End Property
```

```
Public Property Let DegreesF(ByVal new_DegreesF As Single)
Dim new_value As Single

    new_value = (new_DegreesF / 1.8) + 273.15
    If new_value < 0 Then
        ' Raise invalid property value error.
        Error.Raise 380, "Temperature", _
            "Temperature must be at least zero degrees Kelvin."
    Else
        m_DegreesK = new_value
    End If
End Property
```

The programs described throughout this book flagrantly violate the principle of encapsulation by using public class variables. This is not particularly good programming style, but it is done for three reasons.

First, setting the data values directly is faster than using property procedures. Many of the programs already pay a performance penalty for using object references instead of more complex pointer faking techniques. Using property procedures would slow them even further.

Second, many of the programs demonstrate data structure techniques. The network algorithms described in Chapter 12, "Network Algorithms," for example, use object data values explicitly. The pointers that link nodes in a network together are an integral part of the algorithms. It would make little sense to change the way these pointers are stored.

Finally, making data values public keeps the code simpler. It allows you to concentrate on the algorithms without a bunch of property procedures getting in the way.

Polymorphism

The second major benefit of object-oriented programming is polymorphism, which means "having many forms." In Visual Basic it means one object can have different forms depending on the situation. For example, the following code shows a subroutine that can take any kind of object as a parameter. The object obj can be a form, control, or object of some class that you have defined.

```
Private Sub ShowName(obj As Object)
    MsgBox TypeName(obj)
End Sub
```

Polymorphism allows you to create routines that can work with literally any kind of object. That flexibility, however, comes with a price. When you declare an object generically, as in this example, Visual Basic cannot determine what sorts of actions that object can take until run time.

If Visual Basic knows ahead of time what kind of object it will have, it can prepare to use the object most efficiently. If you use a generic object, the program cannot prepare, and it will pay a huge performance penalty.

Example program Generic demonstrates the performance difference between generic and specific object declarations. The following code shows how the program tests a specifically declared object. The generic test is similar except the object is declared to be of type Object instead of type SpecificClass. Setting the object's data value takes more than 200 times longer using the generic object.

```
Private Sub TestSpecific()
Const REPS = 1000000 ' Perform 1 million repetitions.

Dim obj As SpecificClass
Dim i As Long
Dim start_time As Single
Dim stop_time As Single

    Set obj = New SpecificClass
    start_time = Timer
    For i = 1 To REPS
        obj.Value = i
    Next i
    stop_time = Timer
    SpecificLabel.Caption = _
        Format$(1000 * (stop_time - start_time) / REPS, "0.0000")
End Sub
```

Implements

The Implements keyword in Visual Basic 5 allows a program to use polymorphism without using generic objects. For example, a program might define a Vehicle interface. If the Car and Truck classes both implement the Vehicle interface, the program can use objects from either class to perform Vehicle functions.

Start by creating an interface class that declares the public variables the interface will support. It should also define empty public subroutines for any methods it will support. For example, the following code shows how a Vehicle class might define a Speed value and a Drive method.

```
Public Speed Long

Public Sub Drive()

End Sub
```

Next create a class that implements the interface. After the Option Explicit statement in the Declares section, add an Implements statement specifying the name of the interface class. The class should also define any local variables it needs to actually provide the interface features.

The Car class implements the Vehicle interface. The following code shows how it declares its interface and defines the private variable m_Speed.

```
Option Explicit

Implements Vehicle

Private m_Speed As Long
```

When you add the Implements statement to a class, Visual Basic reads the interface defined by the indicated class. It then creates appropriate code stubs for the class. In this example, Visual Basic adds a new Vehicle section to the Car class source code. It defines property get and property let procedures named Vehicle_Speed to represent the Speed variable defined by the Vehicle interface. In property let procedures, Visual Basic uses the variable RHS, which stands for Right Hand Side, to represent the property's new value.

Visual Basic also defines a Vehicle_Drive subroutine. You must write the code to implement the functionality of these routines. The following code shows how the Car class might define the Speed procedures and Drive subroutine.

```
Private Property Let Vehicle_Speed(ByVal RHS As Long)
    m_Speed = RHS
End Property

Private Property Get Vehicle_Speed() As Long
    Vehicle_Speed = m_Speed
End Property

Private Sub Get Vehicle_Drive()
    ' Do whatever is appropriate here.
        :
End Property
```

Once the interface is defined and one or more classes implement the interface, the program can use items of those classes polymorphically. For example, suppose a program has defined Car and Truck classes that both implement the Vehicle interface. The following code shows how a program might initialize the Speed values for a Car object and a Truck object.

```
Dim obj As Vehicle

    Set obj = New Car
    obj.Speed = 55
    Set obj = New Truck
    obj.Speed = 45
```

The object reference obj can point to either a Car or Truck object. Because both implement the Vehicle interface, the program can manipulate the obj.Speed property whether obj points to a Car or a Truck.

Because the obj reference points to an object that implements the Vehicle interface, Visual Basic knows the object provides Speed property procedures. That means it can service requests to the Speed routines more efficiently than it could if the object were a generic object reference.

Example program Implem extends the Generic program described earlier. It compares the speed of setting values using generic objects, specific objects, and objects that implement an interface. In one test on a 166 megahertz Pentium, the program took 0.0007 seconds to set values using specific object types. It took 0.0028 seconds (4 times as long) to set values using an object implementing an interface. The program took 0.0508 seconds (72 times as long) to set values using a generic object. Using an interface is not as fast as using a specific object reference, but it is much faster than using generic objects.

Remember that the Implements keyword is a Visual Basic 5 feature, so program Implem cannot run in Visual Basic 3 or 4.

Reuse and Inheritance

Functions and subroutines support reuse. Instead of writing a bunch of code whenever you need to use it, you can place the code in a subroutine. Rather than rewriting the code, you simply invoke the subroutine.

Similarly defining a routine in a class makes that routine available throughout the program. Using an object that is an instance of the class, the program can use the routine.

To the object-oriented programming community, reuse usually means something more: inheritance. In object-oriented languages like C++ and Delphi, one class can be *derived* from another. The second class *inherits* all the functionality of the first. The programmer can then add, modify, or remove functionality in the derived class. This provides a form of reuse because the programmer does not need to reimplement the features of the parent class to take advantage of them in the derived class.

Even though Visual Basic does not directly allow inheritance, you can achieve similar reuse using *containment* and *delegation*. In delegation an object from one class contains an instance of an object from another. It delegates some of its responsibilities to the contained object.

For example, suppose you have an Employee class that represents employee information such as name, Social Security number, and salary. Suppose you want a Manager class that does everything the Employee class does with an additional secretary property.

To use delegation, the Manager class should include a private object of type Employee named m_Employee. Instead of computing values directly, the Manager's name, Social Security number, and salary property procedures pass requests along to the m_Employee object. The following code shows how the Manager class might handle the name property procedures.

```
Private m_Employee As New Employee

Property Get Name() As String
    Name = m_Employee.Name
End Property

Property Let Name(New_Name As String)
    m_Employee.Name = New_Name
End Property
```

The Manager class can also modify the result returned by a delegated function or generate a completely different result of its own. For example, the following code shows how the Employee class returns a text string displaying data about the employee.

```
Public Function TextValues() As String
Dim txt As String

    txt = m_Name & vbCrLf
    txt = txt & "    " & m_SSN & vbCrLf
    txt = txt & "    " & Format$(m_Salary, "Currency") & vbCrLf
    TextValues = txt
End Function
```

The Manager class uses the Employee object's TextValues function but adds to the result before returning.

```
Public Function TextValues() As String
Dim txt As String

    txt = m_Employee.TextValues
    txt = txt & "    " & m_Secretary & vbCrLf
    TextValues = txt
End Function
```

The Inherit program demonstrates the Employee and Manager classes. The program's interface is not very interesting, but the code includes simple Employee and Manager class definitions.

OOP Paradigms

Chapter 1, "Fundamental Concepts," defined an algorithm as "a set of directions for performing a particular task." A class can certainly use this sort of algorithm in its subroutines and functions. For instance, you can use a class to provide a wrapper encapsulating the behavior of an algorithm. Several of the programs described in earlier chapters use classes to encapsulate complicated algorithms.

Classes also allow a new style of programming where several objects work together to perform a task. In that case, providing a set of directions for performing the task may not make sense. It is more appropriate to provide a model of the objects' behaviors than to reduce the task to a list of steps. To differentiate these collections of behavior from more traditional algorithms, I call them "paradigms."

The following sections describe some useful object-oriented paradigms. Many of these have been drawn from other object-oriented languages such as C++ and Smalltalk, but they can also be used in Visual Basic.

Command

Command objects are also known as action objects, function objects, and functors. A command object represents an action. A program can use the object's Execute method to make the object perform its action. The program does not need to know anything about the action; it just knows the object has an Execute method.

Commands can be used in many interesting ways. A program can use commands to implement the following:

- Generic interfaces

- Macros

- Journaling and recovery

- Undo and redo features

To build a generic interface, a form might contain a control array of buttons. At run time, the form can load the captions displayed by the buttons and create a corresponding array of command objects. When the user clicks on a button, the button's event handler code only needs to invoke the corresponding command object's Execute method. The details of what happens are inside the command object classes, not in the event handler.

Example program Command1 uses command objects to provide a generic interface for several unrelated functions. When you click on a button, the program invokes the corresponding command object's Execute subroutine.

A program can use command objects to create user-defined macros. The user specifies a series of actions that the program stores as Command objects in a collection. Later, when the user invokes the macro, the program calls the Execute methods of the objects in the collection.

Command objects can provide journaling and recovery. Every time a command object executes, it can store information about itself in a log file. If the program crashes, it can later use the log information to recreate the command objects and execute them to repeat the commands it executed before the crash.

Finally, a program can use a series of command objects to provide undo and redo features. Example program Command2 allows you to draw rectangles, ellipses, and lines on a drawing area. Each time you draw a shape, the program stores a drawing command object in a collection. To draw the picture, the program replays the commands in the collection.

The program uses the variable LastCmd to keep track of the last valid command object in the collection. When you select the Draw menu's Undo command, the program decreases LastCmd by one. When the program next draws the picture, it invokes only the objects up to object number LastCmd.

When you select the Draw menu's Redo command, the program increases LastCmd by one. When the program draws the picture, it applies one more command object than it did before, so the restored shape is displayed.

When you add a new shape, the program removes any commands from the collection that lie after position LastCmd. It then adds the new drawing command at the end and disables the Redo command because there are no commands available to redo. Figure 13.1 shows the Command2 program after a new shape has been added.

Visitor

A visitor object visits the items in an *aggregate* object. A routine implemented by the aggregate class traverses its objects passing each as a parameter to the visitor object.

For example, suppose an aggregate object stores items in a linked list. The following code shows how its Visit method traverses the list passing each item as a parameter to a ListVisitor object's Visit method.

```
Public Sub Visit(obj As ListVisitor)
Dim cell As ListCell

    Set cell = TopCell
    Do While Not (cell Is Nothing)
        obj.Visit cell
        Set cell = cell.NextCell
    Loop
End Sub
```

Figure 13.1 Program Command2.

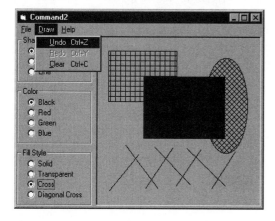

The following code shows how the ListVisitor class might display the values of the list items in the Immediate window.

```
Public Sub Visit(cell As ListCell)
    Debug.Print cell.Value
End Sub
```

When using the visitor paradigm, the aggregate class determines the order in which the items are visited. An aggregate might define more than one method for visiting the items it contains. For example, a tree class might provide VisitPreorder, VisitPostorder, VisitInorder, and VisitBreadthFirst methods to allow visitors to traverse the items in different orders.

Iterator

An iterator provides an alternative method for visiting the items in an aggregate object. An iterator object reaches into an aggregate object to traverse the items it contains. Here the iterator defines the order in which the items are visited. Multiple iterator classes can be associated with an aggregate class to provide different traversals of the items.

To traverse the items, the iterator must understand the way in which the items are stored so it can define its own traversal. If the aggregate is a linked list, the iterator object must know that items are stored in a linked list, and it must know how to maneuver through the list. Because the iterator knows details of the list's internals, it breaks the aggregate's encapsulation.

Rather than make every class that needs to examine the aggregate's items implement its own traversal, you can associate an iterator class with the aggregate class. The iterator should provide simple MoveFirst, MoveNext, EndOfList, and CurrentItem routines to allow indirect access to the list. New classes can include an instance of the iterator class and use the iterator's methods to traverse the aggregate. Figure 13.2 shows conceptually how the new object uses the iterator object to communicate with the list.

The IterTree program, described later in the section "Factory," uses iterators to traverse a complete binary tree. The Traverser class contains a reference to an iterator object. It uses the MoveFirst, MoveNext, CurrentCaption, and EndOfTree routines provided by the iterators to list the nodes in the tree.

Figure 13.2 Using an iterator to communicate indirectly with a list.

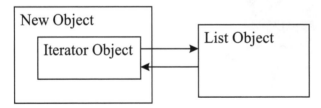

Iterators break the encapsulation of their aggregates, but new classes that contain the iterators do not. Considering the iterator to be an extended part of the aggregate can help limit potential confusion.

Visitors and iterators provide similar functions using different approaches. Because the visitor paradigm keeps the aggregate's details within the aggregate, it provides better encapsulation. Iterators can be useful if the order of traversal must change frequently or if it must be determined at run time. For example, the aggregate can use a factory method (described later) to create an iterator object at run time. The class containing the iterator does not need to know how the iterator is created— it just uses the iterator's methods to access the aggregate's items.

Friend

Many classes work closely with other classes. For example, an iterator class works closely with an aggregate class. To perform its job, the iterator must break the encapsulation of the aggregate. While these related classes must sometimes break each other's encapsulation, other classes should not.

A friend class is a class that has special permission to break another's encapsulation. For example, an iterator class is a friend of the aggregate it traverses. It is allowed to break the aggregate's encapsulation, even though other classes cannot.

Visual Basic 5 provides a Friend keyword that allows restricted access to the variables and routines defined in a module. Items declared with the Friend keyword are accessible to code within the same project but not to code running in other projects. For example, suppose you build LinkedList and ListIterator classes in an ActiveX server project. A program can create a linked list server to manage linked lists. A factory method provided by the LinkedList class creates ListIterator objects for the program to use.

A LinkedList class might provide linked list services for a program. This class declares its properties and methods Public so the main program can use them. The ListIterator class allows the program to iterate over the objects managed by the LinkedList class. Routines used by the ListIterator class to manipulate LinkedList objects are declared Friend in the LinkedList module. If LinkedList and ListIterator are created in the same project, ListIterator can use those Friend routines. Because the main program is contained in a different project, it cannot.

This method is very effective, but it is rather cumbersome. It requires you to manage two projects and to install one as an ActiveX server. It also does not work in versions prior to Visual Basic 5.

The simplest alternative is to make an agreement that only friend classes will break each other's encapsulation. If all developers stick to the agreement, the project will be manageable. The temptation to reach directly inside the LinkedList class may be strong, however, and there will always be a possibility that someone will become lazy or careless and break the encapsulation.

Another alternative is to make the friend object pass itself as a parameter to the other class. By passing itself as a parameter, the friend proves it is of the correct class. Example program FStacks uses this method to implement stacks.

It is still possible to corrupt this method and break the object's encapsulation. A program can create an object of the friend class and use it as a parameter to trick the other object's routines. This is a rather awkward process, however, so it is unlikely that a developer would do this accidentally.

Interface

In this paradigm one object acts as an interface between two others. One object can use the properties and methods of the first object to interact with a second. An interface is sometimes called an adapter, wrapper, or bridge. Figure 13.3 shows how an interface works conceptually.

An interface allows the two objects on either side of it to change independently. For example, if the properties of the object on the left in Figure 13.3 change, the interface must be modified, but the object on the right need not be.

Often in this paradigm the routines used by the two objects are maintained by the developers who maintain those objects. Whoever manages the object on the left also manages the interface routines that interact with the object on the left.

Facade

A facade is similar to an interface except it provides a simple interface to a complicated object or group of objects. A facade is also sometimes called a wrapper. Figure 13.4 shows how a facade works.

The difference between a facade and an interface is mainly conceptual. The focus of an interface is on allowing objects to interact indirectly so they can evolve independently. A facade's main purpose is to make using something complicated easier by hiding details.

Factory

A factory is an object that creates other objects. A factory method is a subroutine or function that creates an object.

Factories are most useful when two classes must work closely together. For example, an aggregate class can provide a factory method that creates iterators for the aggregate. The factory method can initialize the iterator so that it is ready to work with the specific instance of the aggregate that created it.

Example program IterTree creates complete binary trees stored in an array. When you click one of the traversal buttons, the program creates a Traverser object.

Figure 13.3 An interface.

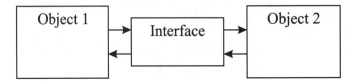

Figure 13.4 A facade.

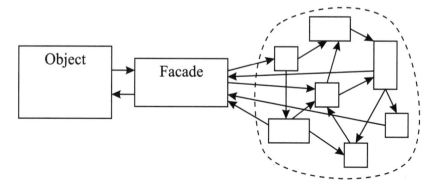

It also uses one of the tree's factory methods to create an appropriate iterator. The Traverser uses the iterator to traverse the tree and list the nodes in the proper order. Figure 13.5 shows program IterTree displaying a tree's postorder traversal.

Singleton

A singleton is an object that is unique in an application. For example, Visual Basic defines a Printer object class. It also defines a singleton object named Printer. That object represents the default printer currently selected on the system. Because only one printer can be selected at a time, it makes sense that the Printer object should be a singleton.

One way to create a singleton is to use a property procedure defined in a BAS module. The procedure returns a reference to an object declared privately within the module. To other parts of the program, the property procedure appears to be just another object.

Figure 13.5 Program IterTree displaying a postorder traversal.

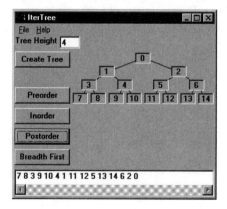

The WinList example program uses this technique to create a singleton of the class WindowListerClass. A WindowListerClass object represents the windows running on the system. There is only one system, so there only needs to be a single WindowListerClass object. The module WinList.BAS uses the following code to provide a singleton named WindowLister.

```
Private m_WindowLister As New WindowListerClass

Property Get WindowLister() As WindowListerClass
    Set WindowLister = m_WindowLister
End Property
```

The WindowLister singleton object is available throughout the project. The following code shows how the main program uses this object's WindowList property to display a list of the windows currently running.

```
WindowListText.Text = WindowLister.WindowList
```

Serialization

Many applications store objects and later rebuild them. For example, an application may save a representation of its objects in a text file. The next time the program runs, it reads the file and reloads the objects.

An object could provide subroutines that read and write it into a file. A more general strategy is to provide routines that save and restore the object's data using a string. Because storing an object's data in a string converts the object into a series of characters, this process is sometimes called *serialization*.

Serializing an object into a string allows the main program greater flexibility. It can save and restore the object using a text file, a database, or a memory location. It can send the serialization across a network or make it available on a Web page. A program or ActiveX control at the other end can use the serialization to re-create the object. The program can also add extra processing to the string. For example, it can encrypt the string after serialization and decrypt it before deserialization.

One approach to serializing an object is to let it write all its data into a string in a predetermined format. For example, suppose a Rectangle class has the properties X1, Y1, X2, and Y2. The following code shows how the class might define the Serialization property procedures.

```
Property Get Serialization() As String
    Serialization = _
        Format$(X1) & ";" & Format$(Y1) & ";" & _
        Format$(X2) & ";" & Format$(Y2) & ";"
End Property

Property Let Serialization(txt As String)
Dim pos1 As Integer
```

```
Dim pos2 As Integer

    pos1 = InStr(txt, ";")
    X1 = CSng(Left$(txt, pos1 - 1))
    pos2 = InStr(pos1 + 1, txt, ";")
    Y1 = CSng(Mid$(txt, pos1 + 1, pos2 - pos1 - 1))
    pos1 = InStr(pos2 + 1, txt, ";")
    X2 = CSng(Mid$(txt, pos2 + 1, pos1 - pos2 - 1))
    pos2 = InStr(pos1 + 1, txt, ";")
    Y2 = CSng(Mid$(txt, pos1 + 1, pos2 - pos1 - 1))
End Property
```

This method is relatively simple, but it is not very flexible. As the program evolves, changes to the object's structure will force you to translate any previously stored serializations. If you have objects stored in files or databases, you will need to write conversion programs to load the old data and store it in the new format.

A more flexible method is to store the names of the object's data items together with their values. When the object reads serialized data, it uses the item names to determine what values to set. If you later add or remove items from the object's definition, you do not need to translate old serialized data. When a new object loads old data, it simply ignores any values that it no longer supports.

By defining default item values, you can sometimes make object serializations shorter. The Serialization property get procedure saves only the items with values that differ from their defaults. Before the property let procedure begins processing a serialization, it initializes all the object's items to default values. Those with nondefault values are updated as the routine processes the serialized data.

Example program Shapes uses this method to save and restore pictures containing ellipses, lines, and rectangles. A ShapePicture object represents the complete picture. It contains a collection of command objects that represent the ellipses, lines, and rectangles.

The following code shows the ShapePicture object's Serialization property procedures. The ShapePicture saves each command object's type name, followed by its serialization in parentheses.

```
Property Get Serialization() As String
Dim txt As String
Dim i As Integer

    For i = 1 To LastCmd
        txt = txt & _
            TypeName(CmdObjects(i)) & "(" & _
            CmdObjects(i).Serialization & ")"
    Next i
    Serialization = txt
End Property
```

The Serialization property let procedure uses the GetSerialization subroutine to read a name followed by a list of information surrounded by parentheses. For example, if the ShapePicture contains a rectangle command, its serialization will include the string "RectangleCmd" followed by the command object's serialization.

The procedure uses the CommandFactory subroutine to create an object of the appropriate type using the command's type name. It then makes the new command object unserialize itself.

```
Property Let Serialization(txt As String)
Dim pos As Integer
Dim token_name As String
Dim token_value As String
Dim cmd As Object

    ' Start a new picture.
    NewPicture

    ' Read values until there are no more.
    GetSerialization txt, pos, token_name, token_value
    Do While token_name <> ""
        ' Make the object and make it unserialize itself.
        Set cmd = CommandFactory(token_name)
        If Not (cmd Is Nothing) Then _
            cmd.Serialization = token_value
        GetSerialization txt, pos, token_name, token_value
    Loop
    LastCmd = CmdObjects.Count
End Property
```

MVC

The Model/View/Controller (MVC) paradigm allows a program to orchestrate complex relationships between objects that store, objects that display, and objects that manipulate data. For example, a finance application might display expense data in a table, pie chart, or line graph. If the user changes the value in a table, the application should automatically update all displays. It might also write the modified data to a hard disk.

For complicated systems, managing the interactions between objects that store, display, and manipulate data can be quite confusing. The MVC paradigm decouples the interactions so that they are easy to handle individually. MVC manages data using three kinds of objects: models, views, and controllers.

Models

A model represents the data. It provides methods other objects use to examine and modify the data. In a finance application, the model stores the expense data.

It provides routines for viewing and changing expense values and creating new values. It might also provide functions that compute aggregate values such as total expenses, total expenses by department, average expenses per month, and so forth.

The model includes a collection of view objects that display the data. Whenever the data is modified, the model notifies the views. The views can then update their displays appropriately.

Views

A view displays the data represented by a model. Because views usually display the data to the user, it is sometimes convenient to build a view using a form instead of a class.

When the program creates a new view, it should add it to the model's view collection.

Controllers

A controller modifies the data in a model. A controller must always access a model's data through its public methods. Those methods can then notify the views that a change has occurred. If a controller modifies the data directly, the model cannot notify its views.

View/Controllers

Many objects both display and modify data. For example, a text box allows the user to view and modify data. A form containing a text box is both a view and a controller. Option buttons, check boxes, scroll bars, and many other user interface elements allow the user to view and manipulate data.

View/controllers are easiest to manage if you can separate the view and controller functions as much as possible. When the object changes the data, it should not update its own display. Later, when the model notifies it as a view that the change has occurred, it can update itself.

This technique is awkward for standard user interface objects such as text boxes. When the user types in a text box, the text box is immediately updated and its Change event handler executes. The event handler can notify the model of the change. The model then notifies the view/controller (acting as a view) that the change has occurred. If the object updates the text box, it will generate a new Change event. It will then notify the model that a change has occurred, and the program will enter an infinite loop.

To prevent this problem, the model's data modification methods should take an optional parameter indicating the controller object that caused the change. When it notifies its views of the change, the model skips that controller. If a view/controller must be notified of a change it causes, it should pass the value Nothing to the update routine. If it should not be notified, it should pass itself as a parameter.

Example program ExpMVC, shown in Figure 13.6, uses the Model/View/Controller paradigm to display expense data. It displays three different kinds of

Figure 13.6 Program ExpMVC.

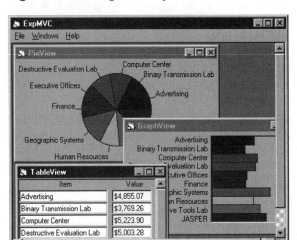

views. The TableView view/controller displays expense data in a table. You can modify expense item names or values by typing in the text boxes.

The GraphView view/controller displays expense data using a bar chart. You can modify expense values by clicking and dragging near the right edge of a bar.

The PieView view displays a pie chart. This is only a view, so you cannot use it to modify the data.

Summary

Classes allow Visual Basic programmers to think about old problems in new ways. Instead of thinking about long lists of tasks performed to accomplish a task, you can think of a group of objects that work in concert to perform the task. If the task is partitioned properly, each of the classes may be quite simple separately, though together they perform a complex function. Using the paradigms described in this chapter, you can decouple the classes so they are individually as simple as possible.

USING THE CD-ROM

A

This appendix outlines the contents of the accompanying CD-ROM and explains how you can use the programs. Appendix B lists and briefly describes the programs.

What's on the CD-ROM

The CD-ROM contains the Visual Basic 4.0 source code for the algorithms and example programs described in this book. The code is saved in Visual Basic 4.0 format so that it can be used by the largest number of readers possible. You can load these files into Visual Basic 4.0 or later. The algorithms have been tested using Visual Basic 4.0 and Visual Basic 5.0.

The example programs described in each chapter are contained in separate subdirectories beneath the Src directory. For example, programs demonstrating algorithms described in Chapter 3, "Stacks and Queues," are stored in the Src\Ch3 directory. Appendix B, "List of Example Programs," details the programs described in this book.

The CD-ROM also includes the source code for the programs in the book's first edition. Those programs are compatible with Visual Basic 3.0, so they are stored in Visual Basic 3.0 format. You can load these programs in Visual Basic 3.0 or later versions of Visual Basic. The old versions are stored in subdirectories of the OldSrc directory. For example, the OldSrc\Ch3 directory contains programs that relate to Chapter 3 in this edition of the book.

The older programs demonstrate many of the same topics covered in this edition of the book, but they use Visual Basic 3.0 code. For example, they do not use collections or classes. This makes some of the algorithms a bit harder to understand, but many of them give better performance.

In particular, the newer versions of the tree and network algorithms use collections and classes extensively. This makes the programs simpler, but it also makes them slower. The older programs use forward star tree and network representations (see Chapter 6, "Trees," for more about forward star) to achieve better performance.

Hardware Requirements

To run and modify the example applications, you need a computer that is reasonably able to run Visual Basic. You also need a compact disk drive to load the programs from the CD-ROM.

Algorithms run at different speeds on different computers with different configurations. A 200 megahertz Pentium Pro with 64Mb of memory will be faster than a 386-based computer with 4Mb of memory. You will quickly learn the limits of your hardware.

Installing Source Code

You can load the example programs into the Visual Basic development environment using the Open Project command in the File menu. You can select the files directly from the CD-ROM, or you can copy them onto your hard disk first.

Files on a CD-ROM are always marked read-only because you cannot normally write files to a compact disk. If you copy files from the CD-ROM onto your hard disk, the copies are also marked as read-only. If you want to modify the files, you must give yourself write permission first.

You can do this with the Windows Explorer. First, copy the files you want onto your hard disk. Then select the files and invoke the Properties command in Windows Explorer's File menu. Uncheck the Read Only check box, and click the Ok button. At this point you can make changes to the copied files and save the changes to your hard disk. Do not worry about making mistakes and accidentally ruining the copied source code. You can always copy the files again from the CD-ROM.

Running the Example Programs

One of the most useful ways to run the example programs is using Visual Basic's debugging capabilities. Load the source code into Visual Basic. Using breakpoints, watches, and other debugging features, you can watch the internals of the algorithms in action. This can be particularly helpful for understanding more complicated algorithms, such as those presented in Chapter 7, "Balanced Trees," and Chapter 12, "Network Algorithms."

Some of the example programs create data or temporary scratch files. These programs place the files in an appropriate directory. For example, some of the sorting programs presented in Chapter 9, "Sorting," create data files in the Src\Ch9 directory. All of these files have a ".DAT" extension so you can find and remove them if you like.

The example programs are for demonstration purposes only. They are intended to help you understand particular algorithmic concepts, and they do not spend a great deal of time validating data and trapping errors. If you enter invalid data, the programs may crash. If you have trouble figuring out what data to enter, use the program's Help menu to get instructions.

User Assistance and Information

The software accompanying this book is being provided as is without warranty or support of any kind. Should you require basic installation assistance, or if your media is defective, please call the Wiley product support number at (212)850-6194 weekdays between 9 A.M. and 4 P.M. Eastern Standard Time. You can also contact product support via e-mail at wprtusw@wiley.com.

To place additional orders or to request information about other Wiley products, please call (800)879-4539.

You can send comments or questions to the author, at RodStephens@ vb-helper.com. Visit www.vb-helper.com or the Wiley Web page www.wiley.com/ compbooks/stephens to learn more about books written by Rod Stephens. These pages include updates and patches to the material presented in the books, as well as descriptions of things readers have done with the material in them.

If you use the material in this book in an interesting way, send e-mail to RodStephens@vb-helper.com. Your achievements may be added to the sites so others can see what you have accomplished.

LIST OF EXAMPLE PROGRAMS

B

The CD-ROM accompanying this book contains 89 example programs, saved in Visual Basic 4.0 format, that demonstrate the algorithms described in the book. This appendix lists the Visual Basic 4.0 programs and briefly describes the concepts each demonstrates.

The CD-ROM also contains 62 programs from the first edition saved in Visual Basic 3.0 format. These programs are not listed here, though they roughly correspond to the newer programs.

Chapter 1—Fundamental Concepts

Pager	Paging and trashing
Faker	Compares linked lists using collections, object references, and pointer faking

Chapter 2—Lists

SimList	Simple resizable array-based list
Garbage	Resizable array-based list with garbage collection
LnkList1	Linked list with sentinel
LnkList2	Linked list encapsulated in a class
LnkList3	Linked list with MoveFirst and MoveNext routines
DblLink	Doubly linked list
Threads	Threaded linked list
FakeList	Linked list implemented using pointer faking

Chapter 3—Stacks and Queues

Stacks	Stacks implemented as linked lists
Stacks2	LinkedListStack class
ArrayQ	Array-based queue
ArrayQ2	Array-based queue class
CircleQ	Circular queue
CircleQ2	Circular queue class

LinkedQ	Linked list queue
LinkedQ2	Linked list queue class
CollectQ	Collection-based queue
PriList	Priority queue
PriList2	Priority queue class
HeadedQ	Multi-headed queue simulation

Chapter 4—Arrays

Triang	Triangular array without diagonal items
TriangC	Triangular array without diagonal items using classes
Triang2	Triangular array with diagonal items
TriangC2	Triangular array with diagonal items using classes
Poly	Linked lists of polygons that contain linked lists of points
Sparse	Sparse arrays
VSparse	Very sparse arrays

Chapter 5—Recursion

Facto	Recursive factorials
GCD	Recursive GCD
Fibo	Recursive Fibonacci numbers
Hilbert	Recursive Hilbert curves
Sierp	Recursive Sierpinski curves
BigAdd	Recursive addition
Facto2	Nonrecursive factorials using tail recursion removal
GCD2	Nonrecursive GCD using tail recursion removal
BigAdd2	Nonrecursive addition using tail recursion removal
Fibo2	Nonrecursive Fibonacci numbers using a lookup table
Fibo3	Nonrecursive Fibonacci numbers using a prefilled lookup table
Fibo4	Nonrecursive Fibonacci numbers using bottom-up calculation
Hilbert2	Nonrecursive Hilbert curve
Sierp2	Nonrecursive Sierpinski curves

Chapter 6—Trees

Binary	Binary tree
NAry	N-ary tree using child collections
FStar	N-ary tree using forward star
Trav1	Tree traversals for a complete binary tree
Trav2	Tree traversals for an N-ary tree

Treesort   Sorted binary tree
Qtree   Quadtree
Qtree2   Quadtree with pointer faking

Chapter 7—Balanced Trees

AVL   AVL trees
Btree   B-tree
Bplus   B+tree

Chapter 8—Decision Trees

TicTac   Game tree searching
TicTac2   Game tree searching with precomputed initial moves
BandB   Exhaustive and branch and bound searching
Heur   Heuristics

Chapter 9—Sorting

Encode   String encoding
Sort   Sorting
FastSort   Sorting with MemCopy
Priority   Heap-based priority queue
Unsort   Randomizing arrays

Chapter 10—Searching

Search   List searching

Chapter 11—Hashing

Chain   Hash table with chaining
Bucket   Hash table with buckets
Bucket2   Hash table with buckets on disk
Linear   Open addressing with linear probing
Ordered   Open addressing with ordered linear probing
Quad   Open addressing with quadratic probing
Rand   Open addressing with pseudo-random probing
Rehash   Open addressing with linear probing, deletion, and rehashing

Chapter 12—Network Algorithms

NetEdit   Network editor
Span   Minimal spanning tree
PathS   Label setting shortest paths

PathC	Label correcting shortest paths
District	Districting using shortest path trees
Flow	Maximum network flow
Work	Work assignment using maximum network flow

Chapter 13—Object-Oriented Techniques

Generic	Generic versus specific object declarations
Implem	The Implements statement (VB5 only)
Inherit	Inheritance through delegation
Command1	User interface using command objects
Command2	Undo/redo using command objects
FStacks	Stacks using friend classes
IterTree	Iterators and factory methods for a complete binary tree
WinList	Use a singleton to list windows
Shapes	Shape drawing using serializable command objects
ExpMVC	Model/view/controller paradigm

WHAT'S ON THE CD-ROM

The CD-ROM contains:

Visual Basic 4.0 source code for the algorithms and example programs described in this book. The code is saved in Visual Basic 4.0 format so it can be used by the largest number of readers possible. You can load these files into Visual Basic 4.0 or later. The algorithms have been tested using Visual Basic 4.0 and Visual Basic 5.0

Source code for the programs in the book's first edition. Those programs are compatible with Visual Basic 3.0 so they are stored in Visual Basic 3.0 format. You can load these programs in Visual Basic 3.0 or later versions of Visual Basic.

CUSTOMER NOTE: IF THIS BOOK IS ACCOMPANIED BY SOFTWARE, PLEASE READ THE FOLLOWING BEFORE OPENING THE PACKAGE.

To use this CD-ROM, your system must meet the following requirements:

IBM-compatible machine running Windows 3.x or higher

CD-ROM Drive